Middle Grades Curriculum

Voices and Visions
of the Self-Enhancing School

A Volume in
Middle Level Education and the Self-Enhancing School

Series Editors:
Kathleen Roney, *University of North Carolina Wilmington*
Richard P. Lipka, *St. Bonaventure University*

Middle Level Education
and the Self-Enhancing School
Kathleen Roney and Richard P. Lipka, Series Editors

*Middle Grades Curriculum: Voices and Visions
of the Self-Enhancing School* (2013)
edited by Kathleen Roney and Richard P. Lipka

Middle Grades Curriculum

Voices and Visions
of the Self-Enhancing School

Edited by

Kathleen Roney
University of North Carolina Wilmington

and

Richard P. Lipka
St. Bonaventure University

Information Age Publishing, Inc.
Charlotte, North Carolina • www.infoagepub.com

Library of Congress Cataloging-in-Publication Data

Roney, Kathleen.
  Middle grades curriculum : voices and visions of the self-enhancing school
/ edited by Kathleen Roney, University of North Carolina Wilmington and
Richard P. Lipka, St. Bonaventure University.
    pages cm
    ISBN 978-1-62396-227-2 (paperback) — ISBN 978-1-62396-228-9 (hardcover) —
ISBN 978-1-62396-229-6 (ebook) 1. Middle schools—Curricula—United
States. 2. Curriculum planning—United States. 3. Educational
change—United States. 4. Academic achievement—United States. I. Lipka,
Richard P.
  LB1628.R59 2013

                                                              373.236—dc23

Dedication

*To Gordon Vars, a valued colleague
who blazed the trail we now trod upon.*

CONTENTS

Foreword
John H. Lounsbury . . . . *ix*

Introduction: The Vision
Kathleen Roney and Richard P. Lipka . . . . *xiii*

1. Should Schools be in the Business
   of Enhancing Student Self-Perceptions?
   Thomas M. Brinthaupt *1*

2. Developing Caring, Humanistic Classrooms:
   Effects on Young Adolescents' Complete Growth
   David F. Brown *17*

3. Grouping Students in the Self-Enhancing School
   David C. Virtue *33*

4. From External Control to Self-Direction
   Kerry Chisnall and Kathleen M. Brown *53*

5. From Self-Isolation to Peer Interaction:
   Building Community in Middle Grades Classrooms
   Clark Power and Ann Marie R. Power *71*

6. From Age Isolation to Multiage Interactions
   Elizabeth Pate *89*

7. From Accepting Failure to Promoting Success
   Patrick Akos, Molly Frommer, and Emily Rinkoski *105*

8. From Avoiding or Blaming Parents
   to Working with Parents
   Lee Shumow and Nancy DeFrates-Densch *119*

9. It Is All About Expectations:
    Moving From Negative to Positive Expectations
    Chris M. Cook and Shawn A. Faulkner *141*

10. From Debilitating Teacher Self-Perceptions
    to Enhancing Teacher Self-Perceptions
    Sara Davis Powell *157*

11. Self-Enhancement Through Self-Transcendence:
    Toward Mindful Middle Schools
    for Teaching and Learning
    Robert W. Roeser, Cynthia Taylor, and Jessica Harrison *179*

12. Understanding Learners: From Confusion
    About Learners to Clear Understanding
    of Learner Characteristics
    David Strahan *213*

13. The Effects on Teachers and Students
    of Using Vague and Specific Learning Constructs
    to Enhance Self-Perceptions
    James E. Calder and Thomas M. Brinthaupt *227*

14. From Subject-Centeredness to Life Centeredness
    Rajni Shankar-Brown *241*

15. From Teacher-Exclusive Planning
    to Teacher-Student Planning: The Promise
    of Partnering in a Connected World
    John M. Downes *253*

16. From Textbooks and Tests to Problems and Projects
    Brianne L. Reck *271*

17. Middle School: A Static Institution Within
    a Dynamic World: Moving the Middle
    School Curriculum Into Our Dynamic World
    Edward N. Brazee *293*

Epilogue: What Have We Learned, and What Must We Do
    Richard P. Lipka and Kathleen Roney *307*

About the Contributors *311*

Author Index *313*

Subject Index *325*

FOREWORD

The Primacy of the Person

John H. Lounsbury

The school should always have as its aim that young people leave it as harmonious personalities, not as specialists.... It is essential that they acquire an understanding of and a lively feeling for values. They must acquire a vivid sense of the beautiful and of the morally good.... The development of general ability for independent thinking and judgment should always be placed foremost, not the acquisition of special knowledge.

—Albert Einstein, adapted

These words were written a long, long time ago by a man who was known as perhaps the world's top intellectual and scientist. They present a point of view that now desperately needs to be considered and in turn implemented as the needed realignment of public education's priorities begins to take place. Public education has strayed too far from its historic, general education mission in the pursuit of narrow, cognitive goals; and our society has suffered as a result. Einstein's opinion on the nature of an education is particularly germane for this volume. Consider:

Beane and Lipka (1987) defined the self-enhancing school as: "one which helps young people to clarify their self-concepts, develop positive self-esteem, formulate values, and understand their relationship to the social world around them" (pp. 1-2).

Middle Grades Curriculum:
Voices and Visions of the Self-Enhancing School, pp. ix–xi
Copyright © 2013 by Information Age Publishing
All rights of reproduction in any form reserved.

Although the words and style of this latter statement by two modern educational leaders are different than Einstein's expression, the two statements parallel one another to an amazing degree. Note Einstein's "harmonious personality" and his references to "a lively feeling for values" and acquiring "the morally good." These words relate directly to a student's self-concept. With just a little tweaking this renowned intellectual giant's statement would be a clarion call for the self-enhancing school that this important and timely resource describes.

Further it is apparent that what Einstein and Beane and Lipka (1987) are talking about is really what an education is all about— helping individuals develop their potential, discover and advance whatever special skills and talents they might possess, identify their particular interests, decide on their values, master the communication skills, and acquire the knowledge to understand how the world has evolved and operates. Such is what education in its full and fundamental sense should encompass.

Public education has in recent decades, however, all but skipped over this historic, general education responsibility that includes character and citizenship education along with the critical social and people skills that are essential in whatever vocation one may pursue. The push to increase the rigor of the academic program has left in its wake schools that have made too limited efforts to help individual students develop as distinct persons, to know themselves and formulate their philosophy of life. Yet middle level educators know the critical nature of these years which place awesome responsibility on teachers, for it is during these years that young adolescents are actively deciding who they are, what they believe, what they might aspire to be, and otherwise firm up the dispositions, values, and attitudes that will largely direct their behavior as adults. The self-concept one develops at this time is the central and critical element in this process. Middle schools should not and cannot fail to help and support young adolescents as they move through their maturation. Every middle school needs to be a self-enhancing school!

The attitude that an individual approaches any learning activity with is determined by the individual's perception of herself or himself as a learner and worthy person. The disposition the student develops colors all learning experiences. For this reason it is embarrassing to recognize that the schools themselves engage in practices that lead directly to many young people acquiring negative self-esteem. While perhaps not intentional, many of our school practices and programs nevertheless do "teach" many students that they are less than able, below par, not as good as some others. Just stop and consider from a students' standpoint the implications of our grouping and grading practices. What conclusion can those students who are always placed in remedial sections and never earn a decent grade reach other than "I am dumb." Where school success seems highly correlated with one's worth and their prior experiences clearly indicate such success is unattainable, apathetic behavior is usually a student's defense mechanism.

As I consider the extensive efforts that have been made in recent decades to improve schools, and recognize how unsuccessful they have been by any standard, I am struck by the realization that these monumental—and very costly in terms of time, personnel, and money—programs overlooked what is, I believe, ultimately the real key to improving education—the students themselves! The best way to improve schools is to improve the students, or to put it simply as a brief maxim, "To improve learning, improve learners."

Edwin Markham's little poem, "Man Making," although set in a larger context than a school, makes the point of the primacy of the person beautifully. Forgive Markham's use of the male gender recognizing that it was written in about 1900.

> We are all blind until we see
> That in the human plan
> Nothing is worth the making if
> It does not make the man.
> Why build these cities glorious
> If man unbuilded goes
> In vain we build the work unless
> The builder also grows.
>
> —Attribution: EDWIN MARKHAM, "Man-Making,"
> *Poems of Edwin Markham* (1950, p. 6)

It is imperative that schools recognize and act on the proposition that they are in the business of building people, not just students. And the center for efforts to make a better person, the foundation from which all else evolves, is an individual's self-concept. Could there be any more direct and successful way to improve education and its students than to establish self-enhancing middle schools? I think not. Educators and, indeed, parents too, really need to spend time with this resource, to soak in its rationales and messages and capture the specific suggestions contained.

REFERENCES

Beane, J. A., & Lipka, R. P. (1987). *When the kids come first: Enhancing self esteem.* Columbus, OH: National Middle School Association.

Markham, E. (1950). *"Man making," Poems of Edwin Markham.* Retrieved from http://www.bartleby.com/73/1149.html

INTRODUCTION

The Vision

Kathleen Roney and Richard P. Lipka

MIDDLE LEVEL CURRICULUM AFFECTS SELF-PERCEPTIONS

From its beginnings, middle level education centered curriculum on the developmental needs of the young people that populated middle grade schools. For example, in the first edition of *This We Believe* (National Middle School Association, 1982) wherein ten "essential elements of a 'true' middle school" (pp. 15-22) were articulated, we read:

> While societal expectations are important and tradition ought not be ignored, a true middle school curriculum will actually be based largely on student needs. The curriculum must carefully balance academic goals and other human development needs. A middle school cannot succeed in fulfilling its educational responsibilities if it ignores noncognitive objectives. Indeed, it cannot succeed in fulfilling its cognitive objectives if it does not recognize the interrelated affective goals. (p. 16)

Our interest in young adolescents and their school setting coincides with the fourth edition of *This We Believe* (NMSA, 2010). Subtitled, *Keys to Educating Young Adolescents*, sixteen characteristics designed around four essential attributes (developmentally responsive, challenging, empower-

Middle Grades Curriculum:
Voices and Visions of the Self-Enhancing School, pp. xiii–xxiii
Copyright © 2013 by Information Age Publishing

ing and equitable) are presented as the model for working with young people ages 10-15 in the 21st century. Of interest to us and our project is the section on characteristics of young adolescents, which addresses physical, cognitive-intellectual, moral, psychological, and social-emotional development. This section has been included in the model since its inception (NMSA, 1982; 1992; 1995; 2003; 2010). The Association for Middle Level Education (formerly known as NMSA) has always kept the academic program and accompanying practices within the context of human development, specifically, young adolescent development.

John Lounsbury (2010) refers to the most recently released *This We Believe* (NMSA, 2010) as a "moral imperative to do what is best for young adolescents" (p. 54). Paul George (2010) identified six principles to help guide us in ensuring the success of every young adolescent (historic commitment, common curriculum, relationships, programs and practices, continuous school improvement, and value-centered operations). James Beane (1993) offered up eight guidelines for a middle school curriculum with guideline number two, "The central purpose of the middle school curriculum should be helping early adolescents explore self and social meanings at this time in their lives" (p. 18). Textbooks abound for teacher educators as they introduce middle grades teacher candidates, first, to an understanding of young adolescents, then to middle level education programs and practices based upon sound theory and rigorous research (See for example, Brown & Knowles, 2007; Kellough & Kellough, 2008; Manning & Bucher, 2012; Powell, 2010).

Emphasizing the need for middle grades educators to understand the effect self-concept has on the transition into and through middle grades years, Parker (2010) provided a summary of the literature relevant to what is referred to as "global self-concept" and "domain-specific self-concepts" in her longitudinal study of self-concepts in the middle grades (pp. 2-3). If "self-esteem is an important marker of general well-being" as noted by Adams, Kuhn, and Rhodes (2006) in the literature that grounded their study of ethnic and gender groups. And, if, "It is critical for middle grades educators to be aware of the tenuous nature of young adolescents' perceptions of self and the role they may play in positively or negatively influencing these various domain-specific self-concepts" (Parker, 2010, p. 10), then we urge those in middle level education to place at the forefront the affective condition of those with whom we work—young people in middle grades schools.

SELF-PERCEPTIONS: OUR VIEW OF THE CONSTRUCTS

For our purposes we will employ the definitions put into the literature by the works of Beane and Lipka. Self-concept is defined as the description an individual attaches to himself or herself. As educators our job is to help young people develop an accurate self-description based upon reality. Young people need our help in discovering the sources of and influences upon the self utilizing the lenses of clarity, accuracy, breadth, and depth.

Self-esteem refers to the judgments one makes of his or her self-concept descriptions. These judgments are based upon values or value indicators such as beliefs, aspirations and interests. To develop prosocial values we as educators must help young people develop the critical thinking skills that will enable them to choose wisely after thoughtful consideration of the alternatives (Raths, Harmin, & Simon, 1978). Finally, educators, parents, and critical observers of early adolescents must not confuse the differences between baseline and barometric self (Rosenberg, 1985). Just as human beings are wired to strive for healthy physical development, so too are they wired to strive for healthy self-development known as baseline self.

Barometric self refers to the moment to moment fluctuations. And, early adolescents with their rapid physical changes and cognitive movement to formal operations have the greatest amplitude to the peaks and valleys of any age group. As educators we must have the dispositions, skills and resolve to foster the healthy development of self known as the baseline self as we deal with the impacts of the barometric self.

Given the preponderance within middle level education literature of a commitment to the self and other aspects of psychosocial development, it seems to us that this should be treated in a most systematic fashion. Therefore that led us to the Self-Enhancing School model in the development of this book.

SELF-ENHANCING SCHOOL

Based upon their experiences as classroom teachers, curriculum theorist and educational psychologist, Beane and Lipka (1986) formulated a model of schooling intended to help young people feel better about themselves—who they are—but through very authentic means. A model of schooling with a strong academic orientation, but not at the expense of the students. A model of schooling that recognized that "cognitive learning is hard won by someone whose life is in affective disarray" (Lipka, 1997, p. 31). Beane and Lipka put forth a model of schooling grounded in authentic learning, for example, young people working on the need for competence in very authentic ways, which they termed the Self-Enhancing School. As summarized in the following Table, the Self-Enhancing School model identified 17 dimensions.

Table 1. Self-Enhancing School Model (1986)

	Dimension	Description
1.	From low priority on self-perceptions to self-perceptions as a focus	Moving from a school where self-perceptions are ignored or deemphasized, and feelings of belonging and participation are minimized. Moving toward a school where care is taken and educators attempt to understand theory and research on self-perceptions in order to act in ways that will enhance self-concept and self-esteem with regard to curriculum planning, decision-making, and interactions
2.	From custodial climate to humanistic climate	Moving from settings that are impersonal and autocratic, with a low emphasis on personal dignity. Moving toward personalness, respect, participation, and human dignity. Students become risk-takers, free from fear and guilt
3.	From attribute grouping to variable grouping	Moving from single attribute grouping where learners feel confused or unclear about themselves. Moving toward variable grouping that provide students opportunities to recognize and build on the multiple dimensions of self.
4.	From external control to self-direction	Moving from learned helplessness when control rests with others. Moving toward cooperative governance. Students participate in curriculum planning and self-directed learning experiences.
5.	From self-isolation to peer interaction	Moving from a place where problems of peer interaction are often compounded in the school by competition for rewards, lack of constructive interaction, and the notion that cooperation is equivalent to cheating. These features of schooling likely hinder the development of clear, positive self-perceptions. Moving to a school that places a premium on developing constructive peer interaction based on the desire for social acceptance.
6.	From age isolation to multiage interactions	Moving from school procedures whereby young people of a particular age are separated from other persons–both younger and older and thus opportunities are limited to learn about and with persons of other ages. Moving toward a school that encourages interaction with other age groups through multiage grouping, older-younger tutoring, community service projects and invitations to older persons to participate in daily school activities.

7. From accepting failure to expecting and assuring success	Moving from curriculum plans that lack meaning and are beyond present achievement levels of learners. Moving to a school that communicates to students the expectation that they can and will succeed.
8. From avoiding or blaming parents to working with parents	The degree to which young people feel adequate and competent as learners may often depend on expectations and feedback from parents regarding education and schooling. Moving to a school that recognizes the powerful role parents may play in their children's learning and makes attempts to improve the expectations and feedback parents provide about educational experiences. A school that is aware of modern family lifestyles and is sensitive to the needs of children from "nonconventional" families in terms of curriculum bias, teacher interaction, and special school events.
9. From negative expectations to positive expectations	Moving from a school where labels and stereotypes are applied to a particular group, suggesting that one or another is better or worse than others, thus contributing nonsensical suggestions to the self-concepts and self-esteem of young people. Moving to a school which has a faculty that accepts all young people unconditionally, without regard for racial, ethnic, socioeconomic, or religious background. A school where all learners are expected to do well, and respect is shown for their personal dignity and sense of self-worth.
10. From debilitating teacher self-perception to enhancing teacher self-perceptions	Moving from confused and negative self-perceptions as teachers and where such overwhelming criticism creates a dangerous atmosphere for learners. Moving toward a school where teachers are treated with professional respect, offered opportunities for professional growth, and provided the best possible support in carrying out their responsibilities.
11. From vague self-perception goals to clear self-perception goals	Moving from a school where self-perception goals are vague, ambiguous, or lost in the shuffle of the everyday life in school. Moving toward a school where self-perceptions goals must be developed in terms of meaning, rationale, and prominence. The school has a clear sense of purpose and priority in the area of self-perceptions.
12. From confusion about learners to clear understanding learner characteristics	Moving from a school where teachers are unsure or vague about the characteristics of learners, thus making instructional decisions on a largely speculative basis and risking the possibility that the selection of resources, activities, and objectives will be appropriate for individuals or groups. Moving to a school where consideration is given to concepts such as developmental tasks and persistent life situations, as well as techniques for identifying problems, interests, needs, and concerns of individuals or groups of learners.

(Table continues on next page.)

Table 1. (Continued)

Dimension	Description
13. From vague learning constructs to learning constructs to enhance self-perceptions	Moving from a school where curriculum and instruction are planned and implemented on the basis of vague notions of how learning, growth, and development take place. Moving toward curriculum and instructional planning which is based on the idea that the salient dimensions of self-perceptions influence the style of learning, approaches to problem solving, perceptions of meaning, reactions to experiences, and the flow of interactions between the individual and the school community.
14. From subject-centeredness to life centeredness	Moving from the approach where learners are expected to master the facts, principles, and concepts associated with various disciplines of knowledge. Moving toward a curriculum organized around problems of living and the emerging needs of young people.
15. From teacher-exclusive planning to teacher-student planning	Moving from curriculum plans that essentially determine the content and process of the time students spend in school. Moving toward a method that allows learners an opportunity to bring their own thoughts to curriculum plans, enhances skills in participation arid decision making, promotes feelings of belonging, and encourages the development of internal locus of control.
16. From textbooks and tests to problems and projects	Moving from teaching and learning situations in schools centered on cognitive objectives, teacher-centered activities, subject-oriented texts, and paper-pencil tests. Moving to a school characterized by concepts and methods that are congruent with self-perceptions and are likely to enhance them.
17. From maintenance of the status quo to continuous development	Moving from a school that has a program based on the past risks and is becoming an anachronism in contemporary life. Moving toward the school that chooses to place a priority on enhancing self-perceptions commits itself to a dynamic and often ambiguous role.

Source: Adapted from Beane and Lipka (1986, pp. 179-188).

xviii

Schools that were going to be serious about dealing with the affective side of schooling had to be involved with these dimensions and get from the *from* perspective to the *to* perspective. In addition, middle grades educators would try to do that in the most systemic way—to see schools that have all seventeen dimensions operating in sync. Nearly 30 years after Beane and Lipka (1986) articulated their model we questioned: Is there such a school in operation today? If there ever were such schools they appear to be few and far between.

When we ask ourselves why not?, we look where we are now in terms of the assault on our profession, the assault on family life, and, the political and cultural assault upon intellect and civic literacy. As Giroux (2012) has so forcefully stated:

> The American public is suffering from an education deficit. By this I mean it exhibits a growing inability to think critically, question authority, be reflective, weigh evidence, discriminate between reasoned arguments and opinions, listen across differences and engage the mutually informing relationship between private problems and broader public issues. (para. 1)

Giroux very succinctly provides a distilled version of the intentions found in *This We Believe* (NMSA, 2010) and the Self-Enhancing School model. To give voice to those intentions we asked authors to share their thinking related to the dimensions of the Self-Enhancing School. It is a challenge for all of our authors as they come from different perspectives. We have authors whose discipline is psychology who in their chapters wrestle with the middle school curriculum side of the issue, and we have authors whose discipline is curriculum who wrestle with self-perception, self-esteem, self-concepts and those types of things as they wrote their chapters.

We were careful not to be overly prescriptive which makes the book strong because authors were asked to give voice from their perspective. They were asked to discuss what is the cost of staying in the *from* position and the benefit of moving to the *to* position in developing a middle grades curriculum based on the Self-Enhancing School dimensions. While the following description does not present a sequential introduction to each chapter, we offer it this way to assist the reader in seeing which authors approached their chapters from the perspective of psychology and which from the perspective of middle level curriculum.

FROM THE VIEWPOINT OF PSYCHOLOGY

Brinthaupt's interest in self-identity led him to wrestle with dimension one—from low priority on self-perception to self-perceptions as a focus

(Chapter 1). The concept of the self itself and how there are negative things associated with that—delinquency, aggression, and in its most extreme form, narcissism—caused Brinthaupt to ponder questions like, should we just ignore the self? Does this mean we want to make self-concept less clear? In what circumstances should self-esteem be lowered?

In addressing dimension five—from self-isolation to peer interaction—Power and Power (Chapter 5), suggest that young people who are transitioning into adolescence are best served by a just community culture in order to flourish socially as well as morally. Although middle level classrooms and schools can and should provide such a culture, administrators and teachers lack an accessible framework for conceptualizing what such a culture might look like or a strategy for bringing it about. Power and Power argue that educators should look to team sports for a model of moral community and responsible peer interaction.

From their vantage point, Akos, Frommer, and Rinkoski address dimension seven—from accepting failure to expecting and assuring success (Chapter 7). They unpack their thesis that educators working with early adolescents should shift from a deficit or failure expectation to a more strengths-oriented, self-enhancing success expectation. Shumow and DeFrates-Densch follow that up with dimension eight—from avoiding or blaming parents to working with parents (Chapter 8). In their chapter they explain why parental engagement matters to middle grades students and educators, present guidelines and principles for engaging parents, and discuss various ways parents are engaged and how educators can utilize that knowledge to design a comprehensive parental engagement program for a self-enhancing middle school.

Roeser, Taylor, and Harrison address dimension eleven—from vague self-perception goals to clear self-perception goals—by focusing on what they refer to as the *mindful middle school* (Chapter 11). They hypothesize that, mindful middle schools are places that orient students, teachers and leaders alike toward seeking self-enhancement and growth through self-transcendence and prosocial behavior, and *moving toward* others (e.g., malleability beliefs, mindfulness, cooperation and self-improvement).

Rounding out the chapters in this book authored from the field of psychology, Calder and Brinthaupt wrestle with dimension thirteen—from vague learning constructs to learning constructs to enhance self-perceptions (Chapter 13). Calder and Brinthaupt first define some of the ways that learning constructs can be vague or specific in the context of middle schools. They then show that the shift toward teacher-centered approaches in the name of "teaching to the test" is not creating better test results, as hoped, but rather is resulting in middle school environments that have drifted away from the self-perception enhancing student-centered approaches. They end with a discussion of the vague/specific construct issue from the perspective of both the teacher and the middle school student.

FROM THE VIEWPOINT OF MIDDLE LEVEL EDUCATION, THEORY, AND RESEARCH

From his experience as a middle level teacher and teacher educator, Brown (Chapter 2) starts us off with his presentation of dimension two—from custodial climate to humanistic climate. Brown emphasizes that learning is always a social, emotional, and cognitive process, and students' genuine cognitive growth is unlikely when middle level educators ignore a responsibility to create caring and mutually respectful classrooms. Virtue (Chapter 3) picks up on this as he deals with dimension three—from attribute grouping to variable grouping. In his chapter, Virtue explains how tracking practices create different schooling experiences for young people. He explores the moral imperative in terms of how we group students. Chisnall and Brown (Chapter 4) approach dimension four—from external control to self-direction—by sharing results of their study of leadership practices, policies and beliefs of middle grades principals. They conclude that schools that possess a humanistic climate are less autocratic and support a transition from external control to self-direction. In wrestling with dimension six—from age isolation to multiage interactions—Pate (Chapter 6) provides examples of multiage interactions as she answers questions such as, what if young adolescents weren't isolated by age, but, instead, grouped intentionally to facilitate multiage interactions? What kinds of grouping would be needed? What curriculum model and strategies could be used?

Cook and Faulkner address issues related to dimension nine—from negative expectations to positive expectations (Chapter 9). They address the theory and research behind expectations, the dangers of negative expectations, the benefits of positive expectations, and provide suggestions for maintaining and creating school environments where high expectations for all is the norm.

With dimension ten—from debilitating teacher self-perceptions to enhancing teacher self-perceptions—Powell (Chapter 10) addresses strategies that strengthen the reciprocal relationship between increased teacher efficacy and enhanced teacher self-efficacy which in turn impacts the reciprocal relationship between increased student learning and increased student self-efficacy. Strahan (Chapter 12) takes on dimension twelve—from confusion about learners to clear understanding of learner characteristics. Strahan argues that the most successful teaching and learning requires a clear understanding of learner characteristics embedded in school and classroom environments characterized by trusting relationships. Shankar-Brown (Chapter 14) establishes that the compartmentalization of knowledge in subject-centered curricula goes against the interconnected reality of the world and life. In her chapter on dimension fourteen—from subject-centeredness to life-centeredness—she concludes that life-centered curricula are essential in supporting the realization of the self-enhancing middle school and imperative for engaging students in the learning process.

In Chapter 15, Downes deals with dimension fifteen—from teacher-exclusive planning to teacher-student planning—as he examines the challenges inherent in teacher-exclusive planning and discusses the role of curriculum integration as a foundation for teacher-student planning. Technology-rich approaches to student-directed and integrated learning are explored as a path toward more relevant, effective, and sustainable teacher-student planning. Addressing dimension sixteen—from textbooks and tests to problems and projects—Reck (Chapter 16) posits that the principles of the self-enhancing school are at the core of most models and recommendations for middle grades educational reform. The fundamental shift that must occur is to place the learner in the center of the learning equation. The paradigm shift needed to affect this change is a shift from textbooks and tests to problems and projects.

The final, seventeenth dimension is addressed by Brazee—from maintenance of the status quo to continuous development (Chapter 17). With an eye toward how technology is changing learning, Brazee takes a look back at curriculum in the middle grades and then offers us a vision for the present and future of middle grades curriculum. His conclusion: the self-enhancing school dimensions clearly point to what middle level educators (researchers, practitioners, theorists) have been saying they wanted all along—student-oriented, democratic, humanistic, and progressive curriculum. To do anything less shortchanges and diminishes our obligations as professionals.

REFERENCES

Adams, S. K., Kuhn, J., & Rhodes, J. (2006). Self-esteem changes in the middle school years: A study of ethnic and gender groups. *RMLE Online, 29*(6),1-9.

Beane, J. A. (1993). *A middle school curriculum. From rhetoric to reality.* Columbus, OH: National Middle School Association.

Beane, J. A., & Lipka, R. P. (1986). *Self-concept, self-esteem and the curriculum.* New York, NY: Teachers College Press.

Brown, D. F., & Knowles, T. (2007). *What every middle school teacher should know.* Portsmouth, NH: Heinemann.

George, P. (2010, January). Renewing the middle school: The lesson of Hansel and Gretel for middle schools. *Middle School Journal, 41*(3), 49-51.

Giroux, H. A. (2012). Beyond the politics of the big lie: The education deficit and the new authoritarianism. *Truthout.* Retrieved from http://truth-out.org/opinion/item/9865-beyond-the-politics-of-the-big-lie-the-education-deficit-and-the-new-authoritarianism

Kellough, R. D., & Kellough, N. G. (2008). *Teaching young adolescents: A guide to methods and resources for middle school teaching* (5th ed.). Upper Saddle River, NJ: Pearson.

Lipka, R. P. (1997). Enhancing self-concept/self-esteem in young adolescents. In J. L. Irvin (Ed.), *What current research says to the middle level practitioner* (pp. 31-37). Columbus, OH: National Middle School Association.

Lounsbury, J. (2010, January). This we believe: Keys to educating young adolescents. *Middle School Journal, 41*(3), 52-53.

Manning, M. L., & Bucher, K. T. (2012). *Teaching in the middle school* (4th ed.). Boston, MA: Pearson.

National Middle School Association. (1982). *This we believe.* Columbus, OH: Author.

National Middle School Association. (1992). *This we believe.* Columbus, OH: Author.

National Middle School Association. (1995). *This we believe: Developmentally responsive middle level schools.* Columbus, OH: Author.

National Middle School Association. (2003). *This we believe: Successful schools for young adolescents.* Westerville, OH: Author.

National Middle School Association. (2010). *This we believe: Keys to educating young adolescents.* Westerville, OH: Author.

Parker, A. K. (2010). A longitudinal investigation of young adolescents' self-concepts in the middle grades. *RMLE Online, 33*(10), 1-13.

Powell, S. D. (2010). *Introduction to middle school* (2nd ed.). Boston, MA: Allyn & Bacon.

Raths, L. E., Harmin, M., & Simon, S. B. (1978). *Values and teaching* (2nd ed.). Columbus, OH: Charles E. Merrill.

Rosenberg, M. (1985). *Self-concept and psychological well-being in adolescence.* In R. Leahy (Ed.), *The development of the self* (pp. 135-162). New York, NY: Academic Press.

CHAPTER 1

SHOULD SCHOOLS BE IN THE BUSINESS OF ENHANCING STUDENT SELF-PERCEPTIONS?

Thomas M. Brinthaupt

Should Schools be in the Business of Enhancing Student Self-Perceptions?

"There is almost zero evidence that failure to learn is tied to low self-esteem or that massaging the psyche can improve learning." (Leo, 1996, p. 25)

"To deny the importance of self-perceptions is to ignore their power as an ongoing influence in living and learning." (Beane & Lipka, 1986, p. 83)

Should it be part of the school's purpose to help students to enhance their self-perceptions and clarify their values? Is it, in any way, the school's job to help students to clarify their self-understanding? If we agree that it is, at least in part, the school's job, is this goal actually achievable? What does the research evidence suggest with regard to the wisdom, necessity, and/or effectiveness of enhancing student self-perceptions? In this chapter, I address these questions primarily within the context of the middle level school.

Middle Grades Curriculum:
Voices and Visions of the Self-Enhancing School, pp. 1–16
Copyright © 2013 by Information Age Publishing

Middle level education in the United States is situated within the current climate of *No Child Left Behind*, with its emphasis on improving student performance, teaching to the test, drill-and-practice, and teachers' accountability for their students' learning outcomes. Given this climate and environment, a focus on self-perceptions appears, at least on the surface, to be misplaced and a waste of time that could be better spent covering material that will be on the test(s).

As the quotes at the start of this chapter illustrate, there are strong opinions about the wisdom or necessity of schools being interested in the selves of their students. In this chapter, I first provide an overview of Beane and Lipka's (1986) recommendations regarding why and how schools should enhance student self-perceptions. Next, I review the literature on the effects of such self-perception enhancement efforts, how schools ended up putting these and related recommendations into practice, and the potential costs of focusing on self-related characteristics and processes. Finally, I propose a set of recommendations for enhancing middle level student self-perceptions, based on the history of such efforts over the past 30 years as well as on the research literature that has delineated the potential drawbacks and difficulties associated with those efforts. As the chapter will show, the question of whether schools should be concerned with student self-perceptions is a complicated one.

THE SELF-ENHANCING SCHOOL: AN OVERVIEW OF PSYCHOLOGICAL COMPONENTS

In their 1986 book, *Self-Concept, Self-Esteem, and the Curriculum*, Beane and Lipka argued for the enhancement and promotion of student self-perceptions in the schools. As they put it, schools can and should "help young people clarify their self-concepts and improve their self-esteem" (p. 2). Among other benefits, enhancing self-perceptions can help "to develop a more constructive and prosocial community in the school" (p. 37). At all levels and for all involved parties, Beane and Lipka were advocating a shift from a custodial school climate to one that is more humanistic and self-enhancing.

By self-perceptions, Beane and Lipka included self-esteem (the more evaluative component of self-views) and self-concept (the more cognitive component of self-views), as well as one's values. The self-enhancing school is characterized by efforts to improve self-esteem (i.e., help students to feel more positively about themselves, their abilities, and their accomplishments) and to clarify values and self-concept (i.e., help students to develop accurate, realistic, and unbiased appraisals of their personal characteristics). The curriculum they recommended did not focus so much on the possibility that these self-perception components are independent as much as it assumed that they are interrelated and operate together in the developing person.

With regard to the major characteristics of the self-enhancing school, it is worthwhile to quote what Beane and Lipka (1986) said about schools moving from having a low priority on self-perceptions to having self-perceptions as a focus:

> In a school where self-perceptions are ignored or deemphasized, we can hardly expect them to be enhanced. More likely, if self-perceptions are not perceived to be of importance, the chance for feelings of belonging and participation are minimized. On the other hand, where self-perceptions are a focal point of the school, learners may feel that they have an important place. This means that in developing curriculum plans, making decisions about institutional features, and interacting among faculty or with learners, care is taken to act in ways that enhance the clarity of self-concept and the quality of self-esteem. It also means that educators will make serious professional attempts to understand theory and research on self-perceptions as those relate to living and learning. (pp. 179-180)

As Beane and Lipka (1986) put it, "self-perceptions ought to be an educational issue not only because they are related to academic achievement, but because they are an integral part of human growth and development (pp. 176-177). In other words, enhancing self-perceptions can play an important role in "helping young people live full, productive lives" (p. 177). The self-enhancing school concept takes an essentially ecological approach, in which the school environment assumes the major responsibility for changing student self-perceptions (see Beane, 1994).

In his historical review of the schools' interest in self-perceptions, Beane (1994) argued that "this area is one of considerable confusion and contradiction as well as tension" (p. 69)—something that continues to be true today. He described three major arguments for why schools might be in the business of enhancing student self-perceptions: (a) the "coping" argument that self-esteem can be used as a buffer to help students cope with stressful life events and conditions; (b) the "achievement" argument that enhanced self-perceptions are associated with improved academic outcomes and doing well in school; and (c) the "human dignity" argument that social institutions are obligated to foster a sense of individual and collective efficacy devoted to improving the common good. As Beane notes, in all three of these arguments, enhancing self-perceptions is viewed as a means to some other goal rather than an end in itself. In other words, "enhancing self-perceptions in the school amounts to asking young people to change themselves or the way they think about themselves so that they are more likely able to do something else" (Beane, p. 76).

Unfortunately, but perhaps not surprisingly, the advent of the self-esteem enhancement movement in schools saw a variety of commercialized or short-cut approaches that were clearly not consistent with the thrust of Beane and Lipka's (1986) arguments. As we will see in the next section, there is a large difference between the notion of everyone getting a star or ribbon regardless of their performance—or everyone being told that they are special—and the notion of everyone gaining improved but accurate self-esteem, self-concept, and values clarity.

THE POTENTIAL COSTS OF ENHANCING STUDENT SELF-PERCEPTIONS IN MIDDLE LEVEL SCHOOLS

Research has amply demonstrated that the middle level school is a time of dramatic cognitive, physical, and social changes for students (for reviews, see Brinthaupt & Lipka, 2002; Simmons & Blyth, 1987). In Harter's (1999) comprehensive review of the development of the self, early and middle adolescence are characterized by the elaboration and differentiation of social-related roles and self attributes. These developments are accompanied by a susceptibility to all-or-none thinking, inaccurate overgeneralizations, and instability and conflict regarding one's self-perceptions and self-evaluations. Based on these changes and issues, it would seem that early adolescence is a crucial time for schools and teachers to provide self-perception guidance to their students. Is the middle level school the most important time and place for enhancing student self-perceptions?

In a review of self-esteem enhancement programs designed specifically for early adolescents, DuBois, Burk-Braxton, and Tevendale (2002) found that multifaceted programs can be effective for young people who are particularly prone to drops in self-esteem or the persistence of low levels of self-esteem. DuBois et al. cited evidence that these programs can successfully increase self-esteem, particularly for at-risk youth. Additionally, they reported that improving self-esteem among students in middle level schools can have positive effects on academic and other behavioral outcomes.

Despite this evidence, there is a great deal of disagreement with the self-esteem enhancement proposition in both the psychological literature and the popular press. For example, taking a very negative view of programs designed to change student self-perceptions, Baumeister, Campbell, Krueger, and Vohs (2005) stated that "efforts to boost people's self-esteem are of little value in fostering academic achievement or preventing undesirable behavior" (p. 84). Nationally-syndicated columnists have taken an even darker view of the self-esteem enhancement movement (e.g., Krauthammer, 1997; Leo, 1996).

In his book, *The Curse of the Self*, Leary (2004) discusses a wide variety of personal and social problems caused by an excessive focus on the self. Admittedly, the self is a useful development for the human species. As Leary notes, "being able to plan, self-evaluate, control one's own responses, introspect, and adopt other people's perspectives not only help people navigate life more successfully but also are responsible for most of the cultural innovations that we think of as human 'progress'" (p. 12). However, according to the psychological research literature he reviews, these advantages are frequently offset by a number of "curses" associated with the self. As Leary puts it, the self "is single-handedly responsible for many, if not most of the problems that human beings face as individuals and as a species" (p. 21) and that it "creates havoc with people's lives, leading to suffering, selfishness, troubled relationships, disastrous decisions, and behavior that is dangerous to ourselves and to others" (p. 24).

As examples of the potential negative aspects of the self, Leary (2004) discusses how a preoccupation with the self can interfere with memory and performance. There are well-documented affective, cognitive, and behavioral deficits associated with excessive rumination, self-talk, and self-reflection. Even among young people, research shows that the self generates a variety of inaccurate but self-serving perceptions and attributions that are biased in ways that protect and enhance our self-feelings. In addition, problems with self-control (such as the inability to resist temptations or controlling impulses) frequently undermine people's everyday lives.

To counter the various curses associated with having a self, Leary (2004) offers several suggestions. First, people can develop an *ego-skepticism* or an active awareness of the ways that the self can bias their perceptions and interpretations. Second, people can learn that many of their negative emotions are the result of the ways that they talk to themselves. Changing this self-talk (with or without therapy) can lead to a healthier regulation of one's emotions. Third, people can learn to cultivate a sense of "self-compassion" (e.g., Neff, 2009). This concept refers to becoming more tolerant and accepting of one's shortcomings and limitations. It can provide resilience for young people, particularly among those with negative self-perceptions (Neff & McGehee, 2010).

In addition to self characteristics that lead people into maladaptive or dysfunctional thinking and behaving, there are certain self-related outcomes that appear to be especially pernicious. Extreme and inaccurate self-perceptions can congeal into unhealthy patterns. As the psychologists

Twenge and Campbell (2009) document in their book, *The Epidemic of Narcissism*, narcissistic tendencies are associated with "aggression, materialism, lack of caring for others, and shallow values" (p. 9). The apparent increases in narcissism in the United States over the past 30 years reflect shifts in cultural values toward self-admiration, self-centeredness, overinflated self-perceptions, a sense of entitlement, and excessive feelings of specialness.

Research indicates that academic achievement rates have remained relatively stable over the past 30 years, but that student narcissism rates as well as global self-esteem rates have shown steady increases (Gentile, Twenge, & Campbell, 2010; Twenge & Campbell, 2009). The research evidence also shows that narcissistic tendencies peak in adolescence (Carlson & Gjerde, 2009). Whereas narcissism is not the same thing as high self-esteem, efforts to increase students' self-esteem can inadvertently lead to increases in narcissistic tendencies. As Twenge and Campbell put it, "you can like yourself just fine without loving yourself to excess" (p. 29).

Young people are bombarded by social and cultural messages that contribute to feelings of specialness and entitlement. Parents and schools deserve some of the blame for this epidemic. Twenge and Campbell (2009) argue that "when parents and teachers protect children from failure to cushion their self-esteem, kids may end up doing worse because they aren't learning from their mistakes.… Having confidence in your true abilities includes knowing your weaknesses and learning from your failures, and that has nothing to do with hating yourself" (p. 49).

With regard to what schools can do to inhibit the development of narcissistic tendencies in young people, Twenge and Campbell (2009) advocate fostering a love of learning and rewarding effort and hard work. Rather than emphasizing "I am special" individual uniqueness and how students are different from one another, they suggest having students identify the ways that they are alike. Additionally, similar to the values and self-concept clarification arguments of Beane and Lipka (1986), Twenge and Campbell propose having students ask their classmates why they have particular likes and dislikes. They also highlight the importance of teaching and learning empathy and the ability to take the perspective of other people.

While there is some controversy about the validity of Twenge and Campbell's (2009) data and interpretations (e.g., Ferguson, 2010; Hill & Roberts, 2011), their review of the roles of generational, cultural, and historical influences on self-views is important for educators to recognize. Teachers do not teach within a vacuum—their efforts are affected in part by the fact that the out-of-school environment sends strong, persuasive, and potentially damaging messages to young people. Within this context, it is important that teachers help their students to understand the accurate, selective, and appropriate use of self-understanding and self-promotion.

Finally, research has shown that praising students can have adverse effects on their subsequent motivation and performance (Dweck, 2007). Blackwell, Trzesniewski, and Dweck (2007) showed that providing praise has very different effects when it is focuses on a student's intelligence (e.g., "You're really smart") and when it focuses on a student's effort (e.g., "You worked really hard at this"). Because of self-presentation concerns and fears of failure, students who are praised for their intelligence are motivated to avoid challenges to this perception by choosing easier subsequent tasks than those who are praised for their effort. When students think they are smart, they are less inclined to put in needed effort; when students think that they are hard workers, they are more inclined to put in needed effort. The liberal use of praise is associated with decreased levels of task persistence as well as with risk aversion and decreased perceptions of autonomy among students (e.g., Henderlong & Lepper, 2002). This research shows that, once again, how teachers and parents respond to students' behaviors can have significant (and sometimes negative) implications for their self-perceptions.

In response to these kinds of criticisms and controversies surrounding the self-esteem construct, Swann, Chang-Schneider, and McClarty (2007) have made the point that a focus on global self-esteem or the affective components of self-perceptions is misplaced (see also Kohn, 1994). Swann et al. propose that there is considerable value in examining self-concepts and metacognitive facets of self-perceptions. In particular, they note that there are several kinds of self-perception "strength" that have been identified by researchers (such as self-certainty, self-clarity, and temporal stability). Each of these characteristics has been shown to have significant impacts on a variety of behaviors.

Swann and colleagues (2007) demonstrate that a major mistake made by self-esteem critics is that they have assumed that *global* esteem measures should predict *specific* outcomes. Research in social and personality psychology has provided convincing evidence that "specific predictors should be used to predict specific behaviors and general predictors should be used to predict general behaviors" (Swann et al., p. 87). In other words, researchers who want to account for specific outcomes (such as math achievement) should use self-perceptions specific to that outcome (such as math self-concept). In fact, there is strong research evidence that specific self-perceptions are predictive of specific academic outcomes across a variety of domains (see Craven & Marsh, 2008; Marsh & Craven, 2006). These findings suggest that teachers' time and effort would be better spent improving their students' self-perceptions within specific academic content areas rather than improving their students' overall self-views.

This does not mean, however, that global self-esteem is unrelated to significant life outcomes. In fact, global self-esteem measured in adolescence has been shown to be predictive of a variety of general behavioral outcomes in adulthood, such as depression, criminality, and problems with money and work (Swann et al. 2007; Trzesniewski, Donnellan, Moffitt, Robins, Poulton, & Caspi, 2006).

Whether these kinds of findings mean that teachers, particularly in middle level schools, should or should not be concerned with the overall self-esteem of their students is an open question. However, Swann and colleagues (2007) argue that there is ample justification for efforts to improve people's self-perceptions. They note that the most effective self-esteem enhancement programs are multifaceted, including not only self-esteem components but also related constructs such as social skills and self-efficacy (see DuBois & Flay, 2004). Such programs also emphasize the development of accurate, realistic, and adaptive self-perceptions. Less effective are programs that rely mainly on self-affirmation exercises and activities.

Swann and colleagues (2007) conclude that the ideal intervention approach is to emphasize both self-perceptions and the behaviors and situations that contribute to and affect those self-perceptions. As they put it, "just as producing lasting changes in self-views requires corresponding changes in the behaviors and social conditions that nourish those self-views, producing lasting changes in people's behaviors and social conditions requires corresponding changes in their self-views" (p. 92). This conclusion is, of course, very consistent with the views expressed by Beane and Lipka (2006).

In summary, despite extensive and well-publicized criticisms of self-esteem enhancement programs in the schools, the research evidence offers good support for the usefulness of such programs. The literature has provided more detailed views of the nature of the self, of the possible negative consequences of self-related activities, and of the ways to foster accurate self-perceptions. Despite the criticisms and responses that have emerged regarding efforts to enhance student self-perceptions, there are several important research questions that have yet to be answered. In the next section of this chapter, I address some of the more interesting of these questions.

UNANSWERED QUESTIONS

Are there qualitative and quantitative differences between schools that do and do not attempt to enhance student self-perceptions? Conducting sound research on this question would, of course, be difficult. Researchers would need to find two schools that are very similar on most relevant dimensions, implement a self-perception enhancement program in one of them (while ensuring that the other school does not include aspects of such a program), and then compare the schools on a variety of perceptual, cognitive, affective, academic, and behavioral outcomes.

Are students who participated in self-esteem enhancement programs in their schools more likely to show unrealistic global self-esteem and higher levels of narcissism compared to students who did not participate in such programs? Critics of self-esteem enhancement programs in the schools have not provided any convincing evidence that participation in these programs is actually the cause of rises in self-esteem and narcissism (see Trzesniewski, Donnellan, & Robins, 2008).

Should a *self-perception* curriculum be considered part of the foundational skills necessary for successful learning? In other words, is the development of clear and accurate self-perceptions as essential to learning as the ability to read, to think critically, and to work with numbers? One might think of a lack of self-perceptual clarity and accuracy as similar to students being disadvantaged or even as having a disability. Can self-related skills be practiced? Are there good and bad ways to *practice* self-perception and values clarity? Does the well-known principle of 10,000 hours of practice to develop expertise (e.g., Gladwell, 2008) also apply to self-perceptions and the development of a sense of self and identity? Similar to artistic, athletic, or academic skills, it may be beneficial to view the development and refinement of self-perceptions as a skill that requires sustained practice (see Twenge & Campbell, 2009, p. 284). Even if it is not appropriate to consider self-perceptions as a domain that involves expertise, the idea that self-perception practice might be useful for young people is worth research consideration.

The "foundational skill" argument is at least implicitly made by those who advocate for schools being in the business of enhancing student self-perceptions. However, what evidence there is for these claims appears to be mainly correlational or anecdotal. There have been few, if any, controlled experimental studies of the specific educational benefits of self-perception interventions. And there are no convincing explanations, to date, of what specific advantages or abilities such interventions provide for the middle level school student, whether or not these are teachable, and if so, how to best teach them in order to enhance student learning and achievement.

What is the role of the *out of school curriculum*, for example, family, community, mass media, and peers) with regard to self-perceptions? As Twenge and Campbell (2009) demonstrated, nonschool influences on self-perceptions are powerful and pervasive. Do these factors outweigh, supplement, or conflict with school effects, particularly school-related self-perception enhancement efforts? What do adolescents and young adults think contributes the most to their sense of self? What are the relative effects of school, extracurricular activities, home life, religious upbringing, peers, extended family, community, unique experiences/life events (i.e., positive or negative things that happen to a person), and romantic relationships on self-perceptions? As Beane (1994) noted, the major shortcoming of the self-enhancing school model is that it "does not clearly speak to conditions outside of the school that enter into the ongoing formation and alteration of self-perception" (p. 81). It appears that no research has addressed the question of the relative impact of in-school and out-of-school influences on middle level school students' self-perceptions.

Do any school-based programs teach students about the psychology of the self-perception process? For example, where do self-concept and self-esteem come from and how do they develop? There is very little literature on teaching the psychology of the self in schools. Some college psychology departments have a "Psychology of the Self" or related course on their books. However, such courses are typically survey, not practical, hands-on courses. The *self* or one's *identity* is assumed to be a result of what happens to a person; the assumption seems to be that self-understanding is almost a capricious process, affected by multiple sources and unlikely to be reliably or predictably directed by the individual person or by his or her significant others.

Is it the teacher's role to *teach*, evaluate, judge, or in some other way facilitate self-understanding? Most students in middle level and high school probably do not think that their teachers (or their parents, for that matter) know them at all. There is clearly a need for research on young people's perceptions of the role of adults in determining or affecting their self-perceptions.

Are the self-perception effects of school more likely (and less likely) at different periods? For example, do self-esteem enhancement programs work better (or make more sense) at particular developmental, age, or grade periods? In their review of self-esteem enhancement programs, DuBois and colleagues (2002) concluded that the need for self-esteem enhancement interventions appears to be strongest during early adolescence. However, systematic studies of the relative benefits of enhancement programs across ages are lacking.

Are there some situations where teachers should strive to *lower* rather than raise student self-esteem? Are there some circumstances where teachers should purposely try to make their students' self-concepts and values *less clear*? As research on narcissism shows, it may sometimes be necessary for teachers (and parents) to ensure that young people's self-perceptions are realistic or accurate. Is it the school's responsibility to do this? When should young people be told that they are thinking too highly of themselves (and what are the factors that will increase the likelihood that they will believe this)? Who should tell them this? Do they need to discover or determine this themselves? It is an intriguing notion that purposely induced self-related uncertainty and lack of clarity might be used to encourage students to engage in critical self-reflection and to acquire more accurate self-knowledge. There appears to be no research on this possibility.

As these questions illustrate, there is a great deal we still do not know about the nature and effectiveness of self-perception enhancement and intervention programs. There is also a great deal of room for growth in the development of these kinds of programs. Despite this lack of information and lack of relevant research studies, there are several recommendations that can be made regarding the enhancement of self-perceptions in the schools. In the final section of this chapter, I describe these emerging "best practices" for self-perception intervention programs.

Recommendations for the School's Involvement in Enhancing Self-Perceptions

First, a word of caution is in order. As always, educators must be careful about implementing personality or self-related concepts into their curriculum. Educational fads (such as the self-esteem enhancement movement) and controversies surrounding those fads come and go at regular intervals. For example, research on learning styles (Coffield, Moseley, Hall, & Ecclestone, 2004; Pashler, McDaniel, Rohrer, & Bjork, 2008) finds little support for the notion that specific "styles" or preferences for learning material are related to actual student performance or achievement. Similar concerns of a lack of empirical support can be directed at other concepts that have found their way into the curriculum, including multiple intelligences (e.g., Gardner, Krechevsky, Sternberg, & Okagaki, 1994) and emotional intelligence (e.g., Doty, 2001). At a time of limited or diminishing resources, educators are best advised to proceed cautiously and to let research dictate their implementation of curriculum changes. Unfortunately, the commercial and competitive nature of the education business and the climate of demonstrating quick and sustained achievement gains do not favor such caution and patience.

Based on the current research literature, there are several recommendations for how middle level schools should conduct their efforts to enhance student self-perceptions. If they are considering purchasing a commercial program, schools or teachers wishing to include a self-perception enhancement component in their curriculum should evaluate which programs are most consistent with the relevant research. If schools or teachers are considering developing their own curriculum, then they should ensure that such programs include certain core elements. In Table 1.1 I provide a listing of these self-perception enhancement program "do's" and "don'ts."

First, self-perceptions that are tied to and aligned with specific academic competencies and abilities are likely to lead to positive outcomes. The research evidence is clear that feeling competent, efficacious, and motivated within a particular academic domain is associated with greater success in that domain. Thus, programs that strive to match specific self-perceptions with specific academic domains are more likely to be successful. However, the matching of self-perceptions with competencies or accomplishments must be made with care (Dweck, 2007).

Second, a focus on raising the general or global self-esteem of students is likely to be misplaced. At the very least, such efforts should be made with caution. In particular, schools should avoid programs that create unrealistic, inaccurate, or unsubstantiated self-views among students. There is clearly some validity to the criticisms of the "every student gets a ribbon" approaches. When self-perceptions are not tied to actual attributes or accomplishments, students are heading for self-confusion rather than clarity. According to Leary (2004), "holding an overly flattering view of one's personality, abilities, and other attributes is often a recipe for personal disaster. Success in life comes largely from matching one's abilities, interests, and inclinations to appropriate situations, jobs, and relationships. To the extent that they misperceive who or what they are really like, people are more likely to make bad decisions" (p. 72). Similarly, Twenge and Campbell (2009) note, "thinking that you're great when you actually stink is a recipe

Table 1.1. Do's and Don'ts for School-Based Self-Enhancement Programs in the Middle Level School

1. *Do* match students' specific self-perceptions with their specific academic competencies and abilities.

2. *Do not* focus on raising the general or global self-esteem of middle level school students.

3. *Do* provide teachers with scientifically accurate material on the nature of the self and its processes.

4. *Do not* implement a self-perception curriculum that ignores or is disconnected from relevant research.

5. *Do* actively teach students how not to be narcissistic.

6. *Do not* ignore the self-perceptions of middle level school students.

for narcissism, yet this is what many parents and teachers encourage in children every day in the name of self-esteem" (p. 83).

Third, teacher training programs would benefit from the inclusion of material on the nature of the self and its processes. This self-related knowledge base could be provided within the intervention program itself, included in preservice teacher education, and/or added to professional development training. Given the potentially crucial role that middle level school teachers play in the selves of their students, having at least a basic understanding of the self-perception process would increase the likelihood that teachers could work effectively with students to achieve clarity and accuracy in their self-views.

Fourth, a self-perception curriculum that is informed by empirical research would be beneficial to middle level school students. In some ways, such a curriculum could be modeled after one that covers the nature and processes of the human body. There is now a developmental and social psychology knowledge base (e.g., Harter, 1999; Leary, 2004) sufficient to address with young people what the self is, how it develops and operates, the positive and negative tendencies it can show, and so on. A strong argument can be made that the middle level school is the most important time and place for enhancing student self-perceptions. This is the time when multiple influences (both good and bad) affect the foundation of a young person's sense of self and when students are likely to have multiple questions about who they are or who they are becoming. The remainder of this book offers many suggestions for how such a curriculum could be developed and implemented.

Fifth, self-perception programs should actively strive to teach students about narcissism and how they can avoid becoming narcissistic. As Twenge and Campbell (2009) have shown, efforts to counter the emerging cultural values of entitlement, specialness, uniqueness, egotism, materialism, self-centeredness, self-admiration, and overly inflated self-views will have positive benefits both for young people and for the adults that they will become. Specific antinarcissism programs could include the teaching of empathy and perspective taking, interpersonal and friendship skills, conflict management and resolution, and the development of self-control, self-discipline, and self-efficacy. Effective praise for academic performance entails an emphasis on students' effort, perseverance, and engagement rather than on some fixed level of intelligence (Dweck, 2007).

Finally, ignoring the self-perceptions of middle level school students is likely to make teaching and learning more difficult. A focus on self-perceptions can be justified by the central role that the self plays in teaching and learning (e.g., Craven & Marsh, 2008). Indeed, that was one of Beane and Lipka's (1986) major arguments. Even if schools devote little attention to self-concept and self-esteem, self-perceptions will still be affected by children's school experiences and their school experiences will still affect their self-perceptions. As Swann and colleagues (2007) concluded, "given that people with negative self-views think and behave in ways that diminish their quality of life, it is incumbent on behavioral scientists to develop and refine strategies for improving these negative self-views" (p. 92). Leary (2004) noted, "I can think of few more important skills than to learn how to minimize the intrusion of the self. If I had my way, all high school students would learn to do so in a life skills course and later receive booster classes in college and in the workplace" (p. 189). Clearly, such efforts could begin in the middle level school through the cultivation of humility, mindfulness, empathy, self-compassion, and more positive self-perceptions.

CONCLUSION

As this chapter has shown, the self is enigmatic in many ways—it can be considered as the core element around which a person's experiences (including learning) are organized, yet it is also the part of the person that can be responsible for inaccurate or dysfunctional perceptions and behaviors. From the middle level educator's perspective, the self can be recruited effectively to help teachers to meet their learning objectives–and it can openly question the necessity for learning specific content, completing assignments or assessments, and taking particular classes. Clearly, some of the self's elements and processes can enhance learning, whereas other aspects can actively work against learning.

On the one hand, educators could *avoid* the selves of their students in their teaching of specific content. On the other hand, educators could *approach* their students' selves by recognizing and teaching the complexities of the self and its processes. This seems like a tall order—compared to the approach option, the avoidance option is surely easier, requires less professional development, does not require a coordinated effort within the school, and is not dependent upon the self-perceptions and self-understanding of the teachers themselves. However, as the remaining chapters in this book demonstrate, there is reason to be optimistic about the approach option. Across all the elements of the self-enhancing school, there are practices and research studies that confirm the possibility and advantages of schools being in the business of enhancing the self-perceptions of middle level school students.

REFERENCES

Baumeister, R. F., Campbell, J. D., Krueger, J. I., & Vohs, K. D. (2005). Exploding the self-esteem myth. *Scientific American, 292,* 84-92.

Beane, J. A. (1994). Cluttered terrain: The schools' interest in the self. In T. M. Brinthaupt & R. P. Lipka (Eds.), *Changing the self: Philosophies, techniques, and experiences* (pp. 69-87). Albany, NY: State University of New York Press.

Beane, J. A., & Lipka, R. P. (1986). *Self-concept, self-esteem, and the curriculum.* New York, NY: Teachers College Press.

Blackwell, L., Trzesniewski, K., & Dweck, C. S. (2007). Implicit theories of intelligence predict achievement across an adolescent transition: A longitudinal study and an intervention. *Child Development, 78,* 246-263.

Brinthaupt, T. M., & Lipka, R. P. (2002). Understanding early adolescent self and identity: An introduction. In T. M. Brinthaupt & R. P. Lipka (Eds.), *Understanding early adolescent self and identity: Applications and Interventions.* Albany, NY: State University of New York Press.

Carlson K. S. & Gjerde, P. F. (2009). Preschool personality antecedents of narcissism in adolescence and young adulthood: A 20-year longitudinal study. *Journal of Research in Personality, 43,* 570-578.

Coffield, F. C., Moseley, D. V. M., Hall, E., & Ecclestone, K. (2004). *Should we be using learning styles? What research has to say to practice.* London, England: Learning and Skills Research Centre.

Craven, R. G., & Marsh, H. W. (2008). The centrality of the self-concept construct for psychological wellbeing and unlocking human potential: Implications for child and educational psychologists. *Educational and Child Psychology, 25*(2), 104-118.

Doty, G. (2001). *Fostering emotional intelligence in K-8 students: Simple strategies and ready-to-use activities.* Thousand Oaks, CA: Corwin Press.

DuBois, D. L., Burk-Braxton, C., & Tevendale, H. D. (2002). Esteem-enhancement interventions during early adolescence. In T. M. Brinthaupt & R. P. Lipka (Eds.), *Understanding early adolescent self and identity: Applications and interventions* (pp. 321-371). Albany, NY: State University of New York Press.

DuBois, D. L., & Flay, B. R. (2004). The healthy pursuit of self-esteem: Comment on and alternative to the Crocker and Park (2004) formulation. *Psychological Bulletin, 130*(3), 415-420. doi:10.1037/0033-2909.130.3.415

Dweck, C. S. (2007). The perils and promises of praise. *Educational Leadership, 65*(2), 34-39.

Ferguson, C. J. (2010). Narcissism run rampant? Let's not flatter ourselves. *The Chronicle of Higher Education.* Retrieved from http://chronicle.com/article/Narcissism-Run-Rampant-Lets/123705/

Gardner, H., Krechevsky, M., Sternberg, R. J., & Okagaki, L. (1994). Intelligence in context: Enhancing students' practical intelligence for school. In K. McGilly (Ed.), *Classroom lessons: Integrating cognitive theory and classroom practice* (pp. 105-127). Cambridge, MA: The MIT Press.

Gentile, B., Twenge, J. M., & Campbell, W. K. (2010). Birth cohort differences in self-esteem, 1988-2008: A cross-temporal meta-analysis. *Review of General Psychology, 14*(3), 261-268. doi:10.1037/a0019919

Gladwell, M. (2008). *Outliers: The story of success.* New York, NY: Little, Brown & Co.

Harter, S. (1999). *The construction of the self: A developmental perspective.* New York, NY: Guilford Press.

Henderlong, J., & Lepper, M. R. (2002). The effects of praise on children's intrinsic motivation: A review and synthesis. *Psychological Bulletin, 128*, 774-795.

Hill, P. L., & Roberts, B. W. (2011). Narcissism, well-being, and observer-rated personality across the lifespan. *Social Psychological and Personality Science*, doi:10.1177/1948550611415867

Kohn, A. (1994). The truth about self-esteem. *Phi Delta Kappan, 76*(4), 272-283.

Krauthammer, C. (1990, February 5). Education: Doing bad and feeling good. *Time, 78*.

Leary, M. L. (2004). *The curse of the self: Self-awareness, egotism, and the quality of human life*. New York, NY: Oxford University Press.

Leo, J. (1996, June 17). Let's lower our self-esteem. *U.S. News and World Report*, 25.

Marsh, H. W., & Craven, R. G. (2006). Reciprocal effects of self-concept and performance from a multidimensional perspective: Beyond seductive pleasure and unidimensional perspectives. *Perspectives On Psychological Science, 1*(2), 133-163. doi:10.1111/j.1745-6916.2006.00010.x

Neff, K. D. (2009). The role of self-compassion in development: A healthier way to relate to oneself. *Human Development, 52*(4), 211-214. doi:10.1159/000215071.

Neff, K. D., & McGehee, P. (2010). Self-compassion and psychological resilience among adolescents and young adults. *Self and Identity, 9*(3), 225-240. doi:10.1080/15298860902979307

Pashler, H., McDaniel, M., Rohrer, D., & Bjork, R. (2008). Learning styles: Concepts and evidence. *Psychological Science in the Public Interest, 9*(3), 105-119. doi:10.1111/j.1539-6053.2009.01038.x

Simmons, R. G., & Blyth, D. A. (1987). *Moving into adolescence: The impact of pubertal change and school context*. Hawthorn, NY: Aldine de Gruyter.

Swann, W. B., Jr., Chang-Schneider, C., & McClarty, C. L. (2007). Do people's self-views matter? Self-concept and self-esteem in everyday life. *American Psychologist, 62*, 84-94.

Trzesniewski, K. H., Donnellan, M. B., & Robins, R. W. (2008). Is 'Me Generation' really more narcissistic than previous generations? *Journal of Personality, 76*(4), 903-918. doi:10.1111/j.1467-6494.2008.00508.x

Trzesniewski, K. H., Donnellan, M., Moffitt, T. E., Robins, R. W., Poulton, R., & Caspi, A. (2006). Low self-esteem during adolescence predicts poor health, criminal behavior, and limited economic prospects during adulthood. *Developmental Psychology, 42*(2), 381-390. doi:10.1037/0012-1649.42.2.381

Twenge, J. M., & Campbell, W. K. (2009). *The narcissism epidemic: Living in an age of entitlement*. New York, NY: Free Press.

CHAPTER 2

DEVELOPING CARING, HUMANISTIC CLASSROOMS

Effects on Young Adolescents' Complete Growth

Dave F. Brown

DEVELOPING CARING, HUMANISTIC CLASSROOMS: POSITIVE EFFECTS ON YOUNG ADOLESCENTS' COMPLETE GROWTH

David Sousa (2010) noted recently, "Schools tend to be so focused on academics and testing that they are often unaware of the powerful effect that social and cultural forces have on students" (p. 16). Perhaps every public school teacher has recognized schools' "cultural" changes initiated by NCLB legislation, and its effects on their instructional behaviors, demeanor toward students, and overall classroom climate.

Talk of providing appropriate professional development for middle level educators was the purpose of a recent meeting of middle level principals. A few principals in attendance suggested the need for a session on *data analyses*. As a parent of an eighth grader, I spoke in opposition to

Middle Grades Curriculum:
Voices and Visions of the Self-Enhancing School, pp. 17–31
Copyright © 2013 by Information Age Publishing

17

offering a professional development session on test score analyses. What many parents want for their 11-15 year-olds each day at school has nothing to do with test scores; but, simultaneously, having an impact on students' test score performance. They want their child to:

- feel psychologically comfortable;
- know that teachers care about and notice their child;
- have academic success in each class;
- be cognitively challenged; and,
- have opportunities to enjoy friendships during the day.

Middle level students have many needs, and cognitive growth is an inherent purpose of schooling; but, young adolescents don't care about their test scores when they enter school each day. Among young adolescents' thoughts each morning are the following:

- Does my hair and skin look good today?
- Do I smell ok?
- Will the clothes I'm wearing appeal to the people I want to notice me, and
- Will they be acceptable to the peer group I want to be a part of?
- Will my teacher notice me today?
- Will I succeed academically today?
- When will I get to eat again?
- When will I see my friends and have a chance to talk to them again?

Parents may see the role of teachers in promoting genuine young adolescent growth as completely opposite of what teachers believe are their responsibilities.

Middle level teachers' focus on covering unrealistic amounts of content, matching each subject's content to state tests, delivering frequent practice tests to prepare students for yearly tests, and limiting student decision-making all in an effort to raise student scores may produce the opposite results among young adolescents than what educators intend. If educators look myopically at student test score data, and interpret them as evidence of teachers' successes, they are likely to ignore the multitude of factors that schools can actually influence that improve students' overall growth.

When students are viewed only as test score data, educators lose their focus on the primary purpose of schooling—the overall healthy growth of young adolescents. The resultant effect of testing emphases may perhaps be a set of slightly better student test scores; but an overwhelming failure of educators to enhance students' social, emotional, identity, and even cognitive developmental processes; all simultaneously screaming for attention during the critical middle level years. Adults want adolescents to be effective decision-makers, creative and critical thinkers, and able problem solvers—narrowing teaching and learning to test score successes diminishes the possibility of promoting cognitive and social adolescent maturity (Brown, 2006).

CHANGES IN ACADEMIC EXPECTATIONS

Young adolescents face many new challenges upon their entry into the middle level schools. Middle level teachers have greater academic expectations than elementary teachers, require students to be more independent learners, often have unrealistic expectations for students' organizational skills, generally have less time to provide individual assistance to students due to teaching several sections, and are thus likely to provide less feedback students need to improve academic performance. Eccles and Midgley (1989) discovered that junior high teachers "Emphasized social comparison and competition more … and were less trusting and more controlling of students compared to the adolescents' elementary teachers" (cited in Roeser & Lau, 2002, p. 110).

These unrealistic expectations often cause academic difficulties for young adolescents. Lower student academic performance initially in middle school is common compared to students' elementary years' successes. These challenges decrease students' confidence and erode previously positive perceptions of their academic capabilities.

Young adolescents become engrossed with other developmental processes causing them to lose focus on their academic responsibilities. Many young adolescents experience daily stress associated with the changing social scene, awkward physical growth, intensified academic expectations, and feelings of academic inadequacy. Stress decreases the probability that students will gain any benefits from being in class.

Young adolescents often lack the organizational strategies necessary for class preparedness and resulting academic success. Their frequent academic miscues (e.g., turning in late assignments, failing to complete difficult homework, reluctance to ask for help) and self-serving doubts lead to an overwhelming drop in self-esteem.

The culmination of these overwhelming negative factors often leads to less overall confidence as learners, a resultant drop in effort, and feelings of cognitive inadequacy that affect positive attitudes needed for academic successes (Kernis, 2002). A familiar childhood event reflects the possible successful path that many young adolescents could experience with effective middle level educators' support.

LESS CONFIDENCE AND MINIMAL
SUPPORT LEAD TO LESS RISK-TAKING

Many recall their first experience climbing the ladder of the high diving board at the local swimming pool. It may have been an intensely stressful scenario for some, experiencing fear of the unknown thought of falling freely into the water from 10 feet above it. If no friends or family members were close by, the swimmer may have walked to the end of the diving board, looked over into the water below, only to return slowly to the ladder where he/she embarrassingly walked backwards down to the cement deck below to never try again. In that scenario, confidence is lost, risk-taking is diminished, and success is unlikely.

If someone were there to support the jumper—to provide guidance and encouragement—he or she probably walked to the edge and slowly stepped off of the end of the board. The feeling of falling was terrifying, but after one enters the water without incident and manages to rise to the surface unscathed, he or she feels a new exhilaration.

Those who succeeded at jumping off the first time, likely did so again almost immediately, returning to the ladder and awaiting their turns with great excitement. The initial success led to repeated risk-taking. Successful jumpers attempted a new way of jumping each time at the end of the board. Some even went from merely jumping, to diving, to somersaults, and to eventually doing one-and-a-half flips into a diving entry. What began as simple fear based on ignorance became a series of successes and greater risk-taking each new time on the high dive. With support, initial fear morphed into risk-taking, success, creative thought, and more advanced growth.

For young adolescents, middle school's daily learning experiences are similar to the high diving board episode. Despite years of repeated successes as learners in the elementary grades, for young adolescents, less academic success during middle level years is often based on a naturally occurring personal obsession with social, emotional, and identity growth processes. Low grades and constant social doubt cause near record levels of low self-esteem during the middle level years (Harter, 2005). The resultant behavior is frequently less risk-taking by students. At a time when cognitive abilities are increasing in strength, young adolescents should not be taking fewer risks at school, but instead many more risks (Walsh, 2004). Little growth occurs among those of any age when risk-taking ceases because cognitive risks challenge learners and lead to further cognitive growth and confidence.

The responsibility for teaching and encouraging young adolescents to adopt the strategies necessary for successful management of behavioral and academic progress lies with every educator. Educators' guidance for overall developmental growth successes looks entirely different than comparing students, setting exceptionally high academic standards, merely issuing poor grades as a warning to improve, or using a traditional teacher-driven instructional and curricular design that often ignores the needs and interests of young adolescents. These traditional and often discouraging strategies have no positive impact on students' efforts, motivation, or cognitive growth.

Ineffective middle level teachers usually accompany these traditional practices with the frequently heard phrase "We've got to get these students ready for the rigor of high school." No philosophy or accompanying strategy could be more feckless in improving young adolescents' many developmental growth processes or cognitive skills.

THE VALUE OF DEMONSTRATING CARE FOR STUDENTS

Sousa (2010) reported "[healthy] School culture is characterized in part by openness of communication, level of expectations, amount of recognition and appreciation for effort, involvement in decision making, and degree of caring" (p. 16). Teachers may have a mistaken belief that young adolescents are too mature or don't need to know that their teachers care about them. Nothing could be further from the truth as young adolescents' emotional states are often in flux, as they search for an ally in their daily academic and social challenges. Students notice whether their teachers care about them on the first day of school, and every day following.

Caring for students is a set of explicit behaviors that effective educators utilize daily. Caring involves

- learning and acknowledging students by name;
- smiling frequently and using humor;
- actively listening to students;
- responding favorably and with empathy to students' anxieties and frustrations;
- knowing and frequently asking about students' personal lives;
- establishing and enforcing a reasonable set of behavioral and academic expectations for each student; and,
- ensuring opportunities for each student's daily academic success.

These effective professional behaviors communicate to young adolescents that the adults in their school are more than mere technicians—that they are genuinely interested in all aspects of students' development. The ways in which teachers demonstrate care are often quite diverse for each student. Some students may need gentle influence and prodding while others expect teachers to hold them to specifically stated expectations such as demanding that homework be completed before the end of the day, or having students meet behavioral goals weekly before being permitted to participate in enrichment activities. Influential teachers discover how each student interprets care and finds ways to meet each one's need for care.

Demonstrations of care enhance student/teacher relationships in significant ways thus improving learning for students. The effects of caring teachers on students have been described by Stipek (2006):

> One of the best predictors of students' efforts and engagement in school is the relationships they have with their teachers. When students have a secure relationship with their teachers they are more comfortable taking risks that enhance learning—tackling challenging tasks, persisting when they run into difficulty, or asking questions when they are confused. (p. 46)

Teaching is a highly social experience. The verbal interactions between teachers and students must be carefully nurtured—on a daily basis. The ability to listen attentively and actively lays the groundwork for ensuring that students comprehend the caring nature of teachers. Congruent communication is another essential component of caring teachers that students clearly recognize and value (Brown, 2005).

Care is a critical aspect of successful learning environments at every level of schooling. The positive effects of care on learning were recognized by Goodman, Sutton, and Harkevy (1995) who noted that caring for students "Promoted learning and overpowered the comparative effects of instructional methodologies" (p. 696). Lipsitz (1995) emphasized "Caring did not substitute for learning; caring established an effective culture for learning" (p. 666). Caring for students is part of the science of effective teaching—not merely the art of effective instruction. Classroom care is imperative to ensure student cognitive growth.

CREATING MUTUALLY RESPECTFUL ENVIRONMENTS

Taking more risks and persisting when challenged are necessary behaviors to ensure genuine learning. Risk taking and persistence are unlikely when students perceive their teachers as undeserving of their respect. Stipek (2006) noted "That students function more effectively when they feel respected and valued and function poorly when they feel disrespected or marginalized" (p. 46).

Every teacher is responsible for creating classrooms of mutual respect. Mutually respectful relationships begin with teachers recognizing students' needs for healthy relationships with teachers and fellow students. Teachers can create relationships with students by developing a classroom atmosphere of psychological safety. When students enter middle level classrooms knowing that they will receive assistance when they need it, have their questions accepted and answered, and know they'll be protected from ridicule, they begin to experience a state of mind needed for enhanced learning. Students recognize mutual respect when teachers

- engage in personal conversations with them;
- recognize their efforts as much as their successes;
- provide specific constructive feedback that encourages more effort; and
- ensure multiple opportunities for academic successes.

Stipek (2006) believes that, "Holding students accountable without this type of support and encouragement is likely to discourage and alienate them rather than motivate them" (p. 48). Students want to be held accountable for learning; but, just as the high diver won't leave the board without confidence and support, neither will young adolescents take the risks needed for academic growth unless they genuinely *feel* the teacher respects them.

When teachers' attitudes toward their students are based on mutual respect, students are treated more like guests rather than as malleable objects to be manipulated. Students know the difference between teachers who respect them and those who merely tolerate them. It's teachers' actions that students notice, as they are always louder than their words in mutually respectful classrooms. Mutual respect among students and teachers creates a learning community in which every student believes he/she belongs in the class, and thus becomes an active member of the learning process.

YOUNG ADOLESCENTS' SOCIAL AND EMOTIONAL CHALLENGES

Any middle level teacher who believes that expert knowledge in a content area alone is sufficient to teach young adolescents will fail to reach and affect academic change in middle level students. The intense growth among young adolescents includes a heightened awareness of their personal attributes and the way in which they either fit or don't fit into the prevailing social milieu of their peers (NMSA, 2010). As fifth or sixth graders, young adolescents usually leave their home community elementary schools to enter an immense building and see hundreds of fellow students whom they have never met. The result of such drastic changes in the location of their new school and the overwhelming population of new students is often fear and a resultant sense of trying to survive daily social encounters. Novel social situations can create fear and worry among adults; so naturally, young adolescents experience similar feelings of distress.

One particular middle level student described the social challenges inherent in every period of a young adolescent's school day:

> I think every middle school teacher should know, or try to understand the social whirlwind of statuses that forms and so quickly hardens with every student in their [sic] place. What may seem, to a teacher, a classroom full of students peacefully working, may be exactly the opposite to a student. It becomes a room full of pitfalls, danger signs, and safe havens situated carefully in familiar territory. Every student, boy or girl, has their [sic] place, their territory, their paths, the people they can stay with on their level. While some students may not be directly aware of it, they always have a subconscious understanding of where they fit. (Doda & Knowles, 2007, p. 29)

This description of the minefields of middle level students' worlds is merely a beginning recognition of the social and emotional challenges inherent in their daily lives.

In their development of socialization skills, young adolescents are attempting to

- develop helpful relationships with their teachers;
- find fellow students who share their academic skills and desires for success;
- find genuine friends who share their interests;
- seek classmates who can help them when they struggle academically;
- find same-sex friends who identify with their interests;
- seek same-sex friends who match their academic and physical talents;
- search for a peer group that accepts them; and
- find same-sex friends who share their interests in developing a sexual identity.

Searching for these *friends* is a constant process, and all along the way, young adolescents judge their successes with either satisfaction or frustration at the end of the day. Their rejection by peers in attempts to join other social groups can be devastating events that usually go unnoticed by the adults in their lives. Cushman and Rogers (2007) noted, "Adolescents tend to lose confidence in their academic abilities in the transition to middle school and find social activities more interesting and more important than academic endeavors" (pp. 14-15). Students and teachers identify socialization skills and making friends as imperative outcomes for young adolescents (Brown & Knowles, 2007).

Socialization challenges create emotional havoc for young adolescents. Middle school students "Have a strong need for approval and may be easily discouraged" (NMSA, 2010, p. 60). Added physical changes, particularly the advent of hormonal effects, can alter young adolescents' moods in unpredictable ways. Personal, as well as, adults' expectations for social and academic success may create even greater turmoil. Young adolescents focus on expanding socialization processes while wrestling with self-awareness that overrides their academic focus. Seiffge-Krenke (1998) noted that young adolescents' needs for social relationships outside the family create possibilities for social inadequacy.

Day-to-day emotional well-being is affected by several other developmental issues during young adolescence:

- dissatisfaction with physical appearance and growth;
- frustration with peer socialization experiences;
- irritation with adults' control over one's decision making opportunities;
- inability to find a balance between dependence and independence from parents;
- responding to an *imaginary audience*; and
- frustration finding and demonstrating the identity they actually want to portray. (Brown & Knowles, 2007).

Brain developmental processes also have an impact on young adolescents' emotional states of mind. Processing of daily events for young adolescents occurs in the amygdala, the emotional center of the brain rather than the prefrontal cortex, the reasoning part of the brain (Walsh, 2004). Immordino-Yang and Faeth (2010) noted that "Factual knowledge alone is useless without a guiding emotional intuition" (p. 78). Teachers must consider their students' emotional states of mind and plan lessons around their emotions.

What appear to be ordinary uneventful daily events to adults actually explode into emotional crises for many young adolescents. Recognition of this brain-processing attribute is essential for teachers to ensure their support for many young adolescent behaviors rather than reacting with anger and frustration toward students who are emotionally charged.

Effective middle level educators don't take the emotional responses from their students personally; have a strong sense of self, are able to laugh at their mistakes and faults, and use humor to diffuse argumentative situations. These responsive teacher behaviors have the power to quell students' emotional outbursts and create a productive learning environment.

PROMOTING POSITIVE SOCIAL AND EMOTIONAL SKILLS

Becoming adept at socialization skills and processes are lifetime goals, as any adult might admit. However, one cannot improve socialization skills unless he or she has an opportunity to "try on" new personas or behaviors. Middle level students *try on* social personalities regularly, but their forays into these new roles are often unsanctioned and cause social unrest with friends or trouble with teachers. Any attempt at improving social skills requires a significant, yet scary move: the willingness to take a risk in a crowd of new people. Risk taking is an essential aspect of growth in all personal areas—including social and cognitive domains. Middle level students need a safe haven for this risk taking to be practiced.

Traditional lunch periods are hardly the venue to ensure socialization successes. Middle level educators must purposely design components of the school day and classroom activities to ensure students have opportunities to practice new socialization skills. Prior to specific teacher interventions, however, is clear understanding and recognition by middle level educators of the need to provide young adolescents with appropriate social and emotional skills. Kohn (1997) reveals,

> Let there be no question then: educators, parents, and other adults are desperately needed to offer guidance, to act as models, to pose challenges that promote moral growth, and to help children understand the effects of their actions on other people, thereby tapping and nurturing a concern for others that is present in children from a very young age. (p. 11)

Young adolescents need specifically designed socialization experiences to learn effective social protocol and encourage the use of appropriate socialization nuances. Advisory sessions are purposely designed nonacademic periods to encourage young adolescents' growth in their social, emotional, identity, and moral developmental processes (MacLaury,

2002). Advisories typically last for 15 to 40 minutes and can meet from once every 2 weeks to even daily in some secondary schools. The ratio of students to teachers is suggested at a maximum of 15 to 1 to meet its objective of providing young adolescents with one adult in the building who knows them well enough to help them with personal social and emotional matters if crises were to occur. MacLaury added, "Advisories are a means of redesigning large, impersonal schools into smaller, caring communities that promote closer relationships between students and staff" (p. 16). Effective advisors also provide academic assistance to students who need help beyond the traditional class meeting times.

Advisories offer middle level educators the forum, time, and curriculum to address young adolescents' many developmental needs (Galassi, Gulledge, & Cox, 1998). Jensen (2009) reported that children need specific instruction in the following emotional responses: "sympathy, patience, shame, cooperation, gratitude, humility, forgiveness, empathy, optimism, and compassion" (p. 18).

Schools are logical places for teaching adolescents these caring emotions due to the constant socialization among many students together for so many hours a day. When teachers engage students in essential conversations about their social and emotional developmental processes through advisory sessions it is likely that students and teachers will develop much closer bonds and the mutual respect needed to promote students' self-confidence and resultant improved academic performance. Advisories are another avenue to creating a self-enhancing school for young adolescents.

THE SIGNIFICANCE OF SHARED DECISION-MAKING IN PROMOTING COGNITIVE GROWTH

Cynthia Mee (1997) noted in interviews with over 2,000 young adolescents that students of middle level age are extremely curious and enjoy asking questions. Children as learners are spoken to from birth, with an expectation that they will be listeners during most of their educational careers. Young adolescents' intense cognitive growth processes, however, create an overwhelming curiosity that teachers can easily use to encourage and increase their motivation for learning. Middle school is the opportune time and place for adults to speak less and listen more to their students for a change.

It is too easy and traditionally common to treat middle level students as merely consumers of facts—especially with the current emphasis on collecting student test score data. With the developing cognitive, moral, and socialization skills of young adolescents, middle school classrooms are the ideal environment for teachers to begin to share decision making. Parents are highly interested in their adolescent children improving their critical analyses and creative thinking processes, but the opportunities for practicing these thinking processes are seldom provided in traditional classrooms.

Many occasions exist for teachers to provide young adolescents with decision-making opportunities throughout the school day. Their need for expanding their moral thinking makes many typical classroom events perfect opportunities for student voice. Some examples of collaborative decision making young adolescents are ready to engage in include:

- establishing classroom rules and expectations at the beginning of the year;
- suggesting a set of reasonable consequences for failure to follow rules;
- developing evaluation rubrics for specific assignments;
- initiating a set of personal academic and behavioral goals for both long and short terms;
- identifying personal areas of needed academic growth;
- establishing guidelines for improving personal academic progress;
- initiating and conducting a conference with their parents on their academic progress; and
- making curricular decisions that reflect their interests and motivate them.

Opportunities for students to determine curricular emphases are imperative for them to make meaningful connections to content. Immordino-Yang and Faeth (2010) reported on the cognitive research supporting student choice in curricular decision-making:

> If students feel no connection to the knowledge they learn in school, then the academic content will seem emotionally meaningless to them. Why not in a serious and responsible manner, involve students in the [curricular] selection process? This participatory approach has the power to instill in students a sense of ownership that can go a long way toward making later learning meaningful and the emotions they experience relevant. (pp. 78-79)

Teachers who provide extensive decision-making opportunities for their students recognize young adolescents' advanced cognitive growth processes, and realize the power of motivating students by offering these chances for engagement. Students engaged in these significant decision-making opportunities easily comprehend the high levels of respect, care, and trust that teachers place in them. The results of sharing decisions lead to an overwhelming confidence in students that transfers to improved academic achievement merely due to the boost in self-confidence that accompanies such respect.

CONCLUSION

Learning is not a solitary event occurring in a cognitive vacuum; it is not merely intellectually based. Every learning situation is a socially and emotionally charged event. Young adolescents' intense and unique developmental growth patterns create a greater need for middle level educators to design learning experiences based primarily on the social and emotional developmental needs of these students than merely on cognitive processes.

The word *rigor* has been used, inappropriately, to describe what some pundits believe to represent and describe significant learning in extremely traditional classrooms of the past. Images of *rigorous* learning denote the very culture of learning that has come to dominate the educational landscape in so many secondary schools across the U. S. since the inception of No Child Left Behind. Instead of creating more learning, the environment that exists in the traditional teacher-directed classroom of note taking, worksheet completing, test taking, and fact regurgitation is actually less intellectually conducive than classrooms where social and emotional student needs are prioritized.

Delivering heavy doses of academic content in a sterile manner is not the most effective means of increasing young adolescents' cognitive growth. Their constantly changing bodies and brains create a challenge for educators unrivaled in the teaching profession. Learning in middle level classrooms must be a shared experience—shared with those who need to grow—young adolescents themselves. Middle level schools should be *opportunity centers*—places where any learning event is planned and delivered with the primary objective of providing unique—not traditional—opportunities for young adolescents to use their social, emotional, and cognitive processes. McEwin, Dickinson, and Jenkins (1996) stated the challenges of teaching middle level students:

> A continuing difficulty in providing developmentally responsive schools for young adolescents is widespread ignorance about the characteristics, needs, and interests of the age group. Many people, both inside and outside the profession, are not only unenlightened about the age group, but hold negative stereotypes about them. (p. 157)

The ignorance of which these researchers speak is demonstrated when teachers rely on traditional teaching methods that focus on content and only students' cognitive processing while neglecting their social and emotional needs in engaging students in learning.

When adults and infants learn outside of schooling contexts, they don't need to experience the *rigor* that many might believe adolescents need to learn well: those factors such as stress, frustration, anxiety, fear, or frequent feelings of incompetence. Adults take control of their learning circumstances. Adults and infants feel comfortable taking risks, look forward to being challenged, embrace a psychologically comfortable environment, and look forward to using their creative and critical thinking processes.

Why should the learning environment for young adolescents be any different? From birth, adults nurture children's learning based on the evidence of developmentally appropriate practices. Young adolescence is also a developmental growth stage. Middle school students need caring and respectful adults to guide their learning each day. They need classrooms in which their voices affect class decisions, and they have opportunities to determine the direction of and personal assessment of their growth. Humanistic teaching is required in middle level schools because young adolescents are humans. Responding to the full range of their developmental needs ensures that they will experience genuine learning—real *rigor*.

REFERENCES

Brown, D. F. (2005). The significance of congruent communication in effective classroom management. *The Clearing House: A Journal of Educational Strategies, Issues, and Ideas, 79*(1), 12-15.

Brown, D. F. (2006). It's the curriculum, stupid: There's something wrong with it. *Phi Delta Kappan, 87*(10), 777-783.

Brown, D. F., & Knowles, T. (2007). *What every middle school teacher should know* (2nd ed.). Portsmouth, NH, and Westerville, OH: Heinemann and National Middle School Association.

Cushman, K., & Rogers, L. (2007). Middle school students talk about social forces in the classroom. *Middle School Journal, 29*(3), 14-24.

Doda, N., & Knowles, T. (2007). Listening to the voices of young adolescents. *Middle School Journal, 29*(3), 26-33.

Eccles, J. S., & Midgley, C. (1989). Stage-environment fit: Developmentally appropriate classrooms for young adolescents. In C. Ames & R. Ames (Eds.), *Research on motivation in education: Goals and cognitions* (Vol. 3, pp. 13-44). New York, NY: Academic Press.

Galassi, J. P., Gulledge, S. A., & Cox, N. D. (1998). *Advisory: Definitions descriptions decisions directions*. Columbus, OH: National Middle School Association.

Goodman, J. F., Sutton, V., & Harkevy, I. (1995). The effectiveness of family workshops in a middle school setting: Respect and caring make a difference. *Phi Delta Kappan, 76*(9), 694-700.

Harter, S. (2005). Self-concepts and self-esteem, children and adolescents. In C. B. Fisher & R. M. Lerner (Eds.), *Encyclopedia of applied development science* (pp. 972-977). Thousand Oaks, CA: SAGE.

Immordino-Yang, M. H., & Faeth, M. (2010). The role of emotion and skilled intuition in learning. In D. A. Sousa (Ed.), *Mind, brain & education: Neuroscience implications for the classroom* (pp. 69-84). Bloomington, IN: Solution Tree Press.

Jensen, E. (2009). *Teaching with poverty in mind: What being poor does to kids' brains and what schools can do about it*. Alexandria, VA: Association of Supervision and Curriculum Development.

Kernis, M. H. (2002). Self-esteem as multifaceted construct. In T. M. Brinthaupt & R. P. Lipka (Eds.), *Understanding early adolescent self and identity: Application and interventions* (pp. 57-88). Albany, NY: State University of New York Press.

Kohn, A. (1997). How not to teach values: A critical look at character education. *Phi Delta Kappan, 78*, 428-439.

Lipsitz, J. (1995). Prologue: Why we should care about caring. *Phi Delta Kappan, 76*(9), 665-666.

MacLaury, S. (2002). *Student advisories in grades 5-12: A facilitator's guide*. Norwood, MA: Christopher-Gordon.

McEwin, C. K., Dickinson, T. S., & Jenkins, D. M. (1996). *America's middle schools: Practices and progress, a 25 year perspective*. Columbus, OH: National Middle School Association.

Mee, C. S. (1997). *2,000 Voices: Young adolescents' perceptions and curriculum implications*. Westerville, OH: National Middle School Association.

National Middle School Association (2010). *This we believe: Keys to educating young adolescents*. Westerville, OH: Author.

Roeser, R. W., & Lau, S. (2002). On academic identity formation in middle school settings during early adolescence. In T. M. Brinthaupt & R. P. Lipka (Eds.), *Understanding early adolescent self and identity: Application and interventions* (pp. 91-131). Albany, NY: State University of New York Press.

Seiffge-Krenke, I. (1998). Secrets and intimacy in adolescence: Their implications for the development of autonomy. In A. Spitznagel (Ed.), *Geheimnis und Geheimhaltung* (pp. 257-266). Gottingen, Germany: Hogrefe.

Sousa, D. A. (Ed.) (2010). *Mind, brain & education: Neuroscience implications for the classroom*. Bloomington, IN: Solution Tree Press.

Stipek, D. (2006). Relationships matter. *Educational Leadership, 64*(1), 46-49.

Walsh, D. (2004). *Why do they act that way? A survival guide for you and your teen*. New York, NY: Free Press.

CHAPTER 3

GROUPING STUDENTS IN THE SELF-ENHANCING SCHOOL

David C. Virtue

Beane and Lipka (1986) proposed the idea of "self-enhancing schools"—schools in which the overall program is oriented toward enhancing students' self-perceptions. They argued that institutional features of schools (e.g., physical setting, social climate, organizational structures) influence the development of students' self-concept and self-esteem. Self-concept refers to the descriptions an individual has of him or herself in terms of his or her roles and responsibilities. Self-concept is multidimensional, so a student may have a self-concept in mathematics that differs dramatically from his or her self-concept in art, science, or physical education. Self-esteem is evaluative and refers to the degree to which a student is satisfied with his or her self-concept. Recent research (e.g., Parker, 2010) highlights the plasticity of young adolescents' self-perceptions and the extent to which they shape students' overall school experiences, thereby underscoring the need for middle level educators to seriously consider the idea of the self-enhancing school.

Beane and Lipka (1986) described the self-enhancing school in terms of shifts from specific self-debilitating factors common in schools to self-enhancing factors supported by research and sound practice. One key fea-

Middle Grades Curriculum:
Voices and Visions of the Self-Enhancing School, pp. 33–52
Copyright © 2013 by Information Age Publishing
33

ture of such schools would be a shift from attribute grouping patterns as a self-debilitating factor to variable grouping patterns as a self-enhancing factor. Attribute grouping occurs "when learners are grouped or tracked according to some supposedly homogeneous attribute such as ability," whereas "variable grouping patterns recognize that in some cases learners benefit most from heterogeneous grouping, while in others they might have better experiences in groups based on such variables as achievement, interest, and social maturity" (Beane & Lipka, 1986, p. 181). Attribute grouping tends to emphasize a single characteristic; however, Beane and Lipka contend that the self is multidimensional and evolving and, therefore, grouping arrangements in schools should allow for these aspects of the self to develop.

This chapter considers the proposed shift from attribute grouping in its most extreme form—tracking—to variable grouping. The practice of tracking students is described and research related to tracking and various student outcomes, including development of self-perceptions, is summarized. The process of moving away from rigid patterns of ability grouping, or detracking, is discussed and examples of variable grouping patterns (e.g., cooperative learning) and practices supporting such groupings (e.g., differentiated instruction) are provided.

FROM ATTRIBUTE GROUPING ...

Attribute grouping, or homogeneous grouping, has been the dominant form of grouping students for instruction in the United States since the 19th century. Students are typically grouped according to academic ability or intelligence, which is often defined in terms of test scores or grades. Such grouping patterns, it has been argued, benefit both teachers and students by allowing teachers to more easily and efficiently focus instruction on the specific needs of the students. Gifted education advocates also claim that attribute grouping by ability is the fairest form of grouping because it allows high-achieving students to be challenged to the limits of their abilities, not to an artificial ceiling set by a standard or test.

Tracking, a rigid form of single attribute grouping in which students are placed in homogeneous ability groups for all or most of the school day, is a very controversial practice that has been hotly debated (Lockwood, 1996). Tracking has been widely criticized for undermining the social and affective aims of school and for reproducing the inequity and stratification that exists in society (see, e.g., Oakes, 1985; Wheelock, 1992). In the middle grades, critics charge that tracking has long served a sorting function, funneling students into academic, vocational, or remedial paths that will shape their educational futures and, ultimately, their lives—a process Andrews (2005) called "schooling as destiny" (p. 70). Tracking has both staunch supporters and vigorous opponents at the middle level (see Figure 1.1), making it what "may be the single most important unresolved issue in education" (George & Alexander, 2003, p. 415). This section discusses the issue of single attribute grouping—and tracking, in particular—in the middle grades and reviews literature related to single attribute grouping and student self-perceptions.

Tracking in the Middle Grades

Attribute grouping is widely used in middle level schools today, especially in mathematics and, to a lesser extent, English language arts (ELA). In a recent national survey of 827 randomly selected and high-performing middle schools, McEwin and Greene (2009) found that 77% of schools were using some form of nonrandom grouping. In an earlier study, McEwin, Dickinson, and Jenkins (2003) found that 77% of middle schools tracked students in mathematics and 25% tracked in ELA and reading. The mathematics findings are consistent with a recent study in which Loveless (2009) used data from the National Assessment of Educational Progress to determine the extent of tracking in Massachusetts middle schools. He found that the percentage of middle schools using tracking in eighth-grade mathematics remained fairly stable between 1992 (73%) and 2007 (75%). In ELA Loveless found that the percentage of Massachusetts schools using tracking dropped slightly from 1992 (48%) to 2007 (43%).

Loveless (1999) argued that systems of rigid tracking have been on the decline, and middle grades students today are less likely than 20 years

For Tracking	Against Tracking
• Tracking helps schools meet the varying needs of students.	• Tracking is detrimental to young adolescent peer relationships.
• Tracking provides low-achieving students with the attention and slower pace they require.	• Tracking is harmful to the self-esteem of low achievers.
• High-achieving students are provided challenges when tracked.	• Tracking perpetuates class and racial inequities.
• Tracking is necessary for individualizing instruction.	• The grouping process for tracking is often biased.
• Tracking will prevent low achievers from hindering the progress of high achievers.	• Tracking reinforces inaccurate assumptions about intelligence.
	• The least experienced teachers are typically assigned to low-achieving classes.

Figure 3.1.   Arguments for and against tracking (adapted from Powell, 2011, pp. 143-144)

ago to remain tracked for all or most of the school day in classes with a group of students who possess a common attribute (i.e., test score or some other measure of academic performance). While all of these studies suggest that tracking has declined in ELA, they all show clear evidence that practice remains common in mathematics classes. The persistence of tracking in middle level mathematics lends credence to the unsettling observation that, "Middle schools earn legitimacy by supplying able students for the high schools' advanced math courses" (Loveless, p. 124). The class schedules of many middle level students are dictated by their mathematics placements, thus the scheduling of mathematics classes may create a *de facto* tracking system across all areas of the curriculum in some schools.

George and Alexander (2003) contended that tracking at the middle level "has little educational value" and noted that it is not implemented as widely "in exemplary middle schools" compared to other schools (p. 417). While many middle level educators would like to move away from tracking and other forms of ability grouping (George & Alexander), teachers often support these practices because they believe they can work more effectively and efficiently with groups of students "whose abilities all fall into the same narrowly defined range" (Marsh & Raywid, 1994, p. 269). While on the surface this may be a reasonable expectation for teachers to hold, the practice of tracking students contradicts middle level philosophy (Powell, 2011). In its position statement *This We Believe*, the Association for Middle Level Education (formerly National Middle School Association [NMSA], 2010) articulates a firm position in opposition to tracking:

> Research indicates the many limiting and negative effects of academic tracking—decreases in student motivation and self-esteem, unequal learning opportunities, and declines in overall quality of education. In its place, successful middle level schools use cooperative learning groups, independent study, enrichment programs, and other practices to respond to the variety of student competencies, interests, and abilities and meet the needs of advanced learners. (NMSA, pp. 32-33)

The NMSA (2010) position echoes research-based evidence from all levels (i.e., early childhood, elementary, secondary, postsecondary) that tracking runs counter to aims for social justice and equity and that the practice has no real academic benefits for students (Collins, 2003; Oakes, 1985; Wheelock, 1992; Yonezawa & Jones, 2006). Doda (2005) described how tracking tends to compromise social equity in the middle grades and argued that the practice must not be considered neutral or benign.

What is often overlooked in understanding the destructive nature of track-ing is the powerful role class composition plays in determining the quality of classroom life ... Class ability groupings ... can reinforce mistaken beliefs that students have about themselves. Young adolescents labeled 'honors' may actually shy away from challenge for fear of failing and thus lose that identity. Likewise, students placed in the low groups may also come to accept that low ability label as accurate. (p. 28)

From a middle level perspective, a main concern with tracking—and various forms of attribute grouping, in general—is the way in which these practices affect student self-perceptions. Beane and Lipka (1986) asserted that "grouping by a singular dimension places the school in a direct attempt to intervene in student self-perception" (p. 39), and the middle level literature is rich with examples of programs, practices, and organiza-tional structures that influence young adolescents' sense of self (Jackson & Davis, 2000; Olafson & Latta, 2002; Strahan, L'Esperance, & Van Hoose, 2009). Middle level organizational structures, such as teams with common planning time and advisory programs, have been associated with enhanced self-perceptions (Johnston, 1997; Killin & Williams, 1995; War-ren & Muth, 1995), and pedagogies including problem-based learning, inquiry methods, and service-learning may also be self-enhancing (Cer-ezo, 2004; Johnson & Notah, 1999; McCaffrey, 2008). Furthermore, grouping arrangements in middle level schools can be self-enhancing, or they can be self-debilitating. The next section summarizes some of the research literature associated with tracking and ability grouping in schools. While studies of grouping in a variety of P-12 settings are consid-ered, the findings are discussed to the extent that they have implications for young adolescent education.

Research on Tracking

Tracking and ability grouping have been the focus of countless studies. This section summarizes a selection of recent studies exploring ways in which self-perceptions may be affected by tracking and related issues, such as labeling, and self-fulfilling prophecies associated with teacher expectations.

Tracking and self-perceptions. Studies have shown grouping patterns to be associated with students' self-perceptions (e.g., Ireson & Hallam, 2009), though the direct effects of grouping on overall self-perceptions appear to be negligible (Kulik, 2004) and the relationship is most visible in academic components of self-concept (Marsh, 2007). This is especially evident in studies examining the big-fish-little-pond effect (BFLPE)—that students show higher self-concept ratings when placed in groups with others of lower academic ability than themselves (Marsh & Parker, 1984).

Trautwein, Ludtke, Marsh, Koller, & Baumert (2006) found that students' self-concept and interest in mathematics were a function of three factors: the achievement of their peers (i.e., their reference group), their own achievement, and the grades they received from their teacher. When the researchers controlled for these three factors, they found no relationship between track level and mathematics self-concept, but the salience of peer references has important implications for grouping considerations.

Chiu and colleagues (2008) also studied relationships between tracking in mathematics and students' self-perceptions. They found that students in lower tracks had lower self-concepts regarding mathematics and school in general and that students tended to compare themselves to other students within the same track rather than with students in other tracks. The kinds of peer comparisons students made within and across tracks did not affect their global self-concepts or self-esteem; however, the grades students received (i.e., the teachers' value judgments of their performance) had a significant impact on their self-concepts of ability in mathematics.

Tracking and labeling effects. Any form of nonrandom grouping in schools involves labeling students—as, for example, *accelerated*, *gifted*, *proficient*, or *remedial*—and the labeling process can have profound impacts on a young adolescent's sense of self. For example, with regards to students labeled as special needs, Walther-Thomas (1997) observed:

> By the time [they] reach the emotionally charged years of middle school, participation in special education has become a source of painful embarrassment. School, at best, is often an unpleasant experience. Their confidence, motivation, and willingness to take on new challenges are all waning. (p. 490)

The impacts grouping and labeling have on students with low academic ability are disturbing, but students at the other end of the academic spectrum also suffer negative effects from these practices. While gifted classes may provide more challenging experiences for high-ability students, they may also be associated with a decrease in academic self-concept (Preckel, Gotz, & Frenzel, 2010), especially for girls (Preckel & Brüll, 2008).

The labeling associated with tracking creates expectancy effects when teachers treat students according to their perceptions of the label. Arguments against tracking and other forms of ability grouping have claimed that groupings impact teacher expectations and that these expectations, in turn, shape student self-perceptions and performance. Teachers behave differently toward low- and high- expectancy students, and this differential treatment may be associated with a self-fulfilling prophecy as students live up (or down) to the expectations teachers communicate to them (Rosenthal & Jacobson, 1968).

Jussim and Harber (2005) revisited the Pygmalion studies (Rosenthal & Jacobson, 1968) that identified the existence of self-fulfilling prophecies associated with labeling in schools. From their critique of this research and analysis of subsequent studies, Jussim and Harber affirmed: "Evidence shows that teacher expectations clearly do influence students— at least sometimes" (p. 131). They noted that there have been "speculative claims emphasizing the negative effects of self-fulfilling prophecies, and their power to accumulate" (p. 132), but they argue that tracking does not appear to be associated with powerful self-fulfilling prophecies. Rather, within-class ability grouping may have a substantive impact on the occurrence of differential treatment and self-fulfilling prophecies. Kulik (as cited in Allan, 1991) drew a similar conclusion regarding the effects of labeling, suggesting that its effects on self-esteem are transitory and eventually overshadowed by the comparisons students make between themselves and the peers with whom they are grouped (see also Chiu et al., 2008).

Tracking and achievement. This review is chiefly concerned with the relationship between grouping patterns (e.g., tracking) and student self-perceptions, not cognitive outcomes. However, because there is a positive relationship between self-esteem and academic performance, a consideration of this relationship is warranted. While some recent research suggested that tracking students may be associated with academic achievement (Duflo, Dupas, & Kremer, 2009; Loveless, 2009), these studies did not identify a causal relationship between grouping patterns and cognitive outcomes. In general, studies of tracked academic programs tend to demonstrate some achievement gains for high-ability groups, which are offset by modest or no achievement gains for low-ability groups (Kulik & Kulik, 1982; Slavin, 1986; 1990). Likewise, low-achieving students demonstrate significant gains when moved from a low-track class to a heterogeneous class while high-achieving students may exhibit a modest disadvantage (Venkatakrishnan & William, 2003). In sum, "tracking tends to exacerbate inequality with little or no contribution to overall productivity" (Gamoran, 2009, p. 4). The effect of tracking on overall academic excellence is, at best, uneven.

Qualitative insights into tracking and ability grouping. The studies discussed thus far have been quantitative studies that have sought to measure effects of grouping on variables of interest, including academic achievement and aspects of students' self-perceptions. While these studies seem to suggest the effects of grouping are small or isolated, they may neglect some very profound impacts of grouping that have been uncovered by a generation of qualitative research. Qualitative studies have provided valuable insights into the ways in which schools, and teachers as agents of schools, reproduce structural inequalities in society through tracking and labeling students (Collins, 2003; Oakes, 1985). A landmark study by Oakes, *Keeping Track: How Schools Structure Inequality*, shook the educational community and put a spotlight on the negative effects of tracking. The study revealed how the quality of instruction was lower and opportunities to learn were fewer in low track classrooms than in high track classrooms. Oakes documented biases in grouping processes associated with tracking; described aspects of daily life in tracked classrooms that affected students' self-perceptions and views of school; and, ultimately, showed how tracking perpetuates class and racial inequities.

Qualitative research has drawn attention to students' perspectives on grouping practices and their effects. For example, qualitative research has revealed that students are very much aware of how and why they are grouped or tracked (Hallam, Ireson, & Davies, 2004), and they may have very clear and strong views regarding issues of equity and social justice associated with grouping and labeling (Yonezawa & Jones, 2006).

Using Bourdieu's concepts of *habitus* and *field*, Zevenbergen (2005) studied how students' interactions with grouping practices, instructional practices, and other school-related factors (the *field*) construct them in particular ways and impact their academic performance and self-perceptions. Through these interactions, students developed a set of dispositions toward mathematics—a mathematics *habitus*—that became a lens through which they interpreted and internalized their school mathematics experiences. *Habitus* predisposed students in different tracks to view mathematics and their futures with the subject in different ways.

Collins (2003) conducted an in-depth case study of an African American young adolescent named Jay whose school experiences seemed to be shaped to a great extent by the perceptions his teachers formed of him. Collins described *ability profiling* as a process through which teachers interpret, or profile, their students according to various characteristics: race, culture, socioeconomic status, gender. Teachers may interpret students "to be either learning disabled, emotionally impaired, or a good learner in the various teaching and learning contexts" in which they encounter students," and these profiles "contribute to the construction of disability and school failure" (p. xiii). Collins contends that ability profiling is "an institutionally and socially sanctioned form of discrimination and segregation" (p. 192). Furthermore, tracking and other arrangements that support the process of profiling position teachers as "agents of an institution that encourages them to 'profile' their students according to their perceived abilities" (p. 190).

In a study of students' science identities in a magnet school setting, Olitsky, Flohr, Gardner, and Billups (2010) found that school structural factors (e.g., the magnet school's selection process; the discourses perpetuated by teachers, administrators, and peers regarding "who belongs" at the school; and negative stereotype threat) were very influential in accentuating student inequalities. They concluded that educators can counter these influences by transforming classrooms into communities of practice that allow students to acquire social capital to help them succeed (see also Sullivan, Mousley, & Zevenbergen, 2006).

Summary

Attribute grouping, or homogeneous grouping, has been a common way to organize students for instruction in the middle grades. Some schools use tracking, a form of attribute grouping in which students are grouped according to academic ability, typically determined by a test score, and remain *tracked* in these groupings for all or most of the school day. Once tracked, students often remain at the same level throughout their schooling. Tracking students has been criticized by middle level educators because decades of quantitative and qualitative studies have found that the practice is associated with negative student self-perceptions, undermines efforts to promote social equity, and has uneven academic outcomes for students.

... TO VARIABLE GROUPING

Instead of tracking or other forms of attribute grouping, middle level advocates have called for detracking schools and reorganizing them into flexible, heterogeneous grouping arrangements that reflect the diverse and varying needs of young adolescent learners (Kasak, 2001; Middle Level Curriculum Project, 1993; NMSA, 2010; Strahan et al., 2009) and promote the democratic way of life (Beane, 2005). Flexible team structures can allow teachers to group students according to individual learning needs or as demanded by specific instructional plans. Teachers may choose to facilitate whole-class, small group, or independent learning or implement various projects, cooperative learning, and differentiation strategies. "The hallmark of these or any other methods is that community is preserved while uniqueness is celebrated" (Middle Level Curriculum Project, pp. 108-109). Variable grouping patterns should support the principle of self-enhancement to the extent that the criteria for variations in groupings are consistent with and supportive of the multidimensional nature of the self.

Detracking

As schools move toward heterogeneous, variable grouping patterns, they must dismantle systems of tracking that may have been in place for decades. Detracking has been a trend in school districts throughout the United States since the 1980s. Loveless (1999; 2009) found that detracking was most likely to occur in urban or rural schools serving low-performing, low socioeconomic status students, while suburban schools and schools serving high-achieving, high socioeconomic status students were more likely to retain multitiered grouping arrangements.

When detracking does occur, schools need to proceed deliberately and carefully because tracking is a practice "deeply embedded" in the cultures of most schools (George & Alexander, 2003, p. 417). George and Alexander attributed problems with detracking to "haste and poor planning" (p. 417).

> The worst possible results should be expected in situations where middle school leaders, even for the best of reasons, take unilateral and impulsive action to end tracking in their school or district. When this happens, ... many teachers will find such plans difficult to implement successfully and will feel frustrated and discontented. (p. 417)

George and Alexander stressed that altering grouping arrangements was and should be a local matter; local interests should be invested in the process; and a solid, systematic plan for professional development must accompany any changes of this sort.

At Cloonan Middle School in the heavily tracked Stamford, Connecticut school district, "parents have long complained that the tracking numbers assigned to students dictate not only their classes but also their friends and cafeteria cliques" (Hu, 2009, para. 14). Stamford is detracking in science and social studies beginning in sixth grade with plans to scale up to seventh and eighth grades, consistent with George and Alexander's (2003) recommendation to start such reforms in the earliest grade.

Zehr (2009) described how Cabin John Middle School in Maryland rearranged its grouping practices in ELA.

> The school decided to do away with a remedial class in English language arts for the lowest performing students and mix the students from that class in with students from two other classes of gifted and talented students. So the school blended the lowest performing and highest performing students in classes to learn English language arts together. [Stacey Kopnitsky, the assistant principal,] said that each class was then taught by a team of two

teachers. In one of the classes, one of the teachers who was part of the team was a special education teacher.

Kopnitsky said that the test scores show that the change benefited the students who had been in the remedial class. Before the change, all of them scored at the lowest of three possible levels on Maryland's English language arts test. After the change, most of them scored at the second of the three levels in English language arts. (para. 3-4)

Mehan, Villanueva, Hubbard, and Lintz (1996) described detracking efforts in San Diego that involved the implementation of a program called Advancement through Individual Determination, or AVID. The AVID program took an incremental approach to detracking, gradually transitioning low-track students into college preparatory courses and providing them with additional academic support throughout the process. Begun in 1980, AVID is one detracking initiative that has been brought to scale; it is now a nationwide program serving more than 20,000 students with a specific curriculum framework and a comprehensive professional development component for teachers.

Variable Grouping in the Self-Enhancing Middle Level School

Teachers in detracked schools should use fluid, flexible, "effective grouping" arrangements that enhance student learning by matching grouping decisions to student needs and specific instructional goals (Caldwell & Ford, 2002, p. 11). Beane and Lipka (1986) conceptualized the self-enhancing school as one in which variable grouping is the norm. Variable or heterogeneous grouping encompasses two types of student groupings: "arrangements in which whole classes of students of varying intellectual ability learn together in one classroom or within-classroom groupings in which students of varying abilities learn together in cooperative learning arrangements" (Daniel, 2007, p. 1). In some instructional contexts, teachers may choose to use ability grouping "with appropriate curricular adjustment" (Tieso, 2003, p. 29), while in other contexts teachers may opt for small heterogeneous groups or groups based on student interests (Manning & Bucher, 2009).

Differentiated instruction. Whichever grouping arrangements they use, teachers in heterogeneous classrooms should employ differentiated instruction to meet the individual needs of diverse learners. Differentiated instruction "provides different avenues to acquiring content, to processing or making sense of ideas, and to developing products so that each student can learn effectively" (Tomlinson, 2001, p. 1). Effective differentiation begins with formative assessment strategies to determine individual student strengths, weaknesses, and learning modalities (Doubet, 2012) and to determine levels of background knowledge (Lapp, Fisher, & Frey, 2012). Teachers in differentiated classrooms should avoid labeling students and not dwell on such categories as "gifted," "advanced," or "grade-level," because the students who fall in a particular category today may be classified in a different way next week. As Tomlinson observed: Some students may be advanced in September and not in May—or in May, but not in September. Some may be advanced in math, but not in reading; or in lab work, but not in memorization of related scientific formulas. Some may be advanced for a short time, others throughout their lives but only in certain endeavors. Some learners are consistently advanced in many areas (Tomlinson, p. 11). Clearly, differentiation works best when teachers know their students well, and middle level organizational structures like interdisciplinary teams and advisory programs help to make this possible (Kasak, 2001).

Once teachers have identified student strengths and needs, they may draw upon a variety of strategies to individualize instruction: "collaborative learning, elaborated helping arrangements, progress-based grading, challenge activities, graphic and learning organizers" (Kasak, 2001, p. 96), to name just a few. Whichever strategy is used, one characteristic of differentiated instruction is essential: learning goals and objectives must be transparent and clearly communicated to the students (Tomlinson, 2001).

Differentiating instruction in heterogeneous, mixed-ability classrooms takes lots of planning, hard work, and determination. Petrilli (2011) portrayed just how challenging it is for teachers to effectively differentiate instruction by describing the program at a diverse school in Maryland that was implementing differentiation as an alternative to homogeneous grouping. The keys to success in this school include strong leadership at the building level, a high level of parent support, and teacher buy-in—teachers at the school overwhelmingly support the differentiation initiative, despite the increased workload.

Cooperative and collaborative learning structures. Opponents of tracking and ability grouping have recommended cooperative learning as an approach for enhancing academic performance and students' self-perceptions in heterogeneous classrooms (Lipka, 1997). Cooperative learning is a form of social learning in which students are grouped into task-oriented teams consisting of heterogeneous groups of students who may have different skills, abilities, or background knowledge (Slavin, 1995). Teams pursue group goals collaboratively, and reward structures in cooperative learning hold both individuals and groups accountable for outcomes. Cooperative learning is associated with improved academic achievement (Stevens & Slavin, 1995) and, with regards to the aims of the self-enhancing school, positive social and attitudinal outcomes (Gillies, 2004; Köse, Sahin, Ergün, & Gezer, 2010; Stevens & Slavin).

Multiage grouping. Multiage groupings are associated with higher self-esteem and self-concept (Elmore & Wisenbaker, 1996; Haynes, 1996; Jensen & Green, 1993), particularly in the domain of happiness and satisfaction (Way, 1981). Brown-Barge Middle School in Florida is an excellent example of a school that teaches a fully integrated curriculum in a multiage setting. Since 1992, Brown-Barge has engaged multiage groups of sixth, seventh, and eight graders in integrated, project-based instructional units called "streams" with great success (Jenkins & Jenkins, 1998; Powell & Skoog, 1995).

Within-class reading groups. Literature circles, book clubs, and peer tutoring are effective grouping arrangements that have supplanted traditional forms of within-class reading groups that labeled students as, for example, "bluebirds" for the more accelerated readers and "redbirds" for the slower readers (Caldwell & Ford, 2002). Literature circles and book clubs involve flexible, temporary groupings of students who engage in natural, student-directed discussions about texts in ELA or other areas of the curriculum (Daniels, 1994). Such strategies may have a positive impact on the development of self (Johnson, 2000; Stringer, Reynolds, & Simpson, 2003). Peer tutoring, specifically peer reading programs, can have positive effects on self-esteem. Miller, Topping, and Thurston (2010) found that students engaged in peer-reading with same-age and cross-age (younger) students experienced enhanced self-esteem, while the cross-age group also showed gains in self-worth.

Summary

Many schools and districts throughout the United States have gradually detracked, moving away from rigid patterns of ability grouping toward more flexible, variable grouping structures. Ideally in such schools, teachers differentiate instruction for heterogeneously grouped students who may possess very diverse backgrounds and mixed abilities. Students may be flexibly organized into cooperative learning groups, literature circles, or peer learning arrangements. When schools move toward such variable grouping patterns, they become places that are better able to support the development of positive, healthy self-perceptions than schools characterized by tracking and homogeneous grouping patterns.

DISCUSSION AND CONCLUSION

Self-enhancing schools are characterized by a shift from single attribute (i.e., homogeneous, tracked) grouping to variable (i.e., heterogeneous, flexible) grouping (Beane & Lipka, 1986). Since the mid-1980s, a major trend in school districts in the United States has been detracking, undoing the rigid grouping practices that have labeled and sorted students into permanent or semipermanent groups that remain together for all or most of the school day. Detracking represents a significant shift in policy; however, in practice other forms of single attribute grouping are flourishing. In some schools, the usual three tracks have been collapsed into two—perhaps called "grade level" and "advanced"—amounting to little more than a relabeling. In many middle level schools, gifted programs and advanced mathematics courses create grouping patterns that have a ripple effect throughout the daily schedule, creating a *de facto* system of tracking. Single gender education programs are on the rise in the United States, as are magnet programs that draw students with a particular aptitude or interest. In sum, while detracking reform has occurred in many schools, attribute grouping practices are so deeply embedded in the culture of U.S. schools these reforms may, in effect, result in little more than old wine in new wineskins.

The research regarding grouping and tracking has been characterized as a "cluttered landscape" (Kulik, 2004, p. 177) as researchers have arrived at conflicting conclusions and divergent recommendations. Gamoran (2009) noted that debates about various approaches to grouping students in school stem from seemingly irreconcilable philosophical viewpoints about the purposes of school.

> Is the purpose of schooling to provide all students with a common socialization? Or is it to differentiate students for varied futures? The former aim is consistent with mixed-ability teaching, whereas the latter is consistent with tracking, and the debate has no simple resolution because school systems embody both goals. (p. 3)

Some view the school as an institution that exists primarily to promote the cognitive development of children and, for some who hold this view, to sort the most able from the least able. Driven by this cognitive imperative, educators and policymakers group students according to a single attribute—typically academic ability determined by some proxy, such as an IQ score. For others, schools should emphasize the social and affective dimensions of development and implement variable grouping patterns that reflect the heterogeneity of the world outside school. Driven by this social/affective imperative, students should learn in heterogeneously grouped classrooms and smaller cooperative learning groups.

Middle level philosophy embraces a multidimensional view of the child and calls upon schools to address cognitive, social, and affective development in a balanced, holistic way. Driven by this developmental imperative, middle level schools should base instructional and programmatic decisions (e.g., grouping) on the developmental needs of the young adolescents they serve (NMSA, 2010). Variable grouping arrangements are supported from this perspective because they take into account the whole learner and, in terms of self-perceptions, the multidimensional nature of the self. The developmentalist imperative is, however, problematic because it imposes certain limitations on the self. Labeling people in middle level schools "young adolescent" (or "sixth grader" or "student") tends to position them as objects to be acted upon (i.e., managed, grouped, etc.) by teachers and other adults, not as authors or coauthors of their own futures. These seemingly benign labels define the roles young people can access in school and delimit the possibilities of who they can become. Beane (2005) reminds educators that:

> Young people are real people living real lives in the real world. The role of "student" is only one of the many they play. They are also members of families, peer groups, and communities; citizens of the society; and participants in cultures that help shape their identities and values. They are of a particular age-group—children, young adolescents, and older adolescents—influenced by both the physical developments and the social and cultural expectations of their age. To respect the dignity of young people means taking them seriously as whole human beings, not just as students. (pp. 71-72)

So, what should grouping arrangements look like in the self-enhancing school? The research on grouping has shown us ways we can hedge our bets, making it more likely that we will enhance self-perceptions (or achieve other educational aims) by implementing a particular form of grouping. However, to judge grouping arrangements based on cognitive, social, or affective outcomes alone misses an important moral dimension of schooling practices in a democratic society. Ultimately, decisions about grouping practices—and all practices and policies in school—should be driven by a moral imperative that acknowledges the personhood of the individuals being grouped, honors their humanity, and respects their dignity (cf. see Beane, 1994; 2005). As Beane (1994) argued, "human beings, including the young, are entitled to a sense of dignity. Therefore, any social institution has the obligation to sponsor experiences that extend the possibility of human dignity and to avoid those that may detract from it" (p. 74).

REFERENCES

Allan, S. D. (1991). Ability-grouping research reviews: What do they say about grouping and the gifted? *Educational Leadership, 48*(6), 60-65.

Andrews, G. (2005). Middle grades education: Back to the future. In V. Anfara, G. Andrews & S. Mertens (Eds.), *The encyclopedia of middle grades education* (pp. 69-78). Greenwich, CT: Information Age.

Beane, J. A. (1994). Cluttered terrain: The schools' interest in the self. In T. M. Brinthaupt & R. P. Lipka (Eds.), *Changing the self: Philosophies, techniques, experiences* (pp. 69-86). Albany, NY: SUNY Press.

Beane, J. A. (2005). *A reason to teach: Creating classrooms of dignity and hope.* Portsmouth, NH: Heinemann.

Beane, J. A., & Lipka, R. P. (1986). *Self-concept, self-esteem and the curriculum.* New York, NY: Teachers College Press.

Caldwell, J. S., & Ford, M. P. (2002). *Where have all the bluebirds gone? How to soar with flexible grouping.* Portsmouth, NH: Heinemann.

Chiu, D., Beru, Y., Watley, E., Wubu, S., Simson, E., Kessinger, R., Rivera, A., Schmidlein, P., & Wigfield, A. (2008). Seventh-grade students' self-beliefs and social comparisons. *Journal of Educational Research, 102*(2), 125-135.

Cerezo, N. (2004). Problem-based learning in the middle school: A research case study of the perceptions of at-risk females. *RMLE Online: Research in Middle Level Education, 27*(1), 1-13.

Collins, K. M. (2003). *Ability profiling and school failure: One child's struggle to be seen as competent.* Mahwah, NJ: Erlbaum.

Daniel, L. (2007). *Research summary: Heterogeneous grouping.* Retrieved from http://www.nmsa.org/Research/ResearchSummaries/HeterogeneousGrouping/tabid/1264/Default.aspx

Daniels, H. (1994). *Literature circles: Voice and choice in the student-centered classroom.* Portland, ME: Stenhouse.

Doda, N. M. (2005). The challenge of middle school equity. In V. Anfara, G. Andrews, & S. Mertens (Eds.), *The encyclopedia of middle grades education* (pp. 25-34). Greenwhich, CT: Information Age.

Doubet, K. J. (2012). Formative assessment jumpstarts a middle level differentiation initiative. *Middle School Journal, 43*(3), 32-38.

Duflo, E., Dupas, P., & Kremer, M. (2009, Summer). Can tracking improve learning?: Evidence from Kenya. *Education Next.* Retrieved from http://www.educationnext.org

Elmore, R., & Wisenbaker, J. (1996, October). *Evaluation of multi-age team (MAT): Implementation at Crabapple Middle.* Paper presented at the annual meeting of the National Middle School Association, Baltimore, MD.

Gamoran, A. (2009). *Tracking and inequality: New directions for research and practice.* (WCER Working Paper No. 2009-6). Madison: University of Wisconsin–Madison, Wisconsin Center for Education Research. Retrieved from http://www.wcer.wisc.edu/publications/workingPapers/papers.php

George, P. S., & Alexander, W. M. (2003). *The exemplary middle school.* Belmont, CA: Thomson/Wadsworth.

Gillies, R. M. (2004). The effects of cooperative learning on junior high school students during small group learning. *Learning and Instruction, 14*(2), 197-213.

Hallam, S., Ireson, J., & Davies, J. (2004). Primary pupils' experiences of different types of grouping in schools. *British Educational Research Journal, 30*, 515-533.

Haynes, H. L. (1996). Observations for the panicked: How to implement a multi-age classroom. *Rural Educator, 17*(3) 41-44.

Hu, W. (2009, June 15). No longer letting scores separate pupils. *The New York Times.* Retrieved from http://www.nytimes.com

Ireson, J., & Hallam, S. (2009). Academic self-concepts in adolescence: Relations with achievement and ability grouping in schools. *Learning and Instruction, 19*(3), 201-213.

Jackson, A. W., & Davis, G. A. (2000). *Turning points 2000: Educating adolescents in the 21st century.* New York, NY: Teachers College Press.

Jenkins, K. D. & Jenkins, D. M. (1998). Integrating curriculum in a total quality school. *Middle School Journal, 29*(4), 14-27.

Jensen, M. K.; & Green, V. P. (1993). The effects of multi-age grouping on young children and teacher preparation. *Early Child Development and Care, 9*(1), 25-31.

Johnson, A. M., & Notah, D. J. (1999). Service learning: History, literature review, and a pilot study of eighth graders. *Elementary School Journal, 99*(5), 453-467.

Johnson, H. (2000). To stand up and say something: "Girls only" literature circles at the middle level. *New Advocate, 13*(4), 375-389.

Johnston, H. (1997). What's going on? From advisory programs to adult-student relationships: Restoring purpose to the guidance program. *Schools in the Middle, 6*(4), 8-15.

Jussim, L., & Harber, K. D. (2005). Teacher expectations and self-fulfilling prophecies: Knowns and unknowns, resolved and unresolved controversies. *Personality and Social Psychology Review, 9*(2), 131-135.

Kasak, D. (2001). Flexible organizational structures. In T. O. Erb (Ed.), *This we believe … and now we must act* (pp. 90-98). Westerville, OH: National Middle School Association.

Killin, T. E., & Williams, R. L. (1995). Making a difference in school climate, counseling services, and student success. *NASSP Bulletin, 79*(570), 44-50.

Köse, S., Sahin, A., Ergün, A., & Gezer, K. (2010). The effects of cooperative learning experience on eighth grade students' achievement and attitude toward science. *Education, 131*(1), 169-181.

Kulik, J. A. (2004). Grouping, tracking, and detracking: Conclusions from experimental, correlational, and ethnographic research. In H. J. Walberg, A. J. Reynolds, & M. C. Wang (Eds.), *Can unlike students learn together? Grade retention, tracking, and grouping* (pp. 157-182). Greenwich, CT: Information Age.

Kulik, C.L., & Kulik, J. A. (1982). Effects of ability grouping on secondary school students: A meta-analysis of evaluation findings. *American Educational Research Journal, 19*, 415-428.

Lapp, D., Fisher, D. & Frey, N. (2012). Building and activating students' background knowledge: It's what they already know that counts. *Middle School Journal, 43*(3), 22-31.

Lipka, R. (1997). Enhancing self-concept/self-esteem in young adolescents. In J. Irvin (Ed.), *What current research says to the middle level practitioner* (pp. 31-40). Columbus, OH: National Middle School Association.

Lockwood, A. T. (1996). *Tracking: Conflicts and resolutions.* Thousand Oaks, CA: Corwin Press.

Loveless, T. (1999). *The tracking wars.* Washington DC: The Brookings Institution.

Loveless, T. (2009). *Tracking and detracking: High achievers in Massachusetts middle schools.* Washington, DC: Thomas B. Fordham Institute.

Manning, M. L., & Bucher, K. T. (2009). *Teaching in the middle school* (3rd ed.). New York, NY: Pearson.

Marsh, H. W. (2007). *Self-concept theory, measurement and research into practice: The role of self-concept in educational psychology.* Leicester, England: British Psychological Society.

Marsh, H. W., & Parker, J W. (1984). Determinants of student self-concept: Is it better to be a relatively large fish in a small pond even if you don't learn to swim as well? *Journal of Personality and Social Psychology, 47,* 213-231.

Marsh, R. S., & Raywid, M. (1994). How to make detracking work. *Phi Delta Kappan, 76,* 268-269.

McCaffrey, K. (2008). Creating an advisory program using Hollywood film clips to promote character development. *Middle School Journal, 40*(2), 21-25.

McEwin, C. K., Dickinson, T. S., & Jenkins, D. M. (2003). *America's middle schools in the new century: Status and progress* (pp. 44-46). Westerville, OH: National Middle School Association.

McEwin, C. K., & Greene, M. W. (2009). Results and recommendations from the 2009 national surveys of randomly selected and highly successful middle level schools. *Middle School Journal, 42*(1), 48-62.

Mehan, H., Villanueva, I., Hubbard, L., & Lintz, A. (1996). *Constructing school success.* New York, NY: Cambridge University Press.

Middle Level Curriculum Project. (1993). Middle level curriculum: The search for self and social meaning. In T. Dickinson (Ed.), *Readings in middle school curriculum: A continuing conversation,* (pp. 105-118). Columbus, OH: National Middle School Association.

Miller, D., Topping, K., & Thurston, A. (2010). Peer tutoring in reading: The effects of role and organization on two dimensions of self-esteem. *British Journal of Educational Psychology, 80*(3), 417-433.

National Middle School Association. (2010). *This we believe: Keys to educating young adolescents.* Westerville, OH: Author.

Oakes, J. (1985). *Keeping track: how schools structure inequality.* New Haven, CT: Yale University Press.

Olafson, L. & Latta, M. M. (2002). Expecting, accepting, and respecting difference in middle school. *Middle School Journal, 34*(1), 43-47.

Olitsky, S., Flohr, L. L., Gardner, J., & Billups, M. (2010). Coherence, contradiction, and the development of school science identities. *Journal of Research in Science Teaching, 47,* 1209-1228.

Parker, A. K. (2010). A longitudinal investigation of young adolescents' self-concepts in the middle grades. *Research in Middle Level Education Online, 33*(10), 1-13.

Petrilli, M. (2011). All together now? Educating high and low achievers in the same classroom. *Education Next, 11*(1), 48-55.

Powell, R., & Skoog, G. (1995). Students' perspectives on integrative curricula: The case of Brown Barge Middle School. *Research in Middle Level Education Quarterly, 19*(1), 85-115.

Powell, S. D. (2011). *Introduction to middle school*. Boston, MA: Pearson.

Preckel, F., & Brüll, M. (2008). Grouping the gifted and talented: Are gifted girls most likely to suffer the consequences? *Journal for the Education of the Gifted, 32*(1), 54-85.

Preckel, F., Gotz, T., & Frenzel, A. (2010). Ability grouping of gifted students: Effects on academic self-concept and boredom. *British Journal of Educational Psychology, 80*(3), 451-472.

Rosenthal, R., & Jacobson, L. (1968). *Pygmalion in the classroom: Teacher expectations and student intellectual development*. New York, NY: Holt.

Slavin, R. E. (1995). *Cooperative learning: Theory, research, and practice*. Boston, MA: Allyn & Bacon.

Slavin, R. E. (1990). Achievement effects of ability grouping in secondary schools: A best-evidence synthesis. *Review of Educational Research, 60*(3), 471-499.

Slavin, R. E. (1986). *Ability grouping and student achievement in elementary schools: A best-evidence synthesis. (Rep. No. 1)*. Baltimore, Md.: Johns Hopkins University, Center for Research on Elementary and Middle Schools.

Strahan, D., L'Esperance, M, & Van Hoose, J. (2009). *Promoting harmony: Young adolescent development & classroom practices*. Westerville, OH: National Middle School Association.

Stevens, R. J., & Slavin, R. E. (1995). The cooperative elementary school: Effects on students' achievement, attitudes, and social relations. *American Educational Research Journal, 32*(2), 321-351.

Stringer, S. J., Reynolds, G. P., & Simpson, F. (2003). Collaboration between classroom teachers and a school counselor through literature circles: Building self-esteem. *Journal of Instructional Psychology, 3*(1), 69-76.

Sullivan, P., Mousley, J., & Zevenbergen, R. (2006). Teacher actions to maximize mathematics learning opportunities in heterogeneous classrooms. *International Journal of Mathematics and Science Education, 4*, 117-143.

Tieso, C. L. (2003). Ability grouping is not just tracking anymore. *Roeper Review, 26*(1), 29-36.

Tomlinson, C. A. (2001). *How to differentiate instruction in mixed ability classrooms*. Alexandria, VA: Association for Supervision and Curriculum Development.

Trautwein, U., Ludtke, O., Marsh, H. W., Koller, O., & Baumert, J. (2006). Tracking, grading, and student motivation: Using group composition and status to predict self-concept and interest in ninth-grade mathematics. *Journal of Educational Psychology, 98*(4), 788-806.

Venkatakrishnan, H., & William, D. (2003). Tracking and mixed-ability grouping in secondary school mathematics classrooms: A case study. *British Educational Research Journal, 29*(2), 189-204.

Walther-Thomas, C. (1997). Inclusion and teaming: Including all students in the mainstream. In T. S. Dickinson & T. O. Erb (Eds.), *We gain more than we give: Teaming in middle schools* (pp. 487-522). Columbus, OH: National Middle School Association.

Warren, L. L., & Muth, K. D. (1995). The impact of common planning time on middle grades students and teachers. *Research in Middle Level Education Quarterly, 18*(3), 41-58.

Way, J. W. (1981). Achievement and self-concept in a multiage classroom. *Educational Research Quarterly, 6*(2), 69-75.

Wheelock, A. (1992). *Crossing the tracks: How "untracking" can save America's schools.* New York. NY: The New Press.

Yonezawa, S., & Jones, M. (2006). Students' perspectives on tracking and detracking. *Theory into Practice, 45*(1), 15-23.

Zehr, M.A. (2009). The problem of tracking in middle schools [Web log post]. Retrieved from http://blogs.edweek.org/edweek/curriculum

Zevenbergen, R. (2005). The construction of mathematical habitus: Implications of ability grouping in the middle years. *Journal of Curriculum Studies, 37*(5), 607-619.

CHAPTER 4

FROM EXTERNAL CONTROL TO SELF-DIRECTION

Kerry Chisnall and Kathleen M. Brown

INTRODUCTION AND BACKGROUND

The middle grades are transformational years that can have a significant impact on the academic, social and emotional development of our youth. Consequently, increased scrutiny of middle level education is necessary, as middle schools frequently represent the last opportunity for many students to be successful (Brown, 2009). Twenty-five years ago, a 1987 California Department of Education report declared the following:

> Middle grades represent the last substantive educational experience for hundreds of thousands of students. If students fail to achieve the integration of their personalities and the motivation required to make a commitment to academic values by the end of the middle grades, many will never do so. (p. 62)

The same is true today. According to Schunk and Pajares (2002), there are a number of variables that can affect students' self-perceptions regarding the transition to middle school. Adapting to a new, widely expanded

Middle Grades Curriculum:
Voices and Visions of the Self-Enhancing School, pp. 53–70
Copyright © 2013 by Information Age Publishing

social reference group, changing classes for the first time, and adjusting to multiple teachers versus one who monitors their progress are a few of the significant changes young adolescents face. Similarly, students transitioning into the middle grades are often confronted with a shift in expectations and evaluation standards which can trigger a reassessment of their academic competence.

How students respond to and handle these transformational years can be significantly affected by the school setting or climate (Beane & Lipka, 1986; Niemiec & Ryan, 2009; Scott, Murray, Mertens, & Dustin, 2001). Schunk and Pajares (2002) attribute a student's middle school success, socially and academically, to how well the school environment contributes to his or her sense of autonomy and ability to relate to teachers and administrators. In his discussion of best practices for schools, Blum (2007) also touted the school environment as critical for students' success. Such success can be positively shaped by a caring environment, a safe and structured environment, an academic environment, and a participatory environment. Blum explained that "a positive school environment creates an optimal setting for teaching and learning ... (it) can be a stabilizing force for young people, both emotionally and academically, particularly when they are experiencing transition or crisis" (p. 2).

School climate was defined by Koran in 1989 as "The total environmental quality within a school building, including physical aspects, social relationships, methods of operation, rules and belief systems" (p. 7). Keefe and Howard (1997) put an emphasis on belief systems and state that a school's climate as perceived by parents, teachers and students is more critical than the lived, or actual, reality. Keefe and Howard add, "The perception, in fact, is often more significant than the reality, since people act and react as they perceive something to be" (p. 35). In 2007, Blum defined it as the personality of a school and its learning context. School climate is influenced and shaped by several factors including student and teacher morale, disciplinary policies and instructional quality.

Howard, Howell and Brainard (1987) claim a positive climate "makes a school a place where both staff and students want to spend a substantial portion of their time; it is a good place to be" (p. 5). Willower (1974) distinguished between two types of school climates that can affect students' self-perceptions negatively or positively: custodial and humanistic pupil control. In his analysis of 70 pupil control studies Willower found a direct relationship between student attitudes and teacher pupil control. Willower reported, "The more humanistic the teacher, the more favorable the student attitudes" (p. 4).

According to Scott and colleagues (2001) custodial (teacher centered) climate places an emphasis on external control and is characterized by autocratic procedures, punitive sanctions and is impersonal and dictatorial. In contrast, the humanistic (child centered) climate is characterized by student involvement in decision-making, democratic procedures, respect, and self-discipline and is personable and facilitative. Many researchers (Beane, 1991; Graham, Halpin, Harris, & Benson, 1985; Scott et al., 2001; Willower 1974) suggest a humanistic climate is more likely to enhance the self-perception of students and support a positive, self-enhancing school.

In 1986, Beane and Lipka explained that a key feature of a self-enhancing school is the transition from external control to self-direction. Accordingly, one's self-perception is enhanced when one feels some control over his or her fate. When responsibility and decision-making power rests solely with others, then individuals are at risk of feeling inadequate and incompetent. The perceived lack of control can ultimately lead to "imbued helplessness" (Beane & Lipka, p. 181). In order to enhance learners' self-perceptions they must be given responsibilities and opportunities to participate in decisions affecting their learning and behavior. When asked 'What does this mean for schools' role in enhancing self-esteem?' Beane (1991) replied, "It means they must place a premium on authentic participation, collaborative action, a problem-centered curriculum, and interdependent diversity" (p. 29).

Several studies since then have found similar results, that is, that school settings that nurture an internal locus of control foster positive student self-perceptions and academic success (Elbaum & Vaughn, 2001; Lan Yong, 1994; Skinner, Wellborn, & Connell, 1990). For example, Tsai, Kunter, Ludtke, Trautwein, and Ryan (2008) found that seventh-grade students' interests in three subjects were enhanced when teachers gave them more autonomy and diminished when they were more controlling. Likewise, Elbaum and Vaughn (2001) found that middle school students' experiences were enhanced when the learning environment was collaborative and maintained high expectations. Lan Yong (1994) similarly found a positive relationship between middle school students' self-concepts and their internal locus of control. Finally, Skinner, Wellborn, & Connell (1990) discovered that students' perceptions were enhanced when they felt a sense of control in the school setting and they were engaged in instructional activities. And, a high level of engagement, as described above, is an important aspect in counteracting the sometimes detrimental impact of transitional times and even failure.

School administrators play a critical role in nurturing and sustaining self-enhancing schools that prioritize internal over external control via their willingness and ability to create humanistic school climates. Albeit indirectly via their values and vision, the potential impact of the school leader "can be especially powerful because of its potent trickle-down effect" (Scott et al., 2001, p. 287). By creating a custodial environment or one centered on external control, the impact on students' self-esteem can be negative and harmful. The opposite is true as well.

A recent study of middle schools highly successful at narrowing the achievement gap highlighted the importance of school leaders in creating and sustaining self-enhancing schools. Chisnall (2010) researched the impact of principals' beliefs, policies and practices on student achievement (through a lens of academic emphasis) in four high performing middle schools. The middle schools were all traditional calendar (all students on same schedule: typically August through late May), consistently high performing as determined by state recognition standards, had diverse student populations, and the principals had been in place at each of the schools for at least 4 consecutive years. Although all four middle schools were classified as "Schools of Distinction" that met Adequate Yearly Progress, two of the middle schools were abnormally successful at narrowing the achievement gap between White and affluent students and minority (Hispanic and African American) and economically disadvantaged students. These schools were referred to as Small Gap [SG] schools with less than a 20% gap. The remaining two middle schools (i.e., the Large Gap [LG] schools) had achievement gaps larger than the state average for the 4-year period researched (2005-2009) with more than a 40% gap.

Where direct quotes are used from Chisnall's (2010) study page numbers are referenced. However, for this chapter Chisnall has accessed supplementary raw data via his transcribed interviews that provide further insight into middle schools that nurture a shift from external control to self-direction. Direct quotes from the raw data, excluded from his dissertation, are not referenced with page numbers in this chapter.

One of the SG schools was in a rural school district while the second was a suburban school located in an urban district (Chisnall, 2010). Both LG schools were suburban schools located in urban districts. The SG middle schools averaged 539 students versus 777 students for the two LG middle schools. However, the average class size was identical for both sets of schools at 21.2 students. The number of minority students (Black, Hispanic and multicultural) averaged 29.8% for the LG schools and 23.9% for the SG schools. Free and Reduced Lunch (economically disadvantaged) students made up 26.2% of the enrollment in the LG schools and 34.4% in the SG schools. The SG middle schools had slightly more students with disabilities at 10.5% versus 9.9% for the LG schools.

The SG middle schools in Chisnall's (2010) study were characterized by humanistic school climates with principals that were focused internally on developing others. For example, both SG principals treated student discipline issues as an opportunity to discuss, reflect and learn from one's actions rather than simply as an opportunity to scold and dissuade a student from repeated infractions through fear of consequences. Discussion about discipline infractions were perceived as teachable moments designed to get at the root of problems, not "got ya" events. As one SG principal explained, "It's all about building relationships … so even though they still get in trouble and have issues, it's about trying to not take it personally and still treating them with respect and building a relationship so that they won't be turned off academically because that's when you do lose them". The other SG principal shared that when a student was sent to her she would discuss the school motto and mascot and then ask the student to explain how he or she had, or had not, satisfied each of the related values and expectations and why. Open discussions such as these helped nurture a sense of ownership, responsibility, and empowerment. Students felt supported by staff and administration, and in turn responded positively to school policies and procedures that were consistently communicated and reinforced. Students also felt cared for and safe enough to take risks in their learning. These findings coincide with claims of Scott and colleagues (2001) that, "An open atmosphere of collegial exchange provides a mechanism for changing behaviors that diminish student self-esteem as well as reinforcing behaviors that enhance student self-esteem" (p. 29). A SG school teacher agreed.

> The environment here is very conducive to middle school kids. It's a very loving environment, it's a caring environment. The teachers understand everyone has issues, but it's not like they blow up and go crazy: "You (a student) messed up? Let's figure out what you did wrong, let's figure out what we can do right." (Chisnall, 2010, p.121)

A clear line of separation did emerge between the self-enhancing, small gap schools versus the more custodial, large gap ones in Chisnall's study (2010). Principals in the Humanistic SG schools viewed themselves as life-long learners, were self-critical, and believed strongly that building respectful relationships with staff and students would reap long-term benefits for all stakeholders. Like their SG counterparts, the LG principals had high expectations, but were described as less modest and more authoritative in nature. For example, in one LG school, the principal's primary leadership team responsible for making major decisions pertaining to academics, scheduling (e.g., block versus traditional), and individual students (i.e., academically and behaviorally) did not include a single regular classroom teacher. And, in reference to the more mundane, day-to-day issues, the principal flippantly explained that "We're not going to sit around talking about trash cans in the hall. There are other committees for that … I don't really care about that." Likewise, the principal in the other LG school exhibited similar autocratic, top down leadership practices. For example, although the School Improvement Team (hereafter referred to as SIT) made a major decision relating to the school's master schedule, it was later arbitrarily overturned by the principal, A teacher in this LG school shared, "We discuss things that come up, but rarely are solutions implemented ... The decisions SIT is supposed to make, the principal kind of makes on her own".

Chisnall's (2010) study used a mixed method design with an initial quantitative phase followed by a second, more dominant qualitative data collection methodology. The first phase entailed equity audits to identify patterns of equity and inequity in terms of resources and student achievement. An equity audit entails an analysis of district and school data to expose the levels of inequity and equity created by their systems of schooling (Skrla, Garcia, Scheurich, & Nolly, 2002). Four main categories were explored in the equity audits utilized for this study: Demographic Equity, Teacher Quality Equity, Programmatic Equity, and Achievement Equity–student performance on end-of-grade testing. Following the data analyses, separate semistructured interviews were conducted with the principal, assistant principal and four teachers in each of the four middle schools. There were a total of 24 interviews.

All four middle schools in the Chisnall (2010) study were generally comparable in terms of student demographics, school programs and resources, and teacher quality, yet very different with respect to student achievement. All four schools outperformed the state proficiency average for the 2005-2009 school years placing them in the top 25% of middle schools for that period. However, the two SG middle schools had consistently maintained a smaller achievement gap versus the two LG schools among Free/Reduced lunch and minority students and White students. The SG schools averaged a disparity of 17.9 percentage points over 4 years versus 29.6 percentage points for the state average and 41.4 percentage points for the two LG schools. It is important to note that while the White students still did outperform their minority and economically disadvantaged peers in the SG schools the latter group of students performed above average (compared to the state and LG schools) which supported a narrowing achievement gap. As such, Chisnall explored why student achievement was more equitable for certain groups of learners in the SG schools as opposed to their counterparts in the LG schools.

According to Beane and Lipka (1986), a self-enhancing school that is transitioning from external control to increased self-direction makes efforts to include "cooperative governance, student involvement in curriculum planning, and self-directed learning" (p. 181). All three themes, and others, emerged as common to the high achieving and more equitable SG schools in the Chisnall (2010) study. Chisnall's study added to Beane's and Lipka's (1986) discussion of self-enhancing schools by focusing on school leadership and revealing the significance of humility and consistency in nurturing a more self-enhancing school.

COOPERATIVE GOVERNANCE WITH HUMILITY

In the Chisnall (2010) study, cooperative governance was a theme common to the two SG middle schools and was evident in part through respect and support for instructional autonomy, within certain parameters. This coincides with Niemiec and Ryan (2009) who reported that when teachers have less external pressures placed on them, especially by administrators, they in turn are more likely to support student autonomy in the classroom (an example of the trickle-down effect). When discussing the degree of instructional autonomy enjoyed in her SG school a teacher stated, "We are very autonomous. We have our own choices to make as far as how we implement our curriculum. We are encouraged to, and do, work closely together within grade levels". Other SG teachers reported that they were free to teach as they pleased as long as they adhered to the state's Standard Course of Study, taught engaging lessons, and achieved desired results.

> We've got our Standard Course of Study that we're expected to teach, I'll break it up into a yearlong schedule by topics and I'll work with my other seventh-grade Science teacher, but what I do with that within my classroom is up to me unless it's not getting the job done and then we'll (administration and teacher) talk and have a conversation about how I need to refocus to meet the needs of the middle school student. (p. 120)
>
> I feel very free to pick my own activities and pick my own assignments ... I am aware of a couple of instances where they (administration) know a good job is not being done with that and in those cases, those teachers are not given quite so much freedom. They are aware of who is not handling their freedom well and they give them a little more direction. (p. 120)

A willingness to delegate instructional leadership duties and other responsibilities was also shared by both SG principals in Chisnall's (2010) study. One SG principal explained that she cannot know everything so she was happy to delegate and viewed herself as working for her staff rather than them working for her. "If I can't do something I will find somebody who can. I've never been afraid to do that. One of my favorite quotes from a movie is a 'man has to know his limitations' and I think that is an important thing. You have to know what you can and cannot do" (p. 143). In the second SG school the principal relied on one of his APs, a former principal to lead and monitor curriculum and instruction initiatives. The principal noted, "I'm the academic leader of the school I realize that.

However, having someone like her on staff ... is such a valuable asset" (p. 116).

Cooperative governance was further evident in one of the SG middle schools through the composition and operational nature of its Leadership Team in Chisnall's (2010) study. According to the principal and staff, many significant decisions were made by the Leadership Team which consisted of a teacher from each grade-level, an AG teacher, administration, parent representatives and two elective teachers. Teachers reported that this body was more collaborative in nature rather than simply consultative.

The significance of a pervasive humility also emerged in Chisnall's (2010) study in relation to the SG principals' key practices, policies and beliefs in developing a self-enhancing school. Indeed, the SG school principals demonstrated beliefs and actions indicative of a modest, self-critical and compassionate approach that further supported the existence of cooperative governance. The principals presented themselves, and were defined by their teachers, as humble, passionate, yet very resolute with high expectations for meeting the needs of the children in their schools. The principal in one SG school described her leadership style as nonconfrontational. She shared that she would avoid conflict when possible and preferred to sit down and talk through issues with personnel and students. A teacher in the same SG middle school referred to this principal as the "Gentle Giant."

> She prides herself on being the 'gentle giant'. At the same time if I went over there right now and said, 'Oh my gosh, my son's car broke down on the way to school this morning and we have the 8th grade dance tonight, my husband's out of town right now, is there anybody that can cover my class?' She (the principal) would cover my class ... I'm sure you've come in contact with leaders that lead with an iron fist and that's not always fun. Whereas she's consistent and has high expectations but in a kinder, gentler way. (p. 142)

The description of this SG principal as a compassionate committed leader was matched by the sentiments and observations of other teachers as well. As one such SG teacher shared,

> In nearly every conversation we have in staff meetings, she always says it's all about the kids, it's not about her, it's not about how the school is so wonderful, it's not about how wonderful the teachers are, she does support and praise us though, but it's about the kids. (p. 143)

Despite leading consistently high performing schools the SG principals were willing to be self-critical (Chisnall, 2010). For example, one confessed that she has not strictly adhered to district benchmark assessment guidelines. "I feel I have not been the best principal when it comes to those types of things" (p. 143). In explanation though this principal shared that she did not want to further expose her students to excess testing and felt the need to cherry pick when possible. Similarly, the other SG middle school principal demonstrated leadership beliefs and actions more supportive of a humanistic school climate oriented to self-direction rather than external control. Once again, humility was again a theme linked to this SG principal who was very calm, soft spoken and emphasized that his vision for his school was one where everyone worked in harmony. "Everybody has a say or some input into what's taking place and working for common goals in a respectful manner and cooperative way" (p. 143). For this principal it was critical to model his vision and beliefs on a frequent basis.

> What I try to do every day, I try to lead by example, I think that's the best way, I try to be a good role model like in the morning announcements I will say, "let's do our best today and I will do my best to be the best principal I can be and with whomever I come in contact to practice respect and dignity and do my best effort in everything I undertake and I want you to make the same commitment and challenge." (pp. 143-144)

This SG principal rarely displayed frustration and went to great efforts to not let others see him upset. He also revealed a modest side by acknowledging his need for professional growth on a continuous basis. "The day that I don't feel I need to improve or do something new is the day that I need to retire. I would say I'm a good principal and I want to be a great principal so that's what I'm looking to do" (p. 144).

Contrary to this, the LG school principals tended to favor a less self-effacing, more direct, and outwardly confident leadership approach (Chisnall, 2010). A LG principal shared her confidence with respect to working with the minority community, "Put it this way: I'm good in the hood" (p. 144). In reflecting on her leadership style and candid approach with ineffective teachers the LG principal added,

> So basically hire the best teachers and support them. Support the ones that can't teach as well, the ones that probably have zero teacher magic, and help them understand that they need to write the Greatest American Southern novel and leave. (p. 145)

Similar outward confidence was displayed by the same principal when discussing her hiring ability. "It's just the most interesting thing ever. We have built the kind of reputation where superstars come to me ... I have one gift for sure and I can hire people" (p. 145). One teacher noted that this LG principal liked and sought publicity and was a high energy cheerleader type.

Similarly, the second LG principal was very direct and confident in defining his leadership policies, practices and beliefs (Chisnall, 2010). As such, he presented himself as very much knowing what he wanted and desired for his staff and students to progress in the same direction.

> I think where we need to move is looking at a business model of professionalism because in education we have people that education is a profession and a career and are ultimate professionals then we have some people that continue going to school their whole lives and they're more in a kid mode. (p. 145)

In describing how his younger teachers need to have a greater appreciation for how to deal with parent communication the LG principal added,

> You know what, you have to talk to that parent, that's what we do! So you have to put your arm around them and at the same time coach them how we do it and as an administrator. So you're holding them firm in one hand and a stick in the other beating them over the head. It's nurturing and directing at the same time. (p. 146)

STUDENT INVOLVEMENT IN CURRICULUM PLANNING

According to Beane and Lipka (1986), a second factor critical to a self-enhancing school shifting from external control to self-direction is involving students in curriculum planning. Sands and Doll (1996) added that self-enhancing independence can be achieved by schools that expand opportunities for students to exercise choice. The notions of choice and involvement were a theme that emerged in the more Humanistic SG middle schools in the Chisnall (2010) study. For example, students in one SG middle school were able to choose from an unusually diverse range of electives that they would then undertake for a 6-week period in the middle of the school year. These mid-year "hobby" electives were tailored to student interests and included the following: rocket building, weaving, and broadcast journalism. Student involvement in curriculum planning was also promoted in the same SG middle school through the opportunity for all students to access special remediation electives throughout the year.

Both SG middle schools provided remediation opportunities for their students to pursue and allowed students and parents to monitor academic progress frequently (Chisnall, 2010). In one SG school the students had study hall on their 6-week elective wheel as a quiet time and place, staffed with caring teachers and supervised by an assistant principal, to help them finish late or incomplete assignments. One SG Principal noted,

> Kids that are not doing well and don't get their work done, rather than giving them elective classes, we may give them one elective class called 'study hall.' They go in there and do their homework because they are not doing their homework at home … we've got kids living in trailers and some bad situations and they're not going to do their homework at home, so we try to make sure they have the opportunity to get it done here. (p. 114)

A teacher in the same school added, "I think it's really helpful. Some of the wheel courses now have remedial math or remedial reading … they get homework done with support rather than attempting it at home and never being able to understand it." The regular elective wheel also included other options for students such as art, music, band, chorus, physical education, technology and Spanish. This elective wheel (or menu of short-term electives) allowed students greater flexibility as they could rotate among a wider range of elective choices (every 6 weeks) rather than being confined to the more orthodox semester or year-long electives which would mean less rotation and choice.

Furthermore, teachers in the SG school gave generously of their planning time and would provide math or reading electives for a 6-week period prior to end-of-grade state testing to ensure students in need had access to comprehensive remediation (Chisnall, 2010). According to the assistant principal, as many as 50% of the core subject teachers participated in this curriculum support program to assist struggling students.

While the one SG school in the Chisnall (2010) study provided a wide array of electives for students to choose from the other SG school ensured that through its schedule students had access to engaging, interdisciplinary instructional units aligned with the state's curriculum Just as Beane (1991) considered student involvement in problem centered curriculum as a step to enhancing their self-perceptions, this SG middle school had 3-week long problem centered interdisciplinary units that were popular with both staff and students. One such unit included creating a crime scene that students would investigate and follow-up on through the study and use of forensics in science, detective novels in language arts, and measurement and geometry in math.

> We had a crime scene set up at the school at a fake bowling alley. We had an outline of a body and fake blood. There were some stands where they had some sliders and they had to measure the angles, so that was a good thing on how they integrated it. In language arts they read Sherlock Holmes. In science they talked about the blood and how all that works. In math they measured the angles. So they really put a lot of neat stuff into it and this

helped the kids to understand relevance and how to put it all together instead of just saying, 'Okay, we're going to talk about angles.' It makes it so much more interactive. (SGS, Principal)

Another example of an interdisciplinary unit in this SG school required students to understand the significance of, and problems attached to, water access in developing countries (Chisnall, 2010). Students carried pails of water in physical education classes to appreciate firsthand the difficulty in locating and transporting water, and in science constructed effective water filter devices. A teacher added,

In science in 8th grade water quality is huge. The students designed their own aquifers to clean their water based on pH, turbidity, and how it looks. Seventh grade designed their own furnaces, how to keep things hot and cold, which worked and which didn't. We do a lot of things that just keep them motivated. In math they designed their own coke cans, needed to know what their volume was and how much they were going to have in there, find the surface area, how much you need to make this product, and what is going to be the final cost of your product.

The SG principal expected his eighth-grade teachers to provide their students with three such units a year, each lasting 3 weeks, and the sixth and seventh-grade teachers had to plan and deliver two interdisciplinary units each school year. Finally, the interdisciplinary units supported cooperative governance as grade-level teachers had to collaborate, for planning purposes, more closely with each other, administration, and elective teachers. As a SG teacher reported, "We do three interdisciplinary units a year, so we have to work together to see how that is all going to mesh."

SELF-DIRECTED LEARNING WITH CONSISTENCY

For Beane and Lipka (1986) self-directed learning entails students having some input into what they will learn and how their knowledge is assessed. The SG schools in Chisnall's (2010) study utilized self-directed learning in a variety of ways. In one SG middle school students were given goal sheets at the start of each school year which showed their performance for the previous 2 school years for standardized assessments in reading and math. The students were expected to review their past performance, set fresh goals and monitor their progress toward those goals. This idea was adapted by administration after learning that the AG teacher had been setting goals with her students and that had motivated them to be more successful. In reference to the goal sheets the AP stated,

So the kids will look at it (goal sheet) and say they have 352 in the 4th grade, they will circle it there and see what their percentile was in the 5th grade and they will come up here and see that maybe they grew and we will say, 'Okay, what do you think you can do this year if you really gave it your best try?' and they are doing that. (p. 134)

Chisnall (2010) reported that self-directed learning was further supported by the practice of students being frequently updated about their academic progress. Both SG schools were aggressive in keeping their students and parents informed. Progress reports went home every 3 weeks in one school and every 6 weeks in the other. This meant that students and parents could attempt to stay on top of concerns and address them proactively rather than learning about them at the end of a quarter.

Another prime example of self-directed control being prioritized over external control was the individualized scheduling practices in one of the Humanistic SG middle schools in Chisnall's (2010) study. First, students could choose from the wide array of electives on an elective wheel. Second, they could request schedule changes. Such changes were not a given as students had to first meet with a counselor, then write a persuasive letter explaining why the requested schedule change was justified. Finally, the assistant principal reviewed the student letters and approved or denied the requested changes.

In addition, it should be noted that both SG middle schools had enjoyed master schedule stability (Chisnall, 2010). Neither SG school had overhauled their master schedules to any significant extent in recent years nor no SG staff in the interviews referred to their schedules in a negative context. In contrast, both LG schools had changed their master schedules in recent times. One LG school had considerable master schedule instability with a teacher acknowledging that her school had three different schedules in the last 4 years. According to the LG principal the master schedule changes were required due to balancing the needs of elective teachers versus core subject teachers, increased student enrollment, and budget considerations. Another teacher in the same school reported that there was still ongoing dissatisfaction over the latest change that had shifted the school to a 90-minute block schedule and differed from the original plan agreed to by the SIT prior to the last summer break. The LG teacher stated, "It made a lot of people mad because it is not what we had decided." The principal acknowledged that the most recent change had been made during that summer break, but in consultation with some of her "generals" or teacher leaders.

It is plausible that the master schedule stability in the SG schools sustained and strengthened the sense of internal control for both staff and students versus the dissatisfaction that was evident in at least one of the

LG schools. There are several studies that indicate organizational or leadership consistency contributes to a more robust and effective workplace (Cole & Bedeian, 2007; Licata & Harper, 1999; Richardson & Piper, 1986). For example, Licata and Harper studied the organizational themes of 38 junior high and middle schools. They noted that when "academic emphasis is compromised, teacher efforts to maintain cohesion and adapt to uncertainty in the internal and external environments may displace academic goals" (p. 474). Chisnall (2010) reported that staff and students in the SG schools benefited from consistency and did not have to experience significant and ongoing changes that were sometimes made with or without input from staff

The theme of consistency was a critical one that separated the two Humanistic SG middle schools from the two LG middle schools in a variety of ways beyond master schedule stability (Chisnall, 2010). The SG principals' leadership policies, practices and beliefs consistently supported an academic emphasis evident in their high expectations and accountability. In one SG school a teacher reported that because they had clear school-wide discipline program students and staff knew what consequences would be for each level of misbehavior.

> Well because we have high expectations and consistency ... so here at school we set the expectation, you meet the expectation and if you don't there are consequences and when you follow through on those consequences it makes a believer out of them. They realize the focus is on their education. (p. 127)

A teacher in the second SG school added, "I think it's part of why we have good kids because we expect that they're going to behave and we treat them with respect and I do think that they respond to that" (p. 128).

In contrast, one of the LG middle schools lacked consistency in both the handling of discipline and expectations for staff (Chisnall, 2010). A teacher in the LG school reported, "sometimes it's (discipline) just not as consistent as it should be, which may lead to more discipline issues which may lead to a decrease in learning" (p. 128). Likewise, another teacher in the same school reported,

> There is a little bit of disconnect between the administrators. One of them is a little more lenient, one treats Black kids a little differently. That is the consensus I guess.... There's tons of announcements and signs up saying if you're play fighting, you're going to get in trouble, but then they don't get in trouble. So there is a little bit of a disconnect with consistency of the disciplinary actions. This gives you ISS, but if you go to the principal, this doesn't give you ISS. (p. 128)

According to Chisnall (2010), a lack of consistency extended beyond discipline and scheduling to staff accountability and the monitoring of instruction in one LG middle school participating in his study. The principal talked of a no-nonsense approach in dealing with staff indiscretions yet a LGS teacher reported the same principal did not appear to address staff members wearing inappropriate attire or arriving late for before-school duties.

> Gosh, I'm on time for my duty every morning yet this guy is not, but ... no one ever says a word to him. Or, this guy wears a t-shirt and shorts to teach in. That would be my biggest complaint of her as a leader.... It's something I've noticed over the years. (pp. 148-149)

Another teacher in the same LG school added that while the principal had high expectations for instruction and the use of data there were few steps taken to ensure teachers actually utilized data. Teachers were instructed to use an assessment tool on a biweekly basis yet when asked if this occurred the teacher responded, "No. The expectation is there, but not the accountability" (p. 118).

Chisnall (2010) surmised that the consistent academic emphasis that existed in the Humanistic SG schools may have offset the lack of structure and consistency that the schools' economically disadvantaged and minority students may have experienced off campus. Lee and Croninger (1994) note that many minority families want their children to be successful, but lack the material resources to assist their children in achieving their aspirations. Groups discriminated against sometimes have difficulty convincing their children that effort can lead to economic and social success, thus low expectations can ensue. However, Lee and Croninger note that schools can overcome such barriers with focused efforts and considerable collaboration.

The Chisnall (2010) study revealed the impact that consistently focused efforts, in tandem with a humanistic climate, can have on students' self-perceptions and academic success. The significance of consistency was reinforced by Scott and colleagues (2001):

> When students receive mixed messages and inadvertent and inconsistent reinforcement from school personnel, they may have more difficulty developing a line of reasoning in relation to their own lives, understanding the concept of boundaries, and applying this concept in the construction of their own values and attitudes. (p. 292)

The two LG middle schools lacked the consistency that was evident in the Humanistic SG schools. They also tended to possess characteristics associated more with custodial rather than humanistic climates. According to

Elmore (2000), "With strong, consistent leadership at all levels, including national study groups, state and local officials, building administrators, and teachers, we can create the middle schools our nation's children deserve and that we all desire" (p. 291).

CONCLUSION

Using a lens of academic emphasis and its three related subcomponents: policies, practices and beliefs, clear themes emerged in the Chisnall (2010) study that were common to the two Humanistic SG middle schools. The themes of high expectations and accountability, in conjunction with humility and consistency, supported a humanistic school climate where staff and students felt safe and empowered. The principals' actions and beliefs also appeared to support cooperative governance, self-directed learning and student involvement in curriculum planning. It was these policies, practices and beliefs of the SG principals that nurtured and sustained Humanistic schools characterized in part by a willingness to relinquish external control for self-direction

What is more, barriers to success were reduced because of the beliefs and actions of the SG principals and teachers who resisted deficit thinking and nurtured self-direction in their students (Chisnall, 2010). According to Scheurich and Skrla (2003), "Really the most important barrier is in our minds, in our beliefs: not in external cause" (p. 24). An ability to combat deficit thinking and develop an enhanced self-perception was well exemplified by the account of the 8th grader in one of the two SG schools. In her mock college application she mentions the impact her Academically Gifted (AG) teacher had on her during her time in middle school.

> Have you ever been told you couldn't do something? When people think of the African American population these things come to mind: drugs, incarceration, thieves, working at a minimum wage job and not amounting to anything. That is what my kindergarten teacher told me at the age of five. She didn't seem to look at my academic ability nor did she seem to notice the eloquence of my speech at my tender age. I went through elementary school with the same mindset of not amounting to anything because that is what I had been told, but in 2007 when I entered my first year of middle school, I met a remarkable woman who has influenced my life tremendously, her name is Sandra Edwards.... Through all of my years at elementary school I had never been pushed so hard in my life. I hated her class, she made me evaluate all of my decisions, she sat with me and tutored me when I needed the help. When I became slack she made sure that I worked to my full potential... I am now in 8th grade and I see the impact Ms. Edwards has

had on my life. I now push myself harder ... I am a better person today because of what she has taught me. She has been, and still is, my greatest inspiration.

The SG teacher who assigned the college application project shared that the above student's work exemplified the school setting within which students learned—that is, one of high expectations, accountability and genuine care for the students. The principals in both self-enhancing middle schools held high expectations for themselves and others, believed all students could be successful, and undertook measures to ensure their success by establishing enduring relationships with staff and students built on a foundation of mutual respect.

REFERENCES

Beane, J. A., & Lipka, R. P. (1986). *Self-concept, self-esteem, and the curriculum*. New York, NY: Teachers College Press.

Beane, J. A. (1991). Sorting out the self-esteem controversy. *Educational Leadership*, *49*(1), 25-30.

Blum, R. (2007). *Best practices: Building blocks for enhancing school environment*. Baltimore, MD: John Hopkins Bloomberg School of Public Health.

Brown, M. C. (2009). Closing the achievement gap: Successful practices at a middle school. *Dissertation Abstracts International,70*(04). (UMI No. 3355235)

California Department of Education. (1987). *Caught in the middle: Educational reform for young adolescents in California public schools*. Sacramento, CA: Author.

Chisnall, K. F. (2010). *Exploring leadership for excellence and equity in high performing middle schools*. (Unpublished doctoral dissertation). University of North Carolina, Chapel Hill, NC.

Cole, M. S., & Bedeian, A. G. (2007). Leadership consensus as a cross-level contextual moderator of the emotional exhaustion-work commitment relationship. *The Leadership Quarterly, 18*(5), 447-462.

Elbaum, B., & Vaughn, S. (2001). School-based interventions to enhance the self-concept of students with learning disabilities. *Elementary School Journal, 101*(3), 303-329.

Elmore, R. (2000). Leadership for effective middle school practice. *Phi Delta Kappan, 82*(4), 291-292.

Graham, S., Halpin, G., Harris, K. R., & Benson, J. (1985). A factor analysis of the pupil control ideology scale. *The Journal of Experimental Education, 53*(4), 202-206.

Howard, E., Howell, B., & Brainard, E. (1987). *Handbook for Conducting School Climate Improvement Projects*. Bloomington, IN: Phi Delta Kappa Educational Foundation.

Keefe, J. W., & Howard, E. R. (1997). The school as a learning organization. *The National Association of Secondary School Principals Bulletin, 81*(35), 35-44.

Koran, C. M. (1989). *School climate and student affective needs: A descriptive study of four junior high schools* (Unpublished master's thesis). University of Lethbridge, Lethbridge, Alberta, Canada.

Lan Yong, F. (1994). Self-concepts, locus of control, and Machiavellianism of ethnically diverse middle school students who are gifted. *Roeper Review, 16*(3), 192-194.

Lee, V. E., & Croninger, R. G. (1994). The relative importance of home and school in the development of literacy skills for middle grade students. *American Journal of Education, 102*(3), 286-329.

Licata, J. W., & Harper, G. W. (1999). Healthy schools, robust schools and academic emphasis as an organizational theme. *Journal of Educational Administration, 37*(5), 463-475.

Niemiec, C. P., & Ryan, R. M. (2009). Autonomy, competence, and relatedness in the classroom: Applying self-determination theory to educational practice. *Theory and Research in Education, 7*(2), 133-144.

Richardson, A. M., & Piper, W. E. (1986). Leader style, leader consistency, and participant personality effects on learning in small groups. *Human Relations, 39*, 817-836.

Sands, D. J., & Doll, B. (1996). Fostering self-determination is a developmental task. *The Journal of Special Education, 30*(1), 58-76.

Scheurich, J. J., & Skrla, L. (2003). *Leadership for equity and excellence: Creating high achievement classrooms, schools, and districts*. Thousand Oaks, CA: Corwin Press.

Schunk, D. H., & Pajares, F. (2002). The development of academic self-efficacy. In A. Wigfield & J. Eccles (Eds.), *Development of achievement motivation* (pp. 15-31). San Diego, CA: Academic Press.

Scott, C. G., Murray, G. C, Mertens, C., & Dustin, E. R. (2001). Student self-esteem and the school system: Perceptions and implications. *The Journal of Educational Research, 89*(5), 286-293.

Skinner, E. A., Wellborn, J. G., & Connell, J. P. (1990). What it takes to do well in school and whether I've got it: A process model of perceived control and children's engagement and achievement in school. *Journal of Educational Psychology, 82*(1), 22-32.

Skrla, L., Garcia, J., Scheurich, J. J., & Nolly, G. (2002, August). *Educational equity profiles: Practical leadership tools for equitable and excellent schools*. Paper presented at the meeting of the National Council of Professors of Educational Administration, Burlington, VT.

Tsai, Y., Kunter, M., Ludtke, O., Trautwein, U., & Ryan, R. M. (2008). What makes lessons interesting? The role of situational and individual factors in three school subjects. *Journal of Educational Psychology, 100*, 460-72.

Willower, D. J. (1974, April). *Some comments on inquiries on schools and pupil control*. Paper presented at the meeting of the American Educational Research Association, Chicago, IL.

CHAPTER 5

FROM SELF-ISOLATION TO PEER INTERACTION

Building Community in Middle Grades Classrooms

Clark Power and Ann Marie R. Power

Educators who have spent time with children in the middle grades know that these students are social to the core, constantly interacting with one another. Educators also know that social interaction at the middle grades level is not always positive; on the contrary, it is frequently fraught with problems ranging from awkwardness to bullying (e.g., Eccles, Lord & Midgley, 1991; Kupersmidt, Coie, & Dodge,1990; Selman, 2003). Considering the relational needs of middle level students, in this chapter we argue that young adolescents are best served by a just community culture to address their social as well as their moral needs. In a just community, teachers and students deliberately work together to create a sense of the common good of the classroom and school and invest themselves into making and maintaining the rules by which they agree to govern themselves. While middle level classrooms and schools can and should provide

Middle Grades Curriculum:
Voices and Visions of the Self-Enhancing School, pp. 71–88
Copyright © 2013 by Information Age Publishing
All rights of reproduction in any form reserved.

such a culture, we recognize that administrators and teachers often lack an accessible framework for imagining such a culture or lack workable strategies for bringing it about. Instead, the conventional practices of schooling combined with a hidden curriculum of "rugged individualism" make it very difficult for educators to conceive of how a moral community might function in a school setting. For this reason, we propose that educators look to sports teams as models for how to build community among adolescents.

OVERCOMING THE "IDIOCY" OF PRIVATISM THROUGH EDUCATION

On the whole, transforming schools into moral communities is not easy because American social and political life is deeply rooted in a culture of privatism which places priority on the self and one's immediate interests rather than on involvement or responsibility toward others. Yet, privatism can be detrimental to the self as well as to the community. Borrowing from the Greek understanding of "idiot," Walter Parker (2002; 2005) describes one's preoccupation with one's own or one's family's interests as "idiocy," explaining, "An idiot is suicidal in a certain way, definitely self-defeating, for the idiot does not know that privacy and individual autonomy are entirely dependent on the community" (pp. 134-135). Idiocy is moral self-isolation. By turning their backs on others, idiots not only undermine the society on which they depend but their own individuality, because community is absolutely necessary for individuals to flourish. To overcome idiocy in an educational environment, students must learn the importance of the common or public good in addition to their own private good.

Drawing on the insights of Vivien Paley (1992) as well as research on the just community approach (Power, Higgins, & Kohlberg, 1989), Parker (2005) argues that schools are the logical place to foster the kind of peer interaction that can transform "idiocy" into democratic citizenship and that the middle grades present a particular opportune moment in student development to engender an appreciation of the common good. Though Parker recognizes the responsibility that schools have at all levels, kindergarten through college, he believes that middle school educators have a special opportunity to develop what he calls the "social consciousness of puberty": "When aimed at democratic ends and supported by the proper democratic conditions, the interaction in schools can help children enter the social consciousness of puberty and develop the habits of thinking and caring necessary for public life" (Parker, 2005, p. 348).

Puberty, which is derived from the Latin word meaning mature, marks the transition into the threshold of adulthood. During this time, the child's body takes on the capacity for work and for reproduction. In other words, the child becomes physically capable of not only independence but care. In our culture, the psychological transition into adulthood takes far longer than the physical and requires much more thought to ensure its healthy development. Ideally, the process of schooling should prepare children to begin to contribute to their society by beginning to take on some of the responsibilities of adulthood. Taking this into consideration, Parker (2005) presses beyond a solely biological focus on puberty to include a sociopolitical one. For Parker, the process of schooling should be "aimed at democratic ends and supported by the proper democratic conditions" (Parker, p. 348).

Democracy is unique among forms of governance in that it depends upon a mature citizenry in order to flourish. Yet, to what extent have we structured schools to prepare children to partake in democratic politics? The institution of public schools grew out of recognition that democracy required a cultivation of the spirit as well as the mind, but we are not always sure of what education for democracy entails. Certainly members of a democracy need to be well-informed about their local and national democratic institutions and what the duties of democratic citizenship include, and such information makes up the content of most "civic education" courses. But merely having information about democratic institutions does not constitute preparation for participating in them. Practicing democratic citizenship includes not only the expression of one's personal views but also participation in an ongoing dialogue about securing justice for all and advancing the common good. Parker (2005) contends that the dialogue that is at the heart of true democracy requires both moral and intellectual virtues. In his view, schools ought to cultivate "habits of thinking and caring necessary for the public life" (Parker, p. 348). Children must learn how to make decisions together that reflect dignity, freedom, and equality. In this way they will come to value and to practice democracy as a "way of life," as John Dewey (1916; 1968) puts it.

If children are to acquire genuine habits of democratic thinking and caring, we need to connect civic education with the discipline and social life of the school, where governance is ongoing. Acquiring habits of citizenship requires actual experience. Moreover, students have to interact with each other over matters that they care about in order to learn how to think and care about the common life. When integrated with daily life and the discipline of the school, citizenship education can form the dispositions necessary for public life. The problem, as we see it, is that we have marginalized citizenship education as simply another subject within a crowded curriculum. Instead of thinking of citizenship education as permeating the way we go about teaching and learning, we have made it into a sterile content area to be studied within a particular class period. Furthermore, concern for citizenship education has taken a backseat to preparing students for standardized tests of achievement. Policies such as "No Child Left Behind" have served to exacerbate the pressure on schools to focus narrowly on math and English tests scores, and major educational reform initiatives going back to a *Nation At Risk* (National Commission on Excellence in Education, 1983) have focused narrowly on economic concerns neglecting to acknowledge the importance of educating for democracy as central to the very aim of education itself.

If citizenship education is to be given its rightful place at the very heart of schooling itself, we must address the cultural idiocy that views schooling as a means to private financial gain. Schools indeed have a critical role to play in establishing the social and political foundations of a just society. In order to overcome the idiocy that narrows our vision about the ends as well as means of education, our schools need to educate children to care about community and the common good.

LESSONS IN CITIZENSHIP EDUCATION FROM SPORTS TEAMS

Because teachers have for the most part viewed classroom instruction in highly individualistic ways, there are few school-based models of how to build community to foster citizenship education in the middle school classroom. Yet outside the classroom there are available models. One place where teachers may consider looking is at team sports, because of their emphasis on team-building. The cliché, "there is no 'I' in team," captures this emphasis on team unity in sports. On sports teams, players learn how to value the common good because in order for teams to be successful, the individual players have to regard themselves as parts of a whole. They must be willing to make sacrifices and to cooperate for the good of the team.

Sports also emphasize experiential learning. All good coaches know the value of practice. Coaches employ "blackboard learning" but know it only goes so far. Athletes develop as team players only through action, by scrimmaging and actually playing together. Good coaches also understand that if athletes are to learn to play together as a team, they have to learn how to make decisions as the game is unfolding. This means that coaches have to help players to understand offensive and defensive strategies well enough so that they can apply these strategies to the novel situations that they encounter in the game. The most effective coaching is not done on the sidelines but on the practice field by creating situations that players are likely to encounter in a game. In addition, significant coaching takes place in team meetings before and after games and practices. The best team meetings are those in which a coach genuinely engages the players in setting goals and in evaluating themselves. Good coaches realize that by seeking players' input and involving them in problem-solving, their players will become more engaged and responsible team members. For example, in teaching players "help defense" in basketball, coaches ask players to change their ordinary defensive assignments in order to assist a player who has gotten "beaten" on defense. This defense requires considerable trust as well as coordination. In order for this defense to work well, all of the players have to take a team, as opposed to an individual, approach to the defense.

Good coaches also involve players in making and enforcing team rules and policies. Coaches understand that players will enforce rules if they have had input into making them and if they feel responsible for enforcing them. Some coaches rely on captains and eighth grade students to build peer support for team rules. Of course, there are some coaches who take an authoritarian approach to rules and try to control players' behavior through intimidation and threat. An authoritarian approach may lead some athletes to comply but not for moral or team-oriented reasons. In our experience, even authoritarian coaches, upon reflection, see the inadequacy of focusing on external conformity. Coaches want to develop their players as leaders who want to do the right thing for the right reason.

Why should teachers think of their classrooms as "teams?" Teams win or lose but there are no collective rewards or punishments for classes of students. Why should teachers think of classrooms as teams when they grade and rank students individually? The parallelism between the classroom and sports field is not obvious. Yet teachers are aware that classrooms have group atmospheres that support or undermine discipline and learning. Although part of the motivation for team-building in sports is winning, coaches understand that team-building is intrinsically valuable apart from the competitive context. Education has its models too; for example, the cooperative learning approach (e.g., Johnson & Johnson, 1994; Slavin, 1990) is a well-established pedagogical practice at all levels of school. Yet some teachers only view cooperative learning instrumentally, as a tool for promoting individual academic progress rather than as a method for developing the classroom community as a whole. In order to understand the importance of the classroom community as an end in its own right, teachers must recognize, first, that learning itself is inherently cooperative and, second, that the development of a classroom community is itself a moral value and a means of moral education. Although coaches do not generally use the language of democracy or community to articulate the importance of team-building, they recognize, if only on an intuitive level, that the individual members of a team are interdependent and that the greater their commitment to the common good, the more likely that they will be to meet their goals as a team, apart from winning. Classroom teachers also recognize the interdependence of the students in their classrooms; developing their students' sense and appreciation of their common good strengthens that interdependence and benefits discipline and learning. Dewey (1916; 1997) described this social approach to education as "democratic" arguing that the means and ends of education ought to be consistent. If we are serious about educating children to become adults in a thoroughly democratic society, then we must provide democratic experiences for children in the context of school. In other words, we must offer them apprenticeships in participatory democracies. In general, an apprenticeship involves learning through practice under the guidance of a master. More specifically, an apprenticeship in democracy entails giving young people the opportunity to learn the skills of democratic deliberation in settings where they can get expert direction and guidance as they learn through experience. Like good coaches, teachers need to give students some ownership of their classrooms so that they can begin to understand what it means to take responsibility for the adult society into which they will soon enter. Students need a first-hand experience of making and enforcing rules that are just and in promoting the welfare of all, particularly the least advantaged. Children need to practice moral citizenry in the *polis* of the classroom while they are still under the direction of those more learned, when their nuclear society is still small and manageable.

Helping students become democratic citizens does not mean turning the governance of classrooms and schools over to the students. Teachers are indispensable as students develop habits of citizenship under their expert tutelage. Just as coaches guide and instruct their players in game situations, so too teachers must guide and instruct their students in their social interactions in the classroom. In this sense, schools offer students an apprenticeship in democracy, an idea which was first put forward by Horace Mann, the Father of the American Public School:

> In order that men may be prepared for self-government their apprenticeship must begin in childhood.... He who has been a serf until the day before he is 21 years of age, cannot be an independent citizen after; and it makes no difference whether he has been a serf in Austria or America. As the fitting apprenticeship for despotism consists in being trained for despotism, so the fitting apprenticeship for democracy consists in being trained for self-government (Mann, 1845, 1957, p. 58).

Approaching middle level education as an apprenticeship in democracy may no doubt go against the grain of many teachers. Wigfield, Eccles, Schiefele, Roeser, and Davis-Kean (2006) report that middle school teachers provide their students with fewer opportunities for decision-making than in the earlier grades. Wigfield et al. also point out that this reluctance to involve children in making decisions about their common life leads the children to feel less engaged in school. Yet, middle school teachers committed to the collaborative and constructivist approaches to teaching advocated in *This We Believe* (National Middle School Association, 2010) should be open to the kind of democratic approach that coaches have shown works to engage young people and to help them to develop morally as well as academically.

SOCIAL AND MORAL CHALLENGES IN MIDDLE LEVEL EDUCATION

Not surprisingly a growing body of research shows that the middle school years present special challenges to students' sense of self (e.g., Eccles, 2004; Eccles & Midgley, 1989; Eccles & Roseser 2010). To a large extent these challenges are rooted in the onset of adolescence itself, which brings significant and often dramatic physical, cognitive, and social changes. For example, as children are adjusting to differences in their appearance, they are developing new capacities for self-reflection and perspective-taking. They are also beginning to differentiate their inner, private selves from outer, public selves (Broughton, 1981; Selman, 1980). These differences in physical and psychological self-perception can and often do lead to feelings of being a stranger even to themselves and of being misunderstood and undervalued by others. Moreover, middle schoolers clearly want to fit in and be a part of the crowd, but they also want to be themselves and not a "phony" or "suck-up."

The dynamics of early adolescence seem to lead children in the middle schools years to feel isolated and alone. Yet this is only half the story. As Eccles (2004) points out, middle schools themselves can help students to feel that they belong and are valued or these schools can exacerbate students' feelings of insecurity and isolation. Research on the school/environment fit (Eccles, 2004; Eccles & Midgley, 1989) as well as from self-determination theory (Deci & Ryan, 1985; 2002) makes clear that we cannot understand how children are developing in the middle school years unless we take into account organizational and cultural characteristics of particular classrooms and schools. The school environment can be relatively nurturing or toxic depending on how well attuned the environment is to the developmental needs of the students.

Research into the social psychological implications of teaching practices at the middle school level gives us reason to be concerned. For example, Roeser, Marachi, and Gehlbach (2002) find that teachers of middle school students becoming increasingly less likely to believe that they are responsible for students' social and emotional well-being. On the other hand, middle school teachers seem to give increasingly greater emphasis to students' academic performance as measured by grades. Eccles and Midgley (1989) show that middle school teachers grade more strictly using social comparison criteria than elementary school teachers do. As grades become more salient, they have greater influence on students' judgments of their competence to succeed in school. Unfortunately, low grades in the middle school years predict to poor performance in high school (Finn, 2006). Of particular concern to us in this chapter is the way in which grading practices reflect a wider cultural pattern of social comparison in which children entering adolescence are forced to measure themselves against others along a number of different criteria, for example, personal appearance, popularity, athletic achievement in addition to grades (Harter, 1998). As Nicholls (1989) and other motivational theorists (e.g., Dweck, 2006) have pointed out, the practice of using social comparison to gauge one's competencies can become self-defeating, especially for those who find themselves at the lower end of the comparison. Moreover, the practice of social comparison can lead to self-isolation as individuals believe they must demonstrate their superiority over others in order to demonstrate their self-worth.

In our view, a classroom climate focused on social comparison should give way to a climate focused on cooperation. Instead of maintaining grade-driven environments in which students ask themselves how they stack up against other students, we propose establishing goal-oriented environments in which students ask themselves what they are accomplishing as a classroom community. This entails understanding the classroom as a community of learners engaged in a common enterprise and committed to each others' development. Our vision of the ideal middle level classroom is informed by sports teams in which the individual members of the team work for the good of the team itself. Sports teams win and lose as teams. The performances of all of the individual members of a team are, of course, important; but ideally individual members of the team value each others' performances as well as their own. What ultimately counts on a sports team is what the team as a whole accomplishes, and on a sports team that is genuinely a community, all members of the team are encouraged to help each other to get better. The same can go for classrooms. Individual learners can take pride in their own accomplishments as well as in their class's as a whole

Several years ago, educators, psychologists, and coaches collaborated to develop an approach to coaching youth and high school sport called, "Play Like a Champion Today" (Power, Sheehan, Crawford, LaVoi, & McBride, 2012). Play Like a Champion Today emphasizes that sports are fundamentally games to be played and, as such, are meant to be fun for all the participants. To play like a champion also connotes something beyond playing for fun. Champions play for the love of the sport, are good teammates and play fairly, and are leaders off as well as on the field. We developed this approach because we observed that some coaches and parents turned the play of sports into high-pressured work and that such an approach too often discouraged rather than encouraged the character development of young champions. We therefore decided to undertake a program of research and coach/parent education.

Play Like a Champion Today draws heavily on Duda and Nicholls' (1992) original theory of achievement orientations in sport and on Duda's (2004) continuing research on coach generated achievement climates. Although this theory had its origins in the classroom (Nicholls, 1989), it has, in our view, been more widely applied on the sports field (Duda & Balaguer, 2007). Coaches readily grasp the importance of tailoring goals to the individual athlete and of focusing on how individual athletes progress toward their own goals. Many teachers, on the other hand, feel constrained to assess students using norm-referenced grading, which compares students with each other. Crooks (1988) shows that norm-referenced grading discourages students who score at the low-end of the class. Low-achieving students would be much more motivated to achieve were they to focus on making progress toward attainable goals that they and their teacher set. Instead of competing against each other for grades, a "team" approach to the classroom suggests that students could be encouraged to support each others' learning with the ultimate goal being the success of the class as a whole.

Taking a "team" approach to learning with an emphasis on making progress to individual and classroom goals can go a long way in overcoming the alienation that students, particularly low achieving students, experience in the classroom. Yet a focus on academic achievement only goes part way in transforming classrooms into genuine communities. Perhaps the greatest challenge in the middle school classroom is overcoming the social isolation and alienation that many middle school students experience. Thus, we need to understand social as well as psychological forces that lead those entering adolescence to struggle to find acceptance and affirmation in their peer groups.

Research in social and moral development indicates that children in early adolescence typically process their social interactions in egoistic ways, which can isolate them from rather than unite them with their classmates and teammates (e.g., Colby & Kohlberg, 1987; Selman, 2003). Colby, Kohlberg and Selman's research describes a sequential pattern of sociomoral cognitive development in which children come to differentiate their own perspective from others and coordinate multiple perspectives. The middle school years, spanning the transition from late childhood to early adolescence, mark perhaps the single most important period in the process of development. In this period, most children progress from a Stage 2 morality based on concrete exchange to a Stage 3 morality based on Golden Rule mutuality and shared interpersonal ideals. The developmental literature suggests that children who fail to make the transition from Stage 2 to Stage 3 in early adolescence are at risk for serious problems with antisocial behavior in later adolescence and adulthood. In fact, Gibbs (2003) notes that developmental delay generally at Stage 2 is at the roots of all antisocial behavior as seen in delinquents and adult offenders.

Stage 2 is a self-centered but not necessarily selfish stage. Individuals at Stage 2 understand morality as based on concrete exchanges with others. Theirs is a morality of "Do unto others as they have done or will do to you." Gibbs (2003) finds that adolescents and adults delayed at Stage 2 adopt a strongly instrumental and self-serving view of right and wrong. For example, they believe that breaking the law is wrong not because the laws are worthy of respect or because society may be harmed but because the lawbreaker may get caught and punished. The development to Stage 3 is based on a concern to uphold mutual values of trust and caring. Individuals at Stage 3 are willing to "be good for goodness sake." They do not need the threat of punishment or the promise of reward to motivate them to be moral. What does motivate them is the recognition that "being good for goodness sake" brings them into a closer relationship with others than was ever possible at Stage 2. The experience of trust and of mutual care is life-transforming and undergirds future relationships with others.

Middle school education can encourage or discourage the transition to Stage 3 depending on the extent to which the culture of the school encourages students to become sensitive to the needs of others and to consider different perspectives in deciding what is right and wrong. Developmental delay typically occurs in environments in which individuals feel threatened, mistrustful, and not cared for. In such environments, individuals feel free to pursue their own needs without regard for the consequences to others. Perhaps the most effective way of assuring that children make the transition to Stage 3 and beyond is to involve them in a group in which they feel they belong but also in which there are shared expectations for sharing and for sacrificing for others and for the group as a whole.

CONFRONTING THE CULTURE OF EXCLUSION

In a study comparing middle school students in 12 Western countries, Juvonen, Le, Kaganoff, Augustine, & Constant (2004) report that U.S. students rate the climate (as measured by pleasantness and belonging) of their middle schools the lowest and the peer culture (as measured by perceptions of their classmates as not kind, helpful, or accepting) of their middle school as the next to lowest. Although we do not have comparative data that can help to explain why students in U.S. middle schools feel more alienated than those in many other countries, Vivien Paley's (1992) classic, *You Can't Say You Can't Play,* provides penetrating insight into how the culture of school itself leads to disconnection and to isolation.   Features of this school culture appear to us to reflect the privatistic culture of the United States itself, which ranks among the lowest of the industrialized countries in the world on indices of income inequality (C.I.A., 2011) and child poverty (UNICEF, 2000). There is a strong ambivalence in the United States over the degree of responsibility that individuals have to promote the common good. There is certainly no shared understanding that being a United States citizen means looking after the welfare of others beyond one's family. Vivien Paley's analysis of the values that inform the way children constitute their play groups gives us an insight into the worlds of both children and adults.

The title of Paley's (1992) book, *You Can't Say You Can't Play,* comes from her attempt to address the painful fact that children begin excluding others from their playgroups as early as kindergarten. Paley writes that one can observe in the kindergarten the erection of a power structure in which "certain children will have the right to limit the social experiences of their classmates" (p. 3). As this structure becomes embedded throughout the elementary level and into the middle grades, "a ruling class will notify others of their acceptability, and the outsiders learn to anticipate the sting of rejection" (p. 3).

Paley (1992) illustrated the dynamics of this structure with an incident from her own kindergarten class. Angelo called her over to comfort "shy" Clara who was crying. Clara explained, "Cynthia and Lisa built a house for their puppies and I said can I play and they said no because I don't have a puppy I only have a kitty. They said I'm not their friend" (p. 14). When Paley suggested that Cynthia and Lisa reconsider, Lisa stood her ground, "It was my game. It was up to me." This troubled Paley and led her to raise a number of serious moral questions. Did Lisa have the "right" to exclude Clara? Should children be free to play with those whom they like? What about the children who are turned away? Concerned about them, Paley proposed a controversial rule for her classroom, "You can't say you can't play."

When she first proposed "You can't say you can't play" as a new rule, only four of the twenty children in Paley's (1992) kindergarten class agreed with it. Not surprisingly those four were those most frequently excluded, the ones psychologists refer to as the "rejected" or "neglected" (Waas, 2006). Children who are rejected and neglected are at risk for serious social and psychological problems throughout school and into adult-hood (Waas). The practice of exclusion comes at a great cost to them.

By the time children get to the fifth grade, peer exclusion has become a fact of life. Yet coupled with a sense that exclusion is inevitable is a dawning realization of the possibility of change. When Paley (1992) discussed her proposed rule with fifth graders, some acknowledged that it would be a good rule in an ideal world. Most of the students, however, thought the rule was impractical or would require a long, deliberate process of implementation. One student noted that "It would take years to get used to. You really have to start in kindergarten" (p. 100). Another student objected to the rule on the grounds that it would lead children to the false hope that exclusion really could be overcome: "In your whole life you're not going to go through life never being excluded. So you may as well learn it now" (p. 100). This student's experience had hardened him to the reality of peer exclusion.

With some gentle prodding from Paley (1992), some students mused about the possibility of changing. If being exclusive was a habit maybe they could develop a habit of inclusion. One student, however, thought that by the fifth grade habits were set in stone. "When you get older, some people really don't care. You're a little meaner" (Paley, p. 100). Others were not so sure. One girl argued, "People can be trained to be nice or to fight. Or both ways, like us" (Paley, p. 100). The children then traded memories about painful rejections. Paley noticed that no one described the experience of doing the rejecting. Although not all children were routinely rejected, many had been snubbed, even by those they thought were their friends. All of the children wanted a classroom environment in which they might count on feeling included. The fifth grade children and those in the earlier grades all appreciated the opportunity to discuss the dynamics of play group inclusion and exclusion.

We might characterize the discussions that Paley (1992) initiated as a form of group therapy. Paley provided a safe and secure context in which children could share painful feelings and frustrations about their social interactions. She was at all times inviting and affirming. Many children spoke up in the group meetings. A few children approached her privately to thank her or to add their own stories. By bringing the phenomenon of peer exclusion into the open, Paley had a better grasp of the extent of the problem and was in a better position to comfort the victims. She was also able to sensitize those who did the excluding, those the younger children described as the "bosses." Although Paley's intervention had demonstrable therapeutic benefits, we miss its significance if we simply classify it as a psychotherapeutic process rather than as a legislative-moral process. By proposing a specific rule directed at children's free play in school, Paley deliberately challenged students to change the way they acted. Engaging children in making a rule that would drastically alter status led students to think about reasons for and against such a rule.

ESTABLISHING SHARED NORMS THROUGH DIRECTED PEER INTERACTION

In the research that we have undertaken on the just community approach (Power 2002; Power, Higgins, & Kohlberg, 1989; Power & Power, 1992), we identified a sequence of phases in the construction of shared norms. The initial phase consists of a proposal for a new norm, which the community is asked to accept. It is important to note that the phase of proposing a norm presupposes a democratic context for adopting the norm. This is a very different process from the teacher imposing rules on students or the teacher asking students to vote on a commonsense rule, such as forbidding fighting, cheating, or stealing with the threat of a penalty.

What is the difference between a shared norm and a rule? They are both similar in the sense that they either proscribe or prescribe a behavior or class of behaviors. Yet we define a shared norm as one in which members of a group agree to try to adhere to the shared norm in spirit as well as in practice. A rule, on the other hand, simply prohibits or commands a behavior and specifies a sanction for noncompliance. Teachers often think of rules as a means of keeping and enforcing order in the classroom. In this sense, rules are tools for management. Norms, on the other hand, have a normative function; they help to define as well as bring about group cohesiveness and identity. Norms and rules can be coextensive. Rules define behavioral requirements while norms address the inner dispositions of the group members. Rules call for conformity while norms call for commitment.

Some teachers formulate a few very general rules, such as Show Respect, Have a Positive Attitude, Be Courteous. Other teachers stress very specific rules, such as don't wear hats in class, shirt tails must be tucked in, and you must always raise your hand before speaking. General rules have the advantage of appealing to a value or virtue, such as respect or courtesy. But these rules suffer from being so general that students and teachers do not always know what is entailed in consenting to them when they are giving their consent. For example, some teachers may presume that not tucking in one's shirt-tail or not raising one's hand to speak is a sign of disrespect or a lack of courtesy; yet many students may not see the connection and regard these rules as arbitrary conventions imposed by the teachers. An approach to discipline that is rooted in a concern for moral education balances a commitment to uphold a value with a somewhat specific expectation for behavior. Paley's (1992) "You can't say...."

rule appeals to the value of caring for others while also linking that value to a range of behaviors associated with including others in play at school.

Although even kindergarten age children saw value in Paley's (1992) rule, many found its prescription for inclusion too demanding. By the fifth grade, as we have seen, many children thought that it was simply unrealistic to turn such caring into a shared expectation. Curiously, Paley found that the teachers in her school acknowledged the problem of exclusion but, like the fifth-graders, balked at Paley's proposed solution. The teachers, however, went further than their students in rationalizing their reluctance to intervene as an unwarranted intrusion into children's freedom. They maintained that all that teachers should do, if they choose to get involved at all, is to help make the "outsiders" more "acceptable" to the insiders (Paley, 1992, p. 33). To Paley's dismay, these teachers accepted exclusion as inevitable, as a defect of human nature, which they were powerless to change. In Paley's estimation, the teachers failed to see that the problem of exclusion was a social construct that could be changed. Moreover, Paley objected to the suggestion that only the outcasts should be forced to change. She argued that if "outcasts" can be asked to change themselves in order to become more pleasing to the group, why can't the group be asked to change itself to embrace the outcasts?

We have found that school administrators and classroom teachers voice many of the sentiments expressed by the teachers in Paley's (1992) school. Yet we have also found that many teachers and school administrators are willing to enact the "You can't say...." rule. All teachers and administrators acknowledge that the rule is deeply countercultural and wonder, for example, why we should be expected to be our sisters' and brothers' keepers? Why should we not respect an individual's freedom to help others if they are so moved? Does helping others actually hurt them by enabling them to get along without having to change themselves to become more successful? Is the greatness of the United States a function of its insistence on the virtues of self-reliance and independence?

Sports teach us that the welfare of the individual is a function of the welfare of the group and vice versa. We are, in fact, not isolated individuals but part of a social whole. United States' greatness, we believe, depends on our commitment to the virtues of justice and shared responsibility. Leadership—in sports, in a classroom, or in society—means taking responsibility for others and the group as a whole. Sport leaders understand that building genuine teams means that all of the members of the team care for each as friends. Few coaches would object to Paley's (1992) "You can't say" rule because they know that sports teams are by their nature inclusive. Coaches typically speak of teams as families in which the members care for one another not because they have chosen to be friends but because they are related in a common enterprise.

Although building classroom communities is very much in vogue among character educators these days (Power & Power, 2012), to what extent do those advocating classroom community have in mind the ideal type of inclusivity that Paley (1992) held out in her "You can't say you can't play" rule?   Classroom communities, no less than sports teams, should be places in which all members of the group can feel that they belong and that they, in turn, have responsibility for each other, even those whom they do not particularly like.   Learning to take an interest in and connect with others not because we have chosen them as friends but because they are fellow members of our society is an important part of what we are calling citizenship education.

As we have noted, one of the advantages that sports teams have over classrooms is that sports teams elicit a sense of pride and loyalty unheard of in most classrooms and even in most schools. It is often on a sports team that children learn that a group is more than the sum of its parts. They find that being a member of a group helps them to develop and to perform their best. They also discover that being a member of a group does not necessarily take away from their individuality; in fact, membership in a group can enhance their sense of who they are. The dawning awareness of the group as an entity including but also transcending the members who compose it is also a part of the transition to a Stage 3 and beyond morality. It is a profoundly new consciousness of one's social reality and obligations that follow from that reality. Experiencing what it means to be a member of a group is crucial if children are to transcend the idiocy of privatism.

CONCLUSION

In our view, middle level education is at a crossroads. We can continue to work within the conventional individualistic model, which reflects a privatistic worldview and leads to a debilitating social isolationism, or we can embrace a vision of education as communal and democratic. The choice does not involve putting the well-being of the group over the good of the individual but recognizing, as coaches do, that individuals are members of a group and that the good of the former can be pursued only by promoting the good of the latter. Middle level teachers have a special opportunity to help young adolescents develop a mature social consciousness in which they extend their concern beyond themselves and their particular peer group to the wider community. Classrooms, like sports teams, should be inclusive communities in which all students feel that they belong, have responsibilities to one another and the group as a whole, and have the power of working democratically to realize the common good. Middle level teachers need to provide students with a vision of a fair and welcoming learning community and to challenge their students to translate that vision into a reality.

REFERENCES

Broughton, J. (1981). The divided self in adolescence. *Human Development, 24*, 13-32.

C. I. A. (2011). *CIA world fact book.* Retrieved from https://www.cia.gov/library/publications/the-world-factbook/fields/2172.html

Colby, A., & Kohlberg, L. (1987). *The measurement of moral judgment* (Vol. 1 & 2). New York, NY: Cambridge University Press.

Crooks, T. (1988). The impact of classroom evaluation on students. *Review of Educational Research. 58*(4), 438-481.

Deci, E. L., & Ryan, R. M. (1985). *Intrinsic motivation and self-determination in human behavior.* New York, NY: Plenum.

Deci, E. L., & Ryan, R. M. (Eds.). (2002). *Handbook of self-determination theory research.* Rochester, NY: University of Rochester Press.

Dewey, J. (1968). *Democracy and education: An introduction to philosophy of education.* New York, NY: Free Press. (Original work published 1916)

Dewey, J. (1997). *Democracy and education.* New York, NY: Simon & Schuster. (Original work published 1916)

Duda, J. L. (2004). Goal setting and achievement motivation in sport. In C. Spielberger (Ed.), *Encyclopedia of Applied Psychology* (pp. 109-119). San Diego, CA: Academic Press.

Duda, J. L., & Nicholls, J. (1992). Dimensions of achievement motivation in schoolwork and sport. *Journal of Educational Psychology, 84*, 1-10.

Duda, J. L., & Balaguer, I. (2007). The coach-created motivational climate. In S. Jowett & D. Lavalee (Eds.), *Social psychology of sport* (pp. 117-130). Champaign, IL: Human Kinetics.

Dweck, C. S. (2006). *Mindset: The new psychology of success.* New York, NY: Random House.

Eccles, J. S. (2004). Schools, academic motivation, and stage-environment fit. In R. M. Lerner & L. Steinberg (Eds.), *Handbook of adolescent psychology* (2nd ed., pp. 125-153). New York, NY: Wiley.

Eccles, J. S., & Midgley, C. (1989). Stage-environment fit: Developmentally appropriate classrooms for young adolescents. In C. Ames & R. Ames (Eds.), *Research on motivation in education: Goals and cognitions* (Vol. 3, pp. 139-186). New York, NY: Academic Press.

Eccles, J., Lord, S., & Midgley, C. (1991). What are we doing to early adolescents? The impacts of educational contexts on early adolescents. *American Educational Journal, August*, 521-542.

Eccles, J. S., & Roeser, R. W. (2010). An ecological view of schools and development. In J. L. Meece & J. S. Eccles (Eds.), *Handbook of research on schools, schooling, and human development* (pp. 6-21). New York, NY: Routledge.

Finn, J. D. (2006). *The adult lives of at-risk students: The roles of attainment and engagement in high school. Statistical analysis report.* U. S. Department of Education, National Center for Education Statistics. Washington, DC: U.S. Government Printing Office.

Gibbs, J. C. (2003). *Moral development and reality: Beyond the theories of Kohlberg and Hoffman.* Thousand Oaks, CA: SAGE.

Harter, S. (1998). The development of self-representations. In W. Damon (Series Ed.) & N. Eisenberg (Vol. Ed.), *Handbook of child psychology: Vol. 3. Social, emotional, and personality development* (5th ed., pp. 553-617). New York, NY: Wiley.

Juvonen, J., Le, V., Kaganoff, T., Augustine, C. H., & Constant, L. (2004). *On the wonder years: Challenges facing the American middle school.* Santa Monica, CA: Rand.

Johnson, D. W. & Johnson, R. T. (1994). *Learning together and alone: Cooperative, competitive, and individualistic learning* (4th ed.). Needham Heights, MA: Allyn & Bacon.

Kupersmidt, J. B., Coie, J. D., & Dodge, K. A. (1990). The role of poor peer relationships in the development of disorder. In S. R. Asher & J. D. Coie (Eds.), *Peer rejection in childhood* (pp. 274-305). Cambridge, MA: Cambridge University Press.

Mann, H. (1845/1957). *The republic and the school: The education of free men.* New York, NY: Teachers College Press, Columbia University.

National Commission on Excellence in Education. (1983). *A nation at risk: The imperative for educational reform.* Washington, DC: U. S. Government Printing Office.

National Middle School Association. (2010). *This we believe: Keys to educating young adolescents.* Westerville, OH: National Middle School Association.

Nicholls, J. G. (1989). *The competitive ethos and democratic education.* Cambridge, MA: Harvard University Press.

Paley, V. (1992). *You can't say you can't play.* Cambridge, MA: Harvard University Press.

Parker, W. (2002). Education for democracy: Contexts, curricula, assessments. Greenwich, CT: Information Age.

Parker, W. (2005). Teaching against idiocy. *Phi Delta Kappan, 86*(5), 344-351.

Power, F. C. (2002). Building democratic community: A radical approach to moral education. In W. Damon (Ed.), *Bringing in a new era in character education* (pp. 129-148).Stanford, CA: Hoover Press, Sanford University.

Power, F. C., Higgins, A., & Kohlberg, L. (1989). *Lawrence Kohlberg's approach to moral education.* New York, NY: Columbia University Press.

Power, F. C., & Power, A. M. R. (1992). A raft of hope: Democratic education and the challenge of pluralism. *Journal of Moral Education, 21*(3), 193-206.

Power F. C., & Power A. M. R. (2012). Moral education. In P. M. Brown, M. W. Corrigan, & A. Higgins-D'Alessandro (Eds.), *The handbook of prosocial education* (Vol. 1., pp. 179-196). Lanham, MD: Rowan & Littlefield.

Power, F. C, Sheehan, K., Crawford, B., LaVoi, N., & McBride, O. (2012). *Play like a champion today: Coaching manual.* Notre Dame, IN: Play Like A Champion Today.

Roeser, R. W., Marachi, R., & Gehlbach, H. (2002). A goal theory perspective on teachers' professional identities and the contexts of teaching. In C. M. Midgley (Ed.). *Goals, goal structures, and patterns of adaptive learning* (pp. 205-241). Mahwah, NJ: Erlbaum.

Slavin, R. E. (1990). *Cooperative learning: Theory, research, and practice.* Upper Saddle River, NJ: Prentice Hall.

Selman, R. L. (1980). *The growth of interpersonal understanding.* New York, NY: Academic press.

Selman, R. L. (2003). *The promotion of social awareness: Powerful lessons from the partnership of developmental theory and classroom practice.* New York, NY: SAGE.

UNICEF. (2000). *A league table of child poverty in rich nations.* Retrieved from http://www.unicef-irc.org/publications/pdf/repcard1e.pdf

Waas, G. A. (2006). Children's peer relations. In G. Bear & K. Minke (Eds.), *Children's needs III: Understanding and addressing the developmental needs of children* (pp. 325-340). Washington, DC: National Association of School Psychologists.

Wigfield, A., Eccles, J. S., Schiefele, U., Roeser, R., & Davis-Kean, P. (2006). Development of achievement motivation. In W. Damon & N. Eisenberg (Eds.), *Handbook of child psychology* (6th ed., Vol. 3, pp. 933-1002). New York, NY: Wiley.

CHAPTER 6

FROM AGE ISOLATION TO MULTIAGE INTERACTIONS

Elizabeth Pate

FROM AGE ISOLATION TO MULTIAGE INTERACTIONS

The middle grades years typically encompass 10- to 15-year-old students, often referred to as young adolescents. Generally, most young adolescents are isolated by age, growing up in age-segregated school systems, and exposed to prescribed curriculum. Many students find the emphasis on academic performance boring and irrelevant to their lives (Jackson & Davis, 2000). Young adolescents want curriculum to be "more up to date with today's society,"; to provide opportunities for choice; to focus on "logic—the students would be given a situation and asked what they would do"; and, engage in debate and dialogue about making responsible decisions and good choices (Homestead & Pate, 2004, p. 3).

What if young adolescents weren't isolated by age, but, instead, grouped intentionally to facilitate multiage interactions? What kinds of grouping would be needed? What curriculum model and strategies could be used? And, finally, what would happen if we moved from "age isolation" to "multiage interactions"? Answers to these questions are provided in this chapter, along with examples of multiage interactions.

Middle Grades Curriculum:
Voices and Visions of the Self-Enhancing School, pp. 89–103
Copyright © 2013 by Information Age Publishing
All rights of reproduction in any form reserved.

MULTIAGE GROUPING

Multiage grouping, in this chapter, refers to young adolescents of different ages intentionally grouped together to enlarge the opportunities for constructive interactions between younger and older students. Multiage grouping is in direct contrast to multigrade grouping (classes in which students from two or more grades are taught by one teacher in one room at the same time) and age-isolated grouping (classes in which students are placed based on age). Multigrade and age-isolated groupings are generally formed for administrative, economic reasons, or because that is the way educational grouping has been handled for centuries.

What grouping opportunities facilitate multiage interactions for middle grades students? Schools within schools, an entire school, and whole classes can be devoted to multiage grouping. Advisory programs, service-learning initiatives, and exploratory programs also serve as opportunities for multiage interactions. Advisory programs, designed to address the affective needs of young adolescents, range from systematically developed units whose organizing center is drawn from the common problems, needs, interests or concerns of students to nonformal interactions between students and teachers (Beane & Lipka, 1987). Service-learning is a methodology involving the application of academic skills to solving real-life problems in the community. Service-learning focuses on problems of life experience as well as mastering content from the subjects involved; learning cuts across multiple subject areas; and, there is a "need to know" with application of learning. Democratic service-learning occurs when the students and teacher collaboratively make decisions and take responsibility for all aspects of the project (see Scenario 1).

Scenario 1. Democratic Service-Learning and Money Management

In an eighth grade language arts classroom, Ms. Hensley overheard her students sharing with each other what kind of car they would have in high school. She asked the students where they would get the money for cars. Some students said they would have a job and others said their parents would buy them a car. When asked about car costs, car payments, car insurance, gasoline, and car upkeep, the students were not nearly as animated. This overheard discussion and question and answer session led into a democratic service-learning project, entitled Money Management: Dollar Sense for Young Adolescents—Future Investors in Training.

Through collaborative decision making, these transitioning middle school students worked with high school students and community entities (e.g., banks) in an effort to educate young people about money management. Through interviews and extensive research, students identified several money issues: financial planning, income, savings and checking accounts, insurance, credit, and debt/loans. They outlined, drafted, edited, and finalized a money management handbook for their peers. In the introduction to the handbook, the students wrote:

> This book was written as a service to young people in Northeast Georgia. We felt that teenagers needed a user friendly book to help them learn sound financial principles. We hope that everyone who uses this book will develop good financial habits that will last a lifetime. We hope that you become financially FIT. (Hensley, 2001, p. 1)

Note—this democratic service-learning project was so *user-friendly* that area banks made copies of the handbook for their adult customers.

Exploratory programs typically provide groupings of young adolescents with opportunities to investigate areas of study not introduced as part of the core curriculum (Whinery & Caskey, 2005). Exploratory examples include such courses as band, choir, art, drama, and career exploration.

CURRICULUM INTEGRATION

Age-isolated groupings generally have rigid curriculum, often derived from professional and state standards and with little, if any, attention to addressing student needs. Grouping intentionally to facilitate multiage interactions, on the other hand, requires a unique curriculum—a curriculum that meets the needs of all students. The curriculum of choice is "curriculum integration." James Beane (2000), historian, scholar of and teacher on curriculum integration, in a position paper entitled "Curriculum Matters: Organizing the Middle School Curriculum" explains that curriculum integration is a "curriculum design that promotes personal and social integration through the organization of curriculum around significant problems and issues, collaboratively identified by educators and young people, without regard for subject area lines" (p.2).

Study, in curriculum integration, is developed around student interests and concerns, as well as, mandated content and skills. Beane (2000) argues that integrated curriculum is more rigorous and relevant than traditional approaches because it challenges young people to think, learn, and tackle issues that are important to them personally. Dewey (1939) argued that learning is the process; not an isolated end.

In curriculum integration, subjects are utilized as needed to answer questions, understand issues, and solve problems. Decisions are made by students and their teachers through consensus rather than teacher or majority rule. Central to curriculum integration is democracy (Beane, 2005). According to Beane (2000), "With its emphasis on real-life themes, contextual application of knowledge, and constructivist learning, the curriculum integration approach is particularly well suited to help students integrate learning experiences into their developing schemes of meaning" (p. 2). According to Nesin and Lounsbury (1999), the integrated curriculum planning process includes nine steps:

1. Students think about questions: Who am I? What are my interests? As individuals, they compile a list of words or phases about themselves.

2. As individuals, students identify questions or concerns they have about themselves and make another list.

3. Small groups of 5 or 6 are formed and students share their lists about themselves. A list of common concerns is compiled.

4. Students are asked to individually make a list of questions they have about the world.

5. Small groups of 5 or 6 are formed and students share their lists about the world. A list of common concerns is compiled.

6. While still in small groups, students study lists and identify possible themes of study that connect questions about self with questions about the world.

7. Post the list of themes around the classroom and discuss. The whole class identifies the first theme to study.

8. The class discusses possible activities the group might engage in and resources they might need.

9. The teacher helps facilitate all aspects and ensures necessary content/standards are addressed.

STRATEGIES FOR MULTIAGE INTERACTIONS

Many strategies can be used to facilitate multiage interactions. A strategy is defined as a plan or course of action selected in pursuit of a specific goal or object. Class meetings, chalk-talk, and consensus building are strategies that foster multiage interactions. Class meetings, as a strategy, is a simple and yet effective way for multiage students to experience a democratic community. Class meetings are designed as a safe forum for students and teachers to brainstorm and share ideas, engage in decision-making and goal-setting, vent frustrations and celebrate successes (see Scenario 2). This is especially important in multiage interactions because of the variety of individual levels of cognitive and social development. Class meetings facilitate the processes of reflection (looking back) and envisioning (looking forward), both important to the health of a community (Thompson & Pate, 2005).

Scenario 2. Class Meeting to Establish a Management Plan

In one middle school multiage classroom, the students and teacher spent over an hour collaboratively deciding on a classroom management plan that focused on student success, rather than behavior management. The meeting began with brainstorming and questioning activities designed to generate discussion about success. Students then broke into small groups (respect, effort, responsibility) to discuss a possible management plan. After 20 minutes of small-group discussion, each group shared their ideas with the larger group. Students and the teacher discussed the merits of each group's plan, and with the agreement of everyone, developed the classroom management plan.

Chalk-talk is a silent way to generate ideas, develop projects, check on learning, solve problems, or reflect. Because it is done completely in silence, chalk-talk allows students to interact visibly and directly with ideas and silently with each other. It encourages thoughtful contemplation, generates questions and ideas, and gives students a change of pace (National School Reform Faculty, 2002). Chalk-talk can be used as a documentation tool to capture the collective thought processes of the participants. For example, multiage students can use the results of the chalk-talk to help categorize ideas, prioritize tasks, and allocate responsibility. The following Table lists the procedures generally used in chalk-talk.

Chalk-talk can also be used as a documentation tool to capture the collective thought processes of the participants. Chalk-talk can be extended for various purposes. For example, participants can use the results of the chalk-talk to help categorize ideas, prioritize tasks, and allocate responsibilities.

Consensus Building is a strategy in which every member (students and teacher) in the group has input in decision making—critical to a democratic multiaged classroom. A democratic classroom is one in which students and teachers collaborate and one in which students' voices are heard and respected. In multiage interactions, Consensus Building allows for productive dialogue, debate, and a better understanding of multiple

Table 6.1. Chalk-Talk Procedures

1. The facilitator explains very briefly that chalk-talk is a silent activity. No one may talk at all and anyone may add to the chalk-talk as they please. Participants can comment on each other's ideas by drawing a connecting line to the comment.

2. The facilitator writes a relevant question, term, or topic in a circle on the board or newsprint taped to the wall. For example, in a 6-7th grade multi-age classroom, students were learning about watersheds. Their chalk-talk question was: What can we do to help our watershed?

3. The facilitator places several markers or pieces of chalk at the board or paper and then hands some out to a few members of the group, or the facilitator provides chalk/markers for everyone. With large groups, it can be helpful to limit the number of people who are writing on the board/paper at the same time. Those who aren't at the board/paper should stand or sit in a position that allows them to see what's being written.

4. Participants write, as they feel moved to write. Allow plenty of wait time before deciding the chalk-talk is over.

5. How the facilitator chooses to interact with the chalk-talk influences its outcome. The facilitator can stand back and let it unfold or expand participants' thinking by:
   - circling interesting ideas to invite comments or note a theme emerging;
   - writing questions about a participant's comment;
   - adding his/her own reflections or ideas; and
   - connecting two interesting ideas/comments together with a line and adding a question mark.

   Active facilitator interaction encourages participants to do the same.

6. Time frame for a chalk-talk is dependent upon the question, attention span of the participants, and group size. Generally, if no one adds anything to the chalk-talk in a period of one to two minutes, then the activity should draw to a close, though the facilitator should say, "Are there any more additions?" before closing. Chalk-talks typically last no more than 10-15 minutes.

7. The facilitator, a participant, or the group as a whole briefly summarizes the results of the chalk-talk, noting significant themes, connections, and questions.

8. In a possible extension of chalk-talk, the facilitator or group can re-format the results into a list or categories to guide future work.

points of view. In addition, Consensus Building aids in negotiation skills, conflict resolution, and group processing.

Consensus Building can be used to develop themes of study. During the first week of the school year, students individually write their responses to four questions: What do I want to learn in this class? How do I want to learn this information? How do I want to be assessed? and, Why is it important to learn this information? Throughout the year, course themes are periodically revisited to see if students are on track in their learning or if adjustments are needed. When simpler decisions need to be made, the strategy of Agree to Agree can be used to build consensus. Simply put, the class "agrees to agree" to a decision. The Agree to Agree strategy is best used when a decision has uncomplicated choices or does not need extensive discussion (see Scenario 3).

Scenario 3. Agree to Agree as Consensus Building

In Bugs of Texas (Foster, 2002), a class of students learned science concepts, reading, writing, and communication skills, geography and history, and art as they researched beneficial and harmful insects of Texas. In this democratic learning experience, each student first chose an insect to research (e.g., habitat, life cycle, food web). During their research, students decided that what they were learning should be community information. Students "agreed to agree" to make their contribution to the community a brochure. They combined their information and, as a class, made decisions about content and title, layout and design, and where to distribute the brochure. Copies of the final brochure were delivered to area nurseries to be provided to customers as they purchased plants.

COMMUNITY OF LEARNERS

Intentional groupings of young adolescents to facilitate interactions become a community of multiage learners. A multiage community of learners is bound together by similar interests (e.g., sports, music, theater), locale (e.g., classroom, school, community site), commonalities (e.g., religion, ethnicity, nationality), or identities (e.g., team of sixth-seventh grade students, service-learning project member, band member). Young adolescents have a chance to have interactions with and form relationships with a wider variety of students than is possible in the age-isolated classroom. This leads to a greater sense of belonging, support, security, and confidence (Veenman, 1995).

Multiage community members are in close proximity to each other; have a social structure resembling intergenerational closure; and foster, model, or explicitly teach shared communal values and a sense of place (Sampson-Cordle, 2001). Intergenerational closure is a social structure in which an extended network of kinship, friendship, and work relations pervade the community (Coleman, 1987). Being a part of a multiage community means that students of all ages feel a sense of belonging and purpose. Students are more committed to learning when they believe that teachers and peers understand and care about them.

The multiage community consists of young adolescents with a range of cultural contexts and personal knowledge they bring to interactions. Cultural contexts include, but are not limited to, geographic locations (e.g., country, state, region, town); cultural norms (e.g., eye contact, personal space, issues of power); school experiences (e.g., home, public, private, progressive, traditional); religion (e.g., Christian, Islamic, Jewish, atheistic, polytheistic); lifestyles (e.g., work, leisure, hobbies); personal, familial, and societal expectations (e.g., family size, marriage expectations); gender distinctions and expectations (e.g., chores, educational opportunity); race, ethnicity, and language (e.g., history, dialect); and socioeconomic class distinctions and expectations (Pate, Powell, Yaksic, & Navarro, 2001). Personal knowledge includes familiarity with, awareness of, and understanding about such things as likes and dislikes, goals and aspirations, practical skills, and interests, needs, and concerns (Pate, in press).

COMMUNITY OF KNOWING

A critical rationale for creating opportunities for multiage interactions is to provide a forum for a "community of knowing." A community of knowing is what is referred to as a dynamic, open system. An open system continuously interacts with its environment. New communities of knowing emerge and change, based on student interactions. Feelings of community in the classroom and school facilitate students' understanding of one another. Self-perceptions develop in a context of social interaction (Beane & Lipka, 1986). In multiage interactions, there is a positive impact on self-esteem and a feeling of bonding within the group when students work together for more than 1 year (Daniel, 2007). Nancy Doda (2002), a pioneer in middle school multiaged teaming, created an open system in which student trust and community were formed. Scenario 4 illustrates highlights of the team.

Scenario 4. A "Community of Knowing" on a Multiaged Team

According to Nancy Doda (2002), a teacher and middle level educator, Lincoln Middle School, Gainesville, Florida, was an exemplary middle school. Every student and teacher was part of a small, stable, caring learning community or team. With students on the team for three consecutive years, it meant that every class would be comprised of a multiage, mixed grouping of students from three grades. This student grouping was designed to facilitate long-term relationships needed to shore up fragile student-teacher relationships, enhance peer relations, dismantle potential racism, discard grade level as an appropriate label for learners, and alter the way less successful students would be perceived and treated.

All teachers served as an advisor to a multiage population of about 18-22 students in grades six through eight. In mathematics, teachers grouped and regrouped students for skill work and support, ensuring that students were able to experience small group work with others tackling the same level of math. As students completed and mastered unit components, they accelerated to the next level regardless of grade level. The learning communities, advisory program, and multiage grouping were about altering the nature and quality of relationships in school.Multiage grouping across three years meant that teachers were unable to dismiss difficult students after one year's challenge. Teachers had to have a long-term view of growth and progress and view their role as agents of social and moral development. Teachers viewed learning as a longitudinal enterprisewith far greater complexity than they would have with traditional grade level expectations. Teachers found that as a result of the multiage context, trust and community were formed (Doda, 2002).

Communication within communities of knowing is known as perspective making (Boland & Tenkasi, 1993). Perspective making is a basis for student transformations within communities of knowing. Within each multiage community of knowing, there are countless opportunities for perspective making. Just think of the wide range of developmental characteristics of young adolescents and opportunities for student transformation within the community. For example, according to the National Middle School Association (2010) and researchers Peter Scales and Nancy Leffert (2004), young adolescents are increasingly able to think abstractly, not only concretely. They commonly face decisions that require more sophisticated cognitive and social-emotional skills. They have varying maturity rates and are acutely aware of the maturation rates of their peers. Young adolescents have a wide range of intellectual pursuits, and are intellectually curious about the world and themselves. They are in transition from moral reasoning that focuses on "what's in it for me" to that which considers the feelings and rights of others. They are generally idealistic, desiring to make the world a better place and to make a meaningful contribution to a cause or issue larger than themselves. They are moving from acceptance of adult moral judgments to developing their own personal values. Young adolescents are searching for adult identity and acceptance and believe that personal problems, feelings, and experiences are unique to themselves. They are both psychologically vulnerable and resilient (at no other stage in development are they more likely to encounter and be aware of so many differences between themselves and others). Young adolescents have a strong need for approval. They are in search of group membership and are socially vulnerable.

Multiage grouping provides younger students with the opportunity to observe, emulate, and imitate a wide range of behaviors; older students have the opportunity to assume responsibility for less mature and less knowledgeable students (Veenman, 1995).

According to John Dewey (1939), all communication is educative. In *Democracy and Education: An Introduction to the Philosophy of Education*, Dewey stated,

> To be a recipient of a communication is to have an enlarged and changed experience. One shares in what another has thought and felt and in so far, meagerly or amply, has his own attitude modified. Nor is the one who communicates left unaffected. The experience has to be formulated in order to be communicated. To formulate requires getting outside of it, seeing it as another would see it, considering what points of contact it has with the life of another so that it may be got into such form that he can appreciate its meaning. Only when it becomes cast in a mold and runs in a routine way does it lose its educative power. (pp. 6-7)

In multiage interactions, the development of a balanced personality is promoted by fostering the attitudes and qualities that enable students to live in a complex and changing social environment (Veenman, 1995). Educative communication, then, becomes perspective making—a basis for student transformations within communities of knowing (see Scenario 5).

Scenario 5. Perspective Making in a Multiaged Project

At Oglethorpe County Middle School, in Oglethorpe County, Georgia, a multiage group of sixth, seventh, and eighth graders held an "Empty Bowl Dinner" to raise awareness about and money to help alleviate the economic problems of some community residents. An "Empty Bowl Dinner" is a community event where citizens purchase a dinner (comparable to what someone might eat at home with few groceries), hear a presentation about the community, and take home an empty bowl (to signify what little food some people may have to eat). Brenda, the exploratory art teacher, and Elizabeth, a university professor, collaborated on a service-learning project using curriculum integration. The project began simply. A few art students were concerned about some of their peers not having enough food at home. As the discussion grew, it became apparent that an awareness campaign should be the focus of the six-week art curriculum. This multiage group of students learned about county demographics, job possibilities (or lack of), and the area food bank. They planned the entire Empty Bowl Dinner event—invited guest speakers, created posters and placements; sold tickets; collected dinner donations; and made over 100 ceramic bowls. On the late afternoon of the event, they worked side by side with parent volunteers and cafeteria workers making chicken noodle soup. Students greeted community members as they arrived, took their tickets, escorted them through the food line (chicken noodle soup, crackers, and water), and directed them to eating locations. Students hosted the formal presentations and presented a check of several hundred dollars to the food bank. As community members left, they each took with them a ceramic bowl of their choosing to remind them of less fortunate neighbors. Students listened to each other and came to consensus about project ideas. Throughout the six weeks, older students assisted younger students with their projects. By the end of the six weeks, a community of knowing was formed—a community of multiage students working on behalf of their community outside of school.

One communication model that can be used with communities of knowing is Wittgenstein's image of communication as "language games in forms of life" (Wittgenstein, 1953). In this model, conversations and activity are language games, and through the exploration of language games students confirm the usefulness of particular words and forms of speech, and continuously evolve new ways of talking and acting out together. Multiage grouping invites cooperation and other forms of prosocial behavior and thus appears to minimize competitive pressures and the need for discipline (Veenman, 1995).

CLIMATE

A climate of communication is fostered in groupings that facilitate multiage interactions for middle grades students. "climate refers to the atmosphere or milieu that permeates or underlies all of the transactions and interactions that take place in the school setting" (Beane & Lipka, 1987, p. 30). In contrast to a custodial climate (teacher-centered, concern for maintenance of order, little emphasis on student voice) often found in graded classrooms, multiage groups generally have a humanistic climate (see Scenario 6). According to Beane and Lipka, a humanistic type of climate is characterized by preference for democratic procedures, high degrees of interaction, personalness, respect for individual dignity, emphasis on self-discipline, flexibility, and participatory decision-making (p. 31). Fewer anxieties may develop because the educational atmosphere is conducive not only to academic progress but also to social growth (Veenman, 1995).

Scenario 6. Humanistic Climate on a Multiaged Team

Alpha, a multiaged middle grades team in Shelburne, Vermont, began over 30 years ago. Teacher Jim Reid began the program because he wanted to know whether or not students could plan their own learning, identifying areas of personal interest and for personal growth. He found out they could. The core of Alpha was centered on student choice. Students of different ages worked together to design units of study that were appropriate for them. Students came together to investigate a topic they were all interested in; presented their idea to the teachers, and with them, decided on a plan for the study, including a timeline. In The Story of Alpha: A multiage, Student-Centered Team—33 Years and Counting, author Susan Kuntz (2005) maintains that multiage grouping (students at one time ranged from 9-14 years of age across 5 grade-levels in one class) in Alpha encouraged a variety of activities at numerous levels and gave students flexibility in finding a place to comfortably work. This flexibility allowed older students to serve as leaders and as role models for younger students and supported continuing relationships between students and teachers. Students found a community of learners in Alpha in which to examine the transformations taking place in their own self. Alpha addressed the variety of individual levels of cognitive and social development through multiage grouping and curriculum integration. The Alpha Team had a humanistic climate.

KNOWLEDGE WORK

Drawn from the fields of business and science is a concept known as "knowledge work." Knowledge work involves the creation of knowledge and its applications in new or improved technologies, products, services, or processes (Boland & Tenkasi, 1993, p. 4). Knowledge work in business and science is conducted by a team of multifaceted workers. Multiage interactions lend themselves to knowledge work. Multiage students, in varying team configurations, brainstorm and share ideas, engage in problem-solving, and transform into learners focused on new or improved products and processes (see Scenario 7). Knowledge work in multiage groupings is in direct contrast to "routine work" in age-graded classrooms–work which is often well-defined, repetitive, and embedded in clear, mostly teacher-directed goals.

Scenario 7. Knowledge Work in a Multiaged Classroom

Students in the multiaged class (seventh and eighth graders) of Teresa Kane and Sharon Littlefield at Warsaw Middle School in Pittsfield, Maine, engaged in knowledge work. The teachers shared the integrated curriculum planning process with students; students examined the list of required state standards, and together, the multiaged class decided they want to focus on settling on the war on terrorism. Student voices were heard and honored by peers and teachers. Students learned geography by studying the countries involved, math by dealing with distances and statistics, and social studies by considering the countries affected by war. In biology, they learned about the human body and bacteria by studying biological weapons. According to the teachers, students were doing interesting, challenging projects and were excited and wanted to come to school (Paterson, 2003).

What would happen if we moved from "age isolation" to "multiage interactions"? A change from impersonalness to personalness would occur; a lack of respect would be changed to respect; autocratic governance would change to participation; and, a low emphasis on personal dignity would change to human dignity (Beane & Lipka, 1987). Teachers would be passionate about shifting from typically impersonal, academically driven, and random relationships to relationships that were sustained, intimate, and linked to school and life (Doda, 2002). Self-perceptions would be viewed as developing rather than developed (Beane & Lipka, 1987). Young adolescents would experience authentic, real-life opportunities to learn from and with their peers. Students would find schooling relevant to their lives.

REFERENCES

Beane, J. A. (2000). *Curriculum matters: Organizing the middle school curriculum.* Retrieved from http://www.nmsa.org/resources/cmorganizing.htm

Beane, J. A. (2005). *A reason to teach: Creating classrooms of dignity and hope—The power of the democratic way.* Portsmouth, NH: Heinemann.

Beane, J. A., & Lipka, R. P. (1986). *Self-concept, self-esteem, and the curriculum.* New York, NY: Teachers College Press.

Beane, J. A., & Lipka, R. P. (1987). *When kids come first: Enhancing self-esteem.* Columbus, OH: National Middle School Association.

Boland, R. J., Jr., & Tenkasi, R. V. (1993). *Perspective making and perspective taking in communities of knowing.* Center for Effective Organizations (CEO). *CEO Publication,* (238), 93-18. Los Angeles, CA: University of Southern California.

Coleman, J. S. (1987). The relations between school and social structure. In M. Hallinan (Ed.), *The social organization of schools: New conceptualizations of the learning process* (pp. 177-204). New York, NY: Plenum Press.

Daniel, L. (2007). Research summary: Multiage grouping. Retrieved from http://www.nmsa.org/Research/ResearchSummaries/MultiageGrouping/tabid/1282/Default.aspx

Dewey, J. (1939). *Democracy and education: An introduction to the philosophy of education.* New York, NY: The Macmillan Company.

Doda, N. M. (2002). A small miracle in the early years: The Lincoln Middle School story. In N. M. Doda & S. C. Thompson (Eds.), *Transforming ourselves, transforming schools: Middle school change* (pp. 21-42). Westerville, OH: National Middle School Association.

Foster, R. (2000). *Bugs of Texas unit plan.* Unpublished project. Boerne, TX.

Hensley, C. C. (2001). *Money management: Dollar sense for young adolescents.* Unpublished project. Toccoa, GA.

Homestead, E. R., & Pate, P. E. (2004). [Anecdotal notes and student reflections in eighth grade social studies classroom.] Unpublished raw data.

Jackson, A., & Davis, G. (2000). *Turning points 2000: Educating adolescents in the 21st century.* New York, NY: Teachers College Press.

Kuntz, S. (2005). *The story of Alpha: A multiage, student-centered team—33 years and counting.* Westerville, OH: National Middle School Association.

National Middle School Association. (2010). *This we believe: Keys to educating young adolescents.* Westerville, OH: Author.

National School Reform Faculty. (March 2002). *Techniques for reflective dialogue.* In National School Reform Faculty, Critical Friends Coaches Institute. Bloomington, IN: Author.

Nesin, G., & Lounsbury, J. (1999). *Curriculum integration: Twenty questions—With answers.* Atlanta, GA: Georgia Middle School Association

Pate, P. E. (in press). Academically excellent curriculum, instruction, and assessment. In P. G. Andrews (Ed.), *Research to guide practice in middle grades education.* Columbus, OH: National Middle School Association.

Pate, P. E., Powell, J. V., Yaksic, D., & Navarro, C. (2001). *Early and young adolescents in cultural contexts: Documenting our voices.* Unpublished manuscript. Department of Elementary Education, University of Georgia, Athens, GA.

Paterson, J. (2003). Curriculum integration in a standards-based world. *Middle Ground: The Magazine of Middle Level Education, 7*(1), 10-12.

Sampson-Cordle, A. V. (2001). *Exploring the relationship between a small rural school in Northeast Georgia and its community: An image-based study using participant-pro-*

duced photographs. Unpublished manuscript. The University of Georgia, Athens, GA.

Scales, P. C., & Leffert, N. (2004). Developmental assets: A synthesis of the scientific research on adolescent development (2nd ed.), Minneapolis, MN: Search Institute.

Thompson, K. F., & Pate, P. E. (2005). Community. In V. A. Anfara, P. G. Andrews, & S. B. Mertens (Eds.), *The encyclopedia of middle level education* (pp. 151-154). Greenwich, CT: Information Age.

Veenman, S. (1995). Cognitive and noncognitive effects of multigrade and multiage classes: A best-evidence synthesis. *Review of Educational Research, 65*(4), 319-381.

Whinery, B., & Caskey, M. M. (2005). Exploratory curriculum. In V. A. Anfara, P. G. Andrews, & S. B. Mertens (Eds.), *The encyclopedia of middle level education* (pp. 195-199). Greenwich, CT: Information Age.

Wittgenstein, L. (1953). *Philosophical investigations.* New York, NY: MacMillan.

CHAPTER 7

FROM ACCEPTING FAILURE TO PROMOTING SUCCESS

Patrick Akos, Molly Frommer, and Emily Rinkoski

FROM ACCEPTING FAILURE TO PROMOTING SUCCESS

When adults reflect on their middle level years, many remember the awkward, difficult, or stressful times in their youth. It is not surprising that the literature frequently refers to this period in a negative light. To describe this transition between childhood and early adulthood, concepts such as storm and stress, risk and rebellion (Guerra & Bradshaw, 2008), and struggle for independence (Beane & Lipka, 1984) still persist in the literature.

Perhaps the primary reason for the deficit focus is the amount of sheer change early adolescents negotiate. Aside from infancy, there is no other stage of life that is characterized by more changes and greater development than early adolescence (Akos, 2005).

> There is probably no more dramatic age period in the human lifespan than transescence or emerging adolescence. This period of development is marked by the onset and achievement of puberty, the emergence of the peer group as 'significant others,' and the onset of formal cognitive operations or

Middle Grades Curriculum:
Voices and Visions of the Self-Enhancing School, pp. 105–118
Copyright © 2013 by Information Age Publishing
All rights of reproduction in any form reserved.

the ability to deal with conceptual, abstract relationships. (Beane & Lipka, 1984, p. 22)

Early adolescents begin to seek independence and have to make autonomous decisions that significantly affect their future in high school and beyond. No two students are ever alike; there is tremendous variability and asynchrony in early adolescent development. Persistence and patience are required to understand student variability in cognitive, moral, and emotional capacity and how this impacts communication and pedagogy (Akos, 2005).

Although the magnitude of the developmental transition may help explain why problems or failures seem normative, more worrisome is the impact of expectations for failure. Schools traditionally focus on addressing problem behaviors after they arise. Common responses in the schools include removal from class, detention, and in- or out-of-school suspension. A problem-based intervention such as the use of punishments may temporarily change a behavior, but they rarely extend benefits beyond that particular behavior or influence dispositions or teach skills to assure success. Further, a deficit-focused approach may elicit a negative relationship and thus lead to disinterest or strengthen an undesirable behavior (Ahmed & Boisvert, 2006). It can also lead to more negative self-perceptions and alienation from the school (Galassi, Griffin, & Akos, 2008). Finally, a punishment or remediation approach often leads to reduced instructional time which does not support students' academic progress.

A prevention or enrichment approach is more promising. A prevention mindset anticipates challenges and seeks to provide programming or instruction to avoid problems or failure before they emerge. These types of prevention programs are effective for reducing some behaviors including alcohol and drug use, dropout and nonattendance (Wilson, Gottfredson, & Najaka, 2001). Although these programs help students acquire skills, they often only address a single, targeted issue. Problem or failure prevention may lead to desirable outcomes in the targeted area, but it is neither the most efficient option nor representative of expecting or assuring success. On the other hand strengths promotion often accomplishes both the goal of problem prevention and reduction while expecting success through the utilization of assets and protective factors in the environment (Galassi et al., 2008). For example, prosocial behavioral lessons should both lessen behavior problems and also enhance a more positive attitude toward the self and school (Beane & Lipka, 1984). Educators working with early adolescents should shift from this deficit or failure expectation to a more strengths-oriented, self-enhancing success expectation.

A SUCCESS OR STRENGTHS BASED APPROACH

A strengths promotion approach does not ignore problems or deficits but addresses these issues by fostering developmental and academic strengths in students. With this focus, school personnel empower all students, rather than only those exhibiting problem behaviors or failure (Galassi & Akos, 2007). Research suggests that certain strengths prevent undesirable outcomes and support healthy development. For example, Park (2009) found that such assets as hope, kindness, social intelligence, self-control, and perspective can minimize the negative effects of stress and trauma and thus minimize the possibility for failure or developmental pathology.

The change and transition still exists, but instead of centering on the challenge of navigating change—the promotion of positive outcomes communicates positive expectations and opportunities available to both students and staff. All middle level students have strengths from which we can build (Park, 2009), and it would be remiss to ignore the additional opportunities afforded with their growth and newly found independence. School personnel should move away from viewing the delays in development and learning as failures during this period and capitalize on the developmental heterogeneity by considering the new possibilities that come with early adolescence. We present examples for expecting and assuring success in individual developmental and academic context.

Individual Development

Young adolescents develop at different rates as some enter puberty much earlier than others. Early adolescents also experience asynchronous development, where the constellation of development within an individual varies. For example, sometimes an individual may be further along in cognitive development but have not changed much physically from childhood. Instead of sheltering students cognitively who appear physically vulnerable, school staff should enable strengths in cognitive development by assigning leadership in academic tasks such as peer tutoring. Similarly, a student with advanced physical development can be engaged in kinesthetic learning and participation in athletic extracurricular activities to enhance self-perceptions and support self-efficacy. Middle level school personnel can educate both the students and families on physical development and healthy strategies (e.g., appropriate health care, sex education) for navigating this period. Neither ignores the variability in development, but strategies such as these maximize student strengths and provide a context to expect and assure success.

Feelings of success and self-efficacy in puberty are especially important due to the significant impact of young adolescents' self-perceptions. The observable changes in capacity that occur during this period effect how they see themselves especially by a new, deeper recognition of comparing oneself to their peers (Beane & Lipka, 1984; Molloy, Gest, & Rulison, 2011). When school staff provide students developmental opportunities that complement strengths, students have the opportunity to thrive in a variety of domains.

Social. During early adolescence, social relationships take on a growing importance. Peer relationships evolve from those dominated by dyadic relationships to larger cliques (Brown & Klute, 2004). Young adolescents differentiate themselves from their parents and other adult influences and rely more heavily on peers. Approval and acceptance from peers is important and peers have a greater influence on dress, behavior, and values (Beane & Lipka, 1984; Daddis, 2008). While peer pressure can lead to poor choices and failure, there is evidence that peer influence can be utilized to increase social capital and social resources (Putnam, 1995). For example, well-structured, adult supervised extracurricular activities provide opportunities for intentional positive peer relationships. Clubs and sports teams foster a collaborative environment in which early adolescents work toward a common goal. This type of social engagement in the school environment is important and correlated to school engagement (Li, Lynch, Kalvin, Liu, & Lerner, 2011).

As young adolescents begin to compare themselves to peers, they more deeply construct a sense of identity. Middle level students explore their talents and capabilities (Akos, 2005). While stressful for the most vulnerable students, it also provides early adolescents a sense of purpose. If schools provide contexts that scaffold opportunities to explore and maximize talents, students develop a sense of self and create positive expectations for their future.

Autonomy and School Connectedness. Becoming autonomous and being able to self-regulate are important developmental markers for young adolescents. Students start by expressing their own decisions and place importance on their clothes and hair choices (Fleming, 2005). Further, early adolescents express autonomy in school by questioning authority and the fairness of school rules. Most often, school staff respond to this normative developmental growth with more restricted classrooms, abundant adult imposed rules and policies, or punishment for insubordination. Expecting and assuring success would instead capitalize on this developmental force by giving students a voice and participation in classroom structure. Engaging early adolescents can lead to improved school connectedness and feelings of belonging, which is linked to a host of positive student outcomes. Feelings of belongingness can lead to elevated school motivation, effort, level of participation, and eventual achievement, as well as the delay of initial encounters with cigarettes, alcohol, marijuana, and sexual intercourse (Lohman, Kaura, & Newman, 2007). Encouraging autonomy is also associated with more positive views of self (Scott, Murray, Mertens, & Dustin, 1996).

Successfully scaffolding and promoting autonomy allows early adolescents to no longer be fully dependent on adults and become better equipped to do things on their own. Although they begin to distance themselves from the adults they previously relied upon (Beane & Lipka, 1984), the independence provides an opportunity for adults to renegotiate rules and responsibilities within the home and school. Most adults and especially parents are uncomfortable with this developmental progression. An expectation of success in the new found independence requires learning through failure and building resiliency. When parents and school personnel involve and engage early adolescent students in decision making, adults support the challenges that accompany autonomy; the students become empowered, and expect success for themselves.

Numerous examples in schools include student government with real decision making power, choice in service learning projects, peer mediation, and participatory classroom management. Perhaps the best example of supporting autonomy and expecting success revolves around the choices early adolescents make in forming early career identities (Akos, 2005). Whether it is career education, offering a variety of electives, or extracurricular activities or clubs, schools can foster this natural desire to explore new areas in their search for purpose. Participation in extracurricular activities is not only associated with increased academic achievement and school connectedness (Akos, 2006), but career identities provide hope and expectations for a successful future.

Cognitive. Finally, our last developmental example of expecting and assuring success centers on the significant growth in cognitive abilities. While younger children think concretely and in black and white terms, abstract thought emerges in early adolescence. During this period, young adolescents develop metacognitive skills that allow them to better understand their own cognitive processes. They can be more aware of how outside influences affect their livelihood, this also allows for more advanced learning (Broderick & Blewitt, 2010, p. 301).

School personnel can build on young adolescents' emerging cognitive processing by teaching and promoting self-regulatory skills. Self-regulation is the ability to internally "regulate affect, attention, and behavior to respond effectively to both internal and environmental demands" (Raffaelli, Crockett, & Shen, 2005, p. 54). The ability to self-regulate is associated with many dimensions of positive development (Gestsdóttir & Lerner, 2008). Parallel to autonomy, research suggests that self-regulation increases through middle childhood and remains stable through early adolescence (Raffaelli, Crockett, & Shen, 2005). Regulatory skills such as attention shifting and inhibitory control increase through early adolescence while impulsivity decreases over the same time period (Murphy, Eisenberg, Fabes, Shepard, & Guthrie, 1999). School personnel can build on these new skills by offering opportunities to practice and learn new self-regulatory strategies so that they can both stay on task and more effectively complete their studies. Asking students to plan and execute plans for multistep projects help early adolescents develop these capabilities. As they autonomously direct academic tasks, they gain awareness when and where help is needed and approach tasks with expectations for success.

We think the primary way middle grades personnel can expect and assure success is to focus on and promote the developmental opportunity of early adolescence. Although we provided some examples of practice connected to individual developmental capacity, several pedagogical or curricular approaches also show promise for nurturing success in academic context.

Academic Context

While families and school support personnel play a part in the success of middle level students, the individuals that interact with students most throughout the school day are classroom teachers. It is therefore incumbent upon teachers to utilize developmental promotion and devise pedagogy and instructional strategies that promote a culture of academic success

Teacher Expectations. All teachers have expectations of their students. The Association of Middle Level Education's vision for successful middle level education includes high expectations for every member of the learning community (NMSA, 2010). Sadly, many instead assume that certain students will fail and it often goes unnoticed when they do (Beane & Lipka, 1984). This negative mindset may cause a deficit-focused approach for lower performing students. Tyler and Boelter (2008) conducted a study that revealed students reports of their teachers' expectations emerged as significant predictors of cognitive engagement, emotional engagement, and behavioral engagement, along with academic efficacy. When a student recognizes that a teacher has low expectations, it decreases confidence and chances of failure increase. At a time when self-perceptions may be most vulnerable, teachers should expect success and clearly communicate and demonstrate those expectations in all student interactions. These high expectations increase chances for academic success and simultaneously meet some of the social needs of young adolescents (Haselhuhn, Al-Mabuk, Gabriele, Groen, & Galloway, 2007).

Teacher-Student Relationships. Communicating positive expectations requires building relationships with middle level students. Research shows that teacher-student relationships improve classroom management, which is vital to high student achievement (Marzano & Marzano, 2003). Powell (2011) explains the concept of wayside teaching, which includes the importance of building and sustaining relationships with middle level students. Wayside teaching involves finding teachable moments inside and outside of the classroom (e.g., cafeteria, carpool line) to demonstrate a high level of interest and commitment to student success.

As these connections build, students also feel more comfortable and are willing to take academic risks. Similarly, when teachers genuinely care about the welfare of each young adolescent, they can guide them to a deeper appreciation for learning (Lachuk & Gomez, 2011). For example, Strahan and Layell (2006) demonstrated that a safe classroom environment that was learner centered fostered warm, supportive relationships with struggling students. Further, these data revealed that these students made more progress in reading and math than the rest of the students (Strahan & Layell). At a stage when learners are "in search of themselves, and they are often, if not always, uncertain" (Tomlinson, 2005, p. 13), educators can make a large impact by expecting that each student can and will succeed through positive relationships.

Meaningful Curriculum. Along with relationships, successful schools for young adolescents provide curriculum that is challenging, exploratory, integrative, and relevant (National Middle School Association, 2010). These themes support the active and meaningful engagement of early adolescents in the curriculum.

In order to promote development in the curriculum, educators "must have some understanding of the needs of middle level students when making decisions about instructional practices" (Hammon & Hess, 2004, p. 6). Some teachers communicate expectations for failure by controlling students in an environment where the students listen and gain knowledge solely from the teacher. In order to challenge students, teachers should elicit and provide content that pushes intellectual growth. For example, if teachers assess and utilize students' prior knowledge, students feel more competent and can better build on knowledge and feel more comfortable brainstorming and sharing with classmates. Challenging instruction helps buffer the decline in motivation commonly expected from early adolescents. It is important that school personnel discover and implement ways to increase student motivation, which will help lead to success. In order to assure success, teachers need to find ways to increase self-efficacy and encourage students in the belief that they can complete academic assignments (Strahan, 2008).

Perhaps more influential for the strengths or success focus, relevant and exploratory learning resonates well with early adolescents. An important piece of exploratory learning involves helping students view their mistakes as an essential and positive part of learning (Haselhuhn et al., 2007). Students should feel comfortable taking risks and realize that errors help to improve and find success academically or personally. In short, early adolescents need to grasp that learning is about the process as much as it is about the result (Pape, Bell, & Yetkin, 2003). In order for exploratory learning to be effective, teachers should take on a more facilitative role and support students as they set out to find and understand the answers to their own questions.

In terms of relevance, students who are developmentally engaged in egocentric thinking (focus on self-perceptions) may succeed most in learning that is connected to their lives. This could mean incorporating local and current events into a daily lesson and stimulating student interest by asking their point of view about that particular topic (Brigman & Campbell, 2003). Further, asking students to consider multifaceted aspects of daily experiences advances cognitive development. Making exploratory learning a reality in the classroom can be as informal as students investigating the social environments in their school and collecting data to present in class or at a science fair (Virtue, Wilson, & Ingram, 2009). When the curriculum provides relevant content, it is more fulfilling not only for the student, but also the teacher.

The best example of relevant curriculum may be career integrated instruction as early adolescents begin to consider their futures. This type of instruction shows students the relationship between the skills acquired in the classroom and the skills necessary for a potential career. Integrating career education into the classroom "has the potential to both promote career development and increase the engagement and relevance of school for students" (Akos, Charles, Orthner, & Cooley, 2011, p. 8). To create a more meaningful experience, teachers may bring in community members to share about their professions or hold school wide job fairs that link to curriculum standards so students can explore their options and hear personal stories relevant to their learning. This also shifts the focus from failure to potential, and allows students to explore and integrate strengths as they may relate to future occupations.

With student help, one teacher created a pollution unit that included a field study component to truly engage the learners. They collected water samples from a nearby creek to relate to what was being studied in the classroom (Virtue et al., 2009). This idea not only met multiple learning styles, but also linked the topic of pollution to a real life situation and potential career paths.

Service learning is another type of exploratory learning that can be integrated into the curriculum to meet the needs of early adolescents and the needs of the community. It also demonstrates measureable growth in all areas of adolescent development, including academic, career, and personal/social (Stott & Jackson, 2005). One study revealed that implementing service-learning practices encouraged critical thinking and genuine instruction, as opposed to conventional learning. Students used what they learned by taking part in group discussions, projects, reflections, and papers based on specific issues that came up in their experiences. (Seitsinger, 2005). In addition, students were forced to shift their focus from themselves to others, which can be challenging, but critical for an egocentric young adolescent.

A teacher or lecture dominated classroom can set students up for failure simply by not allowing them the opportunity to directly engage and investigate new concepts. To help assure success with middle level education, it is important to begin "transferring the responsibility from the teacher to the students" (Hammon & Hess, 2004, p. 8). Teachers should provide them with necessary skills and scaffolding as they journey through the learning process. Scaffolding includes modeling and assisting students with particular skills until they understand the information and feel comfortable working independently. As learners take more control over their learning, they also become more self-regulated (Cleary & Zimmerman, 2004). Self-regulated students set personal goals and make adjustments to those goals along the way in order to be most successful.

Differentiation. Just as we demonstrated the variance in early adolescent development, it follows that cognitive development includes a diverse range of abilities and unique learning needs. Differentiation is specialized student instruction that includes "multiple learning and teaching approaches" that respond to their diversity (NMSA, 2010, p. 14). Teachers who believe in differentiation expect all students to succeed, as failure is mainly a result of instruction that does not correspond to a students learning style. If a student feels overwhelmed or confused during whole group instruction, they may withdraw and lose hope in their abilities. To help students regain lost confidence, educators must find ways for them to repeatedly encounter self-efficacy (Tomlinson, 2005). We recognize the challenge of differentiation in diverse classrooms and understand that differentiation does not mean creating a specific lesson for each student.

Many (e.g., Tomlinson, 2005) have written on differentiation and a full review is beyond the scope of this chapter. However, one way to differentiate and give students experiences planned to review, reteach, or challenge the topic at hand are learning centers. Teachers must be aware of the specific social, emotional, and cognitive needs in the classroom to effectively utilize centers (Hammon & Hess, 2004). Part of this awareness allows teachers to build on the prior knowledge of the students and use scaffolding to help students succeed (Strahan & Layell, 2006).

Many times, differentiation is seen as the solution to struggling students. Expecting success includes challenging academically gifted students as well. Ensuring success should not be bound by grade level expectations and teachers should extend instruction for students to reach their full potential. Academic competitions, such as Odyssey of The Mind or WordMasters, "can expand the scope and depth of content, allowing gifted learners to explore subject areas far beyond the opportunities available in the regular classroom" (Ozturk & Debelak, 2008, p. 47).

There is not one particular way to differentiate instruction in the classroom. The key is to truly observe the diversity of learners in the classroom and take on the responsibility for the success of each of them (Tomlinson, 2005). The ultimate goal of educators is to lead all students to success, but it is important to remember that each learner takes a different path. Understanding this fact helps educators to see each early adolescent as an individual with his or her own strengths and weaknesses and how to best support them.

Heterogeneous Grouping. Although tracking and ability grouping persist in schools, a considerable body of research (Ansalone, 2010) has demonstrated detrimental effects. For example, research suggests that it can support negative perceptions of lower level students that in turn impact students' self-perceptions (Irvin, 1997). Obviously, expecting success for all students would lean more toward heterogeneous grouping. Heterogeneous ability grouping reduces comparisons among and communicates that all learners can be successful (Haselhuhn et al., 2007). It also provides opportunities for valuable programs such as cooperative learning and peer tutoring to help assure success.

Lounsbury (2009) believes that learning how to be part of a team is a necessary element of adolescent success, not only in the classroom, but also in a future career. Beyond team building skills, cooperative learning is also a learning tool that provides middle level students with a sense of belonging, which is critical in a time when peer influence plays such an important role (Willis, 2007). As students work together to solve challenging problems and create projects, they learn from one another and are actively engaged in the process. It has a deeper impact than just passively listening to a lecture or reading a text (Willis, 2007). Students further discover, while developing and utilizing their strengths, how to be a key contributor for group process.

Peer tutoring is another helpful learning tool that can support student success in a group of learners with mixed ability levels (Mastropieri et al., 2001). This provides students the opportunity to use their strengths to help a struggling peer. A student may have a different approach to instructing a confused classmate that is more constructive then traditional pedagogy. Peer tutoring is an evidence-based strategy used to boost student academic achievement (Dufrene et al., 2010), and also can contribute to self-efficacy.

Even though teachers may not have complete control when it comes to actual curriculum development, they do bring dispositions to the classroom and select the pedagogy they use to teach the required material. They can expect success for all students (disposition) and provide strategies that continually place students at the center of the learning process by selecting instructional practices appropriate for young adolescents (Vagle, 2006). As we attempted to demonstrate, a few of the practices designed to assure success in the academic context include positive teacher-student relationships, differentiation, exploratory learning, and heterogeneous grouping.

CONCLUSION

This chapter centered on the self-enhancing school where educators move *from accepting failure to expecting and assuring success.* It is certainly accepted that schools and school personnel cannot accept failure. Although this dispositional shift is essential, it is important to not neglect the learning that can be achieved through making mistakes when time and resources are made available for students to learn from their mistakes. It is also important to distinguish that assuring success does not guarantee success. While educators do not control all of the variables in the success equation, they can relentlessly push the conditions and context that allow for success.

We believe that a self-enhancing school would not only be developmentally responsive but should instead (or in addition to) actively promote development. The optimal way to achieve this goal is to provide an academic context that buffers challenges and both supports developmental assets and enhances protective factors. If early adolescence is a time when self-concept is fragile (Adams, Kuhn, & Rhodes, 2006), middle grades educators must be proactive and focus on the autonomous, self-regulated adolescents we intend to nurture.

REFERENCES

Ahmed, M., & Boisvert, C. (2006). Using positive psychology with special mental health populations. *American Psychologist, 61,* 333-336.

Adams, S., Kuhn, J., & Rhodes, J. (2006). Self-esteem changes in the middle school years: A study of ethnic and gender groups. *RMLE: Research in Middle Level Education, 29*(6), 1-9.

Akos, P. (2005). The unique nature of middle school counseling. *Professional School Counseling, 9*(2), 95-103.

Akos, P. (2006). Extracurricular participation and the transition to middle school. *RMLE Online: Research in Middle Level Education, 29*(9), 1-9.

Akos, P., Charles, P., Orthner, D., & Cooley, V. (2011). Teacher perspectives on career-relevant curriculum in middle school. *RMLE Online: Research in Middle Level Education, 34*(5), 1-9.

Ansalone, G. (2010). Tracking: Educational differentiation or defective strategy. *Educational Research Quarterly, 32*(2), 3-17.

Beane, J., & Lipka, R. (1984). *Self-concept, self-esteem, and the curriculum.* Newton, MA: Allyn & Bacon.

Brigman, G., & Campbell, C. (2003). Helping students improve academic achievement and school success behavior. *Professional School Counseling, 7*(2), 91-98.

Broderick, P. C., & Blewitt, P. (2010). *The life span: Human development for helping professionals* (3rd ed.). Boston, MA: Pearson.

Brown, B., & Klute, C. (2008). Friendships, cliques, and crowds. In G. Adams & M. Berzonsky (Eds.), *Blackwell handbook of adolescence* (pp. 330-348). Oxford, England: Blackwell.

Cleary, T. J., & Zimmerman, B. J. (2004). Self-regulation empowerment program: A school-based program to enhance self-regulated and self-motivated cycles of student learning. *Psychology in the Schools, 41*(5), 537-550.

Daddis, C. (2008). Influence of close friends on the boundaries of adolescent personal authority. *Journal of Research on Adolescence, 18*(1), 75-98.

Dufrene, B. A., Reisener, C. D., Olmi, D., Zoder-Martell, K., McNutt, M. R., & Horn, D. R. (2010). Peer tutoring for reading fluency as a feasible and effective alternative in response to intervention systems. *Journal of Behavioral Education, 19*(3), 239-256.

Fleming, M. (2005). Adolescent autonomy: Desire, achievement and disobeying parents between early and late adolescence. *Australian Journal of Education and Developmental Psychology, 5*, 1-16.

Galassi, J. P., & Akos, P. (2007). *Strengths-based school counseling: Promoting student development and achievement.* New York, NY: Routledge, Taylor & Francis Group.

Galassi, J. P., Griffin, D., & Akos, P. (2008). Strengths-based school counseling and the ASCA model. *Professional School Counseling, 12*(2), 176-181.

Gestsdóttir, S., & Lerner, R. (2008). Positive development in adolescence: The development and role of intentional self-regulation. *Human Development, 51*, 202-224.

Guerra, N. G. & Bradshaw, C. P. (2008). Linking the prevention of problem behaviors and positive youth development: Core competencies for positive youth development and risk prevention. *New Directions for Child and Adolescent Development, 122*, 1-17.

Hammon, A., & Hess, C. (2004). Actively engaging middle school readers: One teacher's story. *Middle School Journal, 35*(3), 5-12.

Haselhuhn, C. W., Al-Mabuk, R., Gabriele, A., Groen, M., & Galloway, S. (2007). Promoting positive achievement in the middle school: A look at teachers' motivational knowledge, beliefs, and teaching practices. *RMLE Online: Research in Middle Level Education, 30*(9), 1-20.

Irvin, J. (1997), *What current research says to the middle level practitioner.* Columbus, OH: NMSA.

Lachuk, A., & Gomez, M. (2011). Listening carefully to the narratives of young adolescent youth of color. *Middle School Journal, 42*(3), 6-14.

Li, Y., Lynch, A. D., Kalvin, C., Liu, J., & Lerner, J. (2011). Peer relationships as a context for the development of school engagement during early adolescence. *International Journal of Behavioral Development, 35*(4), 329-342.

Lohman, B., Kaura, S., & Newman, B. (2007). Matched or mismatched environments? The relationship of family and school differentiation to adolescents' psychosocial adjustment. *Youth & Society, 39*(3), 3-32.

Lounsbury, J. H. (2009). Deferred but not deterred: A middle school manifesto. *Middle School Journal, 40*(5), 31-36.

Molloy, L., Gest, S., & Rulison, K. (2011). Peer influences on academic motivation: Exploring multiple methods of assessing youths' most "influential" peer relationships. *Journal of Early Adolescence, 31*(1), 13-40.

Marzano R. J., & Marzano J. S. (2003). The key to classroom management. *Educational Leadership, 61*, 6-13.

Mastropieri, M. A., Scruggs, T. E., Mohler, L. J., Beranek, M. L., Spencer, V., Boon, R. T., & Talbott, E. (2001). Can middle school students with serious reading difficulties help each other and learn anything? *Learning Disabilities: Research & Practice, 16*(1), 18-27.

Murphy, B., Eisenberg, N., Fabes, R., Shepard, S., & Guthrie, I. (1999). Consistency and change in children's emotionality and regulation: A longitudinal study. *Merrill-Palmer Quarterly, 45*(3), 414-444.

National Middle School Association. (2010). *This we believe: Keys to educating young adolescents.* Columbus, OH: Author.

Ozturk, M., & Debelak, C. (2008). Academic competitions as tools for differentiation in middle school. *Gifted Child Today, 31*(3), 47-53.

Pape, S. J., Bell, C. V., & Yetkin, I. E. (2003). Developing mathematical thinking and self-regulated learning: A teaching experiment in a seventh-grade mathematics classroom. *Educational Studies in Mathematics, 53*(3), 179-202.

Park, N. (2009). Building strengths of character: Keys to positive youth development. *Reclaiming Children and Youth, 18*(2), 42-47.

Powell, S. (2011). Wayside teaching: Focusing on relationships. *Middle School Journal, 42*(5), 48-50.

Putnam, R. (1995). Bowling alone: America's declining social capital. *Journal of Democracy, 6*(1), 65-78.

Raffaelli, M., Crockett, L., & Shen, Y. L. (2005). Developmental stability and change in self-regulation from childhood to adolescence. *The Journal of Genetic Psychology, 166*(1), 54-75.

Seitsinger, A. M. (2005). Service-learning and standards-based instruction in middle schools. *Journal of Educational Research*, *99*(1), 19.

Scott, C., Murray, G., Mertens, C., & Dustin, R. (1996). Student self-esteem and the school system: Perceptions and implications. *Journal of Educational Research*, *89*(5), 286-293.

Stott, K. A., & Jackson, A. P. (2005). Using service learning to achieve middle school comprehensive guidance program goals. *Professional School Counseling*, *9*(2), 156-159.

Strahan, D. (2008). Successful teachers develop academic momentum with reluctant students. *Middle School Journal*, *39*(5), 4-12.

Strahan, D. B., & Layell, K. (2006). Connecting caring and action through responsive teaching: How one team accomplished success in a struggling middle school. *Clearing House: A Journal of Educational Strategies, Issues and Ideas*, *79*(3), 147-153.

Tomlinson, C. A. (2005). Differentiating instruction why bother? *Middle Ground*, *9*(1), 12-14.

Tyler, K. M., & Boelter, C. M. (2008). Linking Black middle school students' perceptions of teachers' expectations to academic engagement and efficacy. *Negro Educational Review*, *59*(1-2), 27-44.

Vagle, M. D. (2006). Dignity and democracy: An exploration of middle school teachers' pedagogy. *RMLE Online: Research in Middle Level Education*, *29*(8), 1-17.

Virtue, D. C., Wilson, J. L., & Ingram, N. (2009). In overcoming obstacles to curriculum integration, L.E.S.S. can be more! *Middle School Journal*, *40*(3), 4-11.

Willis, J. (2007). Cooperative learning is a brain turn-on. *Middle School Journal*, *38*(4), 4-13.

Wilson, D. B. Gottfredson, D. C., & Najaka, S. S. (2001). School-based prevention of problem behaviors: A meta-analysis. *Journal of Quantitative Criminology*, *17*(3), 247-272.

CHAPTER 8

FROM AVOIDING OR BLAMING PARENTS TO WORKING WITH PARENTS

Lee Shumow and Nancy DeFrates-Densch

> Schools and families must work together to provide the best possible learning for every young adolescent. Schools take the initiative in involving and educating families. (Association for Middle Level Education, 2003)

The period of early adolescence can be fraught with difficulty or rife with opportunity, depending to a large extent on how well the people in the contexts in which students live and spend their time work together. For that reason, parent school engagement continues to be as, or even more, important during the middle grades years than it was during the earlier grades. The purpose of this chapter is to explain why parental engagement matters to middle-level students and educators, to present guidelines and principles for engaging parents (adults who are bringing up and responsible for the young adolescent), and to discuss the various ways parents are engaged and how educators can utilize that knowledge to design a comprehensive parental engagement program for a self-enhancing middle level school.

Middle Grades Curriculum:
Voices and Visions of the Self-Enhancing School, pp. 119–139
Copyright © 2013 by Information Age Publishing
All rights of reproduction in any form reserved.

WHY PARENTAL ENGAGEMENT MATTERS

The Association for Middle Level Education (AMLE, 2010) identifies involving parents as one of the sixteen characteristics of successful schools. There are many reasons for identifying parental involvement as a characteristic of successful middle-level schools. For one, engagement contributes to middle-level students' school adjustment, which includes their academic success, motivation, engagement, and social-emotional development. Studies reviewed in this section have tied parent engagement in school with middle-level students' academic success. A meta-analysis of numerous studies (Hill & Tyson, 2009) showed that parent engagement predicted middle-level students' achievement. Similarly, a large, nationally representative study of seventh graders connected parent engagement with students' grade point average (Shumow & Miller, 2001). Motivational benefits also have been documented such that parental involvement predicted middle-level students' learning goals (Duchesne & Ratelle, 2010), cognitive engagement (Mo & Singh, 2008), and orientation to school (Shumow & Miller, 2001). Emotional and behavioral benefits also accrue for students whose parents are engaged. For example, Duchesne and Ratelle found that parental involvement was associated with fewer symptoms of anxiety and depression among young adolescents and another study found that children whose parents encouraged nonviolent conflict resolution were less physically aggressive in middle level schools (Farrell, Henry, Mays, & Schoeny, 2011). Parent involvement during the middle grades has been tied to fewer behavior problems in eighth grade among middle but not lower SES students (Hill, Castellino, Lansford, Nowlin, Dodge, & Bates, 2004). Parent involvement, then, can be a significant source of support for educators in fulfilling their primary mission of educating young adolescents to their fullest possible potential. Indeed, the expectation that parental involvement will pay dividends in child achievement is the fundamental reason that so many educational policies aim to increase parental involvement (Pomerantz, Moorman, & Litwack, 2007).

Conversely, negative consequences are associated with parental disengagement from their young adolescents' schooling. Most studies reviewed in this chapter found a linear relationship between parent school engagement and outcomes for young adolescents. Thus, little or no engagement tends to be associated with behavior problems (both externalizing and internalizing), lack of motivation in school, and academic failure. Avoiding or blaming parents rather than inviting their participation is not in the best interest of young adolescents.

Another reason to identify parental engagement during middle school as important is that parents are instrumental in supporting and responding to their young adolescents' development. Early adolescence is a period of significant developmental changes including the physical changes of puberty, cognitive changes in decision-making and reasoning skills, as well as social changes involving the increased importance of peers; these changes play a role in adolescents' school adjustment and their relationships. Although parents' relationships with their child tends to become temporarily more distant during pubertal maturation (Steinberg, 1987; 1989), there is a widespread misconception that adolescents' burgeoning interests in peers is a result of that distancing from parents and that it inevitably leads adolescents to discount parental influences and succumb to negative peer pressure. To the contrary, researchers have demonstrated that parents play an essential role in managing and guiding young adolescents' peer relationships (Mounts, 2004, 2011) and that these parenting practices foster better academic performance and social skills (Loeber & Stouthamer-Loeber, 1998; Mounts, 2001; Vernberg et al., 1993). Parents also play a critical role in fostering young adolescents' cognitive development and managing their exposure to developmentally instigative experiences, points that will be elaborated on later in this chapter.

Yet another reason for schools to involve parents stems from a basic ethical consideration. In recent history, education has been characterized as a universal human right internationally. Whether that right is characterized as belonging to a child or to his/her parent has been less clear (Englund, Quennerstedt, & Wahlstro, 2009), however. In the United States, numerous laws passed by Congress such as the Individuals with Disabilities Education Act and No Child Left Behind have given parents the right to make decisions and choices about their children's education based on the principle that parents have primary responsibility for a child.

Unfortunately, despite good reasons for middle grades educators to build partnerships with parents, both parent involvement and efforts to involve parents drop off with the transition to middle school (Vaden-Kiernan & Chandler, 1996). Organizational and structural differences between elementary and middle schools often create significant obstacles to maintaining partnerships with parents. During the elementary school grades, public school students are typically assigned to one classroom with one teacher and (in 2007-08) approximately 20 students (U.S. Department of Education, 2009) for all academic subjects. This means that parents have one teacher with whom to form a relationship and communicate and that teachers have approximately 20 families. With the transition to middle school, students generally change classes during the school day—parents, then, need to communicate with three to five academic teachers who each generally have more than 100 students across their classes. This situation makes building relationships and communication more challenging than it was during elementary school. The distance between schools and families is illustrated by the discrepancy between what schools say they are doing to support parents in helping their children with homework or providing information for enriching learning out of school and what parents report that schools are doing. A large study of U.S. schools conducted by the National Center for Educational Statistics found a pronounced and larger difference between middle schools and elementary schools in the discrepant reports (Chen & Chandler, 2001).

Middle level educators who work to build partnerships with parents are likely to find their efforts to be worthwhile. Very few teachers of adolescents, however, have been prepared during their teacher education or during professional development to understand or work with parents (Epstein, Sanders, & Clark, 1999; Hiatt-Michael, 2004; Morgan, 2008; U. S. Department of Education, 1994). The rest of this chapter focuses on guidelines, background information, practices, and resources useful for middle level educators in building partnerships with parents.

GUIDELINES FOR MOVING FROM MARGINALIZING TO ENGAGING PARENTS

General guidelines, synthesized from the work of numerous scholars and educators who have pursued an understanding of how to build collaboration between homes and schools, will help educators move from the present state in which parents are too often marginalized to a state of engaging parents. The guidelines are as follows.

1. *From waiting to initiating.* It is not unusual to hear teachers express the expectation that parents should initiate communication with them. However, the AMLE (2010) explicitly states that schools should initiate partnerships with parents. Teachers are sometimes frustrated with what they perceive as yet another task heaped onto their already prodigious list of responsibilities. Yet, educators are the professionals in the relationship and, as such, have the responsibility to take the lead in promoting partnerships with parents. Parents, especially those who do not have high social status, often wait for *the school* to contact them (Lareau, 2000) and/or to define their role within the classroom or school culture.

2. *From avoiding to welcoming parents.* Most middle level educators choose a profession focused on young adolescents, not adults. Given the considerable time and energy required to meet the needs of educating those young people, it can be easy to avoid con-

tacting parents, especially at the busy start of the school year. However, invitations from either an educator or the student are the key to fostering parental engagement (Hoover-Dempsey, Ice, & Whitaker, 2009). Initial interactions with parents need to be positive, which is most likely to be accomplished if educators have a plan for initiating such interactions at or before the beginning of the school year. It is also crucial to welcome parents and establish a relationship BEFORE problems arise. Parents report that middle schools are less welcoming than elementary schools and that relationship variables are the key components of whether a school is welcoming (Christensen, 2004).

3. *From one to two-way communication.* A central way to build trust, understanding, and partnerships is to recognize, respect, and acknowledge parents' potential contributions to a partnership. Parents and teachers each bring a different form of knowledge and expertise to the table; both forms are essential for educating a child to his/her fullest potential. Parents are experts on their particular child whereas teachers are experts on students in general. Parents know their child's history, interests, personality, and characteristic ways of responding, while teachers know grade level norms, content knowledge, learning strategies, and instructional methods.

4. *From judging to gathering information and generating understanding.* Being quick to judge based on too little information stymies partnership building between educators and parents. Educators sometimes label parents as a way of explaining students' behavior or academic performance, for example, divorced, immigrant, uneducated, poor, minority, working mother. Too often these terms carry judgments that these parents are inadequate (Christensen, 2004). Yet, there is considerable evidence that demographic characteristics are poor predictors of parent engagement at home even though they predict parent engagement at school (Dervarics & O'Brien, 2011). Educators need to ask why parents do not come to school, what might entice parents to school, and how student-centered partnerships might focus on what is done at home. On the other hand, educators sometimes feel blamed, judged, and misunderstood by parents. Getting parents into classrooms and schools can be beneficial in that parents can see the school, interact with teachers, and begin to build an understanding of their child in that context.

5. *From an adversarial to a collaborative stance.* In too many cases, educators and parents became trapped in a win-lose rather than a win-

win position. In fact, almost all parents and teachers share the goal of having students succeed (Hill, Tyson, & Bromell, 2009). Educators can be put off and upset when parents seem to argue for the child against the teacher. Parents have deep enduring emotional ties to their own child and it is often very painful to watch a child struggle or suffer (Rogoff, 1990); it is important to understand that parental advocacy for a child is often rooted in that emotional tie and is a sign of commitment to the child. Acknowledging that it is difficult and interpreting their defense as an indicator of engagement can go a long way in defusing and reframing the situation Identifying the shared goal to parents and students is likely to further discharge tension and set the stage for collaborative problem solving.

6. *From determinism to prevention and problem solution.* Too often, determinism rules—educators expect students and families from certain backgrounds to be unresponsive and parents resign themselves to their child's downward trajectory. A sense of optimism combined with a plan for how a student can improve is critical to preventing that downward spiral. If and when problems arise, they can be better addressed if the parties have shared positive interactions (see point 2) and by taking an optimistic, solution-focused, problem-solving approach is essential.

TYPES OF PARENT ENGAGEMENT

The remainder of the chapter is organized by type of parental engagement. Many scholars have found that parental engagement at-home differs from engagement at-school in terms of both predictors and outcomes. Researchers have found that demographic characteristics like income, race/ethnicity, or immigration status are not good predictors of parent involvement at home (Dervarics & O'Brien, 2011). Findings relevant for educators will be reviewed and ideas for how to facilitate each type of partnership will be presented.

At-Home Engagement

Several types of parental engagement at home are known to impact students' school adjustment. Parents (a) socialize their child, (b) manage informal educational activities and resources, as well as (c) supervise, monitor, assist or extend homework and learning at home. Unbeknownst to many educators, when children struggle in school parents tend to get more involved at home, but less involved at school leading educators to conclude falsely that these parents are not involved because they do not see the parents (Shumow & Miller, 2001).

Socialization. The following studies reviewed associating students' school adjustment with the socialization practices that parents use. Researchers have conceptualized socialization in a variety of ways: rule setting, supervision/monitoring, and orienting students toward school.

Researchers (see Steinberg & Silk, 2003 for a review) have tied the way that parents interact with and discipline their children to how well students function in school. That line of research points to the importance of how, not simply how much parents interact with their children (Pomerantz, Moorman, & Litwack, 2007).

Some studies have shown that the *style*, defined as the intersection of two separate dimensions of parenting (demandingness and responsiveness), is related to how well-adjusted students are in school. Parents who are authoritative are both demanding and responsive; authoritative parents tend to have young adolescents with better behavior, work habits and school performance than parents who are neither or who tend to be one or the other, but not both (see Steinberg & Silk, 2003 for a review). Authoritative parents have high standards for their children, set age appropriate rules and consequences, explain the reason for rules, and are responsive to their children's individuality and are thus perceived as autonomy supporting. Sixth and seventh graders with coercive parents (threatening or authoritarian) were more likely to be anxious at school and to develop performance rather than learning goals (Duchesne & Ratelle, 2010).

Parental rule-setting about things like homework, peer interaction, media use and bedtime has been investigated as a possible contributor to school adjustment among middle school students. A meta-analyses (study that combines and analyzes the findings of many studies) by Patall, Cooper, and Robinson (2008) found that rule setting contributed more to middle school student achievement than any other type of engagement. Interestingly, a meta-analysis of studies on high school students found rule setting to be the weakest type of parent involvement in predicting academic performance. It could be that parents of high school students who are involved in extensive rule setting are doing so because they are controlling parents who have not supported their children's autonomy development or because they are responding to children who are struggling academically or behaviorally. It seems important for parents of middle school students to set reasonable rules that establish habits conducive to school success. Rules about television viewing are a case in point. When parents set rules about how much and what kind of television can be watched, students watch less television (Barradas, Fulton, Blank, & Huhman, 2007). However, a distinct minority of middle-level students' parents (27%) set rules about amount and only slightly more set rules about content (Kaiser Family Foundation, 2010). Many parents are reluctant to set rules about television because they lack resources to otherwise fill the time and fear family discord (Evans, Jordan, & Horner, 2011).

Other researchers (Farrell et al., 2011; Shumow & Lomax, 2002; Steinberg & Silk, 2003) have focused on supervision (often called monitoring, both proximal and distal) of middle school students when they are out-of-school. Not surprisingly, monitoring is an important issue for dual-employed parents in two parent families and for single parents in the United States. Monitoring has been associated with middle school students' academic, behavioral, social, and emotional development in school (Farrell et al.; Shumow & Lomax; Steinberg & Silk). Researchers who have investigated self-care (no adults present) before and after school have found that many middle school students are unsupervised at one time or another during the week (Shumow, Smith, & Smith, 2009). Neighborhood safety, maternal employment, and race/ethnicity are more important factors in predicting how much time middle school students spend in self-care than family income. Parents are far more likely to leave their middle-school children unsupervised in safe than unsafe neighborhoods. White students are most and Hispanic students are least likely to be in self-care before or after school. Importantly, a study with a large nationally representative data set found that middle-level students who experience self-care are more likely to get lower grades and have more school behavior problems than those who do not and these negative effects are more pronounced for middle than elementary school students (Shumow, Smith, & Smith). Those results substantiate the widespread concerns expressed by both parents and educators who are concerned about both the safety and the time use of young adolescents in self-care. Given the individual-level routine activity theory, which posits that problems result from not engaging in developmentally instigative or academically enriching task, the activities of students in self-care are a significant concern. Students who are unsupervised are more likely to watch television and "hang out" and less likely to study or participate in academically enriching activities than students who are supervised (Osgood, Anderson, & Shaffer, 2005).

An important aspect of socialization is that students internalize values and become academically motivated by the behaviors, attitudes, expectations and emotions that parents model and express (Pomerantz, Moorman, & Litwack, 2007; Shumow & Miller, 2001; Taylor, Clayton, & Rowley, 2004). How readily students internalize their parents' values depends on parenting style with the advantage going to authoritative parents. Parents attitudes toward and emotions about school are shaped by their own school experiences (Finders & Lewis, 1994).

Parental Management. Long term academic success depends to no small extent on the resources, routines, planning, and decision-making of parents. Mounts (2001) has studied the important role that parents of middle school students play in managing their children's peer relationships to promote academic and social well-being. More details about parent management of educational planning appear in subsequent sections of this chapter. The financial, cultural and social capital that parents have access to influences how well parents can foster their children's educational success. Yet, it is important to point out that children in well-to-do families do seem to face considerable risk because their parents exert enormous competitive pressure on them and react negatively if they struggle to succeed (Luthar & Sexton, 2004). Emotionally controlling and coercive parenting whether for academic or extracurricular performance results in psychosocial problems, stress, less intrinsic motivation, and less enjoyment (Duchesne & Ratelle, 2010; Luthar & Sexton, 2004; Zarrett & Eccles, 2009).

Given the contributions of parental socialization practices to student adjustment, it is worth considering how schools can work with parents to support socialization practices conducive to school success. Basic information about the middle school child and about socialization practices that have been successful for other parents might be offered on school websites or newsletters. The Collaborative for Early Adolescence at Northern Illinois University (www.niu.edu/cea) has developed one page newsletter inserts for schools (these articles are free of charge but must be cited and cannot be edited by users). Parents of middle school students are often open to valid information because there are so many negative messages about the adolescent period and about middle school students rampant in the mass media. In keeping with the importance of two way communication, parents can be surveyed about the topics that would be most valuable for them and those can be selected. Parent organizations or advisory boards can help generate, and network to promote, contextually appropriate social norms for the middle school community. For example, at the behest of the middle school principal, a Parent Teacher Organization in a middle school serving a broad socioeconomic range of families worked to limit and redirect family expenses for the eighth grade graduation dance by providing the corsages for all students, encouraging donations (financial or in kind) to a class service project, and discouraging the use of limousines to arrive at the dance.

Parent Engagement With Homework. Homework is perhaps the most pervasive avenue through which school enters homes. The mainstream media has repeatedly published articles based on anecdotes suggesting that homework is the bane of parents' existence creating conflict and distress in families. Little evidence substantiates such claims. To the contrary, a study in which adolescent students carried pagers that beeped randomly to signal them to complete reports about their activities, companions, and subjective experience (Shumow, Schmidt, & Kackar, 2008) found that when students were with their parents they concentrated better than they did with peers and were not more angry or stressed than when they were either alone or with friends. A follow up study found that middle school students enjoyed homework more when alone than with parents, whereas high school students enjoyed homework more with parents than when they were alone (Kackar, Shumow, Schmidt, & Grzetich, 2011).

Still the questions persist: Is homework good for students in middle grades? And what role should parents play with homework? An analysis that combined many studies concluded that students who do 90 minutes or less of homework per night during middle school do better than students who do no homework but those students who do more than 90 minutes of homework actually do worse possibly because that much homework signals that the students are having serious problems in school (Cooper, Robinson, & Patall, 2006). The same research team (Patall et al., 2008) then combined 20 studies that examined parent help with homework. They found that, in general, parent assistance predicted higher achievement for both elementary and high school students but lower achievement for middle-level students. Hill and Tyson's (2009) meta-analysis substantiated the findings that parent homework help was associated with lower achievement for middle-level students. A closer look, however, reveals that those general findings depended on subject area. The Patall and colleagues (2008) study showed that parent involvement with homework was actually associated with lower achievement in mathematics but higher achievement in language arts. This might be explained by evidence that parents help young adolescents with homework primarily when the student is struggling academically (Shumow & Miller, 2001). It also might be that parents have more difficulty helping with mathematics homework because they themselves are less competent in mathematics skills than language arts skills or because they are not familiar with the mathematics their children are learning as a result of mathematics reforms instituted after the parents finished school.

Several successful programs and practices have been implemented to help parents of middle-level students assist their children with homework. One program is the Teachers Involve Parents in Schoolwork (TIPS) program (Epstein, Salinas, & Van Voorhis, 2001). TIPS was designed by researchers and middle-school teachers to promote student responsibility and parent engagement with homework. TIPS consists of a series of adaptable homework assignments that inform parents about what students are learning in school through assignments that entail parent-child discussion about or review of the student's work. TIPS was tested in high poverty middle schools; students grades and test scores improved, students reported liking the program, and parents said that the program helped them to understand their children's learning (Epstein & VanVoorhis, 2001). A recent study (VanVoohis, 2011) followed TIPS students for 2 years. There was no difference in the time spent on homework between TIPS participants and the control group. TIPS participants (both parents and students) reported better emotional experiences during homework and more parent involvement in homework; TIPS students received higher scores on achievement tests than the control group.

The Parent Institute for Quality Education (PIQE) program provides 9-week parent education classes that teach parents how to take an active role in their children's education in various ways such as by providing a time and place to do homework. One of the PIQE evaluations focused on parents of middle-level students (Chrispeels, Gonzalez, & Arellano, 2004). The researchers reported that parents who participated in PIQE were more likely to supervise their child's homework than parents who did not take part in the PIQE program. Students' school attendance also improved for students whose parents attended PIQE compared to students whose parents did not. No differences in achievement outcomes were found.

As noted previously, there is some disagreement between parents and school leaders about whether schools provide parents with information that helps them to help their children with homework, suggesting that parents might not receive the information. Technological systems including school websites are one way to provide information about homework and due dates (Rogers & Wright, 2008); many parents report wanting access to such information and rate information on how to help as especially valuable (Christenson, Hurley, Sheridan, & Fenstermacher, 1997). Abdal-Haqq (2002) reported that many families find it convenient and useful to access posted assignments and tips for how to help their children to complete their homework or study. The Transparent School Model program included a voice messaging system for parents. According to an evaluation by Bauch (1998), the program dramatically increased the exchange of information between school and home. Parents said that they accessed the communication system, were better informed about assignments, and thought the information helped their children succeed. Teachers reported an increase in both homework completion rates and better quality homework as a result of parents having access to information.

Academic Enrichment at Home. Middle-level students who are exposed to books and other educationally enriching experiences at home and who visit libraries and museums with their families have higher academic achievement than students who do not have those enrichment experiences (Hill & Tyson, 2009). Lareau (2003) coined the term "concerted cultivation" to describe the approach through which parents who have themselves been successful tend to give their children a competitive edge in school by providing resources and opportunities for knowledge and skill development outside of schools such as after school tutoring, lessons, and other organized activities. One study using a large nationally representative data set found that enrolling middle school students in some structured and supervised activities (e.g., lessons, clubs, youth groups) after school was especially beneficial in offsetting the risks of self-care for young adolescents (Shumow et al., 2009). However, those structured activities often require considerable fees. Not surprisingly then, family socioeconomic status and "social capital" are associated with access to such resources (Ream & Palardy, 2008). Nevertheless, there are examples of parents with low socioeconomic status who have managed to find camps, music programs, mentors and other developmentally beneficial resources for their children (Jarrett, 1999). Historically, church affiliation has been helpful for immigrant and minority populations seeking such programs.

Parent-child discussion of current events and issues in the world, community and personal realms have some developmental benefits for young adolescents. Shumow and Lomax (2002) used a nationally representative data set to show that parent-adolescent communication fostered better social emotional outcomes but was not related to academic performance. Using data from the National Education Longitudinal Study, McNeal (1999) found that how much parents talked with their eighth graders was more predictive of positive student behavior at school than any other form of at-home engagement although it was not related to science achievement.

Computers for Youth is another program that aimed to increase parent involvement with learning at home. Tsikalas, Lee, and Newkirk (2007) studied the program and reported that it promoted the school engagement of middle-level students, which consequently improved their achievement in mathematics. The amount of time that families spent with computers was the strongest predictor of student improvement.

Parent Engagement With Educational Planning

Parent engagement with educational planning spans at-home and at-school involvement. This type of involvement becomes crucial during middle school because students choose ninth grade courses during eighth grade and a student's postsecondary educational trajectory is largely dependent upon which courses are taken in high school. Unfortunately, many parents do not know that high school graduation requirements often differ from college admission requirements; those that did not attend college themselves are least likely to understand the preparation, application process and requirements for college admission (Heredia & Hiatt-Michael, 2009; Wimberly & Noeth, 2004). It is important to note that most parents want their children to attend college including those parents with less social capital (Dounay, 2006).

Interviews conducted by Cousins, Mickelson, Williams, and Velasco (2008) indicated that middle-class White parents were more likely than minority parents to understand how school systems operated, including with whom and when they needed to act to maximize their childrens' academic trajectories. Minority parents, whether middle or working class, were less likely to know the course sequences for mathematics and science, to have networks to inform them, or to have a toolkit of strategies to advocate for their children's educational placement.

Some states have policies which require schools to include parents in educational planning for their children (Dounay, 2006). Educators can play an important role in helping parents assist their children with educational planning. Parents need information about course selection, course sequences, high school graduation requirements, student progress, and college preparation and admission requirements to enable them to effectively help their middle school children with planning (Wimberly & Noeth, 2004, 2005). ACT has sponsored and reviewed studies on how schools can involve parents in educational planning leading them to identify the need for school districts to make formal plans and use systematic strategies to do so (Wimberly & Noeth, 2004; 2005). The study by Cousins, Mickelson, Williams, and Velasco (2008) highlights the importance of cultural sensitivity and targeted attention to parents who are minorities and/or working class.

At-School Engagement

Several types of parental engagement at school are important. Parents (a) conference with teachers, (b) volunteer at school (c) attend school events, and (d) join school organizations. Parents with greater financial, social and cultural capital within U.S. society tend to be more involved at school than their counterparts with less capital. The benefits students derive from their parents involvement at school might result from the networks that parents form through these activities, from parents learning about what is expected by the teachers or by favor that teachers might unconsciously give to students whose parents are involved.

Conferences. Parent teacher conferences are ubiquitous in middle schools. These events tend to be routinely scheduled once or twice a year and offer an opportunity for teachers and parents to exchange information and coordinate efforts. There are fewer studies on parent teacher conferences than on other areas of parental involvement but the existing studies point to some areas of concern in terms of realizing those opportunities. In a study of elementary school conferences, most parents reported that they were relegated to listening and had little opportunity to share their perspective or to ask questions (Murphy, 2009). Another study found that cross-cultural conferences were more difficult and led to miscommunication between teachers and parents more often than intra-cultural conferences (Eberly, Joshi, & Konzal, 2007).

Student-led conferences are an alternative form of conference which has many advantages over the traditional form. The teacher prepares the students to assume the role and responsibility of primary communicator in sharing school work, progress, and goals with their parents. Overall, all parties at middle schools that implemented student led conferences including teachers, administrators, parents and students reported satisfaction with student-led conferences; conference attendance improved dramatically after implanting the student-led conferences in a number of middle schools and all parties associated improvement in student behavior and academic outcomes with the conferences (Tuinstra & Hiatt-Michael, 2004). These conferences also have been implemented with success in urban school districts (Goodman, 2008; Shulkind, 2008). Detailed guidelines for how student-led conferences can be implemented are provided in the articles describing the results of the conferences. Not surprisingly, implementing something new requires forethought, planning, staff development, and time.

Test results need to be shared with parents given the high stakes associated with the results. Explaining these results to parents (and students) might be accomplished during conferences. According to Weiss and Lopez (2011), results must be shared with families in a timely fashion, in a way they can understand the results, with information about how to act on the results. Unfortunately, little is known about how parents understand and react to assessment results.

Parents as Volunteers. Some think of parent involvement in school as synonymous with volunteering in school but volunteering is actually the least frequent type of parent engagement with school; slightly more than a third of middle school students' parents report any instances of volunteering (Herrold & O'Donnell, 2008).

Parents might have difficulty volunteering in a classroom because they are working during school hours. Those parents might be able to contribute valuable skills by doing work outside the classroom (Church & Dollins, 2010). For example, parents can assist with classroom newsletters, organization of activities, finding resources, or with websites and other technology among other things. Moll, Amanti, and Neff (1992) worked with middle school teachers to develop classroom learning activities based on family and community cultural practices and knowledge. Parents came to classrooms to serve as experts on a topic on which they had knowledge; for example, fathers who were carpenters helped students with a mathematical project involving spatial reasoning and related concepts like perimeter and area. As a result, the parents were very engaged and positive relationships were built between families and schools. Hill and Tyson (2009) found that adolescents are particularly accepting of such an approach.

Patel and Stevens (2010) found that the degree to which parents, students, and teachers agree regarding students' scholastic abilities is related to the amount of interaction parents had with the school and their level of volunteerism. Among English-speaking parents, disagreements regarding children's abilities led to less interaction with the school, regardless of who initiated the interaction—teacher or parent—and particularly to less volunteering. Among Spanish-speaking parents, disagreement between parent and student regarding general student scholastic ability was positively related to volunteering activities. This relationship became negative when the disagreement regarding ability was specific to math.

Attending Events. Conventional wisdom among educators is that parents can be induced to come to school to see their child perform more easily than for any other reason. In a recent large, nationally representative sample, a majority (72%) of parents of middle school students reported attending middle school events (Herrold & O'Donnell, 2008). To the extent that these events feature the successes and potential of students in terms of their learning and development, partnerships will be enhanced.

Decision-making. Another form of parent at-school involvement identified by Epstein and colleagues (2002) is parent involvement in school decision-making. Only a few parents can serve on schools boards or advisory committees, yet quite a few parents of middle school students do become involved parent-teacher organizations including the PTA and in booster clubs. According to Herrold and O'Donnell (2008), 76% of middle-level students' parents report having attended such meetings. In a meta-analysis of 58 studies, Ferguson (2008) found that stronger schools result when parents are exposed to activities, knowledge, and tools that enable them to engage effectively in school improvement suggesting that meetings are most effective when they go beyond fundraising and focus on enhancing student learning and development.

CONCLUSION

This chapter has presented the reasons that parental involvement and engagement is critical to the self-enhancing middle school and the important role parents play with young adolescents. Guidelines, principles, knowledge and examples derived from the research literature offered insight into the many ways that parents can be engaged and the ways that a self- enhancing middle school can include parents as partners. Ultimately, middle-level students benefit from such a partnership.

REFERENCES

Abdal-Haqq, I. (2002). *Connecting schools and communities through technology.* Washington, DC: National School Boards Association.

Association for Middle Level Education. (2010). *This we believe: Essential attributes and characteristics of successful schools.* Retrieved from http://www.amle.org/AboutAMLE/ThisWeBelieve/The16Characteristics/tabid/1274/Default.aspx

Barradas, D., Fulton, J., Blanck, H., & Huhman, M. (2007). Parental influences on youth television viewing. *The Journal of Pediatrics, 151*(4), 369-373.

Bauch, J. P. (1998). Applications of technology to linking schools, families, and students. Retrieved from http://ceep.crc.illinois.edu/eecearchive/books/fte/links/bauch.pdf

Chen, X., & Chandler, K. (2001). *Efforts by public K-8 schools to involve parents in children's education: Do school and parent reports agree?* Washington, DC: National Center for Educational Statistics. Retrieved from http://nces.ed.gov/pubs2001/2001076.pdf

Chrispeels, J., Gonzalez, M., & Arellano, B. (2004). *Evaluation of the effectiveness of the parent institute for quality education in Los Angeles Unified School District: September 2003 to May 2004.* Retrieved from http://www.piqe.org/Assets/SpecialPrj/PIQE%202004%20Evaluation/Piqe%20Evaluation%202004.htm

Christenson, S. (2004). The family–school partnership: An opportunity to promote the learning competence of all students. *School Psychology Review, 33*(1), 83-104. Retrieved from http://www.nasponline.org/publications/spr/pdf/spr331christenson.pdf

Christenson, S., Hurly, C., Sheridan, S., & Fenstermacher, K. (1997). Parents' and school psychologists' perspectives on parent involvement activities. *School Psychology Review, 26*, 111-130.

Church, K., & Dollins, C. (2010). Parent engagement at school. In D. Hiatt-Michael (Ed.), *Promising practices to support family involvement in schools* (pp. 75-95). Charlotte NC: Information Age.

Collaborative for Early Adolescence. (2011). *Resources for teachers and parents.* Retrieved from www.niu.edu/cea_

Cooper, H., Robinson, J., & Patall, E. (2006). Does homework improve academic achievement?: A synthesis of research 1987-2003. *Review of Educational Research, 76*(1), 1-62.

Cousins, L. H., Mickelson, R. A., Williams, B., & Velasco, A. (2008). Race and class challenges in community collaboration for educational change. *The School Community Journal, 18*(2), 29-52.

Dervarics, C., & O'Brien, E. (2011). *Back to school: How parent involvement affects student achievement.* Retrieved from http://www.centerforpubliceducation.org/Main-Menu/Public-education/Parent-Involvement/Parent-Involvement.html

Dounay, J. (2006). *Alignment of high school graduation requirements and state-set college admissions requirements.* Retrieved from http://www.ecs.org/clearinghouse/68/60/6860.pdf

Duchesne, S., & Ratelle, C. (2010). Parental behaviors and adolescents' achievement goals at the beginning of middle school: Emotional problems as potential mediators. *Journal of Educational Psychology, 102*(2), 497-507.

Eberly, J. L., Joshi, A., & Konzal, J. (2007). Communicating with families across cultures: An investigation of teacher perceptions and practices. *The School Community Journal, 17*(2), 7-26.

Englund, T., Quennerstedt, A., & Wahlstro, N. (2009). Education as a human and a citizenship right—Parents' rights, children's rights, or ...? The necessity of historical contextualization. *Journal of Human Rights, 8,* 133-138.

Epstein, J. L., Sanders, M. G., Simon, B. S., Salinas, K. C., Jansorn, N. R., & Van Voorhis, F. L. (2002). *School, family, and community partnerships: Your handbook for action* (2nd ed.) Thousand Oaks, CA: Corwin Press.

Epstein, J., Salinas, K., & Van Voorhis, F. (2001). *Teachers involve parents in schoolwork (TIPS) manuals.* Baltimore, MD: Center on School, Family and Community Partnerships, Johns Hopkins University.

Epstein, J. L., Sanders, M. G., & Clark, L. A. (1999). *Preparing educators for school family-community partnerships: Results of a national survey of colleges and universities.* Center Report. Center for Research on the Education of Students Placed at Risk (CRESPAR), Baltimore, MD: Johns Hopkins University.

Epstein, J., & VanVoorhis, F. (2001). More than minutes: Teachers' roles in designing homework. *Educational Psychologist, 36*(3), 181-193.

Evans, C., Jordan, A., & Horner, J. (2011). Only 2 hours? A qualitative study of the challenges parents perceive in restricting child television time. *Journal of Family Issues, 32*(9), 1223-1244.

Farrell, A. D., Henry, D. B., Mays, S. A., & Schoeny, M. E. (2011). Parents as moderators of the impact of school norms and peer influences on aggression in middle school students. *Child Development, 82*(1), 146-161.

Ferguson, C. (2008). "The School-Family Connection: Looking at the Larger Picture" Austin, TX: National Center for Family and Community Connections with Schools at Southwest Educational Development Laboratory. Retrieved from http://www.sedl.org/connections/resources/sfclitrev.pdf

Finders, M., & Lewis, C. (1994). Why some parents don't come to school. *Educational Leadership, 51*(8), 50-54.

Goodman, A. (2008). Student-led, teacher-supported conferences: Improving communication across an urban school district. *Middle School Journal, 39*(3), 48-54.

Heredia, R. C., & Hiatt-Michael, D. B. (2009, April). *Perspectives of Latino parents: Empowered voices*. Paper presented at the Annual Meeting of the American Educational Research Association, San Diego, CA.

Herrold, K., & O'Donnell, K. (2008). *Parent and family involvement in education, 2006-07 school year, from the National Household Education Surveys Program of 2007 (NCES 2008-050)*. Washington, DC: National Center for Education Statistics, Institute of Education Sciences, U.S. Department of Education. Retrieved from http://nces.ed.gov/pubs2008/2008050.pdf

Hiatt-Michael, D. (2004). Preparing teachers for parental involvement: Current practices and possibilities across the nation. *Thresholds in Education, 30*(2), 2-12.

Hill, N., Castellino, D., Lansford, J., Nowlin, P., Dodge, K., & Bates, J. (2004). Parent academic involvement as related to school behavior, achievement, and aspirations: Demographic variation across adolescence. *Child Development, 75*, 1491-1509.

Hill, N., Tyson, D., & Bromell, L. (2009). Developmentally appropriate strategies across ethnicity and socioeconomic status: Parental involvement during middle school. In N. Hill & R. Chao (Eds.), *Families schools and the adolescent: Connecting research, policy, and practice* (pp. 53-72). New York, NY: Teachers College Press.

Hill, N. E., & Tyson, D. F. (2009). Parental involvement in middle school: A meta-analytic assessment of the strategies that promote achievement. *Developmental Psychology, 45*(3), 740-763.

Hoover-Dempsey, K. V., Ice, C. L., & Whitaker, M. W. (2009). "We're way past reading together": Why and how parental involvement in adolescence makes sense. In N. E. Hill & R. K. Chao (Eds.), Families, schools, and the adolescent: Connecting families, schools, and the adolescent (pp. 19-36). New York, NY: Teachers College Press.

Jarrett, R. L. (1999). Successful parenting in high-risk neighborhoods. *The Future of Children, 9*(2), 45-50.

Kackar, H. Z, Shumow, L. Schmidt, J. A., & Grzetich, J. (2011). Age and gender differences in adolescents' homework experiences, *Journal of Applied Developmental Psychology, 32*(2), 70-77.

Kaiser Family Foundation. (2010). *Generation M2: Media in the lives of 8-18 year olds*. Retrieved from http://www.kff.org/entmedia/

Lareau, A. (2000). *Home advantage* (2nd ed.). Lanham, MD: Rowan & Littlefield.

Lareau, A. (2003). *Unequal childhoods: Class, race, and family life*. Berkeley, CA: University of California Press.

Loeber, R., & Stouthamer-Loeber, M. (1998). Development of juvenile aggression and violence: Some common misconceptions and controversies. *American Psychologist, 53*, 242-259.

Luthar S., & Sexton, C. (2004). The high price of affluence. *Advances in Child Development and Behavior, 32*, 125-162.

McNeal, R. (1999). Parental involvement as social capital: Differential effectiveness on science achievement, truancy, and dropping out. *Social Forces, 78*(1), 117-144.

Mo, Y., & Singh, K. (2008). Parents' relationships and involvement: Effects on students' school engagement and performance. *Research in Middle Level Education Online, 31*(10), 1-11

Moll, L., Amanti, C., & Neff, D. (1992). Funds of knowledge for teaching: Using a qualitative approach to connect homes and classroom. *Theory into Practice, 31*(1), 132-141.

Morgan, A. (2008). *Family and parent involvement components in K-12 teacher education: A study of how universities, colleges, schools, and departments of education in a Southeastern state prepare future teachers for work with families and parents* (Unpublished doctoral dissertation). Fielding University, Santa Barbara, CA. (UMI Number: 3350576)

Mounts, N. S. (2001). Young adolescents' perceptions of parental management of peer relationships. *Journal of Early Adolescence, 21*, 92-122.

Mounts, N. S. (2004). Adolescents' perceptions of parental management of peer relationships in an ethnically diverse sample. *Journal of Adolescent Research, 19*, 446-467.

Mounts, N. S. (2011). Parental management of peers and early adolescents' social skills. *Journal of Youth and Adolescence, 40*, 416-427.

Murphy, J. (2009). Survey study of the relationship between parents' and teachers' perception of what constitutes effective school-to-home communications (Doctoral dissertation). Available from Proquest (ATT 3344457).

Northern Illinois University (n.d.) Collaborative for Early Adolescence website, http://www.niu.edu/cea/

Osgood, D. W., Anderson, A., & Shaffer, J. (2005). Unstructured leisure in the after-school hours. In J. Mahoney, R. Larson, & J. Eccles (Eds.), *Organized activities as contexts of development: Extracurricular activities, after-school and community programs* (pp. 45- 64). Mahwah, NJ: Erlbaum.

Patall, E., Cooper, H., & Robinson, J. (2008). Parent involvement in homework: A research synthesis. *Review of Educational Research, 78*(4), 1039-1101.

Patel, N., & Stevens, S. (2010). Parent-teacher-student discrepancies in academic ability beliefs: Influences on parent involvement. *The School Community Journal, 20*(2), 115-136.

Pomerantz, E. Moorman, E., & Litwack, S. (2007). The how, whom, and why of parents' involvement in children's academic lives: More is not always better. *Review of Educational Research, 77*(3), 373-410.

Ream, R. K., & Palardy, G. J. (2008, June). Re-examining social class differences in the availability and the educational utility of parental social capital. *American Educational Research Journal, 45*(2), 238-273.

Rogers, R., & Wright, V. (2008). You've got mail: Using technology to communicate with parents. *Electronic Journal for the Integration of Technology in Education, 7*, 36-58.

Rogoff, B. (1990). *Apprenticeship in thinking: Cognitive development in social context.* New York, NY: Oxford University Press.

Shulkind, S. (2008). New conversations: Student-led conferences. *Principal Leadership, 9*(1), 54-58.

Shumow, L., & Lomax, R. (2002). Parental efficacy: Predictor of parenting behavior and adolescent outcomes. *Parenting: Science and Practice, 2,* 127-150.

Shumow, L., & Miller, J. (2001). Father's and mother's school involvement during early adolescence. *The Journal of Early Adolescence, 21,* 69-92.

Shumow, L., Schmidt, J., & Kackar, H. (2008). Adolescents' experience doing homework: Associations among context, quality of experience, and social-emotional outcomes. *School Community Journal, 18*(2), 9-27.

Shumow, L, Smith, M. C., & Smith, T. (2009). Academic and behavioral characteristics of young adolescents in self care: Moderating effects of family and community characteristics. *Journal of Early Adolescence, 29,* 233-257.

Steinberg, L. (1987). Impact of puberty on family relations: Effects of pubertal status and pubertal timing. *Developmental Psychology, 23*(3), 451-460.

Steinberg, L. (1989). Pubertal maturation and parent-adolescent distance: An evolutionary perspective. In G. Adams, R. Montemayor, & T. Gullotta (Eds.), *Biology of adolescent behavior and development, advances in adolescent development: An annual book series* (Vol. 1, pp. 71-97). Thousand Oaks, CA: SAGE.

Steinberg, L., & Silk, J. (2003). Parenting adolescents. In M. Bornstein (Ed.), *Children and parenting: Vol. 1: Handbook on parenting* (pp. 103-134) Mahwah NJ: Erlbaum. [Electronic Version]

Taylor, L., Clayton, J., & Rowley, S. (2004). Academic socialization: Understanding parental influences on children's school-related development in the early years. *Review of General Psychology, 8*(3), 163-178.

Tsikalas, K. E., Lee, J., & Newkirk, C. (2007). *Home computing, student engagement, and academic achievement of low-income adolescents.* Retrieved from http://www.givewell.net/files/Cause4/Computers%20for%20Youth/EIN%202013-3935309%20Cause%204%20CFY%20Test%20Score%20Study%20Attachment%201.pdf

Tuinstra, C., & Hiatt-Michael, D. (2004). Student-led parent conferences in middle schools. *School Community Journal, 14,* 59-80.

U.S. Department of Education. (1994). *Strong families, strong schools: Building community partnerships for learning.* Washington, DC: Author.

U.S. Department of Education, National Center for Education Statistics. (2009). *Characteristics of Public, Private, and Bureau of Indian Education Elementary and Secondary Teachers in the United States: Results from the 2007-08 Schools and Staffing Survey* (NCES 2009-324). Retrieved from http://nces.ed.gov/fastfacts/display.asp?id=55

Vaden-Kiernan, N., & Chandler, K. (1996). *Parents' reports of school practices to involve families.* Statistics in Brief. Washington, DC: National Center for Educational Statistics.

Van Voorhis, F. L. (2011). Costs and benefits of family involvement in homework. *Journal of Advanced Academics, 22*(2), 220-249.

Vernberg, E., Beery, S., Ewell, K., & Abwender, D. (1993). Parents' use of friendship facilitation strategies and the formation of friendships in early adolescence: A prospective study. *Journal of Family Psychology, 3,* 356-369.

Weiss, H., & Lopez, E. (2011). Making data matter in family engagement. In S. Redding, M. Murphy, & P. Sheley (Eds.), *Handbook on family and community engagement.* Lincoln IL: Academic Development Institute.

Wimberly, G. L., & Noeth, R. J. (2004). *Schools involving parents in early postsecondary planning* (ACT Policy Report). Retrieved from http://www.act.org/research/policymakers/pdf/involve_parents.pdf

Wimberly, G. L., & Noeth, R. J. (2005). *College readiness begins in middle school.* (ACT Policy Report). Retrieved from http://www.act.org/research/policymakers/pdf/CollegeReadiness.pdf

Zarrett, N. R., & Eccles, J. (2009). The role of family and community in extracurricular activity participation: A developmental approach to promoting youth participation in positive activities during the high school years. In L. Shumow (Ed.), *Promising practices for family and community involvement during high school.* Charlotte, NC: Information Age.

CHAPTER 9

IT IS ALL ABOUT EXPECTATIONS

Moving From Negative
to Positive Expectations

Chris M. Cook and Shawn A. Faulkner

Establishing a clear self-concept and positive self-esteem are critical aspects in the developmental maturation of young adolescents. In many ways this formation of self is instrumental in providing a solid foundation for adolescents to both understand and accept the numerous developmental changes taking place during this stage of life. Lipka (1997) contends, "These dimensions of self-represent the central feature of the human personality which in the case of young adolescents unifies the physical, social, and cognitive characteristics into a sense of identity, adequacy, and affirmation" (p. 31). As a result, providing educational environments where young adolescents can nurture this sense of self in a safe and supportive atmosphere becomes a critical component to the purpose of middle level schooling. An essential part to providing this type of environment is the expectations that are placed on the various stakeholders in the school community—students, teachers, and parents. High, positive

Middle Grades Curriculum:
Voices and Visions of the Self-Enhancing School, pp. 141–155
Copyright © 2013 by Information Age Publishing
All rights of reproduction in any form reserved.

expectations for all stakeholders should provide the foundation for every middle level school.

Having high expectations for all is not a unique or new approach, but rather a common belief shared by key organizations concerned with educating young adolescents. It is through these high expectations that students will learn to become successful. The Association for Middle Level Education, formerly known as National Middle School Association (2010), acknowledges that young adolescents need an educational experience that is challenging, "ensuring that every student learns and every member of the learning community is held to high expectations" (p.13). *Turning Points 2000* reveals, "achieving such lofty goals for middle grades education means that educators must have high expectations for all students' success" (Jackson & Davis, 2000, p. 11). *Turning Points 2000* is an in-depth examination of the research on middle level schools sponsored by the Carnegie Corporation. In addition, The National Forum to Accelerate Middle-Grades Reform (n.d.), an alliance of key organizations and researchers focused on promoting the academic performance and healthy development of young adolescents, includes as one of its Schools-to-Watch criteria under social equity that "to the fullest extent possible, all students, including English learners, students with disabilities, gifted and honors students, participate in heterogeneous classes with high academic and behavioral expectations" ("Social Equity," par. 1). Finally, *Breaking Ranks in the Middle*, a comprehensive school reform model grounded in the middle level philosophy developed by The National Association of Secondary School Principals (2006), also emphasized the critical nature of increasing student achievement through having high expectations for all and holding students accountable for meeting these expectations.

Though widely believed to be a critical component of the middle level philosophy, not all school environments are engaging students with high, positive expectations. Jackson and Davis (2000) attest that, "currently, such high expectations for all students do not exist among all middle grades teachers, among the parents of all middle grade students, or among all middle grades students themselves" (p. 11). The question becomes how and why do individual expectations of students change, and it presents the challenge of how middle level schools hold students to high expectations and still maintain a positive environment where students are able to develop their sense of self. Unfortunately, middle level schools have been faced with this challenge since the establishment of the middle level philosophy in the 1960s and numerous misrepresentations and misunderstandings of what this means and how this is accomplished have surfaced. Dickinson (2001) acknowledges this challenge by stating,

One of the most devastating elements of arrested development is an image of middle schools that took hold in the 1960s. This image, like the lie of incremental stage implementation, has been difficult to eradicate. This is the inability to balance the middle school as a good place for young adolescents to learn and grow with challenging and involving academic work in those good places. If middle schools are to reinvent themselves, this is the one element that must be attacked head on. For in no way did the founders and early advocates of this movement ever speak, write, or intend that the school should be less than a positive place to be and a challenging and involving intellectual environment. (p. 8)

As a result, it is critical to define what high, positive expectations look like in the middle grades and how these expectations can be clearly expressed while fostering the self-concept and self-esteem of young adolescents.

Beane and Lipka's (1986) self-enhancing school model highlights 17 dimensions that foster a school environment where students can develop a strong sense of self by moving from a debilitating feature to an enhancing feature. This chapter explores the feature of moving from negative expectations to positive expectations. Specifically, it addresses the theory and research behind expectations, the dangers of negative expectations, the benefits of positive expectations, and provides suggestions for maintaining and creating school environments where high expectations for all is the norm.

THEORY BEHIND EXPECTATIONS

It is no secret that the expectations of teachers and parents for students play a key role in the success or failure of all students. For the past 80 years, researchers have focused on the concept of expectations and the influence they can have on student behavior and academic performance. Edward Tolman was one of the first to research the concept in the 1930s when he observed that organisms learn that certain behaviors lead to certain outcomes, and as such begin to develop specific expectations about those outcomes (as cited in Ormrod, 2004). Rosenthal and Jacobsen's (1968) *Pygmalion in the Classroom* generated more attention by highlighting the relationship between teacher expectations and their influence on student performance. The study highlighted the role of the self-fulfilling prophecy by supposedly identifying which students would excel academically during the year (though there was no specific reason for the identification) and evaluating how students responded to this identification. Rosenthal and Jacobsen concluded that the expectations did have an influence on how students achieved. While the conclusions might be debatable, these studies led the way for additional researchers to explore the role expectations play in the classroom and how teachers and students develop and respond to these expectations.

The theory and research focused around expectations primarily addresses expectancy-value theory and its connection to the self-fulfilling prophecy. Expectancy-value theory is the viewpoint that an individual's performance is shaped both by their belief for success and the perceived value they place on the task (Eccles, 1983; Wigfield & Eccles, 2000), whereas a "self-fulfilling prophecy occurs when teachers' expectations about what students will achieve actually lead to those outcomes" (Anderman & Anderman, 2010, p. 152). While the definitions are similar, the self-fulfilling prophecy becomes a more critical element in the classroom because of the direct role the teacher's expectations play in influencing the beliefs and outcomes of students. Developing an understanding of both terms and the influence they each have on the formation of expectations becomes a critical component of establishing positive expectations for all students.

Good and Brophy (2000) define teachers' expectations as the "inferences that teachers make about the future behavior or academic achievement of their students, based on what they know about these students now" (p. 74). Multiple models of teacher expectations address the effect expectations have on students (Braun, 1976; Brophy & Good, 1974; Cooper & Tom, 1984; Schunk, Pintrich, & Meece, 2008), each confirming that the expectations teachers have for their students can affect achievement and motivation. When expectations are positive and appropriate it can have a positive influence on the achievement and behavior of students. Likewise, when expectations are negative or inappropriate it can decrease achievement and negatively influence motivation and behavior.

Teachers typically convey their expectations to students through four primary means—socioemotional climate, verbal input, verbal output, and feedback (Cooper & Tom, 1984; Rosenthal, 1974; Schunk et al., 2008). The socioemotional climate focuses on the interaction of the teacher with students with behavior such as laughing, smiling, personal eye contact, and displaying supportive and caring gestures. Verbal input refers to the opportunities students have to communicate and interact with the material to make sense of things. Verbal output refers to the frequency of interaction with the teacher. For example, do students get to interact and talk with the teacher on a regular basis? Finally, feedback addresses the praise and criticism received and examples include the specific comments students receive on assignments they complete or on the comments they make in class. Students typically use these interactions to formalize their perceptions of how teachers feel about them and the personal expectations they perceive teachers to have for them.

In addition, numerous factors have been identified that can influence the individual expectations teachers have for students. Good and Brophy (2000) identified context, teachers' personal characteristics, and students' personal characteristics, while Anderman and Anderman (2010) identified gender, ethnicity, and socioeconomic status as having an influence. While the assumption would be that teacher expectations are reasonable and based on the observations and interactions teachers have with students (Schunk et al., 2008), some stereotypes and biases often influence teacher expectations. Beane and Lipka (1986) state,

> At one level, we might explain teacher bias by noting that teachers are human beings and thus subject to typical sources of bias. At another level, however, teachers are professionals entrusted with a large responsibility in the growth and development of young people. Teachers are a select group of human beings who should undertake the planning necessary to rise above ordinary biases. (p. 184)

For example, socioeconomic status is often linked to teacher expectations (Cooper, Baron, & Lowe, 1975), and minority students, particularly in urban areas, are often subject to reduced expectations (Diamond, Randolph, & Spillane, 2004). Each of these factors can influence, both positively and negatively, the outcomes teachers expect from students. Specifically, these expectations can impact whether students believe they can be successful in the classroom setting or not. For example, a student that lives in poverty and is surrounded by higher frequencies of crime is likely to deal with additional pressures and influences that distract from their academic affairs. This not only influences the student's own expectations for success, but can potentially shape what the teacher believes the student is capable of accomplishing. Also, the middle school years are typically where the decline in motivation and academic performance begin to take place for students and potentially influence their personal expectations (Eccles & Midgley, 1989; Eccles & Wigfield, 1997). As a result, the need for caring and stable classroom environments where students experience an important, challenging curriculum and are expected to be successful becomes even more paramount (Jackson & Davis, 2000; NMSA, 2010; Strahan, Smith, McElrath, & Toole, 2001).

Knowing that the specific expectations and beliefs about student potential often become a self-fulfilling prophecy in schools, it is important to make sure positive learning environments are a reality for every student. Brophy (1996) asserts that positive expectations are essential in fostering positive self-concepts and students for whom teachers have positive expectations are more likely to live up to those expectations. Building on Brophy's assertion appears like a logical and practical approach teachers would follow. However, embracing the theory behind the self-fulfilling prophecy and staffing classrooms with teachers who believe all students can be successful, as well as be effective in getting students to believe this themselves, seems to be the challenge. Beane and Lipka (1986) confirm this notion by stating, "research to date suggests that young people tend to succeed to the degree that they are expected to" (p. 184). Unfortunately, a negative self-fulfilling prophecy is an all too familiar component in many schools today (Oakes & Lipton, 2007). As a result, establishing classroom environments where students can experience authentic learning opportunities that are challenging and meaningful, within a structure that is supportive and encouraging, becomes an important approach for teachers to embrace.

The works of Rosenthal (1974), Good and Brophy (2000), and Schunk and colleagues (2008) highlight numerous strategies for establishing positive environments where high expectations are the norm (See Table 1.1). Rosenthal identifies four factors for enhancing student achievement by focusing on positive self-fulfilling prophecy effects on students. Good and Brophy add three. In addition, Schunk et al. document eight principles for enhancing motivation and potentially increasing efficacy toward the learning task. Using these principles as a framework, the ultimate goal is to provide learning opportunities that challenge students and then provide valuable feedback that helps them meet the learning outcomes to the highest expectation possible, all while believing each student is capable of being successful.

A CASE OF NEGATIVE EXPECTATIONS IN ACTION

To help illustrate negative expectations in action, consider the case of *Negative Expectations Middle School*:

> Negative Expectations Middle School (NEMS) has a distinct culture with several elements that are often visible to the guest that walks through the front doors of the school. At first, one might notice the physical features of the school. It doesn't matter if the school building is old or new, the expectations of the administration and staff are evident by the manner in which the buildings are maintained. Visitors might find buildings that are in disrepair—broken furniture, graffiti, general lack of cleanliness, trash around the school grounds and in the hallways. The maintenance of the buildings is not a priority because "the students don't care about the buildings" or "the kids will just tear things up."
>
> Visitors might also notice the low expectations staff have for student behavior. In NEMS, one will find lines painted on the floor. Students are taught to "walk the line" as a means of "teaching" students to move from place to place without causing a disruption. Of course, students practice

Table 1.1. Strategies for Incorporating Positive Expectations

Rosenthal (1974)	*Good and Brophy (2000)*	*Schunk and Colleagues (2008)*
• Develop positive relationships with students. • Provide meaningful feedback about performance to students. • Challenge students academically. • Allow opportunities for students to respond and ask questions.	• Provide students opportunities to achieve success. • Help students recognize the relationship between effort and outcome. • Provide special motivational support to discouraged students.	• Make it clear that students are capable of learning the material being taught. • Point out how the learning will be useful in students' lives. • Teach students learning strategies and show them how their performances have improved as a result of using the strategies. • Present content in ways students understand and tailor instructional presentations to individual differences in learning. • Have students work toward learning goals. • Ensure that feedback is credible. • Provide feedback on progress in learning and link rewards with progress. • Use models that build self-efficacy and enhance motivation.

these procedures and others daily throughout their middle school experience even though practicing these procedures takes away from learning time in the classroom. Students cannot be trusted to use the restroom facilities, and the cafeteria is monitored like a maximum-security prison. Staff members at NEMS believe that one can only control the students' behavior through raising their voices or yelling.

More importantly, negative expectations manifest themselves in the classrooms at NEMS. One might see some teachers focusing on low-level, factual questioning. Students participate in "drill and practice" activities rather than discovery and in-depth inquiry. In other classes, or even school wide, teachers rely on scripted programs that limit student choice and stifle teacher creativity. If not explicitly stated, teachers may believe students at NEMS are poor or from a particular racial or ethnic group; therefore, they lack the skills and ability to achieve at high levels. In order to provide structure, students are not encouraged to collaborate or work in groups to solve real-life, relevant issues because the teachers are convinced that "these students can't handle group work!"

Though the conditions at *Negative Expectation Middle School* are unfathomable, unfortunately, this is the experience of many middle school students.

EXPLORING THE IMPACT OF NEGATIVE EXPECTATIONS

Classroom environments, like those found at NEMS, where negative expectations are common can quickly lead to a toxic atmosphere where students feel success is not an option. Particularly in the middle grades, when significant changes in cognitive, social, and emotional development are taking place, students need an atmosphere that offers a nurturing environment and fosters positive development, especially when students can identify when teachers have reduced expectations for them. Good and Brophy (2000) assert, "Students are aware of differences in teachers' patterns of interaction with different students in the class ... they see their teachers as projecting higher achievement expectations and offering more opportunity and choice to high achievers" (p. 88). In addition, Anderman and Midgley (1997) state, "Students who believe that their poor performance is due to factors out of their control (perceived animosity of teachers) are unlikely to see any reason to hope for an improvement" (p. 42). While most teachers want their students to be successful and most probably believe their students can be successful, that belief is not shared by all teachers.

At first impulse, it seems difficult to grasp the concept that 21st Century classrooms might consist of teachers who have reduced expectations for students. However, as Jackson and Davis (2000) acknowledge, "The hard fact is that many educators believe some groups of students are less able to achieve academically than others because they *see* these groups of students achieving less than others on a daily basis" (p. 13). It is difficult to remove the deficiencies that students bring with them when they begin formal schooling. This is also supported by Jackson and Davis when they add, "Enormous differences in the family and social circumstances of America's young adolescents substantially influence their readiness to master rigorous academic content" (p. 13). Unfortunately, these economic and social differences can lead to lower expectations for students, increase the sense of hopelessness students may feel, and change the manner in which teachers interact with students.

Specifically, Ormrod (2004) indicates that teachers with low expectations tend to provide fewer opportunities for students to speak in class, minimize class assignments and reduce the difficulty of them, provide minimal feedback to improve performance, and seldom recognize when students perform well. Furthermore, Brophy (1998) and Good and Brophy (2000) identified a list of teacher behaviors that highlight numerous discrepancies in how high and low achievers are treated in the classroom. Examples from their list identified that low performing students are often given less wait time to answer questions, placed in seats farthest away from the teacher, are criticized more frequently for failure, receive less praise (or superficial praise) for their performance, experience a low-level repetitive curriculum emphasizing drill and practice, are offered minimal or brief feedback on work, and receive less eye contact from the teacher. Finally, Oakes and Lipton (2007) highlight that students in lower ability classes with reduced academic expectations typically experience a curriculum that addresses low-level facts, experience more worksheets and seatwork, receive few enrichment opportunities, and typically encounter a more hostile and isolating classroom atmosphere. In addition, teachers in these classrooms generally spend more time emphasizing classroom rules and therefore spend more time dealing with discipline issues. Furthermore, these classes are typically taught by the most inexperienced teachers with limited support.

Naturally, regardless of the intent of the teacher, students are able to identify the difference in treatment and become more aware of the variation that exists among students. In fact, as early as 6 years of age, students are able to identify the differential treatment that can take place in the classroom, as well as the difference of ability that exists among students (Anderman & Anderman, 2010). When students begin to learn that teacher expectations are often attached to these abilities, it is easier to understand why students might become disinterested or unmotivated toward exceeding these expectations.

A CASE OF POSITIVE EXPECTATIONS IN ACTION

Positive expectations in action are evident in the following case of *Positive Expectation Middle School*:

> Positive Expectations Middle School greets all visitors who enter the building with a large banner displaying their motto, "Success for All." It is this belief that drives all decisions in the school and provides the foundation administrators use when hiring all faculty and staff, whether it is a cafeteria monitor, custodian, or an Algebra teacher. As visitors move throughout the building, it is clearly evident the building is clean and well-maintained. The entire school community assumes responsibility for maintaining the facilities. Students, teachers, and parents participate in different events throughout the year to touch-up paint, enhance the landscaping, and clean-up litter. The bathrooms are cleaned multiple times each day and students take

pride in their building. Student-created models and projects fill display cases and student artwork hangs on the walls.

The classroom environment at Positive Expectations Middle School emphasizes mutual respect between both students and teachers as its primary foundation. The entire classroom community is expected to represent themselves with pride and behavior management issues are handled quickly and tactfully. Instructionally, students are engaged in meaningful and relevant learning activities. Students consistently engage in classroom discussions and are provided regular opportunities to collaborate with their peers to solve real-life problems and construct knowledge. Teachers meet regularly with one another to discuss individual student progress and develop a plan of action for students who are experiencing academic challenges. Every aspect of the school connects to the overall goal of success for all students.

HIGHLIGHTING POSITIVE EXPECTATIONS IN THE CLASSROOM

Establishing classroom environments where each student is expected to excel academically and behaviorally is a key component to providing developmentally responsive educational experiences for students. Students who attend schools where all students are expected to be successful typically achieve more academically than at schools whose expectations vary (Eggen & Kauchak, 2004). In addition, Oakes and Lipton (2007) document the learning differences for students who are held to high expectations. They indicate that students experience a curriculum that emphasizes inquiry and problem solving, emphasizes development as an autonomous thinker, receives more active and interactive learning activities, utilizes more technology as learning tools, benefits from extra enrichment experiences, and encounters a more positive and friendly classroom environment.

In an effort to assist teachers in establishing these positive classroom environments, Schunk and colleagues (2008) identify five strategies for teachers to help maintain positive expectations in the classroom: 1) Enforce rules fairly and consistently, 2) Assume that all students can learn and convey that expectation to the them, 3) Do not form differential student expectations based on qualities (e.g., gender, ethnicity, parents' background) unrelated to performance, 4) Do not accept excuses for poor performance, and 5) Realize that upper limits of student ability are unknown and not relevant to school learning (pp. 322-323). Anderman and Anderman (2010) also add to be aware of personal expectations for students as well as potential biases, do not learn too much information about students before meeting them, and engage in conversation with colleagues to identify additional strategies for motivating students and maintaining high expectations for them.

PRINCIPLES FOR MOVING TO POSITIVE EXPECTATIONS

1. *All students are capable of performing at high levels is a principle belief among all stakeholders.*

All schools want their students to be successful and excel academically. It seems far-fetched to think schools would want anything else for their students, and in fact, anything else is just not good enough to ensure students receive a quality education. There is no excuse or explanation that could justify anything but quality school experiences. Furthermore, this belief should be reflected in all policies and practices that the school employs and should be an instrumental factor when making all school decisions and hiring new teachers. In addition, teachers in the school must value working with students and should embrace the middle level philosophy. Reflection and formal evaluation might be necessary, at both the school and individual classroom level, to ensure this principle is embedded in all policies and mixed messages are not being communicated. For example, do the school's discipline and behavior policies reflect this belief or is it established under the premise that students will misbehave? It is difficult to express high expectations for all students, but then use behavior management plans that provide no student input or emphasize the need to practice procedures unnecessarily throughout the year. If a school truly has high expectations for all, then students would be taught the procedures from day one and then be expected to follow them. Practicing procedures throughout the year sends a message that students are not capable of following the rules.

2. *Beliefs about expectations must be more than a mission statement—all stakeholders need to put this belief in to action.*

Having high expectations for all students and believing students can then meet those expectations must be the core belief used when making all decisions. All stakeholders in the school community—from the administration, faculty, staff, parents, and students—must reflect this belief in their actions. Furthermore, all school personnel must possess the appropriate dispositions and professional behaviors to work with all students and help them achieve success. Examples of these dispositions and behaviors might focus on the need for teachers to believe that all students can learn, understand how to collaborate to meet the needs of diverse learners, and consistently reflect on personal growth as a professional.

3. *Don't change individual expectations of students; change the manner in which students meet the expectations.*

In an effort to accommodate the individual needs of students and adapt to the different life experiences and challenges students face, sometimes teachers change their expectations of students. While this might reflect a caring and compassionate approach on the teacher's part, it does not reflect a "high expectations for all" mindset. Naturally, the life experiences of students vary greatly, and not all students have the same opportunities. As these experiences surface and begin to interfere with student progress, teachers must explore ways to assist students in meeting their academic demands, such as hosting after or before school tutoring sessions or reducing the quantity of homework. It is important to be clear that this does not mean reducing expectations or decreasing the number of skills or content students need to know. It simply means making adjustments to enhance the likelihood that these students will continue to progress becoming productive citizens who will make positive contributions to society. As a result, working to instill a strong sense of self in students, while providing opportunities for students to face challenges head-on and learn to persevere must become an additional element to the school experience.

In part, this mindset has probably led to some of the decreased expectations for students, as some teachers might believe having students meet reduced expectations could lead to a greater sense of self. However, as the research indicates, students perceive this approach as a lack of faith in their abilities, and it often leads to diminished effort from students. Therefore, it is critical for all administrators, teachers, and parents to maintain high levels of positive expectations for all students.

4. *All stakeholders must have a thorough knowledge of the age-group.*

"Young people undergo more rapid and profound personal changes between the ages of 10 and 15 than at any other time in their lives" (NMSA, 2010, p. 5). As a result, ensuring that all teachers understand, support, and deliver a developmentally responsive educational experience is instrumental in creating an atmosphere where positive expectations flourish. In order to accomplish this, all stakeholders must have a thorough understanding of the developmental needs (cognitive, emotional, moral, physical, and social) of young adolescents, how to respond to these needs, and what this would look like instructionally. Ideally, this can be addressed by hiring teachers who are specifically trained to work with this age group, understand and employ instructional practices that are developmentally responsive, and then requiring teachers who lack this specific information to engage in professional development.

5. *Schools and teachers must consistently reflect on the experiences they provide students and how they interact with students.*

Does the school truly embrace a philosophy that expects all students to be successful? Does the school provide valuable learning opportunities for all students? Are the actions and beliefs of teachers indicative of positive expectations? Are the expectations conveyed sending mixed messages to students? These are just some of the questions schools and teachers should be reflecting on to ensure all students are held to positive expectations. For example, many schools indicate a "positive expectations for all" mantra, but then employ discipline policies and classroom systems that consistently undermine this theme.

FINAL THOUGHTS

At first thought, it seems the concept of positive expectations for all is a relatively simple and common component all schools should embrace. However, after further reflection and analysis of the literature, combined with the current pressures and emphasis schools place on standards and high-stakes testing, it is not too hard to imagine school environments with negative expectations. Far too often in schools, it seems the emphasis is not on the personal development of the child. Regardless of whether it is in the best interest of the children and their self-esteem/self-worth, decisions are made on a regular basis that do not consider the developmental needs of students, but rather focus on simple solutions and quick fixes. Given what is known about the role of expectations and its influence on students' perceptions, it certainly raises the question as to whether this approach does more harm than good for students. In the long run, is the quick-fix worth the impact it will have on the students' self-worth? Are these decisions made because it is truly what is best for the child? Given these questions, it is essential for school leaders to reflect on whether the approach they are taking is enhancing the self-concept of each child and providing a school environment where all students encounter positive expectations. If not, it is essential to change. It is all about the students. It is all about expectations.

REFERENCES

Anderman, E., & Anderman, L. (2010). *Classroom motivation*. Upper Saddle River, NJ: Pearson.

Anderman, L., & Midgley, C. (1997). Motivation and middle school students. In J. Irvin (Ed.), *What current research says to the middle level practitioner* (pp. 41-48). Columbus, OH: National Middle School Association.

Beane, J. A., & Lipka, R. P. (1986). *Self-concept, self-esteem, and the curriculum*. New York, NY: Teachers College Press.

Braun, C. (1976). Teacher expectation: Sociopsychological dynamics. *Review of Educational Research, 46*, 185-213.

Brophy, J. (1996). *Teaching problem students*. New York, NY: Guilford.

Brophy, J. (1998). *Motivating students to learn*. Boston, MA: McGraw-Hill.

Brophy, J., & Good, T. (1974). *Teacher-student relationships: Causes and consequences*. New York, NY: Holt, Rinehart, & Winston.

Cooper, H., Baron, R., & Lowe, C. (1975). The importance of race and social class information on the formation of expectancies about academic performance. *Journal of Educational Psychology, 67*, 312-319.

Cooper, H., & Tom, D. (1984). Teacher expectation research: A review with implications for classroom instruction. *Elementary School Journal, 85*, 77-89.

Diamond, J., Randolph, A., & Spillane, J. (2004). Teachers' expectations and sense of responsibility for student learning: The importance of race, class, and organizational habitus. *Anthropology and Education Quarterly, 35*(1), 75-98.

Dickinson, T. (Ed.). (2001). Reinventing the middle school: A proposal to counter arrested development. In *Reinventing the middle school* (pp. 3-20). New York, NY: Routledge Farmer.

Eccles, J. (1983). Expectancies, values and academic behaviors. In J. T. Spence (Ed.), *Achievement and achievement motivation* (pp. 75-146). San Francisco, CA: W. H. Freeman.

Eccles, J., & Midgley, C. (1989). Stage/environment fit: Developmentally appropriate classrooms for early adolescents. In R. E. Ames & C. Ames (Eds.), *Research on motivation in education* (Vol. 3, pp. 139-186). New York, NY: Academic.

Eccles, J., & Wigfield, A. (1997). Young adolescent development. In J. Irvin (Ed.), *What current research says to the middle level practitioner* (pp. 15-29). Columbus, OH: National Middle School Association.

Eggen, P., & Kauchak, D. (2004). *Educational psychology: Windows on classrooms*. Upper Saddle River, NJ: Pearson Merrill Prentice Hall.

Good, T., & Brophy, J. (2000). *Looking in classrooms*. New York, NY: Longman

Jackson, A. W., & Davis, G. A. (2000). *Turning points 2000: Educating adolescents in the 21st century*. New York, NY: Teachers College Press.

Lipka, R. P. (1997). Enhancing self-concept/self-esteem in young adolescents. In J. Irvin (Ed.), *What current research says to the middle level practitioner* (pp. 31-39). Columbus, OH: National Middle School Association.

National Association of Secondary School Principals. (2006). *Breaking ranks in the middle: Strategies for leading middle level reform*. Reston, VA: Author.

National Forum to Accelerate Middle-Grades Reform. (n.d.). *Schools to Watch Criteria*. Retrieved from http://www.middlegradesforum.org/index.php /school-watch

National Middle School Association. (2010). *This we believe: Keys to educating young adolescents*. Westerville, OH: Author.

Oakes, J., & Lipton, M. (2007). *Teaching to change the world*. Boston, MA: McGraw Hill.

Ormrod, J. (2004). *Human learning*. Upper Saddle River, NJ: Pearson Merrill Prentice Hall.

Rosenthal, R. (1974). *On the social psychology of the self-fulfilling prophecy: Further evidence for Pygmalion effects and their mediating mechanisms.* New York, NY: MSS Modular Publications.

Rosenthal, R., & Jacobsen, L. (1968). *Pygmalion in the classroom.* New York, NY: Holt, Rinehart, and Winston.

Schunk, D., Pintrich, P., & Meece, J. (2008). *Motivation in education: Theory, research, and applications.* Upper Saddle River, NJ: Pearson Merrill Prentice Hall.

Strahan, D., Smith, T., McElrath, M., & Toole, C. (2001). Connecting caring and action: Teachers who create learning communities in their classrooms. In T. Dickinson (Ed.), *Reinventing the middle school* (pp. 96-116). New York, NY: Routledge Farmer.

Wigfield, A., & Eccles, J. (2000). Expectancy-value theory of achievement motivation. *Contemporary Educational Psychology, 25*(1), 68-81.

CHAPTER 10

FROM DEBILITATING TEACHER SELF-PERCEPTIONS TO ENHANCING TEACHER SELF-PERCEPTIONS

Sara Davis Powell

Have you ever been in a social setting where people introduce themselves by telling what they do for a living? Perhaps a bank teller, a construction manager, a nurse, and an accountant are in your circle. If you say you are a kindergarten teacher, the theme of the comments may be "They're so cute at that age." If you say you teach high school math, there may be a certain sense of admiration quickly followed by statements similar to: "I don't know what's wrong with kids today." If you say you teach seventh grade language arts, people have been known to back away, not wanting to "catch" whatever insanity has possessed you to dedicate your life to 13-year-olds they perceive as dysfunctional. And so it goes....

Unlike many other countries, in the United States the teaching profession is often acknowledged only as necessary for the perpetuation of formal education. After all, most adults in the United States completed K-12 education and probably attribute at least some of their development to

Middle Grades Curriculum:
Voices and Visions of the Self-Enhancing School, pp. 157–177
Copyright © 2013 by Information Age Publishing
All rights of reproduction in any form reserved.

their experiences in school. However, by virtue of having been involved in formal education for much of their lives, many consider themselves to be knowledgeable, if not expert, on how schools should function. Public education is just that … public, and open to critique and criticism. Teachers are often maligned, and even blamed, when test results are less than expected or when young adolescents drop out or commit crimes. Still, chances are that anyone you ask about school memories will have a story about the wonderful, unforgettable impact of a special teacher. In kinder moments, noneducators will often agree with, or even express, platitudes such as "Teachers touch the future," and "Teachers make all other professions possible." But ask about U.S. education in general and the tone will likely change to comments like, "Our drop-out rate is atrocious," or "Why are we in the bottom half on international test results?" As educators we know that the answers to these questions are quite nuanced. Even so, the negativity often surfaces and, if persistent, can't help but adversely affect teacher self-perception.

Media sources often contribute to, or cause, the dispersions cast in our direction. We aren't perfect; like any large enterprise there are employees (teachers) who don't fulfill their responsibilities or, even worse, do deliberate harm. When discovered, the teacher misdeeds are spread across television and computer screens and published widely in print media. Things seem to get all out of whack, with the bad apples truly "spoiling the bunch" of hard working, well-meaning, intelligent classroom teachers, at least in the eyes of the beholders. It's tiring and counterproductive.

It's not just the general public that may adversely affect teacher self-perception. Circumstances within a school or district or state may also have negative effects. Lack of support and resources can be damaging. Unproductive relationships or isolation may harm teacher self-perception, as does the inability to consistently bring about desired change in student learning, and the sense of being overwhelmed by our efforts to do so.

This chapter focuses on how to create and perpetuate ways to build rather than tear down, to heal rather than harm, to positively develop rather than allow to stagnate, teachers' confidence in their abilities to perform the tasks involved in teaching and learning. We examine how teacher self-perception links to real accomplishment and to self-efficacy, a term explored in depth. We contextualize and conceptually frame why positive views of self and competency matter in the classroom, along with how to support and promote teacher confidence based on real accomplishment, all with the goal of student learning and growth. We begin with theory and work our way into practice.

The premises of this chapter, as illustrated in Figure 10.1, include: teacher efficacy increases teacher self-efficacy; enhanced teacher self-effi-

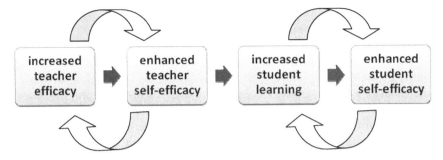

Figure 10.1.   Healthy relationship of increased efficacy and self-efficacy.

cacy increases teacher efficacy; teacher self-efficacy may be enhanced intrinsically; and teacher self-efficacy may be enhanced extrinsically.

HOW ARE SELF-PERCEPTION AND SELF-EFFICACY DEFINED?

The terms self-perception and self-efficacy both refer to a person's view of self and are often used interchangeably by writers and researchers. If not interchangeably, they are frequently used in ways that tend to muddy distinctions between the two. While inextricably linked, for our purposes it's important to define and differentiate these two concepts.

Pajares and Schunk (2002) tell us that examining our own levels of self-perception and self-efficacy require different questions. Self-perception involves questions like "Who am I?" and "How do I feel about ...?" Self-efficacy involves asking questions based on "can," such as, "Can I teach two-step equations?" and "Can I translate this passage from English to Spanish?" The answers people give to the self-efficacy questions reveal "whether they possess high or low confidence to accomplish the task or succeed at the activity in question; the answers to the self-concept questions ... reveal how positively or negatively they view themselves, as well as how they feel, in those areas" (Pajares & Schunk, p. 21).

Self-Perception

Self-perception is a general measure of a person's sense of competence and self-worth. Teacher self-perception is not left in the school parking lot; it is the essence of the person, the teacher. Self-perception is broader than self-efficacy. Personally, I have a positive sense of self, or self-perception, that I often attribute to my parents who never failed to compliment my achievements, even on the most mundane tasks. I distinctly recall washing dishes one Sunday afternoon when my dad remarked, "You really know how to make those dishes shine." On occasions when I was in a school program, Mom and Dad were always front and center, with riding-home-in-the-car comments about how lovely my voice was (although there were 68 fourth graders singing in unison) or how graceful my moves were in a dance recital (even though a tutu was not my best look). Their comments built my self-perception. They gave me a level of confidence that I suppose I knew on some level was not entirely deserved, but that nonetheless gave me the courage to sing in chorus in fifth grade and attend dance classes 1 more year.

A strong and positive self-perception is a good thing, as long as a healthy dose of it is based on real accomplishment, not just empty praise. Layer upon layer of positive feedback builds confidence. Did my early self-perception give me a grandiose view of my abilities? No, but it has served me well. Was it built on real accomplishment? Yes, at least in part and much of the time. But the most significant thing it did, and continues to do, for me is to give me a sort of "Yes, I can" attitude about life.

Self-Efficacy

Self-efficacy is also a sense based on personal appraisal. While self-perception is a general sense, self-efficacy is more specific and may be considered a form of self-perception. Self-perception may or may not be damaged by a decrease in self-efficacy, depending on the specific knowledge or skill involved. However, enhanced teacher self-efficacy adds positively to a teacher's self-perception. Henson (2001) tells us that because self-efficacy judgments refer to the ability to successfully perform a task, self-efficacy is situation-based. Self-efficacy is likely bolstered by self-perception, but doesn't necessarily always align with it. For instance, my self-perception tells me in general that I can teach, that I can successfully handle the tasks involved in the teaching profession. My teacher self-perception is bolstered by my three degrees related to teaching, decades in the classroom, and years as a teacher educator. This is an overall sense. When asked about specifics, I remain optimistic, but to various degrees related to particular situations. My self-efficacy to teach middle school math, or the degree to which I am confident in my ability, is very positive. But my self-efficacy to teach high school math isn't as positive. I understand that my ability to relate concepts at the middle level is greater than my ability to relate concepts at the high school level. Does this understanding harm my self-perception as a teacher? Not significantly. Here are a couple of examples showing that self-perception may remain high, even if self-efficacy in specific venues differs. I can't ice skate. I've tried, but my ankles will have nothing of it. Even with lessons, playing the piano never came naturally to me. While I may have the heart of a great pianist, my skill lags far behind. I have little to no positive self-efficacy regarding ice skating or piano playing, but my positive general self-perception is still intact. These are not activities in which I, nor my employer, expect proficiency. But think about this ... as a math teacher, if my self-efficacy is low regarding solving algebraic equations and that's part of my own and my employer's expectations, there's a problem. Student learning will suffer.

Self-efficacy is grounded in the theoretical framework of social cognitive theory developed in the 1970s by Albert Bandura, Professor Emeritus of Social Science in Psychology at Stanford University. Social cognitive theory analyzes development as impacted by both personal factors and environmental influences. According to Bandura and others who study concepts of social cognition, self-efficacy is the foundation of human motivation, well-being, and accomplishments. Bandura (2006) contends that, "Unless people believe they can produce desired effects by their actions, they have little incentive to act or to persevere in the face of difficulties. Whatever other factors serve as guides and motivators, they are rooted in the core belief that one has the power to effect changes by one's actions" (p. 3). As such, self-efficacy determines goals and behavior, as well as personal responses to, and influence over, conditions in the environment (Schunk & Meece, 2006). *Teacher* self-efficacy consists of beliefs in abilities "to plan, organize, and carry out activities that are required to attain given educational goals" (Skaalvik & Skaalvik, 2010, p. 1059).

Because teacher self-efficacy is a more immediate concept based on specific tasks than teacher self-perception, it is more easily bolstered, but only if actual efficacy is a reality. After decades in the last century when the premise was promulgated that building self-confidence, and the now often maligned term "self-esteem," could be achieved through empty praise and feel-good notions, we now recognize that lasting and effective development of self-efficacy can only come from a strong foundation of verifiable productivity and success (Kohn, 1994). Lemov (2010) tells us that achievement leads to believing in oneself, and not the other way around. "Because mastery experience is the most influential source of self-efficacy information, social cognitive theorists focus on the important task of raising competence *and* confidence in tandem through authentic mastery experiences. An artificial self-concept is naked against challenge and adversity; unwarranted confidence is cocky conceit" (Pajares & Schunk, 2001, Educational Implications section, para. 10).

While we see that self-perception and self-efficacy are similar, yet different, both impact teaching and learning. Figure 10.2 compares and con-

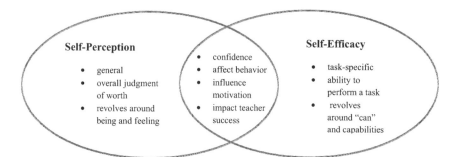

Figure 10.2.   Teacher self-perception and self-efficacy.

trasts some of the characteristics of teacher self-perception and teacher self-efficacy.

Before discussing the value of enhanced teacher self-efficacy, we should acknowledge some dilemmas in researching, or determining empirically, the value of the constructs of self-perception and self-efficacy. The study of constructs related to *self* has been in and out of favor over the years. As previously stated, the terms have been defined in various ways, depending on the theorist. Definitions of both have been based on rationale, lending to the historical problem of measurement (Henson, 2001). Even so, looking at teachers and the work they do with a *self*-lens is important. Most recently, Tschannen-Moran and Woolfolk Hoy (2001) have made advances in the field by both clearly conceptualizing self-efficacy and developing practical measurement instruments that show promise toward empirical study of teacher self-efficacy. Later we examine an instrument and implications for its use in building both efficacy and self-efficacy.

WHY DOES TEACHER SELF-EFFICACY MATTER?

When I was growing up in southeast Texas, my brother had a poster on his closet door that I have thought of frequently over the years. As a pre-teen I remember musing "Who does he think he is?" Looking at Peanuts character Linus saying "There is no burden quite as heavy as a great potential" drove home to me that not only was my older brother brilliant, and recognized as such by others, he also believed it himself. As a sixth grader I thought of it as snobby and stuck-up. As I consider it now, a half century later, I see Linus' statement as wisdom. Having a positive self-perception based on real accomplishment creates a level of responsibility that may, at times, seem to be a burden. You expect more of yourself and others join you in that expectation. When fulfillment of potential has positive results, the burden may seem more like opportunity. In other words, when we accomplish, and subsequently our self-efficacy is bolstered, more opportunities will come our way to repeat success. Fulfilled responsibility leads to opportunity, and opportunity realized leads to greater responsibility.

A strong sense of self-efficacy enhances well-being in many ways. According to Pajares and Schunk (2001), individuals with high levels of self-efficacy:

- approach difficult tasks as challenges to be mastered rather than as threats to be avoided;
- have greater interest and deep engrossment in activities;
- set challenging goals and maintain strong commitment to them;
- heighten and sustain their efforts in the face of failure;
- more quickly recover their confidence after failures or setbacks; and
- attribute failure to insufficient effort or deficient knowledge and skills which are acquirable (Self-Efficacy and Self-Concept—Defining Characteristics section, para. 4).

Imagine teachers who exhibit these characteristics.

Teacher efficacy and teacher self-efficacy are not the same. Teacher efficacy amounts to teacher effectiveness. Because teacher self-efficacy that holds the promise of increased effective practice must be based on the reality of efficacy, it's important to understand what efficacious teachers do. If we can increase efficacious practice, self-efficacy will likely result, leading to the desired positive characteristics in the previous list. The following characteristics are compiled from the research of people who have studied both effective practice and teacher self-efficacy. They tell us that efficacious teachers:

- think optimistically and in self-enhancing ways;
- create classroom climates with academic rigor and intellectual challenge;
- cultivate students' cognitive skills;
- nurture their students' often-fragile egos;
- rethink their teaching mission;
- reflect on the nature of their roles as educators of youth;
- persist with struggling students and criticize less after incorrect student answers;

- experiment with methods of instruction;
- seek improved teaching methods;
- expect and achieve better outcomes; and
- recognize their share of responsibility in nurturing the self-beliefs of their pupils (Henson, 2001; Lopez, 2012; Pajares & Schunk, 2001; Woolfolk, 2004).

When teachers consistently display these characteristics, they perpetuate the healthy relationship illustrated in Figure 10.2. Increased teacher efficacy leads to enhanced teacher self-efficacy. Both of these factors increase levels of student learning that foster enhanced student self-efficacy. According to Pajares and Schunk (2001), "efficacy beliefs [make] a powerful and independent contribution to the prediction of performance" (Self-Concept, Self-Efficacy, and Academic Achievement section, para. 10). In addition, high levels of student self-efficacy impact:

- the choices they make and their confidence in them;
- their engagement in tasks about which they feel confident and avoidance of those in which they do not;
- demonstration of greater control over course and activity selection
- greater effort expended on an activity;
- increased perseverance and persistence; and
- increased success on measures of academic progress (Henson, 2001; Pajares & Schunk, 2001; Woolfolk, 2004).

Considering teachers' levels of self-efficacy as determinants of teaching behavior is a very simple, yet powerful idea (Henson, 2001, p. 4). Goodwin (2011) analyzed three somewhat intangible characteristics of effective teachers, one of which is teacher self-efficacy. Goodwin writes, "A RAND study ... found links between student achievement and teachers' sense of efficacy—their belief in not just their students' ability to succeed, but also their own ability as teachers to help those students succeed" (p. 80). Teacher self-efficacy matters.

> Teachers' self-efficacy for teaching—their perceptions about their own capabilities to foster students' learning and engagement—has proved to be an important teacher characteristic often correlated with positive student and teacher outcomes ... teachers who have a high sense of efficacy and act on it—are more likely to have students who learn. So the question of how to support and not undermine teachers' sense of efficacy is critical. (Woolfolk, 2004, pp. 154, 157)

Given that the more positive the sense of efficacy, the more effort teachers will expend, and the more persistent they will be under difficult circumstances, building teacher self-efficacy is vital. When self-efficacy is enhanced, teacher self-perception is enhanced. Teacher confidence in the tasks of teaching, whether general in the form of self-perception or more task-specific in the form of self-efficacy, is a critical component of school success (Pajares & Miller, 1994).

HOW CAN TEACHER SELF-EFFICACY BE ENHANCED?

We return to the premises stated previously. Teacher efficacy increases teacher self-efficacy; enhanced teacher self-efficacy increases teacher efficacy; teacher self-efficacy may be enhanced intrinsically; and teacher self-efficacy may be enhanced extrinsically. Parker Palmer (1998) wrote, "good teaching cannot be reduced to technique; good teaching comes from the identity and integrity of the teacher" (p. 10). He continues by saying "identity is the moving intersection of the inner and outer forces ..." (p. 13). If we think of a teacher's self-perception and self-efficacy as linked to Palmer's statement about identity, both inner forces (intrinsic) and outer forces (extrinsic) may be sources of increased efficacy.

Increasing Teacher Efficacy

The obvious place to begin when considering how to increase teacher self-efficacy is with efficacy itself. Because self-efficacy is built on actual efficacy, if efficacy increases, so will teacher self-efficacy. Teacher efficacy beliefs, or self-efficacy, are related to instructional practices and to students' achievement and psychological well-being (Tschannen-Moran, Woolfolk Hoy, & Hoy, 1998). After years of research, Tschannen-Moran and Woolfolk (2001) developed an instrument to gauge teacher self-efficacy. The 24 items in the *Teachers' Sense of Efficacy Scale* are built on tasks that teachers consider central to good teaching. They are posed as questions, with response choices on a 0-9 scale. The measures are situation-specific to address the nature of self-efficacy and can be divided into three categories: student engagement, instructional strategies, and classroom management. Because the items correlate with teacher efficacy, it follows that if teachers are more successful accomplishing the tasks listed in Table 1, their self-efficacy will increase. Notice that these are *can* questions, aligning with Pajares and Schunk (2002). Honest teacher self-responses may lead to focused professional development opportunities.

Woolfolk (2004) has made *Teachers' Sense of Efficacy Scale* available for all who wish to use it, with no additional permission required (http://

www.coe.ohio-state.edu/ahoy/researchinstruments.htm#). This very useful instrument can guide teachers to a realization of individual efficacy strengths and needs, as well as an entire staff to collective areas of strengths and needs. Because the tasks in Table 10.1 are basics that every teacher should be conscious of and continually strive to improve, they transcend much of the programmatic professional development emphases.

Professional Development

Meaningful teacher professional development needs to be honest, based on what teachers want to learn, what they need to learn, and what

Table 10.1.   Teachers' Sense of Efficacy Scale Items

Student engagement:

- How much can you do to get through to the most difficult students?
- How much can you do to help your students think critically?
- How much can you do to motivate students who show low interest in school work?
- How much can you do to get students to believe they can do well in school work?
- How much can you do to help your students value learning?
- How much can you do to foster student creativity?
- How much can you do to improve the understanding of a student who is failing?
- How much can you assist families in helping their children do well in school?

Instructional strategies:

- How well can you respond to difficult questions from your students?
- How much can you gauge student comprehension of what you have taught?
- To what extent can you craft good questions for your students?
- How much can you do to adjust your lessons to the proper level for individual students?
- How much can you use a variety of assessment strategies?
- To what extent can you provide an alternative explanation or example when students are confused?
- How well can you implement alternative strategies in your classroom?
- How well can you provide appropriate challenges for very capable students?

Classroom management:

- How much can you do to control disruptive behavior in the classroom?
- To what extent can you make your expectations clear about student behavior?
- How well can you establish routines to keep activities running smoothly?
- How much can you do to get children to follow classroom rules?
- How much can you do to calm a student who is disruptive or noisy?
- How well can you establish a classroom management system with each group of students?
- How well can you keep a few problem students from ruining an entire lesson?
- How well can you respond to defiant students?

Source: Tschannen-Moran and Woolfolk Hoy (2001).

they feel is valuable (Heller, 2004). Makes sense, doesn't it? However, much of what is labeled professional development is far less than what Heller would deem as honest. Before looking at ways to create effective professional development opportunities, let's concede some problematic elements.

Problematic Elements of Professional Development. Teachers are familiar with problems regarding much of what is termed professional development, including relevance, delivery, and timing. After just a few years of experience, teachers have likely lived through several professional development movements that stem from reform efforts aimed at educators. You know what I mean...

> Early childhood is the most important focus because we need to concentrate on readiness skills, or at least until someone decides that reforming high schools is the key to America's future; maybe we need outcome-based education because results are what matter, or perhaps site-based management with stakeholder buy-in will do the trick. How about school choice, charter schools, and magnet schools with vouchers for the poorest children, or maybe vouchers for everyone so private/parochial schools become accessible options. Perhaps we need open schools with school improvement councils, or maybe year-round schools, featuring specialized afterschool schools; how about new math, whole language, cultural literacy, block scheduling, back-to-basics, and vocational arts. Currently we have standards intended to fit all, accountability demanded only of some, and No Child Left Behind that segregates, disaggregates, and aggravates. (Powell, 2010, pp. 135-136)

Douglas Reeves (2006) wisely notes that "Educators are drowning under the weight of initiative fatigue...." (p. 89). With every new initiative comes a slew of professional development topics and experts.

A recurring dilemma with the delivery and substance of professional development involves reliance on *experts* who have no investment past the Wednesday afternoon faculty meeting. When the presenter is gone and the handouts slip beneath tomorrow's lesson plans or are relegated to the recycle bin, the promised results are unrealized. There's no follow-up by the guest speaker and rarely follow-through by participants. Of course, this isn't always the case. There are experts not connected to a school system or school who present relevant topics and do so in ways that are at least palatable. They may raise our consciousness on issues or instruct us on strategies we never thought about. They may cause us to see with new eyes a problem or possibility.

Because traditional professional development practices are only occasionally effective, let's consider some reasons for their failure, along with some more promising practices.

Effective Professional Development. If teachers are not receptive to professional development efforts it could be because they are not convinced the content and skills will make a difference in their professional lives. There are at least three reasons for this. One is that school leaders may fail to make a viable case for the legitimacy of the content and skills. If teachers are not aware of current research or examples of increased student learning resulting from whatever emphasis is to be presented, they will not want to use their time and expend their effort to learn about and implement the focus of the professional development. It is incumbent upon principals and teacher leaders to believe in what's to be presented and make a strong case for the viability of it ... or cancel it. Just because there's a scheduled nonstudent day and funding that needs to be spent because, if not, it won't be justifiable in next year's budget, is not reason enough to pull some professional development session out of a hat, only to be an actual or perceived dead or dying rabbit. A second plausible reason for a lack of receptivity is actually a compliment to teachers. "Thoughtful teachers are not necessarily swayed by gimmicks and fads; they have basic beliefs about teaching and learning that guide their practice, and they can articulate the bases for decisions" (Powell, 2012, p. 230). Teachers who understand curriculum, instruction, assessment, and their own students recognize the "this, too, shall pass" kinds of gatherings. The third reason some professional development efforts hold no real promise is that they are not centered on viable, verifiable premises; they are perhaps rehashes of failed initiatives or faulty in their reasoning or message.

So how do we help teachers increase their efficacy in ways that minimize the chaff in traditional professional development? The answer to this question involves simple, common sense principles that show respect for teachers' intelligence, along with their ability to discern fad from results-oriented practice.

Part of increasing the effectiveness of professional development efforts lies in continually striving to solve the dilemmas posed by issues of relevance, delivery, and timing. For instance, those who organize professional development opportunities can show enough faith in the judgment and self-knowledge of teachers to ask for their guidance in the selection of topics that are relevant to their needs. Those same organizers can acknowledge that as teachers, we are our own best teachers. Read that again ... *we are our own best teachers.* I propose that if you get teachers around a table and give them time and encouragement, they will teach each other what works in their classrooms and, in turn, learn how to be better teachers, even as they enhance their sense of professionalism. The gamut of topics will likely range from attitudinal to practical, from individual-specific to grade-level or subject-matter centered. The old adage

"To teach is to learn twice" applies here. When we teach each other we better understand and hone our own knowledge and skills as we help others learn from our experiences. *Teachers teaching teachers* addresses the issues of relevance and delivery. Giving teachers choices as to when they will meet goes a long way toward eliminating timing dilemmas.

As Woolfolk (2004) contends, helping teachers reach their goal of reaching students is integral to teacher efficacy and teacher self-efficacy. Professional development, then, should be squarely centered on goals directly related to reaching students. We help teachers determine what they need using instruments such as the *Teachers' Sense of Efficacy Scale*. A potentially powerful use of the scale involves the jigsaw strategy. Teachers group according to which of the three categories (student engagement, instructional strategies, classroom management) they perceive to be their greatest strength. They meet and share their successes. They take notes on what works, they organize their experiences and plan ways to talk about and demonstrate their strengths. Then they can do one of two things. Either as a group they present their findings and respond to questions and additional ideas, or they regroup into threes, with one person represented from each category of items. Each then shares their notes in this more intimate setting.

Another possible use of the items in the *Teachers' Sense of Efficacy Scale* is to deal with the items one at a time. Ask teachers in groups of three to prepare to share strategies that address a particular item. This can be done by asking teachers to choose five of the items and then putting teachers together in groups of two or three depending on the size of the faculty, hopefully with teachers getting one of their first five choices. Then in a forum, perhaps for an hour following school one day every other week, teachers share maybe three items per meeting. Each meeting is fresh by virtue of different items and different facilitators. Teachers teaching teachers ... powerful professional development.

One popular form of professional development relies on teacher collaboration to make it work. The professional learning community (PLC) consists of teachers working together to accomplish goals. Richard Dufour and others proposed the formalization of PLCs in the late 1990s. Since then districts and schools across the country have adopted and adapted professional learning community tenants. The PLC format is a professional development initiative that has lasting power and is built on efficacy and self-efficacy enhancing components. According to DuFour, DuFour, and Eaker (2008),

> We define a professional learning community as educators committed to working collaboratively in ongoing processes of collective inquiry and action research to achieve better results for the students they serve. Professional

learning communities operate under the assumption that the key to improved learning for students is continuous job-embedded learning for educators. (p. 14)

The six characteristics of PLCs are:

1. shared mission, vision, goals—all focused on student learning;
2. a collaborative culture with a focus on learning;
3. collective inquiry into best practices and current reality;
4. action orientation: learning by doing;
5. a commitment to continuous learning; and
6. results orientation (pp. 15-17).

This sort of professional development focuses on relevance and teacher-with-teacher delivery. The issue of timing is addressed by many schools that promote PLCs in that time is provided during the school day for teachers to work collaboratively toward the goal of reaching students.

Roland Barth (2000) tells us that adults' learning in schools is basic to effective teaching and learning. When these adults commit to the "heady and hearty goal of promoting their own learning and that of their colleagues" they impact the learning of students (p. v). When teachers act on the principles of professional learning communities, formally or informally, they build both efficacy and teacher self-efficacy. Conversations centered on student learning; book clubs with teachers reading the same book and then discussing its relevance to learners and learning; teachers regularly presenting what works in their classrooms to other teachers ... all these simple, yet productive, means of teachers teaching teachers will positively impact teacher efficacy. The integral involvement of teachers in these and other ways of sharing expertise will build teacher confidence and self-efficacy.

Intrinsic Enhancement of Teacher Self-Perception and Self-Efficacy

Every book and class addressing classroom management probably includes a segment on the value of intrinsic, as opposed to extrinsic, motivation for learning and behavior, and rightly so. We probably all acknowledge the value of self-motivation for our actions. We can build our own self-efficacy in a number of ways, including teaching with our strengths and taking advantage of the do-over factor of teaching.

Teach With Strengths. "More than a job, teaching is a calling, and teaching with strengths helps educators fulfill the mission of that calling. Indeed, teaching with strengths makes teachers happier, more productive, likelier to stay in the field, and far more successful in the classroom – thus helping more students learn and grow" (Liesveld & Miller, 2005, p. 12). Traditional wisdom, in almost every circumstance, says that we look for and improve weak areas; after all, if we are strong in an area, we don't necessarily need to be stronger while other areas are weak. We're striving for balance, aren't we?

The research of Donald Clifton indicates that balance, with regard to teacher strengths, is not necessary for positive student results. "Decades of research have proven that talents are extremely powerful, and the influence of teaching with strengths on students has a dramatic long-term effect. The problem is that teachers haven't had the practical tools they need to use what the scientists have discovered about strengths" (Liesveld & Miller, 2005, p. 13).

Discovering, and then capitalizing on, teaching strengths is mostly an individual enterprise resulting in intrinsic sources of teacher self-efficacy. A strength is the sum of talent, knowledge, and skills. Talent is innate; what we do with the talent is up to us. A person with innate talent for teaching can enhance that talent by increasing knowledge and skill. To achieve sustained effectiveness, talent alone isn't enough, and neither is knowledge or skill.

A Strengths Finder instrument is available with the purchase of the book *Teach with Your Strengths* (Liesveld & Miller, 2005), with 34 determinable strengths and advice on how to capitalize on each. While this may be useful, it isn't necessary. Intuitive teachers are usually adept at recognizing their own strengths. Teachers know when they are in their "effective zones," when they excel in relating concepts and they sense student learning. Chances are these zones are indications of strengths. Building on strengths will lead to even more classroom effectiveness. I have recognized over the years that one of my general teaching strengths is storytelling to make a point. As a math teacher, my strength is recognizing error sources, and then explaining concepts and algorithms in a variety of ways. These are strengths that are effective and result in student learning, so I try to capitalize on them. When I do, and my efficacy increases, my teacher self-efficacy is enhanced as well. Take a few minutes to think about your own strengths. Has considering what you do best and then devising ways to get better at what you already do well ever occurred to you? This question applies to both teachers and administrators.

Understand the Do-Over Factor of Teaching. One of the most beneficial, and yet seldom recognized, aspects of teaching is the fact that most of us start over each August, at least in terms of the students we serve. We keep our talent, knowledge, and skill, along with another year of experiences from which to learn. Think about how exciting the do-over factor can be, but only if we vow to be conscious of the opportunities we have to continually develop and grow. We learn from experience and then have the privilege of applying what we learn to benefit the next group of students coming our way. The do-over factor can also apply on a daily basis in this human enterprise of teaching. What doesn't work one day can be altered and attempted again the next day, all with the intent of increasing student learning and growth.

The do-over factor is personal in nature. I've never been asked by an administrator to deeply reflect on my school year—what I did right and what I did wrong—only to clean up my classroom and turn in my keys. I haven't been asked to link my classroom procedures and strategies to my particular population of students. If I thought reflectively about an individual student and tracked progress or lack of it as it related to my professional responsibility, I did so on my own.

Teachers know what it feels like to regret actions and words that may have lacked careful consideration or resulted from instant reactions. We also know what it feels like to fail to act or plan and realize that opportunities were lost. We can mentally beat ourselves up for both commission and omission. That's natural, but generally unproductive. The do-over factor should encourage us and help build both our efficacy and self-efficacy. Referring to teachers honing their teaching knowledge and skills and then having the opportunity to use them, Steele (2009) says, "the benefits to us are just as great as those that our students accrue; growth keeps us fresh and enthusiastic" (p. 229).

Extrinsic Enhancement of Teacher Self-Perception and Self-Efficacy

Extrinsic enhancement of teacher self-perception and self-efficacy depends on others. Let's consider three sources of impact—principals, teachers, and the community—and just a few of the ways each may enhance or inhibit teacher self-perception and self-efficacy.

Principals. A principal is in a unique position to enhance or inhibit teacher self-efficacy. "The support that matters is not 'cheerleading' or close supervision but help in doing the work of teaching—help in reaching the teachers' goals of reaching the students" (Woolfolk, 2004, p. 163). There's certainly a place for principals to be *cheerleaders* of teachers and students, but without real accomplishment, this sort of encouragement won't have lasting effects on teacher self-efficacy. Let's consider some specific ways principals might enhance teacher self-efficacy.

Much has been written about the problem of teacher isolation and "loneliness that is so typical of the teaching profession" (Heller, 2004, p. 22). Collay (2011) uses the analogy of an egg carton. Teachers are in the same carton, but not touching or interacting, with each classroom a separate compartment. Teacher isolation is limiting and unhealthy. As opposed to isolation, teacher autonomy embraces freedom and independence rather than loneliness. "Autonomy involves a sense of ownership and self-determination.... Being autonomous creates self-confidence" (Powell, 2010, p. 55). Teachers' perception of autonomy in their work is shaped by the organization and the school principal is the leader of the organization in which teachers work (Collay, 2011). Encouraging teachers to make decisions about their instructional practices and the learning environments they maintain indicates trust and confidence in teacher intelligence and expertise. Autonomy builds self-efficacy to do what's best for students and, in turn, helps the teacher be more effective.

Principals have the power to create and maintain an environment that allows teachers to make the most of time with students and, in doing so, promote teacher professionalism. They can shield teachers and students from much of the interferences to teaching and learning that can creep into the school day by:

- minimizing class time interruptions;
- not encroaching on teacher planning time with administrative tasks and duties;
- making necessary resources available;
- supporting teachers' classroom management;
- modeling respect for everyone in the school; and
- asking questions and really listening to responses.

Perhaps one of the most meaningful comments a teacher can make about a principal goes something like this: "My principal supports me as a classroom teacher and makes it possible for me to do my best to reach and teach my students." In that response, we can see both enhanced teacher efficacy and teacher self-efficacy.

Teachers. The adage "We are our own best teachers" radiates a sense of camaraderie and mutual respect so valued by teachers. Roland Barth (2006) tells us, "One incontrovertible finding emerges from my career spent working in and around schools: The nature of relationships among the adults within a school has a greater influence on the character and quality of that school and on student accomplishment than anything else" (p. 9). He continues by defining the four basic relationships among teachers in a school: adversarial, parallel, congenial, and collegial. *Adversarial,* where teachers purposefully sabotage each other's success, is, of course, never desirable. *Parallel* is akin to Collay's (2011) egg carton analogy, with teachers merely coexisting on the same hall, each in a classroom with students, doors closed, never sharing, doing their own thing side-by-side. *Congenial* is the minimum standard for all teachers, friendly with those with whom we have both much and little in common, but still lacking an environment of professional interaction. Barth defines *collegial* relationships by giving us three signs of teacher collegiality:

- educators talking with one another about practice and sharing craft knowledge;
- educators observing one another while they are engaged in practice; and
- educators rooting for one another's success.

Collegiality is the gold standard for teacher relationships. Casey Stengal, beloved baseball manager, reportedly said it's easy to find good players, but what's difficult is getting them to play together. Our schools are full of good players, or competent teachers, but getting them to fulfill their collegial potential is the challenge (Powell, 2012). Imagine a school with collegial relationships among all teachers, supported by a principal who paves the way to exceptional teaching and learning!

Community. Perhaps more than anyone, teachers are the *face* of their schools. Both formally and informally they represent the schools' efforts to make K-12 education work for students and everyone in the community. When something good is publicized, teachers shine as heroes. When something less positive is revealed to the public, be it low test scores or less than professional behavior, teachers bear the brunt of the criticism. Aligning with a school can be exhilarating or demeaning. Some aspects are beyond our direct control, while others can be impacted by us. In the grocery store, at the movies, within community organizations, at places of worship … wherever we are, we represent our schools, our students, and our own professionalism. In this regard, we are our own best, or worst, public relations officers. When the community perceives teachers as energetic, caring, intelligent, and optimistic, teacher self-perception, and even teacher self-efficacy, are enhanced.

It's easy to criticize; it's sometimes difficult to keep challenges "in house" where the problems are, with stakeholders seeing the dilemmas through participant eyes. When we air our dirty laundry in public, those with whom we confide are not in a place to understand the nuances of what we say or grasp the complexity of dilemmas, and negativity spreads. Everyone is harmed, particularly those who are indeed the face of the organization … the teachers. The community's perception is their reality.

If it's negative, it harms teachers' self-perceptions. Let's take this seriously as teachers and help each other be thoughtful and professional ambassadors for our work, our students, their families, and our schools. We will reap the benefits of community respect.

BEYOND SELF-PERCEPTION AND SELF-EFFICACY

Bandura (1997) introduced the concept of *collective efficacy*, possible when "people pool their knowledge, skills, and resources, provide mutual support, form alliances, and work together to secure what they cannot accomplish on their own.... Collective efficacy takes self-efficacy to the social level" (p. 477). According to Bandura, shared beliefs in the collective strength and power of the group is necessary for collective efficacy, resulting in:

- enhanced motivational commitment to endeavors;
- strengthened resilience to adversity; and
- increased group accomplishments.

Teachers with positive self-perceptions and strong self-efficacy for the tasks required in their profession are primed for relationships that take full advantage of collective efficacy, or a kind of synergy that makes the whole more effective than the sum of the individual parts. But teacher self-efficacy is different from collective efficacy in that the former relies on individuals' perceptions of their own capabilities and the latter requires belief in the power of the group as a whole. Henson (2001) tells us that "Collective teacher efficacy is not the simple aggregate of individual perceptions of the self; instead, it is individual perceptions of the capabilities of the entire faculty in a school organization" (p. 10). Think about collective teacher efficacy as teacher beliefs about the "capability of a faculty to influence student achievement; it refers to the perceptions of teachers that the efforts of the faculty of a school will have a positive effect on student achievement" (Goddard, Hoy, & Woolfolk Hoy, 2000, p. 486). Imagine a grade level, a department, and a whole school where collective efficacy, and the self-efficacy/efficacy cycle, are manifested. Powerful, indeed.

CONCLUSION

Given the content of this chapter concerning defining and enhancing teacher self-perception and teacher self-efficacy, and the value of both to teaching and learning, the word *renewal* seems to sum it all up. When we are successful, our sense of confidence increases ... we experience renewal. Renewal, in turn, motivates and encourages us to succeed again. Consider John Lounsbury's (1988) analogy for renewal. "Perhaps what is needed for growth and improvement so earnestly sought on every hand is to report people, to give adequate encouragement to that inherent potential that does exist in all persons, to feed and free those hungry roots from the restrictive psychological pots that bind them" (p. 6). Let's repot ourselves and others as we grow as professional educators, all for the benefit of the students we serve.

REFERENCES

Bandura, A. (1997). *Self-efficacy: The exercise of control.* New York, NY: W. H. Freeman.

Bandura, A. (2006). Adolescent development from an agentic perspective. In F. Pajares & T. Urdan (Eds.), *Self-efficacy beliefs of adolescents* (pp. 1-43). Greenwich, CT: Information Age.

Barth, R. S. (2000). Foreword. In P. Wald & M. S. Castleberry (Eds.), *Educators as Learners* (pp. v-vi). Alexandria, VA: Association for Supervision and Curriculum Development.

Barth, R. S. (2006). Improving relationships within the schoolhouse. *Educational Leadership, 63*(6), 9-13.

Collay, M. (2011). *Everyday teacher leadership: Taking action where you are.* San Francisco, CA: Jossey-Bass.

DuFour, R., DuFour, R., & Eaker, R. (2008). *Revisiting professional learning communities at work: New insights for improving schools.* Bloomington, IN: Solution Tree.

Goddard, R. D., Hoy, W. K., & Woolfolk Hoy, A. (2000). Collective teacher efficacy: Its meaning, measure, and impact on student achievement. *American Educational Research Journal, 37*, 479-507.

Goodwin, B. (2011). Good teachers may not fit the mold. *Educational Leadership, 68*(4), 79-80.

Heller, D. A. (2004). *Teachers wanted: Attracting and retaining good teachers.* Alexandria, VA: Association for Supervision and Curriculum Development.

Henson, R. K. (2001). Proceedings from Educational Research Exchange, College Station, TX. Retrieved from http://des.emory.edu/mfp/EREkeynote.PDF

Kohn, A. (1994). The truth about self-esteem. *Phi Delta Kappan, 76*, 272-283.

Liesveld, R., & Miller, J. A. (2005). *Teach with your strengths.* New York, NY: Gallup Press.

Lemov, D. (2010). *Teach like a champion.* San Francisco, CA: Jossey-Bass.

Lopez, S. J. (2012). Schools could be the happiest places on Earth. *Phi Delta Kappan, 93*(4), 72-73.

Lounsbury, J. H. (1988). *Middle school education: As I see it.* Columbus, OH: National Middle School Association.

Pajares, F., & Miller, M. D. (1994). The role of self-efficacy and self-concept beliefs in mathematical problem-solving: A path analysis. *Journal of Educational Psychology, 86*, 193-203.

Pajares, F., & Schunk, D. H. (2001). Self-beliefs and school success: Self-efficacy, self-concept, and school achievement. In R. Riding & S. Rayner (Eds.), *Perception* (pp. 239-266). London, England: Ablex. Retrieved from http://des.emory.edu/mfp/PajaresSchunk2001.html

Pajares, F., & Schunk, D. H. (2002). Self and self-belief in psychology and education: An historical perspective. In J. Aronson (Ed.), *Improving academic achievement* (pp. 1-31). New York, NY: Academic Press.

Palmer, P. J. (1998). *The courage to teach: Exploring the inner landscape of a teacher's life*. San Francisco, CA: Jossey-Bass.

Powell, S. D. (2010). *Wayside teaching: Connecting with students to support learning*. Thousand Oaks, CA: Corwin Press.

Powell, S. D. (2012). *Your introduction to education: Explorations in teaching*. Upper Saddle River, NJ: Pearson.

Reeves, D. B. (2006). Pull the weeds before you plant the flowers. *Educational Leadership, 64*(1), 89-90.

Schunk, D. H., & Meece, J. L. (2006). Self-efficacy development in adolescence. In F. Pajares & T. Urdan (Eds.), *Self-efficacy beliefs of adolescents* (pp. 71-96). Greenwich, CT: Information Age.

Skaalvik, E. M., & Skaalvik, S. (2010). Teacher self-efficacy and teacher burnout: A study of relations. *Teaching and Teacher Education, 26*, 1059-1069.

Steele, C. F. (2009). *The inspired teacher*. Alexandria, VA: Association for Supervision and Curriculum Development.

Tschannen-Moran, M., Woolfolk Hoy, A. (2001). *Teachers' Sense of Efficacy Scale*. Retrieved from http://people.ehe.ohio-state.edu/ahoy/files/2009/02/tses.pdf

Tschannen-Moran, M., Woolfolk Hoy, A., & Hoy, W. K. (1998). Teacher efficacy: Its meaning and measure. *Review of Educational Research, 68*, 202-248.

Woolfolk, A. (2004). In M. F. Shaughnessy, An interview with Anita Woolfolk: The educational psychology of teacher efficacy. *Educational Psychology Review, 16*(2), 153-176. Retrieved from www.des.emory.edu/mfp/WoolfolkEPRInt.pdf

CHAPTER 11

SELF-ENHANCEMENT THROUGH SELF-TRANSCENDENCE

Toward Mindful Middle Schools for Teaching and Learning

Robert W. Roeser, Cynthia Taylor, and Jessica Harrison

> In looking at the youth of today, one is apt to forget that identity formation, while being 'critical' in youth, is really a generational issue.
>
> (Erikson, 1968, p. 29)

In the spirit of Beane and Lipka's (1986) notion of the "self-enhancing middle school," this chapter takes the reader on a journey in which the middle school is envisioned as a place that optimizes learning and identity development among adolescent students and adult educators alike through the creation of a particular kind of culture for teaching and learning—one that is mindful, caring and focused on mastery through mutual support. Adopting Beane and Lipka's (1986) "from-to articulation" of suggested reforms in middle school education, we envision the "mindful middle school" as a place in which, over time and with intention and effort, school leaders, teachers and students alike *move away from* par-

Middle Grades Curriculum:
Voices and Visions of the Self-Enhancing School, pp. 179–211
Copyright © 2013 by Information Age Publishing
All rights of reproduction in any form reserved.

ticular mindsets (e.g., belief in the fixed nature of ability), habits (e.g., mindlessness), and social norms (e.g., competition and social comparison during learning) common in many schools today, and *move toward* other rarer, but ultimately more effective ones (e.g., belief in malleability of ability, habit of mindfulness, norms of cooperation and mutual support). These arguably less common mindsets, habits and social norms are, collectively, what we see as constituting the heart of a new culture of education, one that is mindful and compassionate in outlook and activity.

Mindfulness has been described at the level of the person as a mental state or trait characterized by focused attention, a calm and clear awareness of what is happening in the present moment, and an absence of emotional reactions or conceptual elaborations to what is occurring that tend to take attention and awareness out of the present moment as it unfolds (Kabat-Zinn, 2003). In addition, in some renderings, mindfulness is associated not only with a curious and open-minded, but also a warm-hearted attitude toward the present moment and toward others with whom we share it (Cullen, 2011). To be mindful is to be awake, aware, adaptively present, and empathically concerned for others. As such, mindfulness has been hypothesized to have benefits for learning, health, and social relationships among adults and adolescents alike (Mind and Life Educational Research Network (MLERN), 2012; Roeser & Peck, 2009).

In this chapter, we explore the potential benefits of mindfulness in the education of early adolescents in terms of a "mindful middle school." We conceptualize the mindful middle school in terms of (a) mindful school leadership in which there is a focus on the whole school learning and the development of students and educators alike; (b) mindful schoolwide cultures for teaching and learning that emphasize awareness and self-regulation, malleability of skills, mastery as the goal of learning, and cooperation; and (c) the presence of school-based mindfulness and compassion programs that directly teach students and educators mindfulness and compassion skills (see Figure 11.1).

A basic premise of this chapter is mindfulness and compassion are educable skills, and that adults and adolescents can learn these skills and use them in the service of both personal development and prosocial contributions to family, friends, school, community and society (MLERN, 2012). Furthermore, by learning and embodying these qualities, school leaders, teachers, and adolescents are in a position to create and maintain mindful and compassionate classrooms and schools—to cultivate mindful awareness and compassion not only within and for oneself, but also within and for others in the daily social settings of life such as the school. The mindful middle school that we envision in this chapter is a kind of thought experiment regarding how we might go about preparing young adolescents, and the adults who educate them, for the demands of 21st century

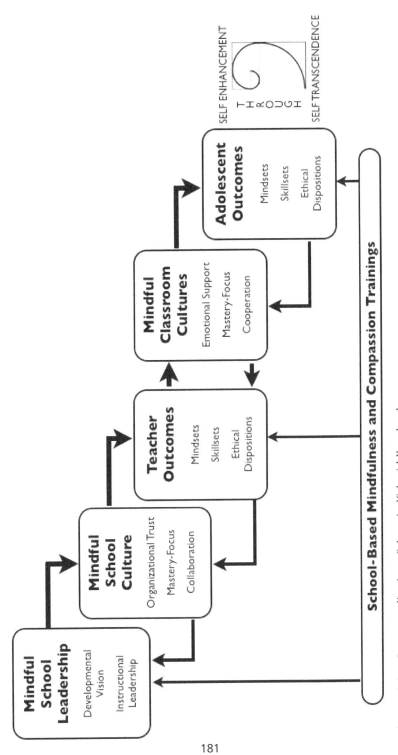

Figure 11.1.   Conceptualization of the mindful middle school.

life in a global community (Ryan, 2012). We begin our journey by outlining some historical reasons for why mindful and compassionate approaches to middle grades education are particularly needed now, and then proceed to envision the key features of a mindful and compassionate middle school.

HISTORICAL CHANGE AND SCHOOLING IN THE 21ST CENTURY

In the face of globalization, climate change and increasing social, technological and economic interdependence, theorists have argued that we need to educate young people, and the teachers who teach them, in new ways and toward novel ends (Dalai Lama, 1999; Darling-Hammond & Bransford, 2005; Goleman, 1995; Heckman, 2007; Noddings, 2005). The overarching goal of these new educational approaches is the cultivation of human qualities that are necessary for future generations to meet the economic, moral and leadership challenges confronting the United States today. Such challenges are evident at this particular moment in history. As economist Jeffrey Sachs (2011) sees it:

> At the root of America's economic crisis lies a moral crisis: the decline of civic virtue among America's political and economic elite. A society of markets, laws and elections is not enough if the rich and powerful fail to behave with respect, honesty, and compassion toward the rest of society and toward the world. America has developed the world's most competitive market society but has squandered its civic virtue along the way. Without restoring an ethos of social responsibility, there can be no meaningful and sustained economic recovery. (p. 3)

> We need to reconceive the idea of a good society in the early 21st century and find a creative path toward it. Most important, we need to be ready to pay the price of civilization through multiple acts of good citizenship: bearing our fair share of taxes, educating ourselves deeply about society's needs, acting as vigilant stewards for future generations, and remembering that compassion is the glue that holds society together. (p. 5)

Schools and educators, arguably, play an instrumental role in preparing young people for these contemporary and future challenges by focusing on student development of relevant kinds of mindsets, skills and ethical dispositions (MLERN, 2012). From this point of view, schools are conceptualized as contexts for holistic human development, and therefore are about more than academic knowledge and skill formation, though academic goals are central to the mission of the middle school. Beyond academics, some envision middle schools as places that also educate adolescents, as well as the adults who teach them, in certain kinds of identities, social-emotional skills, and ethical values (Eccles & Roeser, 2010). In the best case scenario, our schools are instrumental in preparing young American adolescents to participate in our democracy and to prosper and flourish in a world that is increasingly hot, flat and crowded (Friedman, 2008).

CONCEPTUALIZING 21ST CENTURY EDUCATIONAL OUTCOMES

Theorists have offered various descriptions of the kinds of educational outcomes that schools should aim for to meet the unique challenges of the 21st century (see Table 11.1). Though these conceptualizations differ, there is both a growing scientific consensus and empirical data showing

Table 11.1.   Conceptualizations of Educational Aims for 21st Century

Social and Emotional Competencies[1]

- Self-awareness
- Self-management
- Social awareness
- Relationship skills
- Responsible and ethical decision-making

Cognitive and Noncognitive Skills[2]

- Self-control
- Self-regulation and time perspective
- Motivation and confidence
- Dispositions like open-mindedness and conscientiousness

Self-Regulated Learning Skills[3]

- Forethought and goal setting
- Retrieval and activation of relevant prior knowledge
- Resource and task appraisal, planning and strategy selection
- Monitoring of goal pursuit during problem-solving
- Flexibility and adaptation of learning strategies
- Knowledge and skillful use of strategies for overcoming obstacles during learning
- Reflection

Sources: [1]Zins, Weissberg, Wang, and Walberg (2004); [2]Heckman (2007); [3]Zimmerman (2000).

that factors such as self-control, emotion regulation, self-awareness, empathy and responsible behavior toward others matter significantly for both the educational and economic success of students and their nations (see Durlak, Weissberg, Dymnicki, Taylor, & Schellinger, 2011; Heckman, 2007; Moffitt et al., 2011), as well as for teachers and teacher effectiveness (Jennings & Greenberg, 2009; Roeser, Skinner, Beers, & Jennings, 2012).

For purposes of this chapter, we simplify these diverse characterizations of contemporary educational outcomes presented in Table 11.1 into three main areas that research shows to be most impactful for effective teaching and learning during adolescence: (a) motivational mindsets that emphasize malleability, mastery and improvement, and self-compassion (see Dweck, 2008; Neff, 2003); (b) skill sets associated with mindfulness, mental focus and flexibility (e.g., present-focused awareness of mental and physical experience, acting with awareness, nonreactivity to experience, an empathic concern for others; see Baer, Smith, Hopkins, Krietemeyer, & Toney, 2006; Kabat-Zinn, 2003); and (c) normative dispositions such as cooperation and prosociality rather than competition and individualism during teaching and learning (see Roseth, Johnson, & Johnson, 2008). Using a "from-to" framework, the next section presents the kinds of prevailing mindsets, skills and dispositions we propose that mindful middle school leaders, teachers, and students move away from, as well as those that we propose they move toward based on extant research (see Tables 11.2 & 11.3).

A key first step in efforts to learn new ways of leading, teaching and learning in the mindful middle school involves adults' and adolescents' orientation toward particular motivating and revitalizing mindsets. Two key mindsets have been identified in the literature on motivation; mindsets that are more and less beneficial with regard to learning in schools. First, school leaders and educators need to encourage themselves and adolescent students to move away from a Fixed Mindset—the pessimistic view that "you can't teach an old dog new tricks" or that one's abilities are fixed by nature or developmental history or some other external factor. At the same time, school members need to move toward a Malleable Mindset that holds that the skills necessary to improve leadership, teaching and learning are understood to be plastic, educable, and modifiable through sustained intention, effort and mutual support. Supporting school members to shift from a Fixed to a Malleable Mindset with regard to their personal or professional abilities (e.g., verbal ability or teaching ability) and social-emotional habits and dispositions (e.g., social skills, emotion regulation) is critical for motivating lasting behavioral change (Dweck, 2008). Such belief systems are not only scientifically valid with respect to what we know about the development of expertise (Ericsson & Charness, 1994), but also moti-

Table 11.2.   Shifts in Motivational Mindsets and Social Norms

	From	*To*
Motivational	Fixed Mindset	Malleable Mindset
Mindsets	Belief that one's personal abilities and qualities are relatively fixed by nature and therefore not subject to very much change.	Belief that one's personal abilities and qualities are relatively malleable by nature and therefore subject to change through self-effort and mutual support.
	Proving Mindset	Improving Mindset
	Desire to receive prove one's abilities or talents through superior performance as one's motivation for behavior.	Desire to improve one's abilities and talents through sustained engagement and resilience as one's motivation for behavior.
	Self-Critical Mindset	Self-Compassionate Mindset
	A non-conscious tendency to be critical or judgmental of oneself or one's abilities in the face of setbacks or failures.	A conscious attitude of acceptance and non-judgment of oneself or one's abilities in the face of setbacks or failures because they are recognized as "part of being human."
Social	Demonstration of Ability Norms	Cooperative Development of Ability Norms
Norms	Use of leadership and teaching practices to emphasize the public demonstration of competence, social comparisons when learning, and in essence, competition and superior performance as valued goals and ways of conceiving "success".	Use of leadership and teaching practices to emphasize the shared development of competence, self-to-self temporal comparisons when learning, and in essence, cooperation and progressive mastery over time as valued goals and ways of conceiving "success".

vating and empowering because they foster a sense of personal efficacy in affecting the events and course of one's life (Bandura, 1997).

Dweck (2008) reviewed decades of research showing that individuals with a Malleability Mindset are more likely to pursue "mastery-oriented goals"—goals in which mastery and improvement of one's malleable qualities through sustained effort and support are the aims—what we call an Improving Mindset during learning. In contrast, when individuals hold a Fixed Mindset they are more oriented toward the *proving* of ability—what we call a Proving Mindset during learning. If individuals hold a Fixed Mindset and have low perceived or actual ability, or encounter challenges or situations where their superior relative ability cannot be proven, then they are more likely to give up. On the other hand, the Malleable Mindset suggests the necessity of "beginning again" in the face of challenge and difficulty—that improvement includes setbacks. Thus, the Malleability

Mindset is associated with longer term resilience and persistence than the Fixed Mindset, which is more vulnerable to failure-related feedback (see Lau & Roeser, 2007). Again, we envision members of mindful middle schools as moving toward an Improving Mindset while at the same time moving away from a Proving Mindset by considering their deeply held beliefs and their practices of leadership and teaching that may emphasize one or the other of these mindsets (see Table 11.2).

Research has demonstrated the importance of these mindsets for motivation and learning among early adolescents. In a recent intervention study with early adolescents, results showed how the alteration of such mindsets in adolescent students can be beneficial with respect to engagement and achievement after the transition from elementary to middle school. In this study, researchers exposed half of the students to an intervention that emphasized the malleability of intelligence (e.g., Malleability and Improving Mindsets) just before the transition to middle school, whereas the controls did not receive the intervention. Follow-up data showed that the intervention promoted positive change in students' classroom motivation and seemed to ameliorate the downward trend in academic grades normally found after the transition to secondary school (Blackwell, Trzesniekwski & Dweck, 2007). By emphasizing the malleability of one's ability, and the need to stay focused on personal improvement over time, many of the negative changes associated with students' transition into school environments that emphasize relative ability, social comparison, and the demonstration of ability (see Midgley, Anderman & Hicks, 1995) were reversed.

Similarly, in a review of three rigorously designed intervention studies aimed at reducing the detrimental effects of stereotype threats on the achievement of African American students, Aronson, Cohen, McColskey, Montrosse, Lewis, & Mooney (2009) identified three main components of the interventions that seemed the most crucial: (a) the reinforcement of the idea that intelligence is malleable and, like a muscle, grows stronger when exercised; (b) the reinforcement of the idea that difficulties in school are often part of a normal learning curve or adjustment process, rather than something unique to a particular student or his/her racial group and (c) provisions of opportunities for students to reflect on other values in their lives beyond school that are sources of self-worth for them. The Malleability and Improving Mindsets, therefore, seem particularly important for reducing achievement gaps that arise from debilitating stereotypes that impugn the intellectual intelligence of members of various racial and ethnic groups in U.S. society.

In addition to these key mindsets, research has shown that the attitude one takes toward oneself in the aftermath of challenge, difficulty or even seeming "failure" is another critical, malleable factor related to the quality of leadership, teaching and learning. Specifically, many of us adopt nonconsciously an attitude of self-criticism when we fail (or, alternatively, we may inappropriately blame others instead of some aspect of self). In contrast, Neff (2003) has described a more adaptive and resilience-enhancing mindset that she calls "self-compassion." Self-compassion is defined in terms of three components: (a) being aware of and open to one's own suffering, as in being willing to observe painful experiences, thoughts, and feelings without identifying with or fixating on them; (b) taking a kind, nonjudgmental, and understanding attitude toward oneself in instances of pain or difficulty rather than being self-critical; and (c) framing one's difficulties in light of the shared human experience of challenge and suffering rather than as something that isolates us from others. In a study of college students, Neff, Hsieh, and Dejitterat (2005) found that self-compassion was positively associated with the pursuit of perceived competence and mastery achievement goals, in which the focus of awareness is on learning and improvement, and negatively associated with fears of failure and the pursuit of socially comparative achievement goals in which the focus of awareness is divided between learning and one's ego-status and performance compared to others. Further, Neff and colleagues found that among college students who perceived their midterm grades as indications of "failure," self-compassion was associated with more adaptive coping strategies for raising grades (e.g., applying more effort, seeking academic support). This research highlights the importance of assisting all members of a mindful school in moving toward a Self-Compassionate Mindset and in moving away from a Self-Critical Mindset is another important aspect of the mindful middle school.

A key way for school leaders and teachers to create cultures of teaching and learning in the school that focus on malleability of skills, improvement as the goal of learning, and self-compassion as the attitude to adopt toward oneself while learning is to begin to move away from practices that implicitly or explicitly emphasize Demonstration of Ability Norms and to begin to move toward practices that emphasize the Cooperative Development of Ability Norms with a focus on progressive mastery of multiple abilities over time through mutual support and collaboration as the keys to learning and success at all levels of the middle school system (Maehr & Midgley, 1991, 1996). In a review of 25 years of research in Achievement Goal Theory on motivation and school environments, Meece, Anderman and Anderman (2005) concluded that, "whereas school environments that are focused on demonstrating high ability and competing for grades can increase the academic performance of some students, research suggests that many young people experience diminished motivation under these conditions" (p. 487). At the same time, research over those same 25 years has clearly demonstrated the importance of helping students to develop motivational mindsets in which the goals of effort, self-improvement and the progressive development of malleable abilities leading to mastery are salient (see Table 11.2).

> Students who pursue mastery goals, compared to those who do not, often find their classes interesting, persist when facing difficulty, value cooperativeness, seek help when confused, self-regulate effectively, use deep learning strategies (i.e., elaborating the material, connecting it to other concepts), navigate decisional conflict well, experience positive emotion, and perceive tasks as valuable. (Senko, Hulleman & Harackiewicz, 2011, p. 27)

Lending even more support to the idea that schools should move away from emphasizing Fixed Mindsets and Proving Mindsets based on reliance on Demonstration of Ability Norms, a meta-analysis on the effects of competitive, cooperative, and individualistic goal structures on student achievement and peer relationships among over 17,000 adolescents in 100 countries showed that higher achievement and more positive peer relationships were associated with cooperative rather than competitive or individualistic goal structures (Roseth, Johnson & Johnson, 2008). This work shows that learning and achievement are actually maximized during adolescence when educators move away from Demonstration of Ability Norms and move toward Cooperative Development of Ability Norms.

These mindsets are useful for motivating and sustaining long-term engagement in learning new and complex skills. In that sense, such mindsets set the stage for kinds of learning of new skill sets that we propose are essential in a mindful middle school and in the 21st century. In Table 11.3, we describe these key self-regulatory skills. Central to our concept of the mindful middle school is finding ways to assist all members of the middle school to move toward the Habit of Mindfulness (Kabat-Zinn, 2003), a form of conscious, present-moment awareness relatively unbiased by emotional reactions or conceptual elaborations or judgments. At the same time, it is important for school members to move away from the Habit of Mindlessness (Langer, 1989), a form of nonconscious moment-to-moment awareness in which one automatically applies previous memories and habitual emotional and behavioral reactions to current task environments. Whereas mindlessness is a highly efficient form of information processing once right understanding or wholesome habits are developed or novel situations mastered, it is not a particularly useful mode of information processing when learning new things or unlearning old ways of doing things in new task environments. Furthermore, in the uncertain and emotionally complex world of schooling, mindlessness is often not that helpful in social interactions. For teaching, learning and many social

Table 11.3.   Shifts in Self-Regulatory Skillsets and Social Norms

	From	*To*
Self-Regulatory	Habit of Mindlessness	Habit of Mindfulness
Skills	A nonconscious form of information processing and perception of current task environments via automatically activated feelings, beliefs and expectations stored in long-term memory (e.g., automatic emotional and mental habits)	A conscious form of information processing and perception of current task environments in a manner that is relatively free from identifications with and biases arising form emotional reactions or conceptual elaborations of the present based upon memory (e.g., mindfulness).
	Habit of Mind Wandering A nonconscious tendency to switch attention from one object of focus to another without attending to any particular one for very long time.	Habit of Focused Attention A conscious, effortful capacity for attending to a specific object of focus for an extended period of time and/or bringing attention back to an object of focus when the mind wanders away from it.
	Habit of Mental Fixation A nonconscious tendency to perseverate and have difficulty "switching" rules or mental sets when problem-solving.	Habit of Mental Flexibility A conscious, fluid capacity to "switch" rules or mental sets when problem-solving.
	Habit of Impulsivity A nonconscious tendency to pursue short-term goals, often at the expense of longer-term goals.	Habit of Self-Control A conscious, effortful tendency to delay gratification of short-term goals in favor of longer-term goals.
Social	Habit of Egocentricity	Habit of Empathy/Perspective Taking
Norms	A nonconscious tendency to view life from a primarily personal point of view in the service of looking out for one's own welfare.	A conscious, effortful tendency to view life from others' points of view, in addition to one's own in the service of being concerned for the welfare of the other.

activities, mindful awareness is indispensable. We consider it the master self-regulatory habit of mind in mindful middle schools.

Developing a Habit of Mindfulness also would assist middle school educators and students in moving away from the Habit of Mind Wandering, a widespread habit in schools today. This refers to an effortless, nonconscious tendency for attention to shift from one object to another in a daydreaming or ruminative fashion without attending to any particular object for very long (Smallwood & Schooler, 2006). In mindful middle schools, adults and adolescents are trained using exercises that specifically help them to move toward the Habit of Focused Attention—an intentional and conscious capacity for attending to a specific object of focus for an extended period of time and/or bringing attention back to an object of focus when the mind wanders away from it. We discuss such trainings further below.

In addition, we see mindful middle schools as place where adults and adolescents move away from the Habit of Mental Fixation—a nonconscious tendency to perseverate and have difficulty "switching" rules, mental sets, or perspectives when problem-solving; and move toward a Habit of Mental Flexibility—a conscious, fluid capacity to "switch" rules, mental sets, or perspectives when problem-solving. Mental flexibility of this kind is associated with creativity, problem-solving and learning (e.g., Diamond & Lee, 2011).

Another key feature of the mindful middle school is a movement away from the Habit of Impulsivity, a nonconscious tendency to pursue short-term, emotionally-salient goals, often at the expense of longer term values; and movement toward the Habit of Self-Control, a conscious, effortful tendency to delay gratification of short-term goals in favor of longer term values (see Table 11.3). By encouraging student autonomy through affordances for voice and choice, we see school climates as capable of scaffolding the development of emotion and behavioral regulation (Eccles & Roeser, 2010).

Finally, we propose mindful middle schools as places in which adults and adolescents move away from a Habit of Egocentrism, a nonconscious tendency to view life from a primarily personal, self-interested point of view with the aim of insuring personal welfare; and move toward a Habit of Empathy/Perspective Taking, a conscious, effortful tendency to view life empathically from others' points of view in addition to one's own with the aims of insuring the welfare of others in addition to oneself. It is clear that education in care and compassion is needed in an increasingly interconnected, warm and crowded planet (Friedman, 2008, Noddings, 2005.

In the next section, we describe how the multilevel contexts of the middle school can be designed so as to support the development of these mindsets, skill sets and ethical dispositions on the part of adults and adolescents alike. Furthermore, we briefly describe data suggesting that each of the desirable self-regulatory habits described in Table 11.2 can be cultivated through mindfulness training (see MLERN, 2012).

CONCEPTUALIZING THE MINDFUL MIDDLE SCHOOL

How does one work to cultivate and sustain the kinds of habits of mind, skills, and normative dispositions just described? In this section, we present our conceptual model of the Mindful Middle School (see Figure 11.1), as well as the key dimensions of such schools that help to cultivate the novel educational outcomes presented in Tables 11.2 and 11.3. A mindful middle school, in our definition, does not just exist for the development of its students. Rather, such a school is grounded in a vision of education that encompasses the lifelong learning and development of adult educators as well as adolescent students, and aims to cultivate the same mindsets, skill sets and ethics among adults as among students. Indeed, it is hard to understand how adult educators could prepare adolescent students for the future unless they themselves have developed and embodied so-called 21st century mindsets and skill sets themselves (MLERN, 2012).

Based on a selected synthesis of research on adolescent and adult development, schooling and motivation to learn, we conceptualize the mindful middle school in terms of (a) mindful school leadership in which there is a focus on the whole school learning and the development of students and educators alike; (b) mindful schoolwide cultures for teaching and learning that emphasize awareness and self-regulation, malleability of skills, mastery as the goal of learning, and cooperation; and (c) the presence of school-based mindfulness and compassion programs that directly teach students and educators mindfulness and compassion skills (see Figure 11.1).

Based on the interdependence of these three essential characteristics, we propose that mindful schools, through the cultivation of the mindsets, skill sets and normative ethical dispositions reviewed above, ultimately lead adult and adolescent members of the school community to seek enhancement of self through self-transcendence and prosociality, rather than through social-comparison and competition with others for resources or recognition (Dweck, 2008, Roseth et al., 2008). The mindful middle school, in other words, is about mutual support and the simultaneous attainment of personal and collective well-being through the avenues of self-transcendence (continually striving to go beyond current capacities and knowledge) and prosociality (continually striving to look beyond purely self-interests to consider those of others alongside one's own).

1. MINDFUL SCHOOL LEADERSHIP

The first hypothesized characteristic of mindful middle schools is *mindful school leadership*. Research has clearly demonstrated that effective schools are run by school leaders who have a vision of education that is strongly focused on the improvement of teaching and learning (Lee, 2000). Recent meta-analyses show that when school leaders have a clear vision of the school's mission, and focus resources on the cultivation of mindsets and skills needed to create a school culture and professional learning community that are consistent with that vision, they can significantly improve student learning outcomes (Lomos, Hofman & Bosker, 2011; MacNeil, Prater & Busch, 2009; Mills, McDowelle, & Rouse, 2011). Based on this research, we propose that two key aspects of mindful school leadership are (a) the articulation of a developmental vision of the mission of the middle school; and (b) a sustained focus on the cultivation of staff mindsets and skill sets that align with and support that vision through the exercise of instructional leadership.

A Developmental Vision of School

One mindset we have not yet discussed that is key for school leaders to have in a mindful middle school is vision—specifically, a vision that comes from school leaders' answers to the seemingly obvious question "For whom do middle schools exist?" An nondevelopmental vision or mindset with regard to answering this question is the tacit, widespread assumption that schools exist solely for the learning and development of students. This idea has become such a truism that we do not question it with regard to the aims of primary and secondary schools. Educators and their needs are often left out of school reform debates, and this contributes significantly to the lack of any sustained reform in education over historical time (e.g., Tyack & Cuban, 1995). Consider Seymour Sarason's (1998) thought experiment in this regard:

> If we asked university professors to justify the existence of a university, the answer will be that the obligation of the university is to create and sustain contexts in which its faculty learns, changes and grows in relation to his or her interests. You can have a university with no or very few students. The assumption is that the faculty will create a similar context for their students.
>
> If you ask schoolteachers to justify the existence of an elementary, middle, or high school, the answer will be that it is for students; it is not for the learning and development of teachers. Yet if contexts for productive learning do not exist for teachers, they cannot create and sustain those contexts for students. And that is precisely the case for the students and teachers in the modal American classroom, and especially so in our urban schools. (pp. 9-10)

Sarason's (1990) longstanding hypothesis, seemingly supported by the "predictable failure of school reform," is that if school reform is to be effective in transforming everyday routines of teaching and learning in the classroom, school leaders need create and sustain positive work environments for teachers in the same kinds of ways that leaders wish for their teachers to create and sustain positive learning environments for students. Research on the history of school reform provides support for the idea that when school leaders adopt the vision and mindset that schools exist for the growth, learning and development of educators as well as students, their ability to implement and sustain reform efforts is improved substantially (e.g., Connell & Broom, 2004; Sarason, 1990). We call such a vision a Developmental Mindset and posit it as a cornerstone of the mindful middle school. Such a vision acknowledges the basic fact that both learning and development are life-long, and educational institutions from the preschool to the graduate school benefit from adherence in design and process to this basic assumption (Sarason, 1998).

Why is this so? From a developmental perspective on schooling, one could argue that although the rate of developmental change is different among adolescents (fast) and the adults who teach them (slow), the developmental life tasks of adolescent students and educators in middle schools are nonetheless strongly interdependent (Roeser, Eccles, & Sameroff, 2000). As Erikson (1973) once proposed, whereas the core life task of adolescence is the discovery of what one *cared to do* and who one *cared to be* (e.g., identity task); a core part of adulthood development involves the discovery of whom one *takes care of* (e.g., the generativist task p. 124). Mindful schools are places in which, one could say, adolescents are learning about what they care to do and who they care to be, and adults are learning about how best to take care of the young people in their charge by helping them find these answers for themselves in a fast-changing, globally interconnected world. Moving away from Nondevelopmental Vision of the middle school and moving toward a Developmental Vision is a key hypothesized aspect of mindful school leadership.

A Focus on Teacher Professional Development

In addition to encouraging change in the mindsets of oneself and staff members, mindful school leaders must also develop and assist their teaching staff in the development of new instructional skill sets that are consistent with the developmental vision of the school and effective teaching of adolescents. These changes require what has been described as "instructional leadership" by others (Robinson, Lloyd & Rowe, 2008). Instructional leadership refers to activities in which the school leader actively supports teachers emotionally and collaborates with them on the planning, coordinating, and evaluating of their teaching and curriculum (Robinson et al., 2008). The results of a recent meta-analysis of leadership factors concluded:

Leaders in schools where students performed above expected levels were more likely to be involved with their staff in curriculum planning, visiting classrooms, and reviewing evidence about student learning. Staff welcomed leaders' involvement in teacher evaluation and classroom observation because it resulted in useful feedback.

The leadership dimension that is most strongly associated with positive student outcomes is that of promoting and participating in teacher learning and development. Because the agenda for teacher professional learning is endless, goal setting should play an important part in determining the teacher learning agenda.

Leaders' involvement in teacher learning provides them with a deep understanding of the conditions required to enable staff to make and sustain the changes required for improved outcomes. It is the responsibility of leaders at all levels of the system to create those conditions. (Robinson et al., 2008; p. 667)

The ability of school leaders to effectively manage and foster change in the middle school through instructional leadership is key in our model of the mindful middle school. But school leaders need not do this work alone. Rather, they can harness the collective efficacy of their teachers and staff to collaborate with them in charting a new and more mindful and compassionate course for the school. Thus, the next key dimension of mindful school leadership is the ability of principals to organize their school staff for organizational trust, learning and actual reform.

2. MINDFUL SCHOOL CULTURE

The ability of a school leader to create a support, mindful school culture for change, as well as to organize professional development (PD) activities in ways that cultivate the mindsets and skill sets that teachers need to align with the vision of a mindful school, are two key aspects of mindful school leadership. Hoy (2002) has described the importance of principals' creating of a mindful, participatory organizational culture in schools. He defines a mindful school culture as one in which the principal, teachers, and staff, as members of a professional learning community, practice five qualities together as they work to improve teaching and learning in their school: a normalization of and curiosity regarding the reasons for failure, a reluctance to simplify interpretations of challenges, sensitivity to issues of teaching and learning (e.g., daily operations), commitment to resilience in the face of situational demands, and deference to expertise when problem solving. In mindful schools, members of the administration and faculty in a mindful school do not focus on their successes alone, but rather continually scan for potential problems or failures. They remain close to the day-to-day operations of the classroom and the school and are able to bounce back resiliently from challenging situations that inevitably occur in schools because of a mindset that sees challenges not as "failures" but "opportunities to learn." When a problem arises, leaders and teachers in mindful schools defer to the person who is an expert in the area needed, rather than, as is traditional, to the person at the highest level of authority. Just as individual mindfulness can facilitate a person's capacity for self-awareness and self-regulation in the form of responding vs. reacting to stressful events, organizational mindfulness can facilitate a school staff's ability to be aware of and regulate day-to-day operations with regard to teaching and learning in a problem-focused, prevention oriented (as opposed to an emotionally reactive) manner.

Mindfulness at the organizational level necessarily rests on organizational trust between teachers, staff, and the school leader (Bryk & Schneider, 2002). A trusting culture in which teachers believe that their principal and their fellow teachers have common goals, good intentions, and the capacity to realize those goals is essential for creating a context for honesty, in which people can discuss problems or mistakes openly, and where individuals support one another in solving or rectifying them. Through organizational trust, a sense of openness is cultivated that directly facilitates an organization's ability to stay close to the day to day operations of the school and to bounce back resiliently from any mistakes that do occur. Hoy, Sweetland and Smith (2002) found that mindfulness of the principal, the faculty, and the school as a whole was associated with teachers' trust for one another, for their principal, and for students. Thus, mutual support, cooperation and trust go hand and hand with mindful awareness, openness, and resilience in a mindful school organization.

Another key aspect of mindful leadership and a mindful school culture is insuring that teachers and principals get the professional development and skill sets they need to practice mindful and compassionate forms of leadership and education. Unfortunately, research shows that current forms of PD activities are often ineffective (Ball & Cohen, 1999). Ironically, one reason for this is that these activities are often not designed with regard to the principles and best practices of adult learning. Specifically, PD often involves short—rather than long-term workshops and the presentation of knowledge or techniques rather than experiential or practice-based exercises with feedback cycles on how to use the knowledge/techniques. These types of "one-shot" workshops, without any follow-through in terms of sustained practice and mentorship, are not particularly motivating or effective for teachers, nor do they have a positive impact on students (Birman, Desimone, Porter, & Garet, 2000; Garet, Porter, Andrew, & Desimone, 2001).

One solution has been for school leaders to eschew participation in traditional kinds of PD and instead develop within-school professional communities of learners wherein all of the educators in the school come together to inquire into challenges facing the school and to collectively problem-solve and implement changes to address those challenges (Lieberman & Miller, 2008). These horizontal structures in schools serve as a cultural space for the principal and teachers to provide emotional support to one another, develop a sense of shared community in addressing the needs of all the inhabitants of the school, share instructional challenges and solutions, select and modify curricula, and review, discuss, and act on the basis of data regarding student learning and achievement in a school. Helping to organize and make possible these kinds of professional learning communities at the school level is one useful strategy for school leaders who wish to create mindful organizational cultures, and may be a more effective use of professional development days (MacDonald & Shirley, 2009).

3. MINDFUL CLASSROOM CULTURES

Because there is an interdependence between the work culture school leaders create for teachers and the classroom cultures teachers create for students (Sarason, 1998), we hypothesize that mindful school cultures will promote mindful classroom cultures (see Figure 11.1). Drawing on Langer's (1989) work, Hoy (2002) proposed that teachers in mindful schools may be more likely to adopt a mindful approach to classroom teaching by encouraging their students to (a) create new categories for experience as a fundamental part of learning; (b) remain open to new information; and (c) attend to and try to understand multiple perspectives on a single issue. These factors are hypothesized, in turn, to reduce student boredom, promote interest, and to make learning more like play than work. In addition, by teaching teachers mindfulness and compassion directly (see below), they may also be more likely to bring these qualities into their everyday instruction and relationships with students (see Roeser & Zelazo, 2012). Although these hypotheses have not yet been researched, the notion of a mindful approach to teaching is quite close to what others have termed mastery-focused, autonomy-supportive, emotionally supportive classroom environments (Ames, 1992; Pianta & Hamre, 2009).

Achievement Goal Theorists have discussed how teachers can create mindful, intrinsically motivational climates for student learning. In this work, teachers, through their mindsets and related pedagogical practices, are hypothesized to create climates that focus students on the demonstration of relative ability or on mastery, self-improvement and mutual support during learning in the classroom (see Ames, 1992; Midgley, 2002). Above, we called labeled these two different motivational approaches to teaching either (a) the Demonstration of Ability Norms or (b) the Cooperative Development of Ability classroom norms, respectively.

Research has shown that through teachers' use of practices such as grouping by ability, differential rewards for high achievers, public evaluative feedback, academic competitions, and other practices, teachers enact a Demonstration of Ability Norm in their classrooms such that academic success is understood by students as outperforming others and proving one's superior ability. Performance and ability are what is valued, rewarded and expected when teaching practices emphasize these norms (Midgley, 2002). Alternatively, through teachers' use of practices such as heterogeneous grouping, recognition for improvement over time, nonpublic evaluative feedback (including formative assessments), interest-based choices in work, and collaborative work assignments, teachers can foster Cooperative Development of Ability Norm in the classroom and thereby communicate to students that it is these things that are valued, rewarded and expected among students (Midgley, 2002).

Based on this work, we propose that another key aspect of the mindful middle school is classroom cultures that nurture the Malleable and Improving Mindsets through an emphasis on classroom norms in which the Cooperative Development of Ability is the focus. This requires a rethinking of most aspects of pedagogical practice, including how teachers use time, evaluate students, distribute authority in the classroom, recognize students, group students, and design academic tasks (Ames, 1992).

Furthermore, as depicted in Figure 11.1, teachers' practices tend to align with the overall ethos of the school in which they work (Lee, Bryk, & Smith, 1993; Talbert & McLaughlin, 1999). Thus, the importance of school principals in creating a mindful school culture that can support school teachers in creating mindful classroom cultures cannot be overestimated. For instance, Roeser, Marachi, and Gehlbach (2002) found that when elementary and middle school teachers perceived their school culture in terms of differential treatment of teachers by school leaders and a sense of competitiveness among their colleagues regarding who were the "best teachers," they were also more likely to say they used teaching practices in the classroom that highlighted differential treatment and competition between students (e.g., Demonstration of Ability Norms). On the other hand, when teachers in elementary and middle schools perceived their school culture in terms of support for innovation and cooperation from school leaders and colleagues, they were more likely to emphasize these ideas in their own approaches to motivating students to learn in the classroom (Codevelopment of Ability Norms).

The implication of this work is that the school organizational culture affects teachers' mindsets, skills and norms; which in turn affects the classroom cultures that teachers create for students. The classroom culture, in turn, affects the development of students' mindsets. Roeser and colleagues (2000) found such a chain of relationships moving from principal reports of the school culture, to teacher reports of their own practices in the classroom, to student reports of their perceptions of the classroom and their own motivational mindsets. Dweck (2008) have also argued that when teachers hold the mindset that intelligence is a fixed entity rather than a modifiable skill, they are likely to use performance-oriented (i.e., Demonstration of Ability Norm) pedagogical strategies. Students, in turn, who come to see their intelligence as a fixed entity, are likely to adopt a relative ability-focused motivational orientation to learning (Roeser et al., 2000). If they are doing very well academically, this orientation may not cause them problems but if they are not doing very well, such an orientation is likely undermine their engagement in learning and in school (Roeser et al., 2000).

Unfortunately, research has shown increases in the salience of Demonstration of Ability Norms in schools as adolescents move from elementary to middle school, and a decrease in their sense of emotional support from teachers (Roeser et al., 2000). That is, students are increasingly exposed to schools and teachers that place emphasis on social comparison, relative ability, and competition as a means of motivating learning in a context of diminished social support. This increased emphasis on superior performance and relative ability is paralleled by increases in students' own orientation toward performance-oriented, relative ability goals when learning and decreases in a sense of belonging in school settings (Midgley, Anderman, & Hicks, 1995).

Several studies have documented the relations between the nature of the classrooms in middle school and students' motivation, well-being and achievement. Harter, Whitesell, and Kowalski (1992), in a study of middle school students (Grades 6-8), found that "students who characterized the school environment as (increasingly) emphasizing and externally evaluating performance and competence relative to others had higher extrinsic motivation, reported a much higher level of scholastic anxiety, and rated academic success as more important than did those not sharing these perceptions of the educational environment" (p. 797). Roeser, Midgley, and Urdan (1996) found that adolescent students' who perceived their schools as emphasizing relative ability also were more likely to adopt the Proving Mindset (see Table 11.2), which in turn predicted their feelings of self-consciousness in school. Interestingly, students who perceived a strong focus on relative ability and superior performance in their middle school were less likely to perceive that their teachers cared for them. In contrast, student perceptions of an emphasis on mastery, malleability and self-improvement in their middle school were also more likely to adopt an Improving Mindset while learning, which, in turn, positively predicted their academic self-efficacy beliefs and positive affect in school. Such a perceived emphasis on mastery was also strongly correlated with students' sense that their teachers cared for them.

In another study, Roeser, Eccles, and Sameroff (2000) found that adolescent students' perceptions of their school as focused on relative ability and superior performance (e.g., Demonstration of Ability Norms) showed diminished feelings of academic competence and valuing of school, increased feelings of emotional distress, and decreased grades over time; whereas those who perceived an emphasis on mastery, improvement and support (e.g., Cooperative Development of Ability Norms) showed increased valuing of school and diminished emotional distress over time after controlling for student background characteristics (Roeser, Eccles, & Sameroff, 1998). Similarly, Kaplan and Maehr (1999) reported that students' perceptions of a focus on mastery in their school were associated with greater sense of well-being and less misconduct than when students perceived an emphasis on performance goals in their school.

In summary, the work reviewed on school leadership, school culture, classroom culture, and student outcomes show that these levels of analysis are interrelated in schools in theoretically predictable ways. As depicted in Figure 11.1, a mindful school is a multilevel system characterized by mindful leadership; a mindful and collaborative school culture for teaching, and classroom cultures that are emotionally supportive, mastery-focused, and characterized by cooperative goal structures for students. In order for school leaders, teachers, and students to have the skills to participate productively in the creation and maintenance of the mindful middle school, we believe specialized mindfulness training programs for adults and adolescents are also useful.

4. SCHOOL-BASED MINDFULNESS TRAINING PROGRAMS

Over the past decade or so, there has been an explosion in research and interest in the introduction of mindfulness and compassion-oriented skills training programs in education and child development settings (see Roeser & Peck, 2009; Roeser & Zelazo, 2012). These programs are being studied with respect to whether or not they are actually efficacious with respect to cultivating the kinds of mindsets, skills and ethical dispositions described in Tables 11.2 and 11.3. The quest for these kinds of programs is long-standing in psychology. Over 100 years ago, William James (1890) noted that:

The faculty of voluntarily bringing back a wandering attention, over and over again, is the very root of judgment, character, and will…. An education which should improve this faculty would be *the* education *par excellence*. (p. 424).

There is growing evidence in adult samples that mindfulness training strengthens brain functions that are responsible for attention regulation, emotion regulation and resilience, and empathy and compassion for self and others (MLERN, 2012). This evidence has lead to questions about whether there exist potential benefits to introducing mindfulness training into teacher professional development programs and social-emotional learning and positive youth development programs for students (Greenberg & Harris, 2012; Roeser & Peck, 2009; Zelazo & Lyons, 2012). To date, relatively few studies of the effects of mindfulness and compassion practices on teachers and students, however. Thus, we are only now beginning to address questions such as: How can we understand the ways in which contemplative practices may affect brain and behavior across time during childhood (Zelazo & Lyons, 2012)? What are the prospects for designing age-appropriate forms of training to scaffold and support the development of mindsets and skill sets associated with executive function and attention, emotion regulation, and empathy and compassion in children and adolescents (Greenberg & Harris; 2012)? How can we support key adult figures in young people's lives such as teachers or parents to develop and thereby teach these same mindsets and skill sets (Benn, Akiva, Arel, & Roeser, 2012; Roeser et al., 2012)? Can trainings be feasibly and effectively delivered in secular settings like schools?

Mindfulness Programs for Educators

Mindfulness training (MT) has been hypothesized to support school leaders and teachers in directly developing the kinds of mindsets, skills and dispositions described above (Jennings & Greenberg, 2009, Roeser et al., 2012). Indeed, it appears that MT might fill a crucial gap in educators' knowledge bases and skill sets in that the kinds of habits of mind MT cultivates are not a focus in most preservice and in-service teacher professional development programs. One way to describe such habits of mind is in terms of what Darling-Hammond and Bransford (2005) call "adaptive expertise." Adaptive expertise refers to teachers who are both highly efficient and highly innovative on the job. Efficiency on the job involves the automatization of particular habits of practice and ways of knowing, whereas innovation requires training the mind, in essence, to let go of particular habits of practice, simply observe habitual thoughts, beliefs, and feelings; and befriend ambiguity and uncertainty as a ground for novelty, creativity, and transformation. Roeser and colleagues (2012) enumerated several mindfulness-based habits of mind that seem essential to teachers' adaptive expertise, including focused attention, mindful awareness, mental flexibility, emotion regulation (nonreactivity), curiosity, compassion and tolerance for ambiguity.

Given the uncertain, emotional, and socially-demanding nature of teaching, when teachers do not develop habits of mind useful for managing professional demands effectively, their occupational wellbeing and instructional practice, as well as the school's attainment of broader educational goals with students, can suffer (Jennings & Greenberg, 2009). With regard to the economic bottom-line in education, for instance, unmanaged teacher stress may not only undermine teacher wellbeing and spiral into occupational burnout, but likely also engenders significant health care and human resource costs for school districts due to teacher illness, absenteeism and desistence from the profession. With regard to the student achievement bottom-line in education, teachers who have not developed the kinds of habits of mind discussed thus far may not be reaching their full potential with regard to creating emotionally supportive, motivating classroom climates for student learning (e.g., Briner & Dewberry, 2007).

A handful of studies of MT with teachers have been published to date. In one, Winzelberg and Luskin (1999) found that 21 preservice teachers who participated in four 45-mindfulness-based stress reduction training sessions across 4 weeks time reported significant reductions in somatic, emotional and behavioral indicators of stress. Jennings, Snowberg, Coccia and Greenberg (2011) reported the effects of a mindfulness-based occupational health program for teachers that included 4 day-long sessions taking place over 4-5 weeks. The program, designed to reduce teachers' stress and promote well-being, was assessed in two studies using samples of teachers in a lower SES urban setting, and student teachers in a suburban setting. Researchers reported mixed results regarding changes in mindfulness and stress. Kemeny and her colleagues (2012) evaluated the effects of a mindfulness intervention on the wellbeing of teachers. Teachers took part in an 8-week, 42-hour meditation/emotion regulation training, and analyses showed self-reported declines in symptoms of depression and anxiety, increases in positive affect, and improvement in a behavioral task requiring recognition of emotions.

In our own work, we have conducted three randomized trials of a MT program for teachers—one in Vancouver, Canada (2009), one in Boulder, Colorado (2010), and one in Ann Arbor, Michigan (2011). With respect to the Vancouver and Boulder studies, after establishing group equivalence following randomization, we found evidence for good program feasibility

(88% program completion rate) and efficacy with regard to mindfulness and the reduction of occupational stress and burnout among the teachers (Roeser, 2012). Results showed that teachers randomized to MT reported greater mindfulness, less occupational stress and burnout, and fewer sick days at postprogram and follow-up compared to controls. In half the sample, postprogram improvements in a behavioral measure of working memory were found among teachers receiving MT, but not among teachers in the waitlist control condition. Mediational analyses showed group differences in mindfulness at postprogram due to randomization to treatment or control were responsible for longer term reductions in occupational stress, burnout and sick days at follow-up (Roeser, 2012). In the Ann Arbor Study, Benn, Akiva, Arel and Roeser (2012) looked at the effects of the same MT training (twice a week for 5 weeks) for teachers and parents of children with special needs. Results showed reductions in distress and increases in various measures of well-being for both parents and teachers that persisted at 3-month follow-up.

These preliminary studies suggest the potential of direct mindfulness training programs a key means by which school leaders can foster the creation of mindful middle schools by developing their own capacity, and the capacity of their teachers, for mindful and empathic awareness at work. Although the evidence is still preliminary, there are indications that MT for educators may promote the kinds of mindsets and skills/habits described in Tables 11.2 and 11.3, and in that way prepare teachers to meet the unique demands of educating youth in and for the 21st century.

Mindfulness Program for Adolescents

The benefits of direct MT for health, well being and success may not be limited to only the adult educators in middle schools. Consistent with a Developmental Vision in which middle schools are assumed to exist for the life-long learning, health and development of adolescents and adults alike, we think it is fruitful to explore the potential benefits of direct mindfulness training for adolescent students (Greenberg & Harris, 2012; Roeser & Peck, 2009). From the perspective of primary prevention and the cultivation of positive youth development, MT and yoga may be unique ways to assist adolescents in developing focused attention, emotion regulation and social skills, and healthy identities during the many changes of these years in a manner that is cost-effective. Promoting focused attention, emotion regulation and social skills as part of the broader aims of public education may prove to have many individual and social benefits across lifetimes and generations, respectively (Greenberg & Rhoades, 2008).

The scientific investigation of the effects of mindfulness training on adolescent development is just beginning (Greenberg & Harris, 2012; MLERN, 2012). The studies that have been completed and published to date are small and often lacking in experimental rigor, but they are suggestive of considerable acceptance of these practices among youth when they are delivered in developmentally and culturally appropriate ways. What evidence that exists suggests that MT for adolescents are feasible in that youth enjoy and accept the practices (Greenberg & Harris, 2012; Roeser & Peck, 2009). Furthermore, there is some indication that mindfulness training may be efficacious with respect to cultivating the mindsets and skill sets described in Tables 11.2 and 11.3, especially focused attention and its use to regulate emotion and see the world from others' perspectives.

In a study of preadolescents ($M = 8.23$ years of age), Flook and her colleagues (2010) found that preadolescents who had been rated as low on self-regulatory ability by their parents and teachers showed significant improvement in the regulation of behavior, self-control, and metacognition following an 8-week mindfulness program. Improvements in self-regulation and self-awareness also can also positively affect adolescents' well-being. Among clinically-referred adolescents in an out-patient clinic, results of a randomized control study showed that compared to treatment-as-usual, those adolescents who received treatment-as-usual plus mindfulness training showed greater reductions in anxiety and depression (Biegel, Brown, Shapiro, & Schubert, 2009). Broderick and Metz (2009) found a significant reduction in negative affect and a significant increase in feelings of relaxation, calm, and self-acceptance among 12th grade high school girls following a mindfulness program targeting awareness of the body, awareness of feelings and reductions in self-judgment. Qualitative data revealed that adolescents said the training increased their awareness of and ability to regulate emotion. In 9 to 11 year-old boys and girls, a mindful yoga program was associated with decreases in youth self-reported rumination, intrusive thoughts, and emotional arousal to stressful events (Mendelson et al., 2010). Schonert-Reichl and Lawlor (2010) found increases in optimism for students in 4th-7th grades following a 10-week Mindfulness Education program compared to those randomized to control conditions. Teachers of students who received the mindfulness training also reported significant reductions in students' aggressive and oppositional behavior, and increases in focused attention and social competence in the classroom. Teachers were not blind to students' condition in the study, however.

In sum, although the evidence is still preliminary, there is some indication that MT for adolescents may promote the kinds of mindsets, skills sets and dispositions described in Tables 11.2 and 11.3. The mindful school embodies the idea the development of mindfulness and compassion are lifelong endeavors that can improve learning, health and well-being; and that adults and adolescents might fruitfully learn these skills together across the generations in schools that see themselves as existing for the lifelong development of all of their members.

SELF-ENHANCEMENT THROUGH SELF-TRANSCENDENCE

Throughout this chapter, we have described the mindful middle school as a kind of place that (a) is concerned with the holistic development of all and (b) that places great value on personal development and prosociality through mindfulness, motivation and perspective, and mutual support. Mindful schools are places where people are aware of themselves and others, and care for themselves and others as they go about the daily activities of leading, teaching and learning.

As such, this work has followed in the footsteps of Beane (1986), Beane and Lipka (1986), and Beane, Lipka, and, Ludewig (1980), who articulated a vision of middle schools and the middle grades curriculum with reference to the core life task that begins in a self-reflective, narratively coherent way in adolescence—the development of a sense of identity (see Pasupathi & McLean, 2010). These authors contributed significantly to a decades long discussion on the kinds of middle schools that enhance rather than undermine the development of healthy self-perceptions and senses of purpose among early adolescents given the many physical and mental changes that occur with puberty during this period. This chapter is itself an extension of that dialogue, and so we wish to end by discussing how what we are calling the "mindful middle school" relates to the idea that middle schools should focus on and foster healthy forms of self-enhancement and development among adolescents, and by extension, the adults who educate them in middle school. Specifically, we suggest that ideally, mindful middle schools are places that orient students, teachers and leaders alike toward self-enhancement through self-transcendence and prosocial behavior. What does this mean?

We define self-enhancement as a process by which individuals develop a sense of identity, belonging and positive esteem through the elaboration of their personal qualities and resources (e.g., mindsets and skill sets) and the extension of their networks of social support and social ties. Research has demonstrated that individuals pursue the enhancement of self during adolescence and adulthood through various differing means (Dweck, 2008). For some, self-enhancement comes primarily as a function of *improving* one's skills, knowledge and abilities over time compared to oneself. For others, self-enhancement comes primarily as a function of *proving* one's skills, knowledge, or abilities compared to others. Similarly, some individuals tend to build their social relationships around cooperation and mutual support to be *one's best*, whereas others develop their relationships around competition and a mutual striving to be *the best*. Whereas achievement, social comparison, competition and winning are clearly central to the American way of life (Kitayama, Markus, Matusmoto & Norasakkunkit, 1997), we propose that self-improvement, concern for others, and cooperation are actually the ways of life Americans need to adopt to be resilient and to work together collectively to address important social and ecological problems facing the nation and the world (Sachs, 2011). School, especially during adolescence, is the perfect training ground for teaching young people ways to participate later in society. It "trains" students by cultivating particular mindsets, skills and values.

With regard to the mindful middle school, we envision an organizational ethos that promotes the idea to adults and adolescents alike that one can enhance oneself by working to transcend oneself and to make positive contributions to the well-being of others. Self-transcendence refers to a striving for that which is beyond the ego-self, including our current identities, habits, knowledge and capabilities, as well as our self-centered interests regarding "me and mine." Victor Frankl (1984), a Jewish psychiatrist who survived the Nazi concentration camps, described self-transcendence in this way:

> being human always points, and is directed, to something, or someone, other than oneself—be it a meaning to fulfill or another human being to encounter. The more one forgets himself [sic]—by giving himself to a cause to serve or another person to love—the more human he is and the more he actualizes himself … self-actualization is possible only as a side effect of self-transcendence. (p. 115)

On this view, self-transcendence is about having a long-term purpose, an ideal, a beloved person toward which or whom one is constantly moving, and in which one is constantly losing oneself, such that one can fully become oneself. Mindful schools, through the cultivation of mindful awareness and compassion; through practices and norms that emphasize malleability, self-improvement, mastery, and cooperation; and through the valuing of kindness to self and others, provide an implicit education in Frankl's notion of self-actualization through self-transcendence.

His Holiness the 14th Dalai Lama (1999) has also referred to the need for a "spiritual revolution" in our times in which there is a re-orientation of values from self-centeredness to mutual concern for others.

> My call for a spiritual revolution is thus not a call for a religious revolution. Nor is it a reference to a way of life that is somehow otherworldly, still less to

something magical or mysterious. Rather, it is a call for a radical reorientation away from our habitual preoccupation with self. It is a call to turn toward the wider community of beings with whom we are connected, and for conduct which recognizes others' interests alongside our own. (pp. 23-24)

To work with others for collective—and not just self-interests; to work cooperatively and not competitively only; and to concern oneself with the needs of others as much as ourselves is the kind of reorientation of skills, perspectives, values that thinkers posit are necessary for our country to prosper in the 21st century (Sachs, 2011). What are needed, this line of thinking goes, are mindful, compassionate and innovative organizations that revitalize our nation (Ryan, 2012). In this chapter, we have attempted to sketch out a vision of the kind of middle grades schools that might help to prepare educators and adolescent students alike for this challenge and a fast-arriving future. We hope our visioning of the mindful middle school is helpful in this on-going dialogue about the culture of education we need in the 21st century.

REFERENCES

Ames, C. (1992). Classrooms: goals, structures, and student motivation. *Journal of Educational Psychology, 84*, 261-271.

Aronson, J., Cohen, G., McColskey, W., Montrosse, B., Lewis, K., & Mooney, K. (2009). *Reducing stereotype threat in classrooms*. Washington, DC: U.S. Department of Education, Institute of Education Sciences, National Center for Education Evaluation and Regional Assistance, Regional Educational Laboratory Southeast. Retrieved from http://ies.ed.gov/ncee/edlabs

Baer, R. A., Smith, G. T., Hopkins, J., Krietemeyer, J., & Toney, L. (2006). Using self-report assessment methods to explore facets of mindfulness. *Assessment, 13*, 27-45.

Ball, D. L., & Cohen, D. K. (1999). Developing practice, developing practitioners: Toward a practice-based theory of professional development. In L. Darling-Hammond & G. Skyes (Eds.), *Teaching as the learning professional: Handbook of policy and practice* (pp. 3-32). San Francisco, CA: Jossey-Bass.

Bandura, A. (1997). *Self-efficacy: The exercise of control*. New York, NY: Freeman.

Beane, J. A. (1986). The self-enhancing middle grade school. *The School Counselor, 33*, 189-195.

Beane, J. A., & Lipka, R. P. (1986). *Self-concept, self-esteem and the curriculum*. New York, NY: Teacher's College Press.

Beane, J. A., Lipka, R. P., & Ludewig, J. W. (1980, October). Synthesis of research on self concept. *Educational Leadership, 38*(1), 80-89.

Benn, R., Akiva, T., Arel, S., & Roeser, R. W. (2012). Mindfulness training effects for parents and educators of children with special needs. *Developmental Psychology*. Advance online publication. doi:10.1037/a0027537

Biegel, G. M., Brown, K. W., Shapiro, S. L, & Schubert, C. M. (2009). Mindfulness-based stress reduction for the treatment of adolescent psychiatric outpatients: A randomized clinical trial. *Journal of Counseling and Clinical Psychology, 77*(5), 855-66.

Birman, B., Desimone, L., Porter, A. C., & Garet, M. (2000). Designing professional development that works. *Educational Leadership, 57*(8), 28-33.

Blackwell, L. S., Trzesniewski, K. H., & Dweck, C. S. (2007). Implicit theories of intelligence predict achievement across an adolescent transition: A longitudinal study and an intervention. *Child Development, 78*(1), 246-263.

Briner, R., & Dewberry, C. (2007). *Staff wellbeing is key to school success.* Research summary prepared for Worklife Support, London, England.

Broderick, P. C., & Metz, S. (2009). Learning to BREATHE: Pilot trial of a mindfulness curriculum for adolescents. *Advances in School Mental Health Promotion, 2*, 35-46.

Bryk, A. S., & Schneider, B. H. (2002). *Trust in schools: A core resource for improvement.* New York, NY: SAGE.

Connell, J. P., & Broom, J. (2004). *The toughest nut to crack: First things first approach to improving teaching and learning* (Unpublished manuscript). Institute for Research and Reform in Education, Toms River, NJ.

Cullen, M. (2011). Mindfulness-based interventions: An emerging phenomena. *Mindfulness, 2*, 186-193.

Dalai Lama. (1999). *Ethics for a new millennium.* New York, NY: Penguin Putnam.

Darling-Hammond, L., & Bransford, J. (Eds.). (2005). *Preparing teachers for a changing world: What teachers should learn and be able to do.* San Francisco, CA: Jossey-Bass.

Diamond, A., & Lee, K. (2011). Interventions shown to aid executive function development in children 4-12 years old. *Science, 333*, 959-964.

Durlak, J. A., Weissberg, R. P., Dymnicki, A. B., Taylor, R. D., & Schellinger, K. B. (2011). The impact of enhancing students' social and emotional learning: A meta-analysis of school-based universal interventions. *Child Development, 82*, 405-432.

Dweck, C. (2008). Can personality be changed? The role of beliefs in personality and change. *Current Directions in Psychological Science, 17*, 391-394.

Eccles, J. S., & Roeser, R. W. (2010). School and community influences on human development. In M. H. Boorstein & M. E. Lamb (Eds.), *Developmental psychology: An advanced textbook* (6th ed., pp. 361-434). Hillsdale, NJ: Erlbaum.

Ericsson, K. A., & Charness, N. (1994). Expert performance: Its structure and acquisition. *American Psychologist, 8*, 725-747.

Erikson, E. H. (1968). *Identity, youth and crisis.* New York, NY: Norton.

Erikson, E. H. (1973). *Dimensions of a new identity.* New York, NY: Norton.

Flook, L. Smalley, S. L., Kitil, M. J., Galla, B. M., Kaiser Greenland, S., Locke, J., Ishijima, E., & Kasari, C. (2010). Effects of mindful awareness practices on executive functions in elementary school children. *Journal of Applied School Psychology, 26*, 70-95.

Frankl, V. E. (1984). *Man's search for meaning.* New York, NY: Beacon Press.

Friedman T. (2008). *Hot, flat, and crowded.* New York, NY: Farrar, Straus and Giroux.

Garet, M., Porter, S., Andrew, C., & Desimone, L. (2001). What makes professional development effective? Results from a national sample of teachers. *American Educational Research Journal, 38*, 915–945.

Goleman, D. (1995). *Emotional intelligence.* New York, NY: Bantam.

Greenberg, M. T., & Harris, A. R. (2012). Nurturing mindfulness in children and youth: Current state of research. *Child Development Perspectives, 6*, 161-166.

Greenberg, M. T., & Rhoades, B. L. (2008). *State-of-science review: Self regulation and executive function-what can teachers and schools do?* Foresight project: Mental capital and mental wellbeing. London, England: Office of Science and Innovation.

Harter, S., Whitesell, N. R., & Kowalski, P. (1992). Individual differences in the effects of educational transitions on young adolescents' perceptions of competence and motivational orientation. *American Educational Research Journal, 29*, 809-835

Heckman, J. J. (2007). The economics, technology and neuroscience of human capability formation. *Proceedings of the National Academic of Sciences, 104*, 13250-13255.

Hoy, W. K. (2002). An analysis of enabling and mindful school structures: Some theoretical, research and practical considerations. *Journal of Educational Administration, 41*, 87-108.

Hoy, W. K., Sweetland, S. R., & Smith, P. A. (2002). Toward an organizational model of achievement in high schools: The significance of collective efficacy. *Educational Administration Quarterly, 38*, 77-93.

James, W. (1890). *The principles of psychology.* New York, NY: Holt.

Jennings, P. A., & Greenberg, M. (2009). The prosocial classroom: Teacher social and emotional competence in relation to child and classroom outcomes. *Review of Educational Research, 79*, 491-525.

Jennings, P. A., Snowberg, K. E., Coccia, M. A., & Greenberg, M. T. (2011). Improving classroom learning environments by cultivating awareness and resilience in education: Results of two pilot studies. *Journal of Classroom Interaction, 46*, 37-48.

Kabat-Zinn, J. (2003). Mindfulness-based interventions in context: Past, present, and future. *Clinical Psychology: Science and Practice, 10*, 144-156.

Kaplan, A., & Maehr, M. L. (1999). Achievement goals and student well-being. *Contemporary Educational Psychology, 24*, 330-358.

Kemeny, M. E., Foltz, C., Cullen, M., Jennings, P., Gillath, O., Wallace, B. A., … Ekman, P. (2012). Contemplative/emotion training reduces negative emotional behavior and promotes prosocial responses. *Emotion, 12*, 338-350.

Kitayama, S., Markus, H. R, Matusmoto, H., & Norasakkunkit, V. (1997). Individual and collective processes in the construction of the self: Self-enhancement in the United States and self-criticism in Japan. *Journal of Personality and Social Psychology, 72*, 1245-1267.

Langer, E. J. (1989). *Mindfulness.* Reading, MA: Addison Wesley.

Lau, S., & Roeser, R. W. (2007). Cognitive abilities and motivational processes in science achievement and engagement: A person-centered analysis. *Learning and Individual Differences, 18*, 497-504.

Lee, V. E. (2000). Using hierarchical linear modeling to study social contexts: The case of school effects. *Educational Psychologist, 35*, 125-142.

Lee, V. E., Bryk, A., & Smith, J. (1993). The organization of effective secondary schools. In L. Darling-Hammond (Ed.), *Research in education 19* (pp. 171-226. Washington, DC: American Educational Research Association.

Lieberman, A., & Miller, L., (Eds.). (2008). *Teachers in professional communities.* New York, NY: Teachers College Press.

Lomos, C., Hofman, R. H., & Bosker, R. J. (2011). Professional communities and student achievement. *School effectiveness and school improvement: An International Journal of Research, Policy and Practice, 22*, 121-148.

MacDonald, E., & Shirley, D. (2009) *The mindful teacher.* New York, NY: Teachers College Press.

MacNeil, A. J., Prater, D. L., & Busch, S. (2009). The effects of school culture and climate on student achievement. *International Journal of Leadership in Education, 12*, 73-84.

Maehr, M. L., & Midgley, C. (1991). Enhancing student motivation: A schoolwide approach. *Educational Psychologist. 26*, 399-427.

Maehr M. L., & Midgley C. (1996). *Transforming school cultures.* Boulder, CO: Westview.

Meece, J. L., Anderman, E. M., & Anderman, L. H. (2005). Classroom goal structure, student motivation and academic achievement. *Annual Review of Psychology, 57*, 487-503.

Mendelson, T., Greenberg, M. T., Dariotis, J., Gould, L. F., Rhoades, B., & Leaf, P. J. (2010). Feasibility and preliminary outcomes of a school-based mindfulness intervention for urban youth. *Journal of Abnormal Child Psychology, 38*, 985-994.

Midgley, C. (2002). *Goals, goal structures, and patterns of adaptive learning.* Mahwah, NJ: Erlbaum.

Midgley, C., Anderman, E., & Hicks, L. (1995). Differences between elementary and middle school teachers and students: A goal theory approach. *Journal of Early Adolescence, 15*, 90-113.

Mills, L. B., McDowelle, J. O., & Rouse, W. A. (2011). A meta-analysis of research on the mediated effects of principal leadership on student achievement. In E. H. Reames (Ed.), *Southern Regional Council on Educational Administration 2011 Yearbook: Leading in the decade of challenges and opportunities* (pp. 23-30). Auburn, AL: Auburn University College of Education.

Mind and Life Education Research Network. (2012). Contemplative practices and mental training: Prospects for American education. *Child Development Perspectives, 6*, 146-153.

Moffitt, T. E., Arseneault, L., Belsky, D., Dickson, N., Hancox, R. J., Harrington, H., Houts, ... Caspi, A. (2011). A gradient of childhood self-control predicts health, wealth, and public safety. *Proceedings of the National Academy of Sciences, 108*, 2693-2698.

Neff, K. D. (2003). The development and validation of a scale to measure self-compassion. *Self and Identity, 2*, 223-250.

Neff, K. D., Hsieh, Y. P., & Dejitterat, K. (2005). Self-compassion, achievement goals, and coping with academic failure. *Self and Identity, 4*, 263-287.

Noddings, N. (2005). *The challenge to care in schools.* New York, NY: Teachers College Press.

Pasupathi, M., & McLean, K. C. (2010). Introduction. In M. Pasupathi & K. C. McLean (Eds.), *Narrative development in adolescence: Creating the storied self* (pp. xix-xxxiii). New York, NY: Springer.

Pianta, R. C., & Hamre, B. K. (2009). Conceptualization, measurement and improvement of classroom processes: Standardized observation can leverage capacity. *Educational Researcher, 38*, 109-119.

Robinson, V. M. J., Lloyd, C. A., & Rowe, K. J. (2008). The impact of leadership on student outcomes: An analysis of the differential effects of leadership types. *Educational Administration Quarterly, 44*, 635-674.

Roeser, R. W. (2012, April). *Mindfulness training for public school teachers: Rationales, processes and outcomes.* Paper presented at the biennial International Symposia for Contemplative Studies, Denver, Colorado.

Roeser, R. W., Eccles, J. S., & Sameroff, A. J. (1998). Academic and emotional functioning in early adolescence: Longitudinal relations, patterns, and prediction by experience in middle school. *Development and Psychopathology, 10*, 321-352.

Roeser, R. W., Eccles, J. S., & Sameroff, A. J. (2000). School as a context of social-emotional development: A summary of research findings. *Elementary School Journal, 100*, 443-471.

Roeser, R. W., Marachi, R., & Gehlbach, H. (2002). A goal theory perspective on teachers' professional identities and the contexts of teaching. In C. M. Midgley (Ed.), *Goals, goal structures, and patterns of adaptive learning* (pp. 205-241). Mahwah, NJ: Erlbaum.

Roeser, R. W., Midgley, C. M., & Urdan, T. C. (1996). Perceptions of the school psychological environment and early adolescents' psychological and behavioral functioning in school: The mediating role of goals and belonging. *Journal of Educational Psychology, 88*, 408-422.

Roeser, R. W., & Peck, S. C. (2009). An education in awareness: Self, motivation, and self- regulated learning in contemplative perspective. *Educational Psychologist, 44*, 119-136.

Roeser, R. W., Skinner, E., Beers, J., & Jennings, P. A. (2012). Mindfulness training and teachers' professional development: An emerging area of research and practice. *Child Development Perspectives, 6*, 167-173.

Roeser, R. W., & Zelazo, P. D. R. (2012). Contemplative science, education and child development: Introduction to the Special Section. *Child Development Perspectives, 6*, 143-145.

Roseth, C. J., Johnson, D. W., & Johnson, R. T. (2008). Promoting early adolescents' achievement and peer relationships: The effects of cooperative, competitive and individualistic goal structures. *Psychological Bulletin, 134*, 223-246.

Ryan, T. (2012). *A mindful nation.* Carlsbad, CA: Hay House.

Sachs, J. D. (2011). *The price of civilization.* New York, NY: Random House.

Sarason, S. B. (1990). *The predictable failure of school reform.* San Francisco, CA: Jossey-Bass.

Sarason, S. B. (1998). Some features of a flawed educational system. *Daedalus, 127,* 1-12.

Schonert-Reichl, K. A., & Lawlor, M. S. (2010). The effects of a mindfulness-based education program on pre- and early adolescents' wellbeing and social and emotional competence. *Mindfulness, 1,* 137-151.

Senko, C., Hulleman, C. S., & Harackiewicz, J. M. (2011). Achievement goal theory at the crossroads: Old controversies, current challenges, new directions. *Educational Psychologist, 46,* 26-47.

Smallwood, J., & Schooler, J. W. (2006). The restless mind. *Psychological Bulletin, 132,* 946-958.

Talbert, J. E., & McLaughlin, M. W. (1999). Assessing the school environment: Embedded contexts and bottom-up research strategies. In American Psychological Association (Ed.), *Measuring environment across the life span: Emerging methods and concepts* (pp. 197-227). Washington DC: APA.

Tyack, D. B., & Cuban, L. (1995). *Tinkering toward utopia: A century of public school reform.* Cambridge, MA: President and Fellows of Harvard College.

Winzelberg, A. J., & Luskin, F. M. (1999). The effects of a meditation training in stress levels in secondary school teachers. *Stress Medicine, 15,* 69-77.

Zelazo, P. D., & Lyons, K. E. (2012). The potential benefits of mindfulness training in early childhood: A developmental social cognitive neuroscience perspective. *Child Development Perspectives, 6,* 154-160.

Zimmerman, B. J. (2000). Attainment of self-regulation: A social cognitive perspective. In M. Boekaerts, P. R. Pintrich, & M. Zeidner (Eds.), *Handbook of self-regulation* (pp. 13-39). San Diego, CA: Academic Press.

Zins, J. E., Weissberg, R. P., Wang, M. C., & Walberg, H. J. (2004). *Building academic success on social and emotional learning.* New York, NY: Teachers College Press.

CHAPTER 12

UNDERSTANDING LEARNERS

From Confusion About Learners to Clear Understanding of Learner Characteristics

David Strahan

The complexity of the developmental changes that young adolescents experience underscores our commitment to provide programs and practices that are specifically designed for young adolescents themselves. Because these changes are so dynamic, middle level classrooms must be responsive and supportive.... Becoming a responsive teacher begins with gaining a full understanding of young adolescents and an appreciation for their individuality. (Strahan, L'Esperance, & Van Hoose, 2009, p. 85)

Understanding and responding to the developmental needs of young adolescents has long been the bedrock of the middle school concept. As stated in *This We Believe* (National Middle School Association, 2010), "The curriculum, pedagogy, and programs of middle grades schools must be based upon the developmental readiness, needs, and interests of young adolescents. This concept is at the heart of middle level education" (p. 5).

Consequently, middle level educators have assembled a wealth of information from research on young adolescent development and organized it in ways that help classroom teachers better understand their students.

Middle Grades Curriculum:
Voices and Visions of the Self-Enhancing School, pp. 213–225
Copyright © 2013 by Information Age Publishing
All rights of reproduction in any form reserved.

Caskey and Anfara (2007) compiled a useful synthesis of these efforts. They noted that, while research summaries often feature categories of characteristics such as physical, intellectual, emotional/psychological, moral/ethical, and social domains, "these characteristics are interrelated and overlap" (p. 1). In *Self-Concept, Self-Esteem, and the Curriculum*, Beane and Lipka (1986) emphasized the fundamental importance of this understanding:

> One characteristic of the self-enhancing school is that the professional staff has a clear understanding of the developmental characteristics of the learners with whom they work. This means that consideration is given to concepts such as developmental tasks and persistent life situations, as well as techniques for identifying problems, interests, needs, and concerns of individuals or groups of learners. (p. 185)

Since the publication of their book, evidence for the importance of this understanding has grown stronger. Researchers (Alvermann, 2009; Intrator & Kunzman, 2009) in the developmental arena have continued to examine how the changes students experience with the onset of puberty impact their views of themselves and of their interactions with others. At the same time, classroom researchers have analyzed the strategies teachers use to base instructional decisions on their understanding of students. An earlier analysis of developmental responsiveness and classroom practices concluded that good teachers demonstrate "theories of action" which draw from their personal values, observations, and professional wisdom to guide the decisions they make (Strahan, L'Esperance, & Van Hoose, 2009, p. 86). In this chapter, I will draw from a number of research syntheses and case studies to describe some of the ways that good teachers put their understanding of students into action in their classrooms.

UNDERSTANDING STUDENTS AS THE FOUNDATION OF SUCCESSFUL TEACHING

Over the past 3 decades, I have had an opportunity to document some of the ways that successful teachers create caring communities in their classrooms. I began my career in a large junior high with colleagues that inspired me to learn as much as I could about students and find ways to engage them in lessons. I decided to pursue graduate studies to extend my understanding through scholarship. As I began my own research, I found ways to collaborate with inspiring teachers and learn more about them. I soon found that while their classrooms were different in many ways, the underlying dynamics were often very similar, especially in terms of relationships among teachers and students.

One of our most detailed case studies compared the perceptions of two groups of students who had entered seventh grade with very little academic momentum (Strahan, 1988). One group *bounced back* to do well that year and the other continued to struggle. Students who made little progress most often expressed a *survival orientation* in their interviews. Some described ways that they tried to look busy. Others created disruptions, recalling freely ways they would *get into it* with classmates and teachers to avoid work. The students who made progress could describe the strategies they used for completing assignments and avoiding trouble. More specifically, they attributed their progress to supportive relationships with their teachers and to academic tasks they could accomplish.

A number of large-scale investigations have emphasized the power of these intertwined factors. Blum (2005) reported an extensive synthesis of research on school connectedness. He concluded:

> Students are more likely to succeed when they feel connected to school. School connection is the belief by students that adults in the school care about their learning as well as about them as individuals. The critical requirements for feeling connected include students' experiencing:

- high academic expectations and rigor coupled with support for learning;
- positive adult-student relationships; and
- physical and emotional safety (p. 20).

Intrator and Kunzman (2009), reported parallel results from their synthesis of more than a dozen investigations: "Across the studies we reviewed, youth express the perception that adults who can engage them in supportive and affirmative relationships matter in how they experience the curriculum" (p. 39).

To learn more about these dynamics as they occur in the flow of classroom events, I have conducted a series of intensive case studies with colleagues (Binkley, Keiser, & Strahan, 2011; Kronenberg & Strahan, 2010; Smith & Strahan, 2004; Strahan, Faircloth, Cope, & Hundley, 2007; Strahan & Layell, 2006; Strahan, Smith, McElrath, & Toole, 2001). Situated in a variety of settings over extended periods of time, these studies have documented four recurring patterns of success.

These good teachers addressed students' basic needs for physical and emotional safety. They created classroom communities that nurtured trusting relationships. Participants built trust with students in conversations that helped them learn more about students as individuals. They also promoted positive relationships among students so that they could support each other.

1. These good teachers planned instructional activities that were responsive to students' academic needs and interests. They developed assignments that linked inquiry and collaboration. These assignments provided rich data for assessing students' progress in learning strategies and concepts. Participants implemented challenging curricula by integrating content and procedures to foster a sense of "connectedness." They focused attention to social and ethical dimensions of learning by extending the community beyond the walls of their classrooms. Family and community activities provided opportunities for real-world experiences.

2. These good teachers provided ongoing personal support to students. Not only could they describe in detail the emotional, physical, intellectual and family needs and circumstances of students, they addressed these needs by responding to students as individuals.

3. These good teachers engaged students in dialogue that helped them make personal connections with their classroom experiences. They encouraged students to reflect on how they learned as well as what they learned. Participants nurtured intrinsic motivation by involving students in classroom decisions on a continuous basis. As students gained confidence, participants encouraged them to set goals and assume more responsibility for their learning.

4. In our case studies, we had many rich conversations with participants and were often present when they met with their colleagues. In these conversations, we rarely heard teachers use the language of researchers to express their understanding of their students. Formal terms like *developmental needs, physical changes, cognitive growth*, or *identity development* were seldom spoken. Informally, teachers often made comments like:

- students this age are so different;
- some seventh graders look like high schoolers; others still seem so young;
- puberty brings all sorts of changes and issues;
- hormones kick in at awkward times;
- middle school students think differently;
- they need to find out who they are;
- what their peers think of them is so important; and
- sometimes everything is black or white with students; they have a hard time seeing shades of gray.

Comments like these provide glimpses of the theories of action that guide good teachers' decisions. In the next section of this chapter, I will illustrate some of the ways that one team of teachers used their understanding of students to invite them to succeed.

UNDERSTANDING INTO ACTION

Two case studies conducted with the same team of teachers have provided a rich description of successful teaching across time. Richard and Jen were our collaborators in these investigations. For 3 years, they taught seventh grade as a two-teacher team at a middle school in a small southern city which serves just over 600 students, 35% of whom are members of minority groups and 45% of whom qualify for free and reduced meals. Richard taught math and science; Jen taught language arts and social studies.

In the first report (Strahan & Hedt, 2009), we examined how Richard and Jen learned to teach more responsively through collaboration. We documented ways that they integrated reading and writing across the curriculum to create connections with reluctant students during the 2007-2008 school year. Analysis of observations, interviews, and archival documents showed that their professional growth accelerated with discussions of instructional practices and student performance, guided by informal assessments of student achievement. At the end of the year, students on their team showed strong growth on statewide achievement tests in both mathematics and reading, exceeding the expected growth set by the state and showing gains that were higher on average than the other seventh grade teams at their school.

In the second study (Strahan, Kronenberg, Burgner, Doherty, & Hedt, 2012), we focused more specifically on ways the team differentiated instruction by chronicling the learning experiences of five seventh graders in an integrated unit. During the fall semester 2008, Richard and Jen worked with their fellow seventh grade teachers to develop and implement an interdisciplinary unit entitled "Hungry Planet" to integrate concepts from science and social studies with learning strategies using technology. This month-long unit was guided by five main themes that were linked to world hunger through lessons in math, science, language arts and social studies: nature, education, economics, population, and politics. We selected this unit as the focus of the study so that we could examine students' development of concepts in the context of specific content. Richard and Jen identified five students who represented a range of academic performance and would respond to the Hungry Planet unit from different perspectives.

- Juan and his family had recently moved to the area from Latin America and he seemed curious about other cultures. An excellent student, he was almost always engaged in lessons and eager to participate.

- Liz was also a good student, although she was often not as overtly engaged with social studies lessons as Juan. Jen noted, "She will push away the intellectual side of herself to look cool" (p. 14).

- James had engaged with lessons in a somewhat inconsistent fashion. Sometimes he was focused and inquisitive. Other days, he seemed disinterested.

- Mariah was also a bit of an enigma, occasionally demonstrating moments of keen insights while appearing distracted at other times. Her assignments sometimes featured perceptive comments, yet were often incomplete.

- Michael seemed to struggle with many concepts and rarely engaged with lesson activities.

We obtained consent from these students and their parents to participate in a study of their responses to instruction. We observed lesson activities, analyzed work products, and interviewed students about their perception of events and their understanding of concepts. Data showed that Richard and Jen encouraged engagement by identifying students' strengths, tapping interests, and extending their thoughts. Students' engagement with the unit varied according to connections they made with teachers and information. Results illuminated some of the dynamics of differentiation and provided rich illustrations of the four recurring patterns of success emphasized in all of our case studies:

- creating safe classroom communities that nurture trust;
- planning instruction that responds to needs and interests;
- providing ongoing personal support to students; and
- engaging students in dialogue that connects learning experiences.

Creating Safe Classroom Communities That Nurture Trust

In our first case study, we described how Richard and Jen made a conscious effort to create classroom-learning communities. From the first days of school, they worked together to promote shared responsibility for learning. As Richard suggested, "We have managed to stay positive and not let the dangerous attitude of 'it's not cool to be smart—it's not cool to be motivated by school' get started" (Strahan & Hedt, 2009, p. 10). In regular dialogue sessions, he and Jen collaborated "to get students to accept the fact that they need to come into the classroom and give it their best shot" (p. 7). By modeling positive interpersonal dynamics with students and with each other, they invited students to trust them and trust each other. As the year progressed, students' sense of community grew stronger. Peer relationships became more supportive and students expressed a team identity.

> Richard and Jen put a great deal of effort in developing cooperative groups, seating students so that they built relationships and supported each other. They met with each other daily, discussing the progress of individual students and developing strategies/interventions.... They conferred with students individually and worked with them in small-group settings both during instructional time and before and after school. They can tell you a wealth of information about every single student on their team and incorporate that understanding into instructional design. (Strahan & Hedt, 2009, p. 12)

In the first study, Jen emphasized strategy journals as an important source of information:

> I have been keeping strategy journals this year where they write up their experience after a project. It is very simple—what did you like? What didn't you like? There is not much more to the journals than that. I keep those journals because I like to take them home and respond back to them while the lesson is still fresh in their minds. That has been one of the best tools I have had. (Strahan & Hedt, 2009, p. 9).

As teachers in our other case studies had done, Richard and Jen made a conscious effort to get to know their students and create a supportive climate for learning. Learning more about students as individuals enabled them to better understand their needs and interests. They could then use this knowledge to plan instruction more precisely.

Planning Instruction That Responds to Needs and Interests

In planning the Hungry Planet unit, Richard and Jen used their knowledge of students' needs and interests to design lessons that scaffolded instruction and taught strategies explicitly. Introductory activities featured a video of graphic images of human hunger around the world, a speaker from a local food bank, and a presentation on the work of Doctors without Borders in countries afflicted by hunger. In their social studies classes, students used the book, *Hungry Planet* (Menzel & D'Aluisio, 2007), to learn about food consumption in a variety of countries around the world. Several math and technology lessons focused on the 2007 World Population Data Sheet produced by the Population Reference Bureau. Students worked in groups to make graphs of the information. The World Population Data Sheet was also the basis for a related technology lesson. Students went to the computer lab (or worked on classroom laptops) to learn new spreadsheet skills in Microsoft Excel. In their Language Arts and Social Studies classes, students learned about the genocide in Sudan and how it related to hunger. With the details they learned from the articles they read, students completed a writing assignment related to these current events. The basic assignment was a graphic organizer including categories such as government and geography. More advanced assignments required a letter to the United Nations including statistics and a solution to the problem or to a celebrity to convince him or her to put on a charity event to benefit the Sudanese refugees.

As they implemented these activities, Richard and Jen made adjustments based on students' responses. For example, Richard was not sure that some students saw connections between the dew point lab activity and concepts of food growth. He decided to show a United Streaming video on dew point and humidity. "It was short and they watched it twice to be sure we all understood the connection between dew point, the lab, and climate in Africa" (Strahan & Hedt, 2009, p. 20). After introducing a lesson on Sudan, Jen incorporated a simulated *walk to a refugee camp in a high state of malnourishment* to give kinesthetic learners a chance to move. She asked students to walk as though they were protein deprived. After this walk, she led a discussion of atrophied muscles and the importance of protein in brain function—making connections with the science curriculum. She also added more explicit reading strategies into the passages from the *Hungry Planet* books, encouraging students to compare details regarding packaged vs. nonpackaged foods from around the world (Strahan & Hedt, p. 20).

Providing Ongoing Personal Support to Students

Richard and Jen planned activities and discussions that helped them learn more about their students as individuals. They worked together to develop a sophisticated set of formal and informal assessments. Using data from weekly assignments and the district's benchmark tests, they collaborated with Melissa to develop a stronger system for monitoring individual performance. They created a portfolio of work samples in which students did a math or science activity that incorporated writing. During lessons, they engaged in habitual *kidwatching,* a process Jen described as "just visually seeing the difference in the kids' attitudes in what you are doing. When the piece of the puzzle falls into place for them, it is really obvious in how they approach the product" (p. 8).

Richard and Jen used this information about individuals to provide ongoing support to them. For example, they noted that James's reasoning on the Hungry Planet Unit as well as on other lessons was inconsistent. They began to investigate his work patterns more closely. They encouraged one of the teacher assistants to spend more time with James during the flow of lessons. Ms. J. worked with James during group assignments and occasionally pulled him aside for one-to-one support. In an interview toward the end of the year, Ms. J. noted:

> I try to follow Jen's example of being very fair and as consistent as possible. James was motivated when he wanted to be—and had his days when he's uninterested in everything. He can also be very focused. Anything visual really helps him. The integration of visual elements seems to make a big difference for him. (p. 26)

When asked to share perceptions of James and his work, Jen and Richard noted that the individualized support he received from Ms. J. helped him to simplify big ideas into smaller parts that were more digestible for him academically. Jen recalled that James thrived on classroom participation and being called on during class. "He's one of the few students who really enjoyed preferential seating. He enjoyed sitting in the front and being close to the action. He worked very well with anything visual—it seemed to tap into the artist in him, anything art-based he connected with" (p. 27)

When asked to reflect on his experiences, James expressed appreciation for the way Richard would "always help with simplifying things. We studied as a class and he would give us some easier ways to do problems." He added that his teachers gave him "a lot of one-on-one help and would help me afterschool. They have done a lot of things to show me they care" (p. 27).

Mariah's varied responses to activities led her teachers to spend more time with her individually. Richard noted "for math, it was always a bit of a mystery that she did as well as she did. I just had to trust she understood it all when she said she did." Jen recalled "We knew we had to put her with the person she knew best in the class or she'd just shut down; she's shy like that" (p. 28). Jen learned that Mariah often tried to hide her reading ability from her friends.

> It was seen as not cool to read, but she found ways to get it done. One reason she improved her reading so much is that she is a secret reader. I learned not to talk with her about books in front of other students. She is super shy. If we offered to work with her during class, she would say "I don't need help." I found that if I talked with her off-stage, she loved talking about books. I ordered a few things just for her and made sure she got to keep them. (p. 28)

When asked, "What were the most helpful things your teachers did?" Mariah's responses included "Ms. D. would help us learn things using videos and making us do big projects. Mr. B. put things on the board and walked us through problems, then gave us some problems to work on our own or like in pairs, which would help me. They would check in on us when we worked alone and answered questions, gave us more time too if we needed it" (p. 29).

Knowing students as individuals enabled Richard and Jen to interpret their responses to lesson activities with increasing precision. They tailored interventions to address their needs and interests. Students appreciated their efforts to engage them in lessons and strengthened their views of themselves as learners.

Engaging Students in Dialogue That Connects Learning Experiences

In the first case study, Jen described how students' responses to classroom discussions led her to place more emphasis on heightening their explicit attention to learning strategies:

> I learned this last year that if you let students know from the beginning that they are going to write about strategy and about how well that lesson worked for you, eventually they can start talking about it on their own. By the end of this year, if it works as well as last year, they will be able to really evaluate themselves critically and get to a point they are pulling from text, comparing themselves with others, and finding strategies that will work better for them. (Strahan & Hedt, 2009, p. 8)

Richard and Jen planned seminars as integral activities for the Hungry Planet unit. The opening seminar followed the presentation from Doctors without Borders and featured the Bracelet of Life, a paper bracelet used to determine the level of malnourishment experienced by a patient. Teachers presented students with a Bracelet of Life and asked them to guess what its purpose might be in relation to doctors working with malnourished patients. They then used it on themselves and discussed ways their levels of health compared with those of the malnourished. For the closing seminar, students examined two photographs, the first of a city and the second an image of an adult and children, possibly a family, collecting or scavenging in what looks like a large pile of rubble along a river. Students then put the photographs together to see that they were really one image cut in two. Teachers then asked questions such as "How do these photos relate to our study of hunger during Hungry Planet? And, what are specific actions we could take at school, home or in our communities to help end poverty?"

Richard and Jen extended these reflections with written assignments. For the final assessment of the unit, students created a concept map that linked hunger to the guiding themes: economics, politics, population, education, and nature. Their assignment was then to write a letter to the United Nations that proposed a plan to solve world hunger with supportive information from the unit. Their plans were to be supported by information they learned during the unit and were to include details such as the necessity for their plan and its logistics.

In addition to these formal discussions, Jen and Richard regularly encouraged dialogue about students' reflections. Questions such as "what do you think?" and "what does that mean to you?" recurred in almost every lesson. Their emphasis on reflection and interpretation encouraged students to make personal connections. Debriefing interviews included the following insights:

> For Economics, I related to what we were talking about in Ms. Doherty's class about colonialism. We just talked about the Berlin Conference. It relates economics and hunger. The Africans couldn't get all their raw materials, like iron and diamonds, because the Europeans took it all and made money off of it. This would make them poor and hungry. I think homelessness and charity are also related to economics. (Juan)
>
> (It) was interesting because it was fun to work with the numbers and charts. We only chose one region to make the charts but we looked at a lot of them to make our choice. It was cool to see all the differences … I liked looking for information, instead of just writing it down … I felt like I got a lot out of it because there was so much information to see. It was challenging because it took a long time. It was important to see things like life expectancy; some comparisons were surprising, too. (Liz)
>
> I used the data sheet with all the numbers on it. I made it connect to hunger because there was a column that was like 'percent of hungry people.' I used that to compare it to the whole population of a place. I thought it was like using facts mainly. But it also makes a connection to hunger because of those percents. (James)

These responses demonstrate some of the personal connections that students made with their classroom experiences. They became more reflective about ways they learned best, gained confidence in themselves as students, and began to assume more responsibility for their learning.

CONCLUSIONS

Richard, Jen, and the other teachers who have collaborated in our classroom case studies over the years have provided me a continuing source of inspiration. Their interactions with students affirm the power of caring adults to encourage academic and personal connections in school. In many ways, they demonstrate that much of good teaching flows from understanding students. The examples from our case studies that I have shared in this chapter suggest several insights about the theories of action that guide good teachers' decisions.

First, theories of action reflect an understanding of developmental needs in general and individual needs in particular. Good teachers know that middle school students are as different from each other as they are from elementary children or older adolescents. They know that puberty triggers major changes, some predictable, others less so. They know that middle school students learn to think in new ways, especially so about themselves and how they relate to the world. They understand the fragile nature of peer dynamics and moral judgments. Although they have internalized these insights, these teachers are more likely to talk about what Juan wants to know about Latin America, why Liz wants to look cool, when James is engaged in activities, why Mariah appears distracted, or how to bring Michael into discussions.

We can also infer that theories of action reflect core values. Good teachers value a sense of community in the classroom because students need to feel safe. They treasure activities that spark curiosity because inquiry matters. They find time to work with individuals because students learn to care by example. They promote thoughtful conversation because dialogue provides opportunities to consider their own values and the values of others.

For all of these reasons, understanding learners is essential to the self-enhancing school. A central element in the vision of a school in which every facet of the environment is self-enhancing is that "young adolescents gradually exercise more control over their lives in school" (Lipka, 1997, p. 34). Experiencing a school in which all of the teachers care about students as much as Richard and Jen do would make such a transition more likely. Interacting each day with teachers who put caring into action with their level of sophistication would be self-enhancing. Having an opportunity to document such experiences would increase the probability that other teachers in other schools would embrace this vision.

REFERENCES

Alvermann, D. E. (2009). Sociocultural constructions of adolescence and young people's literacies. In L. Christenbury, R. Bomer, & P. Smagorinsky (Eds.), *Handbook of adolescent literacy research* (pp. 14-28). New York, NY: The Guilford Press.

Beane, J. A., & Lipka, R. P. (1986). *Self-concept, self-esteem, and the curriculum*. New York, NY: Teachers College Press.

Binkley, R., Keiser, M., & Strahan, D. (2011). Connected coaching: How three middle school teachers responded to the challenge to integrate social studies and literacy. *The Journal of Social Studies Research, 35*(2), 131-162.

Blum, R. W. (2005, April). A case for school connectedness. *Educational Leadership,* 16-20.

Caskey, M. M., & Anfara, V. A., Jr. (2007). Research summary: Young adolescents' developmental characteristics. *Association for Middle Level Education.* Retrieved from http://www.nmsa.org/Research/ResearchSummaries/ DevelopmentalCharacteristics/tabid/1414/Default.aspx

Intrator, S. M., & Kunzman, R. (2009). Who are adolescents today? Youth voices and what they tell us. In L. Christenbury, R. Bomer, & P. Smagorinsky (Eds.), *Handbook of adolescent literacy research* (pp. 29-47). New York, NY: The Guilford Press.

Kronenberg, J., & Strahan, D. (2010). Responsive teaching: A framework for inviting success with students who "Fly below the radar" in middle school classrooms. *Journal of Invitational Theory and Practice, 16,* 77-86.

Lipka, R. P. (1997). Enhancing self-concept/self-esteem in young adolescents. In J. L. Irvin (Ed.), *What current research says to the middle level practitioner* (pp. 31-39). Westerville, OH: National Middle School Association.

Menzel, P., & D'Aluisio, F. (2007). *Hungry planet: What the world eats.* Napa, CA: Material World Books.

National Middle School Association. (2010). *This we believe: Keys to educating young adolescents.* Westerville, OH: Author.

Smith, T. W., & Strahan, D. (2004). Toward a prototype of expertise in teaching: A descriptive case study. *Journal of Teacher Education, 55*(4), 357-371.

Strahan, D. (1988). Life on the margins: How academically at-risk early adolescents view themselves and school. *Journal of Early Adolescence, 8*(4), 373-390.

Strahan, D., Faircloth, C. V., Cope, M., & Hundley, S. (2007). Exploring the dynamics of academic reconnections: A case study of middle school teachers' efforts and students' responses. *Middle Grades Research Journal, 2*(2), 19-41.

Strahan, D., & Hedt, M. (2009). Teaching and teaming more responsively: Case studies in professional growth at the middle level. *RMLE Online—Research in Middle Level Education, 32*(8), 1-14. Retrieved from http://www.amle.org/ Publications/RMLEOnline/Articles/Vol32No8/tabid/1894/Default.aspx

Strahan, D., Kronenberg, J., Burgner, R., Doherty, J., & Hedt, M. (2012). Differentiation in action: Developing a logic model for responsive teaching in an urban middle school. *Research in Middle Level Education Online, 35*(8), 1-17.

Strahan, D., & Layell, K. (2006). Connecting caring and action through responsive teaching: How one team accomplished success in a struggling middle school. *The Clearing House, 9*(3), 147-154.

Strahan, D., L'Esperance, M., & Van Hoose, J. (2009). *Promoting harmony: Young adolescent development and classroom practices.* Westerville, OH: National Middle School Association.

Strahan, D., Smith, T., McElrath, M., & Toole, C. (2001). Connecting caring and action: Teachers who create learning communities in their classrooms. In T. Dickinson (Ed.), *Reinventing the Middle School* (pp. 96-116). New York, NY: Routledge Press.

CHAPTER 13

THE EFFECTS ON TEACHERS AND STUDENTS OF USING VAGUE AND SPECIFIC LEARNING CONSTRUCTS TO ENHANCE SELF-PERCEPTIONS

James E. Calder and Thomas M. Brinthaupt

Education is a social process; education is growth; education is not a preparation for life but is life itself.

—John Dewey

Too often students are given answers to remember, rather than problems to solve.

—Roger Lewin

The most important function of education at any level is to develop the personality of the individual and the significance of his life to himself and to others.

—Grayson Kirk

In their view of the Self-Enhancing School, Beane and Lipka (1986) identified a variety of characteristics for "moving *from* some debilitating feature *to* an enhancing feature" (p. 179). In their illustration, they identified

Middle Grades Curriculum:
Voices and Visions of the Self-Enhancing School, pp. 227–240
Copyright © 2013 by Information Age Publishing

learning constructs that are vague about student self-perceptions as debilitating and learning constructs that are specific about student self-perceptions as enhancing. In this chapter, we will focus on vague and specific learning constructs as they relate to the current school climate being dominated by state and federal legislation, including *No Child Left Behind*, state standards, and state-mandated assessments. In this context, we will supplement Beane and Lipka's points by arguing that vague overall learning constructs can have enhancing features while specific learning constructs can be debilitating in terms of student self-perceptions.

In order to develop our argument, we need first to define some of the ways that learning constructs can be vague or specific in the context of middle schools. The vague/specific continuum can be applied in different ways to the activities of teachers (e.g., their lesson plans and class activities). For example, teacher activities can be vague or specific in terms of being teacher-centered, structured, directed, clear-cut, and so on. An example of a vague general learning activity would be the use of problem-based or collaborative learning. Class activities can also be vague or specific in terms of whether they actively and directly address student self-perceptions. An example of a specific self-perception related activity would be organizing a content module around the ways that it helps students to define their selves or identities. Seen in this light, it is possible for either vague or specific general teaching activities to be either vague or specific with regard to their self-enhancing qualities.

There seems to be very little room in today's educational reform climate of teacher/student accountability to specifically include the characteristics of the self-enhancing school as described by Beane and Lipka (1986). Emphasis in high schools and middle schools is focused on the acquisition of academic content at the expense of the individual student's self-development. Research highlights the movement in schools toward teacher-centered approaches and away from student-centered learning activities in response to the pressures emanating from current school reforms (Faulkner & Cook, 2006). This movement can be characterized as using increasingly specific teaching approaches that are at the same time vague about (or completely ignore) self-perception related constructs.

The evidence indicates that, in addition to the physical, emotional, and social changes that students experience (Brinthaupt & Lipka, 2002; Harter, 1999), the structure of middle school requires significant adjustments for students (Arowosafe & Irvin, 1992; Eccles, Lord, & Midgley, 1991; Simmons & Blyth, 1987). Compared to elementary school students, new middle school students are accountable to multiple teachers rather than one teacher in a self-contained classroom; they experience greater performance expectations; and they are expected to show greater behavioral control and to assume increased personal responsibility (Association for

Middle Level Education, 2002). In addition, it is clear that there are differences among schools' cultures or climates in the tendency to prefer vague or specific self-related learning constructs due to historical, cultural, and leadership factors (for a review, see Beane, 1994).

In the current climate of high-stakes testing, attention to student self-perceptions and values takes a back seat to drill-and-practice activities (Moon, Brighton, Jarvis, & Hall, 2007). Goals for both teachers and students come down from the top, whether from local, state or federal administrators. In essence, it is increasingly likely that control is being externally applied from the perspective of both teachers and students. Middle school students have very little control over their educational experiences; middle school teachers have control over their students, but they increasingly, in the current educational climate, have very little control over what and how they can teach those students. It seems as though federal legislation, such as *No Child Left Behind,* has created a top-down atmosphere in educational reform fostering a trickle down mentality where State Departments of Education are trying to keep the U.S. Department of Education *off their ass,* which results in superintendents trying to keep State Departments *off their ass,* further resulting in principals trying to keep superintendents *off their ass,* resulting in teachers trying to keep principals *off their ass.* It is ironic that the most important stake holders in this entire process, the students, are left holding the *short end of the stick!* Throughout this chapter, we will show that the shift toward teacher-centered approaches in the name of *teaching to the test* is not creating better test results, as hoped, but rather is resulting in middle school environments that have drifted away from the self-perception enhancing student-centered approaches.

Under these circumstances, the implementation of an inclusive curriculum that focuses on the whole person is very difficult. The attitudes of both teachers and students are likely to be changing due to these top-down directives. What factors affect teachers' willingness or ability to include content that enhances student self-perceptions in their classes? What factors affect students' willingness or ability to achieve self-perception clarity and accuracy from their middle school classes? In the remainder of this chapter, we discuss the vague/specific construct issue from the perspective of both the teacher and the middle school student.

THE TEACHER'S PERSPECTIVE

Compared to elementary school teachers, the curriculum of middle school teachers is less likely to have a *love children* emphasis and more likely to have a content emphasis (Fitzsimmons & Lanphar, 2011). In

230 J. E. CALDER and T. M. BRINTHAUPT

today's climate of school reform, middle school teachers focus more on the student's acquisition of curriculum content (History, Algebra I, English, Geography, etc.) than the student's development of self. In fact, except for their responsibilities to their homeroom students, teachers' entire days in the classroom may be spent providing instruction in their specialized content areas to a large number of students who they are unlikely to know very well (e.g., Brown & Knowles, 2007).

Beane (1991) points out that, historically, programs that presented the authentic integration of affect and cognition "usually disappeared as new academic demands found a place in the schedule" (p. 12). The utilization of such approaches as thematic units and block scheduling have been abandoned in the face of federal legislation and state-mandated testing and replaced with the employment of drill and practice, worksheets, lectures, and whole class discussions as teachers feel more pressure to *teach to the test*. However, this is in direct contrast to the tenets of the middle school philosophy which asserts that early adolescents must experience a variety of instructional strategies that transcend teacher-centered approaches to fully receive a quality educational experience (Amrein & Berliner, 2003; Faulkner & Cook, 2006; Leonard, 1968; Nichols & Berliner, 2007, 2008).

Even though proponents believe that high-stakes testing will lead to improved instructional practice and student progress, such practices lead to neither increased student motivation nor increased student achievement (Amrein & Berliner, 2003; Nichols & Berliner, 2007). In light of this research, we question whether the decision by teachers to rely on teacher-centered instructional practices in the name of academic progress should not be seriously reconsidered. As other chapters in this book demonstrate, there is much research support for adopting those student-centered activities that directly support academic success and that directly or indirectly support the growth of student self-esteem and the clarification of their self-perceptions.

It is likely to be the case that, all things considered, it takes more work for teachers to use specific, self-enhancing learning constructs than to use vague ones. In their study, Faulkner and Cook (2006) indicated that middle school teachers reported widespread "use of often ineffective strategies such as lecture and worksheets to the exclusion of more developmentally responsive and academically engaging strategies like hands-on experiments, reflective writing, inquiry, integrated units, literature circles, and Socratic seminars" (p. 10). These engaging strategies require more preparation time and the development and use of authentic assessment by the teacher than the utilized lecture and worksheet strategies. However, research indicates that these student-centered strategies result in middle school students experiencing greater academic success and achieving higher scores on high stakes tests than the teacher-centered strategies (Eggen & Kauchak, 2001; McCombs, 2004; McEwin, Dickinson, & Jenkins, 2003; Needles & Knapp, 1994), as well as students reporting more positive changes in attitudes and self-perceptions (Hall, 2006; Huber, Smith, & Shotsberger, 2000).

One of the ways we are defining vague/specific is in terms of the effort made to integrate course content with student experiences and interests. Early adolescent middle school students are by nature inquisitive and particularly prone to ask *why* they need to learn something. In fact, research investigating the involvement of students in decision making (e.g., Gould, 2011; McCuddy, Pinar, & Gingerich, 2008; Patmor & McIntyre, 1999) supports the concept of building on this natural inquisitiveness as a way to develop an inclusive curriculum based on middle school students' experiences and interests. In discussing his vision for an integrated curriculum, Beane (1991) refers to the need to engage in new curriculum conversations that "view early adolescents as real human beings who, whole at this stage, are also participants in the larger world" (p. 10). In fact, Huber and colleagues (2000) acknowledge that learning "is something students do, not what is done to them" and "where students ask questions, acquire knowledge, construct explanations … and test explanations in many ways" (p. 4). When teachers fail to make learning authentic and engaging, their students will find themselves on the *vague* side of the learning construct continuum—both in the general sense and with regard to self-perceptions.

What are examples of teacher activities that are specific to the enhancement of student self-perception? As Faulkner and Cook (2006) point out, actively involving middle school students throughout the learning process, including being a part of the decision making, results in greater academic success. Fitzsimmons and Lanphar (2011) found that in an authentic learning environment, "each student felt their voice was heard, and they realized the collective voice of the class was also being heard with genuine care and respect, each interaction with their teacher, and ultimately their peers, not only gave them a sense of feeling valued, but also a belief in their competence" (p. 38). In addition, they found that through authentic learning "the role of emotion in classroom learning is not one of simply being a 'feel good' experience, but the psycho-socioemotional glue that has the potential to take middle school students to new areas of reflective and practical capabilities" (p. 39). Simply stated by one student, authentic learning provided an "open learning place I can do what I want to do without a map telling me what to do. The teachers here guide you but you can really choose. You have the freedom to choose" (p. 39). According to Moos and Honkomp (2011), the foundation of authentic learning includes three basic needs: autonomy, competence, and relatedness. Thus, learning must provide students with an opportunity to have a voice in choosing what they will learn, to actively engage in the learning process, and to interact and collaborate with classmates. However, as stated repeatedly throughout this chapter, in today's climate of standards, high-stakes testing, and teacher and student accountability, teachers continue feel pressure to *teach the test* and to gravitate toward more teacher-centered strategies such as lectures, whole class instruction, worksheets, and drill and practice as a way of achieving this outcome (Faulkner & Cook, 2006; Nichols & Berliner, 2008). As we have also noted, these strategies are very specific with regard to the content; however, they are vague about how that content relates to student self-perceptions.

As we have shown, the middle school philosophy is based on tenets that value actively engaging early adolescents in student-centered activities, including being involved in the decision making process. Zemelman, Daniels, and Hyde (1998) support the value of engaging middle school students in active learning experiences because these experiences allow students to learn by doing rather than by hearing about the content. Philosophically, middle school teachers are prepared to embrace a curriculum that is relevant and challenging, using a variety of strategies that support *best practices* in teaching and learning and that use authentic assessments. Yet, there seems to be very little teacher training that focuses on the self-perception process or on ways that teachers can help their students to obtain self-perceptual and values clarity (see Brinthaupt, this volume). There is even less time for (and importance attached to) middle school teachers being concerned with the developing selves of their students. The lack of training, time, or importance devoted to self-related issues means that teachers will continue to teach in ways that fail to integrate content and learning objectives with students' efforts to learn about and understand themselves. At best, attention to student self-perceptions appears to be an afterthought or is not thought about at all.

Although there is little training for teachers in understanding and working with personality and self-perceptual differences, with regard to both themselves and their students, there are ways to integrate teacher self-understanding effectively into preservice and professional development programs (Kelchtermans, 2009). Despite interest in and attention devoted to diversity, the bottom line is that teacher attitudes and willingness to work with diverse students is the key to teaching and learning success. The tendency to attend to student self-issues is likely to be a function of the teacher's professional identity or commitment to the profession. However, we are unaware of any research that addresses this possibility. In the current climate, we are moving in the opposite direction, away from acknowledging and integrating both the teachers' and the students' self-perceptions and values in the classroom.

It takes more than trying to train prospective teachers to work with diverse students to effectively impact student self-perceptions. According to Steer (1984), "the most effective middle/junior high school teacher is one who genuinely likes and respects people, and who is committed to working with 'transescents,' or young people in transition from childhood to adolescents; listening to and talking with them; and assisting in their development of positive self concepts" (p. 1). Gullatt (1995) adds that middle school teachers should also be able to "work effectively as a member of an instructional team; design and implement interdisciplinary programs of study; understand and utilize sound principles of guidance; use a variety of teaching styles and instructional techniques; and foster leadership potentiality of adolescents" (p. 1). These qualities seem to be the important lynch pin between the curriculum and the student. Teachers possessing these qualities inherently embrace and utilize strategies and techniques that engage early adolescents in active student-centered learning activities within the middle school curriculum (McCombs, 2004).

In the current No Child Left Behind climate of emphasizing student test scores, teacher self-perceptions are also likely to be negatively affected. We cannot overlook the influence of teachers' conceptualization of themselves as teachers in playing a contributing role in the vague/specific continuum discussed in this chapter (see Lipka & Brinthaupt, 1999). Research reveals that just as a teacher's behavior influences a student's self-concept, so are teachers' self-concepts affected by their professional relationships with significant others (Borich, 1999). These significant others include, but are not limited to, principals and supervisors. In today's climate of high stakes testing and teacher accountability, teacher evaluations are heavily weighted by the test scores of their students and their evaluations by their professional significant others. The effect of these evaluations on teacher self-perceptions is a natural experiment in the making.

In summary, because of the pressures middle school teachers are experiencing to be successful, many are abandoning student-centered instructional activities for building test-taking skills and the memorization of facts. It is, however, student-centered learning activities that engage students in hands-on experiences such as problem-based learning (Cerezo, 2004), cooperative learning (Johnson, Johnson, & Scott, 1978), and team building (Gibbons & Ebbeck, 2011) that are fundamental to the development of students' self-perceptions. However, as we have argued, teacher-centered instructional activities are inherently poorer than student-centered activities at enhancing student self-perceptions. It is seemingly paradoxical that student-centered instruction, while frequently vague in terms of techniques and teacher-directedness, is actually more specific about student self-perceptions. The teacher-directed approaches are frequently quite clear-cut, efficient, and specific, yet these approaches offer little in the way of helping students to understand themselves and their educational experiences.

THE STUDENT'S PERSPECTIVE

Because of the wide variety of physical, social, cognitive, and psychological changes they are undergoing (Brinthaupt & Lipka, 2002; Harter, 1999), middle school students are also likely to vacillate between the need for adult guidance and the need to assert their independence and autonomy. Working with young people who can be unpredictable, inconsistent, moody, and stubborn makes the job of middle school teacher particularly challenging. Within this context, teaching approaches that are vague or specific can have multiple effects.

Middle school students show clear preferences for student-centered teaching approaches (e.g., Huber et al., 2000; Patmor & McIntyre, 1999). What is the effect on students' learning and motivation when they perceive their teachers as uninterested in or unable/unwilling to address their self and identity concerns? One likely effect is to show students that school is more of a job than an adventure. When externally directed goals and criteria (that teachers may not agree with or believe in) come to dominate the implicit and explicit classroom dialogue, students are likely to avoid and discount rather than approach and embrace their learning.

If teachers are under increased pressure to ensure that their students perform well on standardized tests, then it is logical that they will try to manage their classrooms in controlling and heavily rule-oriented ways. Middle school students are unlikely to respond favorably to these teacher behaviors. Rather, students are likely to show defiance, disinterest, reactance, resistance, and defensiveness (Eccles et al., 1991). These student behaviors can be expressed either covertly and passively or overtly and actively. As Moon and colleagues (2007) found with gifted and talented students, the pressure to produce high test scores is associated with disengagement from the learning process and resentment and frustration toward the slow pace and repetitive aspects of daily classroom activities.

Middle school students are likely to be particularly bothered by learning constructs that are taught in very structured and specific ways but that are simultaneously vague or indifferent to their self-perceptions and self-understanding. There is some evidence that teachers expect their students to show increasing abilities to engage in cooperative learning and to demonstrate self-control and self-assertion skills (e.g., Lane, Pierson, Stang, & Carter, 2010; Lane, Wehby, & Cooley, 2006). Students also show greater motivation and interest in learning when their teachers are supportive and caring (e.g., Wentzel, 1997). Similarly, students who have high-quality relationships with their teachers are more willing to follow school and classroom rules and require less discipline than students who have poor relationships with their teachers (Beaty-O'Ferrall, Green, & Hanna, 2010; Marzano, Marzano, & Pickering, 2003). There is also some evidence that parental involvement can increase middle level school students' self-concepts and locus of control (e.g., You & Nguyen, 2011). Additionally, research has demonstrated that when middle level school students have positive views about their parents, teachers, and school support, this can have a strong effect on their achievement (Marchant, Paulson, & Rothlisberg, 2001).

It may also be a common experience that students have teachers who vary in their use of vague and specific teaching approaches. Regardless of their typical approach, these teachers could conceivably integrate content that specifically enhances students' self-perceptions. How to do this in ways that will engage students while at the same time satisfy the high stakes testing gatekeepers is an open question. Research on teaching both traditional and nontraditional competencies finds little support for the idea that a focus on nontraditional competencies (such as civic and social competence and self-concept) detracts from academic competencies (van der Wal & Waslander, 2007).

One of the drawbacks of high stakes testing is that it induces in students an attitude of only wanting to know what is on the test, just as it induces in teachers an attitude of only being able to teach exactly what will be on the test (whether or not they want to do this). Middle level school students want to know what their teachers expect them to learn; teachers who are teaching to the test are telling students that this is what they need to learn. Such a climate has been shown to foster discipline and behavioral problems and a passive approach to learning (Hempel-Jorgensen, 2009). If teachers want their students to learn more than what is on the test, then they must identify adequate approaches to facilitate this additional learning within the current climate. It is difficult for middle level school students to express their unhappiness with the current educational climate, in part because many of them are still motivated to please the significant others in their lives, which includes their teachers.

What are the qualities of good students in middle level education? Or, even more to the point, what would happen if we left middle level school students up to their own devices? There would probably be a good deal of chaos. Some students might be productive, but most students probably would not be able function well without greater direction. Students might not clamor for teacher-centered instruction, but they would probably gravitate toward it. In essence, the ideal balance seems to be between developing students who are skilled academically and developing students who are well-rounded with regard to their self-perceptions. One of the goals of the middle level school is to facilitate the development of this balance. In the current climate, students hear increasingly less about such balance, and *good* has become dependent upon how students perform on high stakes tests.

CONCLUSIONS AND RECOMMENDATIONS

As we have noted in this chapter, there remains several questions about the use and nonuse of learning constructs that enhance self-perceptions. From the perspective of both teachers and students, there are numerous ways that attention to self-perception could affect school-related attitudes, behaviors, and thoughts. Another important point to recognize is that many of the issues surrounding the movement away from student-centered teaching approaches have yet to be studied systematically, at least in terms of the effects on students' self-perceptions and their school-related identities.

There are times when student-centered activities enable students to take content and grow with it, applying it to themselves and making it more meaningful for them. There are also times when teacher-centered activities are needed for the development of fundamental skill sets. Understanding the basic content is often necessary before applying and generalizing that content to new problems more metacognitively. This implies that there can be a happy median—teachers should apply both teacher-centered and student-centered activities as often as appropriate. Everything that is covered in middle level education does not need to use student-centered approaches, just as everything does not need to use teacher-centered approaches.

Applying these arguments to the vague/specific continuum, teacher-centered activities are typically specific (i.e., structured, routine, directed), whereas student-centered activities are typically vague (i.e., open-ended, undirected, less structured). Self-perceptions are likely to be involved with either specific or vague classroom activities. In particular, students do need to learn to function in situations where others (potentially powerful others) are making decisions for them, just as they need to learn to function in situations where they need to make decisions themselves and function autonomously. Both contexts can be effective at helping students to obtain accurate and unbiased self-perceptions (see Brinthaupt, this volume).

When students' learning is primarily experienced through teacher-centered instruction that is specific to test behavior, students have fewer opportunities to relate their learning to themselves and to align that learning with their self-perceptions. This is an opportunity lost—the whole person is shuttled to the side and the school is far away from a self-enhancing school.

We would strongly encourage teachers to also consider the relative advantages of teaching activities that are vague as well as specific to student self-perceptions. Middle level school students are developing from childhood to adolescence. As they make this transition, they need both direction and opportunities to develop independence. They need to move from dependent to independent learners. The middle level school can, and frequently does, provide both structure and leeway so that children can begin moving into adolescence. Having learning experiences that are vague about self-perceptions (but that encourage the exercise of self-related processes) can be as valuable as providing learning constructs that are specific to self-perceptions.

Teachers need not always tell students what to do, but they do need to guide their students as they make mistakes and learn from them and to provide students an opportunity to explore new identities in an environment that is relatively tolerant. Vague self-perception approaches can be beneficial to students when those approaches do not dictate or direct the nature of student self-perception, but rather allow students to flounder (with some minimal level of structure). Specific self-perception approaches can be more directive or reflective. In other words, both structure and lack of structure can be valuable to provide students with a successful learning experience, whether we are talking about students learning content or learning about themselves.

REFERENCES

AMLE. (2002). *Supporting students in their transition to middle school.* Retrieved from PositionStatements/TransitioningStudents/tabid/283/Default.aspx

Amrein, A. T., & Berliner, D. C. (2003). The effects of high-stakes testing on student motivation and learning. *Educational Leadership, 60*(5), 32-38.

Arowosafe, D. S., & Irvin, J. E. (1992). Transition to a middle level school: What kids say. *Middle School Journal, 24*(2), 15-19.

Beane, J. (1991). The middle school: The natural home of integrated curriculum. *Educational Leadership, 49*(2), 9-13.

Beane, J. A. (1994). Cluttered terrain: The schools' interest in the self. In T. M. Brinthaupt & R. P. Lipka (Eds.), *Changing the self: Philosophies, techniques, and experiences* (pp. 69-87). Albany, NY: State University of New York Press.

Beane, J. A., & Lipka, R. P. (1986). *Self-concept, self-esteem, and the curriculum.* New York, NY: Teachers College Press.

Beaty-O'Ferrall, M. E., Green, A., & Hanna, F. (2010). Classroom management strategies for difficult students: Promoting change through relationships. *Middle School Journal, 41*(4), 4-11.

Borich, G. (1999). Dimensions of self that influence effective teaching. In R. P. Lipka & T. M. Brinthaupt (Eds.), *The role of self in teacher development* (pp. 92-117). Albany, NY: State University of New York Press.

Brinthaupt, T. M., & Lipka, R. P. (2002). Understanding early adolescent self and identity: An introduction. In T. M. Brinthaupt & R. P. Lipka (Eds.), *Understanding early adolescent self and identity: Applications and interventions*. Albany, NY: State University of New York Press.

Brown, D. F., & Knowles, T. (2007). *What every middle school teacher should know* (2nd ed.). Portsmouth, NH: Heinemann.

Cerezo, N. (2004). Problem-based learning in the middle school: A research case study of the Perceptions of at-risk females. *Research in Middle Level Education Online, 27*(1), 1-13. Retrieved from http://www.nmsa.org/Publications/RMLEOnline/tabid/101/Default.aspx

Eccles, J. S., Lord, S., & Midgley, C. (1991). What are we doing to early adolescents? The impact of educational contexts on early adolescents. *American Journal of Education, 99*(4), 521-543.

Eggen, P., & Kauchak, D. (2001). *Educational psychology: Windows on classrooms*. Upper Saddle River, NJ: Merrill.

Faulkner, S. A., & Cook, C. M. (2006). Testing versus teaching: The perceived impact of assessment demands on middle grade instructional practices. *Research in Middle Level Education, 29*(7), 1-13.

Fitzsimmons, P., & Lanphar, E. (2011). Where there's love inside there's a reason why: Emotion as the core of authentic learning in one middle school classroom. *Australian Journal of Language & Literacy, 34* (2), 35-40.

Gullatt, D. (1995). Effective leadership in the middle school classroom. ERIC ED388454.

Gibbons, S. L., & Ebbeck, V. (2011). Team building through physical challenges in gender segregated classes and student self-conceptions. *Journal of Experiential Education, 34*(1), 71-86. doi:10.5193/ JEE34.1.71

Gould, J. (2011). Does it really take a village to raise a child (or just one parent?): An examination of the relationship between the members of the residence of a middle school student and the student's satisfaction with school. *Education, 123*(1), 28-38.

Hall, L. (2006). Anything but lazy: New understanding about struggling readers, teaching, and text. *Reading Research Quarterly, 4*, 424-426.

Harter, S. (1999). *The construction of the self: A developmental perspective*. New York, NY: Guilford Press.

Hempel-Jorgensen, A. (2009). The construction of the 'ideal pupil' and pupils' perceptions of 'misbehavior' and discipline: Contrasting experiences from a low-socioeconomic and a high-socioeconomic primary school. *British Journal of Sociology of Education, 30*(4), 435-448.

Huber, R. A., Smith, R. W., & Shotsberger, P. G. (2000). The impact of standards guided equity and problem solving on participation teachers and their students, ERIC ED442621.

Johnson, D. W., Johnson, R. T., & Scott, L. (1978). The effects of cooperative and individualistic instruction on students' attitudes and achievement. *Journal of Social Psychology, 12*(3), 3-15.

Kelchtermans, G. (2009). Who I am in how I teach is the message: Self-understanding, vulnerability and reflection. *Teachers and Teaching: Theory and Practice, 15*(2), 257-272. doi:10.1080/13540600902875332

Lane, K. L., Pierson, M. R., Stang, K. K., & Carter, E. W. (2010). Teacher expectations of students' classroom behavior: Do expectations vary as a function of school risk? *Remedial and Special Education, 31*(3), 163-174.

Lane, K. L., Wehby, J. H., & Cooley, C. (2006). Teacher expectations of students' classroom behavior across the grade span: Which social skills are necessary for success? *Exceptional Children, 72*(2), 153-167.

Leonard, G. (1968). *Successful schools for young adolescents.* New York, NY: Delacorte Press.

Lipka, R. P., & Brinthaupt, T. M. (Eds.). (1999). *The role of self in teacher development.* Albany, NY: State University of New York Press.

Marchant, G. J., Paulson, S. E., & Rothlisberg, B. A. (2001). Relations of middle school students' perceptions of family and school contexts with academic achievement. *Psychology in the Schools, 38*(6), 505-519.

Marzano, R. J., Marzano, J. S., & Pickering, D. J. (2003). *Classroom management that works.* Alexandria, VA: Association for Supervision and Curriculum Development.

McCombs, B. L. (2004). The learner-centered psychological principles: A framework for balancing a focus on academic achievement with a focus on social and emotional learning needs. In E. Zins, R. P. Weissberg, M. C., & Wang, H. J. Walberg (Eds.), *Building academic success on social emotional learning: What does the research say?* (pp. 23-39). New York, NY: Teachers College Press.

McCuddy, M. K., Pinar, M., & Gingerich, E. F. R., (2008). Using student feedback in designing student focused curriculum. *International Journal of Educational Management, 22*(7), 611-637.

McEwin, C. K., Dickinson, T. S., & Jenkins, D. M. (2003). *America's middle schools in the new century: Status and progress.* Westerville, OH: National Middle School Association.

Moon, T. R., Brighton, C. M., Jarvis, J. M., & Hall, C. J. (2007). *State standardized testing programs: Their effects on teachers and students.* Storrs, CT: The National Research Center on the Gifted and Talented, University of Connecticut.

Moos, D. C., & Honkomp, B. (2011). Adventure learning: Motivating students in a Minnesota middle school. *Journal of Research on Technology in Education, 43*(3), 231-252.

Needles, M., & Knapp, M. (1994). Teaching writing to children who are underserved. *Journal of Educational Psychology, 86,* 339-349.

Nichols, S., & Berliner, D. (2007). *Collateral damage: How high-stakes testing corrupts America's schools.* Cambridge, MA: Harvard Education Press.

Nichols, S., & Berliner, D. (2008). Testing the joy out of learning. *Educational Leadership, 65*(6), 14-18.

Patmor, G. L., II, & McIntyre, D. J. (1999). Involving students in school decision making. *NASSP Bulletin, 83*(607), 74-78.

Simmons, R. G., & Blyth, D. A. (1987). *Moving into adolescence: The impact of pubertal change and school context.* Hawthorn, NY: Aldine de Gruyter.

Steer, D. (1984). Effective teachers of early adolescents. Report: ERIC ED242698.

van der Wal, M., & Waslander, S. (2007). Traditional and nontraditional educational outcomes: Trade-Off or complementarity? *School Effectiveness and School Improvement, 18*(4), 4-9-428.

Wentzel, K. R. (1997). Student motivation in middle school: The role of perceived pedagogical caring. *Journal of Educational Psychology, 89*(3), 411-419. doi:10.1037/0022-0663.89.3.411.

You, S., & Nguyen, J. T. (2011). Parents' involvement in adolescents' schooling: A multidimensional conceptualization and meditational model. *Educational Psychology, 31*(5), 547-558.

Zemelman, S., Daniels, H., & Hyde, A. (1998). *New standards for teaching and learning in America's schools.* Portsmouth, NH: Heinemann.

CHAPTER 14

FROM SUBJECT-CENTEREDNESS TO LIFE-CENTEREDNESS

Rajni Shankar-Brown

Today public school curricula in the United States are organized using a separate-subjects approach, which focuses on concepts and facts associated with specific content areas. Although middle level education strongly supports the use of a student and life-centered curricula, the prevailing approach used in United States public middle schools remains subject-centered.

This subject-centered approach is exemplified by the responses given by middle school teachers to the following question: "What do you teach?" When posing this question to middle school teachers they generally state their content area or areas. Rarely, has a middle school teacher responded by saying, "I teach promising young adolescents!" or "I teach life-centered, thematic units!" In addition to middle level teachers declaring a subject area or areas, I have also encountered disturbing responses on various occasions. For example, I recently met a middle school social studies teacher at a workshop and upon inquiring about her teaching, she loudly sighed and said, "What do I teach? Hormones. Yes, code for middle school students. Yes, code for oh how I wish they would shut up and go away." Unfortunately, our society is full of negative messages about

Middle Grades Curriculum:
Voices and Visions of the Self-Enhancing School, pp. 241–252
Copyright © 2013 by Information Age Publishing
All rights of reproduction in any form reserved.

middle school and young adolescence. Such jaundiced perspectives are even visible within middle school walls and teacher preparation environments. I cannot begin to count how many times someone has called me "crazy" for choosing middle school teaching. During my years as a middle grades teacher and even now as a middle grades teacher educator at the university level, people (including education colleagues at the elementary and secondary levels) inform me that the mere thought of teaching middle school is dreadful and that anyone willing to working with "that age group" deserves a medal. I am saddened and outraged by the common public response to middle level education, primarily because I know that middle school is far from dreadful, but in fact deeply rewarding and fun! Fortunately, there are countless, fellow middle level educators who share my love for teaching young adolescents and understand why this *crazy* decision is beyond worthwhile.

Young adolescents are often silenced in United States public schools and given little consideration in regards to curriculum and instruction, which becomes increasingly clear when examining the perpetuation of subject-centeredness, particularly in light of the middle school that Beane and Lipka (1986) explain "young adolescents need and deserve" (p. 31). The fourteenth characteristic of Beane and Lipka's definition of the self-enhancing school is "From subject-centeredness to life-centeredness" (p. 186). In the vision of the self-enhancing school, curriculum is centered on the personal needs of learners, successfully acknowledging and affirming the students' barometric and baseline self. In this chapter I examine the 14th dimension of the self-enhancing school, "From subject-centeredness to life-centeredness", as outlined in *Self-Concept, Self-Esteem, and the Curriculum* (Beane & Lipka, p. 186).

Life-centeredness is a viable means to support the realization of the self-enhancing school by positively impacting the ongoing development of *self* during early adolescence. Drawing from literature and my own life experiences I will specifically attempt to accomplish the following in this chapter: (a) define the terms subject-centeredness and life-centeredness; (b) present rationale for, and significance of, using a life-centered curriculum in middle level education; and, (c) discuss the challenges and opportunities that exist for middle level practitioners moving from subject-centeredness to life-centeredness in the 21st century.

DEFINING SUBJECT-CENTEREDNESS AND LIFE-CENTEREDNESS

A subject-centered curriculum compartmentalizes knowledge by dividing content into representative specialized fields or departments (Ellis, 2003; Erikson, 2002). Subject-centeredness is based on the concept of knowledge organized by specific subject areas or disciplines, such as language arts, math, science, social studies, art, music, technology, foreign language, and physical education. Historically, even from a global lens, education has been largely organized around distinct subject areas. United States public schools have traditionally used a subject-centered approach, especially at the middle, secondary, and university levels. Subject-centeredness became increasingly popular during the 1890's when the National Education Association made recommendations for standardizing curriculum and instruction; the subject-centered approach continues to dominate public school configurations today (Beane, 1993).

In a subject-centered curriculum the emphasis is on uniformity of learning and the curriculum is controlled by authority figures external to the learner and the learning context, i.e. state, school district, school administration and teacher. Therefore, in a subject-centered approach the content is selected and planned external to the learning situation or before the teaching situation occurs.

In contrast, life-centered curriculum is rooted in progressive educational movements and fosters curriculum integration—the organization of curriculum around life issues, which are collaboratively recognized by teachers and students (Beane, 1993; Ellis, 2003). A life-centered approach focuses on making learning relevant to students' everyday lives. This approach still uses knowledge from traditional disciplines, but blurs subject area divisions and encourages interdisciplinary or thematic learning. Beane (1995) describes a life-centered curriculum as "coherent" and he explains that, "a 'coherent' curriculum is one that holds together, makes sense as a whole; and its parts, whatever they are, are unified and connected by the sense of the whole" (p. 3). In a life-centered approach, content is selected collaboratively and includes the learners' perspectives or interests. Unlike subject-centeredness, the emphasis in a life-centered approach is on meaningful student learning.

RATIONALE AND SIGNIFICANCE
FOR A LIFE-CENTERED APPROACH

I vividly remember sitting through most of my middle school, separate, subject-centered classes wondering how what I was learning was relevant to my life. I often asked questions such as, *Why does this matter?* and *Why should we care?* in my mind. Theorists (Brophy, 2004; Vallerand et al., 1993) find that apathy is one of the greatest demotivational factors in schools resulting from the disconnect between the student and the curriculum. In their research on middle school academic identity formation, Roeser and Lau (2002) illuminate this mismatch between middle school environments and the developmental needs of young adolescents. They explain that several "opportunities associated with structure, autonomy support, and quality relationships that would support adolescents' fulfillment of needs and attainment of related goals in middle school, and thereby promote positive academic identity formation and behavior, are often lacking" (p. 109). The mismatch between school and life as described by Roeser and Lau, particularly a lack support of autonomy or "curricula that speak to the developmental, cultural, and contemporary interests of early adolescents" (p. 108), undoubtedly decreased my affective experience of middle school. I often found myself wishing I had a voice in the curriculum and dreading the isolated teaching of facts between subject areas. Like a herd of sheep, we would move between classrooms and we would be force-fed facts of little relevance to my daily life. I agree with James Beane (1993) who asserts that the separate subject-centered curriculum approach has, "seriously failed the middle schools and so frequently helped to create a deadening effect on teaching and learning" (p. 3).

This life-centered view of curriculum makes it possible to incorporate radical curriculum theory into the design of the education of students. Life-centered curricula can better incorporate progressive-experimentalist theory, which emphasizes the social gains of society, as well as critical theory, which incorporate the social injustices of society (Hlebowitsh, 1993). This flexibility further demonstrates the superiority of life-centered curricula as the incorporation of these theories is much more difficult in a subject centered approach (DeLeon & Ross, 2010; Ross, 2006).

Like many middle school students, I felt severely disconnected with the curriculum and instructional practices in school (Eccles et al., 1993; Roeser & Lau, 2002; Roeser, Eccles, & Sameroff, 2000). Additionally, the transition from the elementary to middle school and its "less personal and positive teacher-student relationship" (Eccles & Roeser, 2009, p. 421) created a poorer experience for me in middle school, just as it has done and does for others (Feldlaufer, Midgley, & Eccles, 1988). As a young adolescent I constantly wished school provided more visible connections between subject areas and life. Schoolwork was meaningless drudgery that usually felt like punishment for a crime that I had never done.

During some middle school visits, I frequently observe students lingering in the halls long after the bell rings and entering classrooms with bleak expressions. The expressions on middle school students' faces as they enter the classroom all too often look as if they are at a funeral, forlorn and wanting to be somewhere else. It is a distressing image and one I observe repeatedly in public middle schools across the United States. Clearly, this is connected to a lack of engaging curricula and the prevalence of subject-centered education. When talking to young adolescents, I often ask them to describe school and I find that "boring" is the most commonly used description.

CHALLENGES AND OPPORTUNITIES OF MOVING FROM SUBJECT TO LIFE-CENTEREDNESS

As a rule a subject-centered approach lacks connection to the voices, interests, and needs of the learners. Beane and Lipka (1986) remind us that, "early adolescence is the period when issues of continuity in the self-concept are most salient to the individual" (p. 32). Unfortunately, the subject-centered approach rarely impacts the development of positive self-perceptions among young adolescent learners. As mentioned previously in his book, *A Middle School Curriculum: From Rhetoric to Reality,* James Beane (1993) asserts that the separate subject-centered curriculum approach has, "seriously failed the middle schools and so frequently helped to create a deadening effect on teaching and learning" (p. 3). Yet, compartmentalizing knowledge into distinct subject areas continues to dominate curriculum and instruction at the middle and secondary levels. Why? While there are many reasons for the continuation of subject-centeredness, the highs stakes and accountability era presents great challenges for educators committed to the middle level concept. Since the 1960's, the middle school movement has argued for an integrated, problem-based curriculum as opposed to subject-centeredness. In fact, in *The Emergent Middle School*, Alexander, Williams, Compton, Hines, and Prescott (1968) advised that curriculum should include real issues relevant to students and provide opportunities for applied learning based on authentic problems. One of the fundamental principles upon which the middle school movement is founded is the design and implementation of developmentally appropriate and interdisciplinary, team-taught curriculum (Lounsbury & Vars, 1978; Vars, 1998). However our nation's obsession with standardized testing elicits conservative, subject-centeredness in schools (Cuban, 2008), which naturally presents challenges for teachers wishing to shift from subject-centeredness to life-centeredness. The standards-based reform movement advocates for conventional, standardized, subject-centeredness, even to the point of scripted teaching lessons as visible in some school districts, especially in urban areas. The fact remains that most state standards and proficiency exams are structured around separate subject areas such as reading and math, which further encourages subject-centeredness in schools.

Fortunately, life-centeredness is reflected in the new Common Core State Standards Initiative, a state-led effort that was released in June 2010. Thus far, the Common Core State Standards have been adopted by

48 states and calls for instruction to prepare students for real life experiences by engaging them in complex thought processes based on life-centered curriculum (National Governor Association Center for Best Practices and Council of Chief State School Officers, 2010). The Common Core Standards are designed to ensure that, "students make progress each year and graduate from school prepared to succeed in college and in a modern workforce" (Common Core State Standards Initiative, 2012). Life-centered curriculum has four primary advantages (Jacobs, 1989):

1. It stops the fragmented schedules of moving from subject to subject. Gone are the 50-minute blocks of math, science, etc. Replacing this schedule would be the construction of time necessary for the unit. Imagine a teaching world in which the teacher did not have to plan a lesson around an artificial timer designed to move students from one subject to another.

2. It creates relevance for students. Students are obviously frustrated with school. Embedding lessons within life-centered content enables learners to relate to the material resulting in an increased level of motivation.

3. Society is not fragmented this way. By teaching students the methods in which the real world works, in which engineers write papers and reports regularly use mathematics, students become better prepared for their future. With the teaching through the life-centered lens, students become better prepared for life.

4. Society is constantly adding to its knowledge base. It is impossible to keep up with the advances in knowledge. With this, the skills to navigate the unprecedented amount of knowledge become paramount. Through life-centered curriculum, the skills to thrive in a knowledge-saturated society emerge.

The change from subject-centered education to life-centered education is not without its perils. The history of United States education is littered with failed attempts of curriculum change. Most notably, John Dewey (1966) expresses this by observing that these attempts are mired in the lack of proper measurement and Dewey argues for authentic assessment to measure student learning, preferably through inquiry-based curriculum grounded in a life centered approach. As curriculum changes, so must the devices that measure it (Kliebard, 2002). In terms of this life-centered curriculum, how can we as educators, assess our effectiveness. Grades are still being reported based on the subjects, effectively ensuring the doom of life-centered curriculum and the revival of a subject centered one. This type of curriculum change dictates that all of the components of the curriculum change, not merely the instructional part of it.

Clearly, there are challenges for teachers moving from subject-centeredness to life-centeredness, yet these challenges can equally be viewed as opportunities. Teachers have the incredible opportunity to practice and advocate for curriculum and instruction that values students' interests, perspectives, and diverse learning needs, all of which are essential to the middle school concept (National Middle School Association, 2010). By making teaching and learning more life-centered, teachers have the opportunity to engage students in authentic learning with a social justice framework and instill a lifelong joy for learning, which is generally absent in subject-centered schools as evidenced through my own schooling experience. I wish that my middle school math teachers taught math concepts through life lenses as opposed to isolated facts geared toward an arbitrary standardized test that resulted in high math anxiety and decreased learning motivation. A life-centered approach to math would have increased my interest and retention of the concepts. For example, why not teach algebra through an interdisciplinary, financial perspective collaboratively developed with students—covering essential life topics such as saving, budgeting, investing, frugality, credit, social wealth disparities, and charity. In addition, a math teacher could work with students on a life-centered project that uses math skills and covers essential math concepts in a purposeful way, such as raising money for a class event dedicated to helping families experiencing homelessness or building a public garden in an impoverished neighborhood—ultimately, addressing the needs of diverse learners, integrating the curriculum, and making math education more meaningful.

A unit that I designed and helped team-teach at a local middle school exemplifies another example of a life-centered approach. Hurricanes are a part of living on the coast and in my city I quickly discovered that the topic of Hurricanes is relevant to students' lives. I encouraged a team of teachers to teach specific content topics through a life-centered approach and focus on teaching from the lens of hurricanes. Table 14.1 offers a 1-day snapshot of this creation:

Life-centeredness is also beautifully exemplified in the Waldorf curriculum. The Waldorf curriculum is based on the philosophy of Rudolph Steiner (1996), who advocated for a humanistic and interdisciplinary approach to education. While visiting Waldorf schools, I observed young adolescents applying specific content skills while engaged in meaningful, integrated projects. For example, a group of middle school students worked together to build multilevel birdhouses for their school and to share with the surrounding community. These students were highly motivated and focused, which was further evidenced by the minimal amount

Table 14.1.   Hurricane Unit Plan

Language Arts	Facilitate a Socratic seminar on the government response to *Hurricane Katrina*
Math	Graph the number of hurricanes in their city and make predictions for the future
Science	Collaboratively design a building model that would be conducive for a hurricane zone and write an argumentative essay for your design
Social Studies	Research and document individual and family hurricane stories in the community.
Special Education	Research and begin creating a hurricane safety kit
Art	Collage an aspect of a hurricane
Music	Write hurricane haikus and put the words to music
Technology	Create a Prezi (2012) on the causes of hurricanes
Physical Education	Transform "red rover" to "hurricane roar"

of classroom management issues, especially when compared to what I have observed in subject-centered middle level classrooms in the United States.

Before attempting to build their own bird feeding structures, the students discussed wildlife conservation, researched types of birds, identifying those present in their local area, and they explored birdhouse designs from architectural perspectives. While decorating and personalizing their creations, the students also learned about different art styles and the science behind the creation of paint mediums, such as outdoor versus indoor oil primers. Students learned from one another and from life. For instance, one of the students reminded the group that the placement of their birdhouses was as important as the actual construction. After an elderly man wrote the students a thank you note for placing a birdhouse at the local nursing home, this group of students stayed after school with their teacher to collaboratively create extra birdhouses for the local nursing home. The students were actively using literacy, math, science, social studies, art, and physical education skills, in addition to civic engagement. Students were encouraged to explore ideas and make connections between content and life. Learning was meaningful and the students' enthusiasm for learning was remarkable, the type of enthusiasm all young adolescents should experience in school. Students were actively engaged in 21st century skills such as collaboration, critical thinking, and creativity.

The Waldorf curriculum is founded in the belief that learning is continuous and interconnected; teachers are empowered to design curriculum with their students; and the needs and interests of the learners are given first priority in the classroom (Petrash, 2002), as opposed to focusing on external accountability standards and assessments. There are 44 public Waldorf schools in the United States, most of them situated in California (Costello-Dougherty, 2009). The Waldorf curriculum is just one example of a life-centered approach to teaching and learning. Unfortunately, most public school teachers are not empowered to collaboratively design curriculum with their students and are expected to follow the conventional, subject-centered approach to curriculum and instruction. However, the myriad benefits of moving from subject-centeredness to life-centeredness, demands the immediate attention of all educators, especially those at the middle level.

AN INVITATION TO PRACTICE AND ADVOCATE FOR LIFE-CENTEREDNESS AT THE MIDDLE LEVEL

Our 21st century, global landscape makes the shift to life-centeredness even more imperative. I invite middle level teacher educators and practicing middle school teachers to join me in empowering young adolescent learners by actively using and advocating for a life-centered approach in curriculum and instruction. Learning, just as life, is organic and interconnected. The middle school curriculum must reflect students' everyday lives, perspectives, and the world in which they live. As educators, we must commit ourselves to reprioritizing the traditional subject-centered approach to engage students first and foremost, as opposed to engaging subjects first and foremost. William Butler Yeats' sentiment, "Education is not the filling of a pail but the lighting of a fire" (Lothstein & Brodrick, 2008, p. 77), is the underpinning of life-centered curricula. For the most part, memorizing facts in the 21st century is archaic because we have the Internet, where we can access facts at our fingertips anytime of day. With a plethora of information available on the Internet, teaching our students critical literacy skills becomes increasingly more important. Students must be able to draw evidence-based conclusions, and they need the ability to decipher whether information is valid during the inquiry process. In addition, as evident by the new Common Core State Standards (Common Core State Standards Initiative, 2012), we need to teach students how to be resourceful citizens and innovative thinkers who celebrate creativity and know how to work collaboratively.

The popular subject-centered school structure is immensely disconcerting. However, my concerns are transformed into rays of hope as I work with passionate preservice and practicing teachers who are dedicated to providing students with meaningful learning experiences. In the book *My*

Spiritual Journey by Dalai Lama and Sofia Stril-Rever (2010), the Dalai Lama explains,

> If a teacher doesn't limit himself to academic teaching, if he also takes on the responsibility of preparing his students for life, they will have respect for him and confidence in him. The things they learn from him will leave an indelible print in their minds. Conversely, subjects taught by someone who doesn't care about his students' well-being will be of only passing interest to them and will soon be forgotten. (p. 7)

By using a life-centered approach, teachers have the opportunity to open their students' minds and hearts to lifelong learning. May we work together to advocate for life-centered curricula in order to educate students to be successful in an exponentially interconnected and complex world. May we address the needs of diverse learners and ensure that what they are learning will not soon be forgotten.

Thanks to my older brother, I was as a young adolescent introduced to the magical and adventurous writing of Antoine de Saint-Exupery (1971). The French poet, illustrator and aviator immediately captured my attention. In retrospect, I realize that my immediate and enduring connection with his work was a result of his life-centered stories. More than an adored book, *The Little Prince* (de Saint-Exupery; originally published 1943) was a translated companion that helped me survive the drudgery of subject-centered middle school curriculum, as well as ponder the wondrous experiences of life. Seven years later, I shared *The Little Prince* with my younger sister as she struggled to navigate herself through the same subject-centered, *mismatched* middle school. Since my first middle school encounter with *The Little Prince*, I have discovered many other gems created by Antoine de Saint-Exupery; perhaps none greater than the following paraphrase from an English translation of his unfinished work, *Wisdom of the Sands (Citadelle)*, originally published in 1948/1984. "If you want to build a ship, don't drum up people to gather wood, divide the work, and give orders. Instead, teach them to yearn for the vast and endless immensity of the sea" (Naslund, 2011).

Life-centered curricula are essential in supporting the realization of the self-enhancing middle school and imperative for engaging students in the learning process. The compartmentalization of knowledge in subject-centered curricula goes against the interconnected reality of the world and life, often resulting in a dangerous disconnect between the students and the curriculum. Middle level education, as illuminated by the National Middle School Association (2010), is grounded on a life-centered approach to teaching and learning. Just as Antoine de Saint-Exupery's *Wisdom of the Sands* (Naslund, 2011) remains an unfinished masterwork, so does the fulfillment of the middle school concept. I believe the wisdom of the self-envisioning middle school teaches us, to paraphrase Antoine de Saint-Exupery ... *If you want to build education, don't drum up students to gather disconnected facts, divide the subjects, and give orders. Instead, teach students to yearn for the vast and endless immensity of knowledge.* May we foster, in ourselves and in our students, an unrelenting hunger for learning and commitment to service, ultimately making life the center of learning and learning the center of life!

REFERENCES

Alexander, W. M., Williams, E. L., Compton, M., Hines, V. A., & Prescott, D. (1968). *The emergent middle school*. New York, NY: Holt, Rinehart, & Winston.

Beane, J. A. (1993). *A middle school curriculum: From rhetoric to reality* (2nd ed.). Columbus, OH: National Middle School Association.

Beane, J. A. (1995). *Toward a coherent curriculum: The 1985 ASCD Yearbook*. Alexandria, VA: ASCD.

Beane, J. A., & Lipka, R. P. (1986). *Self-concept, self-esteem, and the curriculum*. New York, NY: Teachers College Press.

Brophy, J. E. (2004). *Motivating students to learn* (2nd ed.). Mahwah, NJ: Erlbaum.

Common Core State Standards Initiative. (2012). Retrieved from http://www .corestandards.org/the-standards

Costello-Dougherty, M. (2009). *Waldorf public schools are on the rise*. Retrieved from http://www.edutopia.org/waldorf-public-school-morse

Cuban, L. (2008). *Hugging the middle: How teachers teach in an era of testing and accountability*. New York, NY: Teachers College Press.

Dalai Lama, & Stril-Rever, S. (2010). *My spiritual journey*. New York, NY: Harper Collins.

DeLeon, A. P., & Ross, W. E. (2010). *Critical theories, radical pedagogies, and social education: New perspectives for social studies education*. Rotterdam, The Netherlands: Sense.

de Saint-Exupery, A. (1971). *The little prince* (K. Woods, Trans.). New York, NY: Harcourt Brace & Company. (Original work published 1943)

de Saint-Exupery, A. (1984). *The wisdom of the sands, Citadelle* (S. Gilbert, Trans.). Chicago, IL: University of Chicago Press. (Original work published 1948)

Dewey, J. (1966). *Democracy and education: An introduction to the philosophy of education*. New York, NY: Free Press.

Eccles, J. S., Midgley, C., Wigfield, A., Buchanan, C. M., Reuman, D., Flanagan, C., & Iver, D. M. (1993). Development during adolescence: The impact of stage—environment fit on adolescents' experiences in schools and families. *American Psychologist, 48*, 90-101.

Eccles, J. S., & Roeser, R. W. (2009). Schools, academic motivation, and stage-environment fit. In R. M. Lerner & L. Steinberg (Eds.), *Handbook of adolescent psychology* (3rd ed., pp. 404-427). Hoboken, NJ: Wiley.

Ellis, A. K. (2003). *Exemplars of curriculum theory*. Larchmont, NY: Eye on Education.

Erikson, L. H. (2002). *Concept-based curriculum and instruction: Teaching beyond the facts.* Thousand Oaks, CA: Corwin Press.

Feldlaufer, H., Midgley, C. & Eccles, J. S. (1988). Student, teacher and observer perceptions of the classroom environment before and after the transition to junior high school. *Journal of Early Adolescence, 8,* 133-156.

Hlebowitsh, P. S. (1993). *Radical curriculum theory reconsidered: A historical approach.* NewYork, NY: Teachers College Press.

Jacobs, H. H. (1989). *Interdisciplinary curriculum: Design and implementation.* Alexandria, VA: ASCD.

Kliebard, H. M. (2002). *Changing course: American curriculum reform in the 20th century.* New York, NY: Teachers College Press.

Lothstein, A. S., & Brodrick, M. (2008). *New morning: Emerson in the 21st century.* New York, NY: State University of New York Press.

Lounsbury, J. H., & Vars, G. F. (1978). *A curriculum for the middle school years.* New York, NY: Harper.

Naslund, A. (2011, September 19). *Our era of wayfinding.* Retrieved from http://www.brasstackthinking.com/2011/09/our-era-of-wayfinding/

National Governors Association Center for Best Practices, Council of Chief State School Officers. (2010). *Common core standards.* Washington, DC: National Association Center for Best Practices Council of Chief State School Officers.

National Middle School Association. (2010). *This we believe: Keys to educating young adolescents.* Westerville, OH: Author.

Petrash, J. (2002). *Understanding Waldorf education: Teaching from the inside out.* Beltsville, MD: Gryphon House.

Roeser, R. W., & Lau, S. (2002). On academic identity formation in middle school settings during early adolescence: A motivational-contextual perspective. In T. M. Brinthaupt & R. P. Lipka (Eds.), *Understanding early adolescent self and identity: Applications and interventions* (pp. 91-131). Albany, NY: State University of New York Press.

Roeser, R. W., Eccles, J. S., & Sameroff, A. J. (2000). School as a context of social-emotional development: A summary of research findings. *Elementary School Journal, 100,* 443-4.

Ross, W. E. (2006). The struggle for the social studies curriculum. In W. E. Ross (Ed.), *The social studies curriculum: Purposes, problems and possibilities* (pp. 17-36). Albany, NY: State University of New York Press.

Steiner, R. (1996). *The education of the child and early lectures on education.* Hudson, NY: Anthroposophic Press.

Vallerand, R. J., Pelletier, L. G., Blais, M. R., Brière, N. M., Senécal, C. B., & Vallières, E. F. (1993). On the assessment of intrinsic, extrinsic, and amotivation in education: Evidence on the concurrent and construct validity of the Academic Motivation Scale. *Educational and Psychological Measurement, 53,* 159-172.

Vars, G. F. (1998). You've come a long way, baby! In R. David (Ed.), *Moving forward from the past: Early writing and current reflections of middle school founders* (pp. 222-233). Columbus, OH: National Middle School Association & Pittsburgh, PA: Pennsylvania Middle School Association.

CHAPTER 15

FROM TEACHER-EXCLUSIVE PLANNING TO TEACHER-STUDENT PLANNING

The Promise of Partnering in a Connected World

John M. Downes

The role of curriculum planning in a self-enhancing school remains a compelling yet remarkably elusive aspect of middle grades reform. Lipka (1997) framed curriculum as central to young adolescents' self-concept—their perception of self in terms of roles and attributes—and self-esteem—the assessment they make regarding personal satisfaction with those roles and attributes. Stevenson (2002) entwined curriculum with students' self-efficacy, including their senses of competence, awareness, affiliation, ethical sense of self, and responsibility. James' theory of *Need Polarities* (1974) describes the complex, and at times competing, needs of the young adolescent self, including: the need to need/the need to be needed; the need to move inwards/the need to affect the outer world; the

Middle Grades Curriculum:
Voices and Visions of the Self-Enhancing School, pp. 253–270
Copyright © 2013 by Information Age Publishing

need for routine/the need for intensity; the need for myth and legend/the need for fact; the need for stillness/the need for activity; and the need for separateness/the need for belonging.

These rich psychological perspectives on the young adolescent challenge us to think boldly about how curriculum can enhance the self of middle schoolers. They beg for a curriculum intimately connected to each young adolescent and the wider world. It seems an impossible task for any individual teacher as architect of curriculum; indeed, it seems an improbable task for any group of adults, unless, that is, students are invited into the design process. For curriculum to serve its vital role in a self-enhancing school, it must emanate from students themselves. The vision and work of schooling must move from teacher-exclusive planning to teacher-student planning.

Teacher-student planning arises as a provocative and proven approach to enhancing the young adolescent self, whether framed as self-concept/ self-esteem, personal efficacy (Bishop & Downes, 2008), or need polarities (Brinegar & Bishop, 2011). A common theme across these analyses is the remarkable benefits to the young adolescent self when teachers and students plan curriculum together, benefits that elude far too many students when they are left out of curriculum development.

Today, however, another perspective lends still greater urgency to teacher-student planning. The gap between students' in-school and out-of-school lives always complicated efforts to design engaging curriculum. That gap has widened profoundly with the rapid diffusion of technology throughout youth culture and the surrounding world. However, the prospect of engaging students in closing that gap with compelling and challenging learning is more promising than ever. Tested strategies for negotiating curriculum with students now can be combined with readily available technologies to further transform curriculum development, student and teacher learning, and the selves of all partners in schooling.

In this Chapter 1 briefly examine the long-running challenges inherent in teacher-exclusive planning. I then discuss the role of curriculum integration as a foundation for teacher-student planning. Next, technology-rich approaches to more student-directed and integrated learning are explored. Finally I consider the organizational implications of moving in such a direction, and offer several critical lenses that may guide our path forward.

TEACHER-EXCLUSIVE PLANNING DEFINED

Dewey's 1938 (1998) description of teacher-exclusive planning all too well captures the prevailing adult-driven mode of curriculum design and delivery today.

The traditional scheme is, in essence, one of imposition from above and from outside. It imposes adult standards, subject-matter, and methods upon those who are only growing slowly toward maturity. The gap is so great that the required subject-matter, the methods of learning and of behaving are foreign to the existing capacities of the young.... Consequently, they must be imposed; even though good teachers will use devices of art to cover up the imposition so as to relieve it of obviously brutal features. (p. 4)

The gap Dewey observed, echoed nearly a half century later by Beane and Lipka (1986, pp. 188-189), has been exacerbated by the rapid diffusion of technology in the lives of youth, creating an ever "widening gap between children's everyday 'life worlds' outside of school and the emphases of many educational systems" (Buckingham, 2007, p. 96). A teacher's own memories of adolescence are a poor guide, particularly when it comes to technology and how young adolescents learn today. As Ball and Cohen (1999) observed, some of what teachers need to know about their students is general, such as their stage in human development, but understanding children's beliefs and work, "requires expertise beyond what one gathers from one's own experience. What one enjoyed, thought, or felt as a child may afford helpful speculation about one's students, but is insufficient as a professional resource for knowing learners" (pp. 8-9).

It is precisely the disconnect between what teachers think they know about their students and what the students truly care about that undercuts teachers' efforts to cultivate student self-concept and self-esteem through curriculum design. Addressing this disconnect requires an intimate and unfolding insight into each student that cannot be clearly mapped out ahead of time. Closing that gap between what we think we know about our students and the lives they actually lead is no less daunting than closing the gap between students in-school and out-of-school lives. Trying to do so without enlisting students as codesigners of curriculum in particular, and schooling in general, is absurd.

CURRICULUM INTEGRATION

In contrast to teacher-exclusive planning, teacher-student planning involves "working in a partnership to articulate a problem/concern, develop objectives, locate resources, and evaluate progress in fulfilling objectives" (Lipka, 1997, p. 35). Beane (1993) viewed curriculum integration as integral to generating a middle-years curriculum that should emphasize "general education; help students explore self and social meanings; respect students' dignity; be grounded in democracy; honor diversity; be of great personal and social significance; be lifelike and lively; and enhance knowledge and skills for all young people" (p. 17).

Connecting with students' concerns and transforming them into effective learning opportunities, then, becomes a central challenge of curriculum design and implementation. When a curriculum of topics is designed by committees of adults and implemented without students' input, it is likely to fall short of this complex task (Bishop & Downes, 2008).

Curriculum integration, grounded in the questions and concerns raised by students, provides a unique route to authentically engaging curriculum—"work that students believe to be worth doing" (Schlechty, 2001, p. 10). It helps us transcend simple subject-area boundaries and instead embrace disciplinary knowledge to addresses the real and purposeful questions humans ask, including young people (Beane, 1997). Seeking the real concerns of adolescents draws students and teachers into critical human inquiry, where simple answers are elusive; collaboration and humility are essential; and the facts and strategies of fields and disciplines are intellectual lifelines (Beane, 1993).

Brazee (1997) argued that this type of curriculum integration is particularly well suited to meeting the developmental needs of young adolescents. Too often our curriculum fails to engage young adolescents because it "asks students to give answers to questions they do not ask" (Brazee, p. 187). In contrast, a curriculum built on significant self and social issues is inherently challenging and relevant. As Beane (1997) asserted, "personal and social concerns are quite literally the 'stuff' of life" (p. 15)." These concerns constitute human inquiry itself: to seek meaning and respond to the meanings we derive. Justice, freedom, and peace are meanings we have created, as are enterprise, work and family. Aesthetics, art, and story are also meanings we hold dear, as are joy and play. The list continues and is shared by young and old alike, more than we generally acknowledge (Bishop & Downes, 2008). Curriculum integration holds the potential to capitalize on these shared concerns and meanings and to tap into "students' desire to do things they cannot do *unless* they learn" (Schlechty, 2001, p. 9). Springer (2006) and Kuntz (2005) present vivid examples of curriculum integration and the schooling that supports it.

TEACHER-STUDENT PLANNING

An integrated curriculum—developed collaboratively with students and focused on the real issues and concerns of young adolescents—exhibits important elements of a democratic learning environment (Apple & Beane, 1995). Negotiating curriculum can take many forms but generally requires teachers and students to rethink their relationship (Boomer, Lester, Onore, & Cook, 1992). Cook-Sather and Youens (2007) describe a process of "repositioning" students from merely "beneficiaries—or victims—of whatever pedagogical commitments and approaches prospective teachers develop" to "stakeholders who have a right to play an active role in the coconstruction of their learning, the development of pedagogical commitments and approaches, and the critical revision of educational and social structures" (p. 62). These more recent works build on a rich history of curriculum theory that argues for involving students in the construction of schooling, including the work of John Dewey, L. Thomas Hopkins, and Joseph Schwab. In spite of this foundation, Schultz and Banks (2011) wonder, "Why is it that with such theoretical guidance over the century in curriculum history and the history of public education in the United States, we cannot find it in ourselves to leverage the insights, imaginations, and creativity of our students" (p. 46)?

Recent research illustrated the benefits of collaboratively planned curriculum integration for students. Brown and Canniff (2007) pointed to the extended, flexible time and the interconnection of concepts and principles as bolstering cognitive processing, as well as creating an environment that fosters independence, self-confidence, and the exploration of questions about self and life. Brown (2011) highlighted benefits to students' motivation, ability to make critical decisions about learning, development of advanced thinking processes, and metacognitive and self-assessment skills. Brinegar and Bishop (2011) noted the considerable growth over time in students' self-assessment of their learning styles, motivation, engagement, leadership and time management skills. They noted, however, that students only gradually came to appreciate and articulate these insights over several years of emersion in a collaborative planning environment.

Benefits accrue to teachers as well when they consult their students about curriculum and school improvement. Rudduck noted that teachers gained "a more open perception of young people's capabilities, the capacity to see the familiar from a different angle, a readiness to change thinking and practice in the light of these perceptions, a renewed sense of excitement in teaching, a practical agenda for improvement, and confidence in the possibility of developing a more partnership-oriented relationship with their students" (Rudduck, 2007, pp. 599-600).

As we consider both Dewey's long ago perspectives and Beane's (1993) more recent yet classic work on teacher-student planning—although decades apart—the resources and social opportunities for learning were remarkably similar. Teachers and their students could collaborate with each other to identify questions and concerns, design activities in their classrooms or communities and avail themselves of locally available texts and human resources to enrich their investigations. Today, however, the dynamic is changing rapidly. Increasingly, students are already engaged in learning and knowledge construction using tech-

nologies their teachers know little about. And many teachers are missing out on powerful tools to cultivate questioning, collaboration, and
challenging learning with their students. In 1938, Dewey (1998) warned
that "the gulf between the mature or adult products and the experience
and abilities of the young is so wide that the very situation forbids much
active participation by pupils in the development of what is taught" (p.
4). In contrast, today collaborating with students may be the only way to
keep up with rapidly evolving knowledge and the technologies in which
it is thoroughly intertwined.

THE FUTURE OF TEACHER-STUDENT PLANNING

A number of social and technological trends raise exciting opportunities
and challenges for advocates of teacher-student planning and curriculum
integration, including the following:

- The abundance of resources and relationships made easily accessible via the Internet is increasingly challenging us to revisit our roles
  as educators.
- Technology continues to profoundly affect the way we work, collaborate, communicate, and succeed.
- People expect to be able to work, learn, and study whenever and
  wherever they want to.
- The perceived value of innovation and creativity is increasing
  (Johnson, Adams, & Haywood, 2011).

These trends introduce critical challenges to education:

- Digital media literacy continues its rise in importance as a key skill
  in every discipline and profession.
- Economic pressures and new models of education are presenting
  unprecedented competition to traditional models of schools.
- The demand for personalized learning is not adequately supported
  by current technology or practices.
- A key challenge is the fundamental structure of the K-12 education
  establishment—aka *the system*.
- Many activities related to learning and education take place outside
  the walls of the classroom [e.g., through online games, learning
  communities and social networks] and are thus not part of our
  learning metrics (Johnson et al., 2011).

These trends and challenges invite us to think proactively about how teacher-student planning will necessarily look different in the years to come and how educators can build a sustainable infrastructure for the practice. A synergy exists between the theories and practice of teacher-student planning and emerging technologies, many with which students are already engaged for their out-of-school purposes. Technology rapidly is enhancing the feasibility and capacity of teacher-student planning and curriculum integration. For instance, there long has been an appropriate concern that some educators lacked the knowledge and skills necessary to depart from boxed, but nonetheless expert-created, curriculum. However, contemporary technologies make available sufficient expertise and quality of resources to anyone who knows how to find them. An increasing number of teachers are experimenting with these new technologies, yielding at least four promising directions, all of which could benefit teacher-student planning: (a) crowd sourcing curriculum; (b) Personal Learning Networks (PLN); (c) electronic portfolios; and (d) Learning Management Systems (LMS). Running throughout each of these directions are the common threads of relevance, personalization and differentiation, and the prospect of enhancing the self of all our students.

Crowdsourcing Near and Far: The World at Our Fingertips

The concept of crowdsourcing (Howe, 2009), taking a function once performed by employees and outsourcing it to an undefined (and generally large) network of people, typically using online social media tools, should resonate with readers familiar with Beane's (1993, 1997) curriculum development process. Once students have generated questions and distilled a theme for study, the next step is essentially within-team crowdsourcing on the resources, expertise and activities that can be brought to bear on the theme. Teachers who practice curriculum integration invite their students to consider who in their family, school and community can bring unique skills, insights, and expertise to the study. These often are the vibrant and authentic resources that invigorate thematic inquiry with field trips, service learning opportunities, community-based projects and interviews with experts.

Crowdsourcing curriculum with social networking tools broadens the pool of contacts to include people and places all over the world. Through the use of Twitter (twitter.com) or ePals (epals.com), for instance, or social bookmarking tools like Diigo (diigo.com) and Delicious (delicious.com), students can solicit input from fellow young adolescents in other countries and cultures, from scientists in laboratories, and from experts at world-renowned museums. Teachers as well can garner expertise from far and wide, filling crucial gaps in prior knowledge that are frequently exposed when teachers follow the inquiring lead of young adolescents. We are no longer merely as smart as we've become; we are in fact as smart as the global crowd.

Personal Learning Networks: A Lifetime of Engaged and Connected Learning

Thoughtfully designed and managed Personal Learning Networks (PLNs) lend structure to this practice of crowdsourcing. PLNs "allow us to build global learning networks where ... we can pursue our intellectual or creative passions or needs with others who share them" (Richardson & Mancabelli, 2011, p. 2). Warlick (2009) portrays how a PLN can tame myriad social networking opportunities that can inform teacher and student learning. Using freely available tools, such as iGoogle (google.com/ig), Netvibes (netvibes.com) and Pageflakes (pageflakes.com) users can aggregate latest information on specific topics from multiple sources, including reputable news media, bloggers, Twitter feeds, and social bookmarking sites, into a single, personalized start page or "dashboard" available from any computer or mobile device anywhere on the Internet. A PLN, sometimes referred to as a Personal Learning Environment (Johnson et al., 2011), provides a framework for sustained and evolving collaborative learning. As Richardson and Mancabelli proclaimed,

> Right now, assuming we have an Internet connection, we can start to create a personal learning network—a set of connections to people and resources both on line and off line who enrich our learning—at a moment's notice. With a PLN, we can learn anytime, anywhere, with potentially anyone around the world who shares our passion or interest. We can literally build global, online classrooms of our own making on the Web that include networks and communities of learners with whom we interact on a regular basis. (p. 2)

Teachers have discovered the power of interest-driven social networking to enrich their own teaching practice (Richardson & Mancabelli, 2011; Warlick, 2009). A unique facet of this approach is that teachers can narrowly define challenges they confront in their practice and tap thousands of educators around the world facing similar issues. Teachers frequently feel isolated or marginalized when changes in their practice, including curriculum integration, strain local relationships and norms. PLNs and a constantly growing array of communication tools can extend and sustain vital collegial networks.

Students as well can avail themselves of PLNs, using these same tools to delve deeply and independently into rich learning (Drexler, 2008). The intentional use of PLNs taps into organic trends in adolescent online life. Youth engage in friendship-driven and interest-driven online activities, sometimes simply "messing around" with new media and acquiring new technology skills along the way. At other times, they "geek out," delving deeply into personal interests, engaging wide networks of fellow enthusiasts, networks in which age or other traditional signs of status have little importance (Ito et al., 2008). Students want to personalize their learning by creating networks of experts using emerging tools (Project Tomorrow, 2010). With adult modeling and guidance, students can embrace "connectivism" (Siemens, 2010) in the context of their integrated curriculum. Moreover, developing and maintaining a PLN is likely to become an essential skill for passionate and lifelong learning. Richardson and Mancabelli (2011) point out that "unlike traditional learning environments, each of our networks is unique, created and developed to our personalized learning goals that evolve and grow throughout our lives" (p. 3).

Electronic Portfolio Assessment

The idea of portfolios often resonates with educators committed to curriculum integration; they offer students the opportunity to communicate their learning and growth in multiple ways, stretching beyond traditional measures like multiple choice tests and essays to include problem solving, artistic representation, and more recently multimedia. More important, when portfolios are structured around individual goal setting, they can paint a vivid and compelling picture of each student's growth over time, particularly in hard to measure domains such as communication, critical thinking, and problem solving. Portfolios can also be an important source of dialogue about learning. Student led portfolio conferences that highlight goal-setting and reflection on growth over time benefit students' self-concept, self-esteem, and sense of efficacy (Bailey & Guskey, 2001; Belgrad, Burke, & Fogarty, 2008; Berckemeyer & Kinney, 2005). Further, portfolios are likely a necessary complement to a growing emphasis on personalized learning plans and proficiency-based graduation and accountability systems in secondary education (Tung, 2010).

Electronic portfolios have the potential for a multitude of benefits (Barrett, 2007). They extend the traditional portfolio processes of collecting, selecting, reflecting, projecting and celebrating to include archiving, linking/thinking, storytelling, collaborating, and publishing (Barrett, 2007). They offer more manageable storage of learning artifacts, particularly the increasing and broadening array of electronic products students are generating. An electronic format also bolsters portfolios as sources of formative assessment for use by teachers and students from day to day and across students' school and work careers. Electronic portfolios can enrich the role of parents as collaborators in the portfolio process by providing routine and convenient access to their child's running record of work and reflection. And they expand the prospect of peer, mentor and expert involvement in portfolio work to include any trusted person in the world. As more high schools adopt proficiency based assessment and accountability (Tung, 2010), school systems will need an electronic approach to managing student artifacts and reflection. We may be on the verge of best practices in high school assessment actually driving broad implementation of long frustrated assessment reform in the middle grades.

Initiating an electronic portfolio process invites familiar as well as novel challenges and opportunities. It should respond to the demands of effective and comprehensive portfolio systems, including audiences served, standards and curriculum, developmental stages of the students, artifacts to be selected, reflection and self-assessment, and conferencing and showcasing (Belgrad, Burke, & Fogarty, 2008). Particularly when integrated into an online database system or LMS, electronic portfolios can incorporate an array of tools to enhance their benefits. Just as burgeoning collections of photos can be tagged, searched and selectively retrieved in Flickr or Facebook, entries in an electronic portfolio can be tagged for various purposes and audiences. For instance, an essay or portion of an essay could be tagged 'Standard 3.7' as part of the school's standards and curriculum assessment; "Growth in Writing" to facilitate student-teacher-family dialogue about growth over time; "Mom's Favorite" for review during a student-led portfolio conference; "Best Dialogue" so the student can easily return to an successful example; and "Fun Assignments" as part of ongoing student-teacher dialogue about creating more engaging learning experiences. Document-level privacy settings, available in Google Docs and many other Web 2.0 tools, and increasingly integrated into LMSs, give students the ability to control which entries are shared with which audiences and when. A student can electronically invite a peer or expert to view and comment upon only a specific piece of artwork in a portfolio. Students can regulate access to reflection blogs, portfolio sections still in development, and the revision history of their documents. They can enrich their reflections by using electronic highlighters and markup tools, electronic sticky notes, and a wide range of commenting techniques. The opportunities for ambitious use of electronic portfolios are considerable and growing. But they hinge on our commitment to the higher purposes of portfolio assessment as we design portfolio initiatives, design and select portfolio platforms, and support students, teachers and families in their use.

Learning Management Systems

With everything from resources, expertise, activities, and artifacts predominantly online, it is not surprising that a growing number of educators and systems designers are attempting to package the whole process of curriculum, instruction and assessment into a manageable online format. From these attempts have evolved what we now term the Learning Management System. A LMS provides ubiquitous access to a central portal for day-to-day learning. A key feature of an effective LMS includes easy and instant updating of online content by teachers and students. Through a LMS, teachers and students also enjoy embedded or linked access to popular Web 2.0 tools, differentiated tasks, and flexible grouping. Some LMSs also integrate goal setting, rubrics, portfolios and standards-based evaluation and reporting. A centralized, automated administration for routine tasks such as parent and student notifications, online calendaring, and work submission adds to the efficiency and benefits of these tools. Emerging LMSs, such as EDU2.0 (edu20.org) and Haiku (haikulearning.com) are beginning to bridge the cultural and pedagogical gap between middle schooling and earlier, postsecondary-oriented LMSs such as Moodle and Blackboard. Indeed, now is the time for advocates of curriculum integration and teacher-student planning to press for LMS designs that meet their needs.

Taken together, these four directions in educational technology work synergistically to assist in the process of teachers collaborating with students in the design of schooling. The collaboration of crowdsourcing combines with the information management of PLNs, the flexibility and accessibility of electronic portfolios, and the personalization of an LMS. With these, proponents of curriculum integration possess powerful tools to embark on learning that is more relevant, authentic, and worldly than ever previously imagined.

REVISITING ASSUMPTIONS

A Partnership With New Roles and Skills

Contemporary technologies, and the ways in which many students already engage those technologies in their out-of-school lives, augur exciting opportunities for modeling updated, and perhaps wholly new, teaching roles with young adolescents. Teachers must relinquish to a considerable degree their traditional role as content and curriculum expert. In its place, they should develop and honor a new role as expert facilitator and curriculum negotiator. Students must relinquish their role as expert consumer of teacher-produced curriculum and develop their new role as creator of personalized learning and negotiator of class curriculum. The transition for students and teachers alike is made all the more difficult given that neither can turn to the other for established expertise. Cook-Sather and Alter (2011) described how teachers and students enter a liminal state, "betwixt and between" (p. 37) their traditional relationship and one aligned with their emerging sense of partnership. Everyone in the classroom may be encountering the ambiguity of change at the same time, creating a potentially fragile and stressful—and potentially rewarding—classroom setting.

Siemens (2010) emphasized that effective teaching is "a critical and needed activity in the chaotic and ambiguous information climate created by [learning] networks" (p. 10). Siemens suggested that rather than controlling a classroom, teachers now must work to influence or shape the networks with which they and their students engage. Accordingly, new teacher roles include "amplifying" high quality streams of information to make them more readily available to students and "curating" key concepts and resources so that students "bump into" them repeatedly as they explore issues and develop ideas (Siemens, 2010, pp. 16-19). Teachers now must facilitate "wayfinding and socially-driven sensemaking" that steers students to diverse opinions and supports them as they grapple with that diversity (Siemens, 2010, pp. 20-23). They concentrate on "aggregating" information to help students cope with abundance and monitor the impact of aggregation on their exploration (Siemens, 2010, pp. 24-27). By "filtering" information, teachers acknowledge that they are now only one of many streams to which a student has access (Siemens, 2010, pp. 28-29). Finally, new teacher roles include "modeling" critical skills of learning and networking and being a "persistent presence" online, through blogs, wikis, Twitter, and other modes (Siemens, 2010, pp. 30-32).

The Organization of Middle Grades

What would it look like to organize schools in response to what we value for students and the technology and resources we have available? How might common planning time differ if we fully embraced teacher-student planning? How might student work time change if learners could collaborate face to face—virtually, perhaps—with classmates, peers, and experts anytime, anywhere in the world? Having imagined the many ways that teacher-student planning, curriculum integration, and 21st century technology can enhance students' self concept and self esteem, how might we rethink the structure of middle schooling to maximize these benefits?

Although the structural reforms long advocated for by the middle grades movement won't necessarily bring about needed curricular reforms, they can nonetheless create conditions supportive of teacher-student planning and integrated curriculum. For example, middle school advocates for years have emphasized the need for teacher common planning time (Mertens, Flowers, Anfara, & Caskey, 2010). Yet we seem to be a long way away from managing schooling time in such a way that values student participation in curriculum development—and schooling more generally. Too often, administrators, parents, students, and even the teachers themselves pit the 2 or more weeks spent planning curriculum with students against instructional time. This false dichotomy belies the intimate and powerful connections between curriculum negotiation, integrated curriculum, and the quality of learning that students ultimately experience. The values shift, from teacher-exclusive planning to teacher-student planning, must incorporate the ways we value and use school time.

Educators in general, and middle grades classrooms and schools in particular, need to embrace the wholesale reengineering of their organizations and systems in order to "race with" rather than against technological innovation (Brynjolfsson & McAfee, 2011). Conditions such as ubiquitous access to technology, and tools such as the LMS, can help to reframe learning previously bound by the traditional organization of schools. We must begin to imagine the vast potential benefits of technological change, embrace them wholeheartedly, and respond with the organizational transformations—not simply the hardware purchases—necessary to bring them to reality.

Teacher-student planning frequently reveals organizational constraints. Teachers may reduce time for planning in order to cover mandated content or prepare for high stakes tests. Students may be forced to choose between participation in school improvement initiatives and sports, music, or lunch. The strain of such institutional forces points to the arbitrary constraints of school structure on educational innovation. Our research agenda must include the examination of such fundamental systems and critical reflection on any initiatives related to student involvement. In short, we need to update our recommendations for middle grades school organization. In light of teacher-student planning, student involvement and emerging technologies, what should common planning time look like? What should teaming look like? Grouping? Scheduling? Advisories? Are these still viable constructs for thinking about how we organize the middle grades? Absolutely. Do their current iterations in policy recommendations and research reflect a bold embrace of student involvement and contemporary technologies? No.

Student Involvement and School Improvement

We need to see curriculum integration and teacher-student planning as part of a broader ethic of honoring the intellectual and affective needs of young adolescents. The literature on student involvement and consultation may contribute to our thinking about teacher-student planning in the 21st century.

First, Fielding (2001) challenged us with a series of pointed questions about efforts to involve students. "How do the systems enshrining the value and necessity of student voice mesh with or *relate to other organizational arrangements* (particularly those involving adults)? Do the *cultural norms and values* of the school proclaim the centrality of student voice within the context of education as a shared responsibility and shared achievement? Do the *practices, traditions and routine daily encounters* demonstrate values supportive of student voice? *Where* are the public spaces (physical and metaphorical) in which these encounters might take place" (pp. 134-135)?

Second, Fletcher (2010) challenges us to climb the Ladder of Student Involvement in School, from adult-led to student-led decision making, as we critically examine our collaborations with students. Students and teachers can examine the ladder as they reflect on the quality of their partnership, tasks and activities—and the motivations behind them. More important, subsequent conversations can drive practice toward richer, student-led partnerships with adults.

Fielding (2001) and Fletcher (2010) invite us to critically consider our strategies, conditions and purposes as we undertake teacher-student planning. We need reflective frameworks that signal to students and educators that the practical and democratic purposes of collaborative planning are valued among the other goals of schooling. Valid frameworks may also make it easier for others to chart a path toward genuine and democratic student participation. This quest takes on greater significance in the context of the rapidly developing field of learning analytics. Learning analytics "loosely joins a variety of data gathering tools and analytic techniques to study student engagement, performance, and progress in practice, with the goal of using what is learned to revise curricula, teaching, and assessment in real time" (Johnson et al., 2011, p. 7). These tools and techniques are well adapted to examining large data sets drawn from previously elusive learning behaviors, such as online social interactions, content viewing, game play, and reading and writing, and mining them for purposes of ongoing improvement of teaching and learning. The field holds promise for helping educators discern which learning methods work best for specific students or groups of students. An ethic of teacher-student planning and curriculum integration should inform the algorithms in learning analytics, valuing authentic student engagement, student-directed learning, and student self-efficacy. Imagine, for instance, how analytics might inform weekly student self-reflections about their personal learning network. "This week I noticed that my interactivity score was up from last week, which is what I was aiming for. But next week I want to raise my diversity of opinion score." Now is the time to integrate student involvement into evaluation and performance metrics—a partnering analytics—as if students' voices were vital to educational quality and student performance.

CONCLUDING THOUGHTS

We are witnessing a remarkable convergence of thinking about the roles students can play in shaping their own learning. Secondary school reform is emphasizing personalized learning plans and student involvement in school change (Tung, 2010); educators are realizing the powerful role students can play as collaborators in initial teacher preparation (Cook-Sather & Youens, 2007), continuing professional learning (Downes, Nagle, & Bishop, 2010), and school improvement (Mitra, 2008); and curriculum theorists find ever growing evidence that engaging and challenging learning experiences are hard-won but natural byproducts of negotiated and student-directed curriculum (Brinegar & Bishop, 2011; Brown, 2011). This convergence begs for an integrated approach to teacher-student planning, one that reframes schooling structures, assessment, accountability schemes in terms that foster these proven yet nascent roles for teachers and students. We need to identify and cultivate the skills and dispositions that are essential for teacher and student success in collaborative planning, including modeling teacher-student planning in teacher preparation programs (Pate & Nesin, 2011).

Throughout this chapter I have suggested that teacher-student planning can contribute to other characteristics of self-enhancing schools. Shifting toward a genuine planning partnership creates a more humanistic environment for teachers and students. A curriculum grounded in students' real-life questions and concerns, played out with personal learning networks and collaborative technologies, creates boundless space for self-direction, peer and multiage interactions. And learning management systems that couple standards, personalized goal setting and comprehensive portfolio assessment raise new hopes for systematic implementation of self-directed learning. These pathways embrace learner characteristics, welcome parents into substantive dialogue about their children's growth, and value students' self-perception. With such a holistic approach to honoring the innate value of each member of the learning community—the truly democratic school—we may embark boldly together upon continuous and rewarding growth as selves and community.

REFERENCES

Apple, M. W., & Beane, J. A. (Eds.). (1995). *Democratic schools*. Alexandria, VA: Association for Supervision and Curriculum Development.

Bailey, J. M., & Guskey, T. R. (2001). *Implementing student led parent conferences*. Thousand Oaks, CA: Corwin.

Ball, D. L., & Cohen, D. K. (1999). Developing practice, developing practitioners: Toward a practice-based theory of professional education. In L. Darling-Hammond & G. Sykes (Eds.), *Teaching as the learning profession: Handbook of policy and practice* (pp. 3-32). San Francisco,CA: Jossey-Bass.

Barrett, H. C. (2007). Researching electronic portfolios and learner engagement: The REFLECT Initiative. *Journal of Adolescent and Adult Literacy, 50*(6), 436-449.

Beane, J. A. (1993). *A middle school curriculum: From rhetoric to reality*. Columbus, OH: National Middle School Association.

Beane, J. A. (1997). *Curriculum integration: Designing the core of democratic education*. New York, NY: Teachers College Press.

Beane, J. A., & Lipka, R. P. (1986). *Self-concept, self-esteem, and the curriculum*. New York, NY: Teachers College Press.

Belgrad, S., Burke, K., & Fogarty, R. (2008). *The portfolio connection: Student work linked to standards*. Thousand Oaks, CA: Corwin Press.

Berckemeyer, J., & Kinney, P. (2005). *Professional development kit: The what, why and how of student-led conferences*. Westerville, OH: National Middle School Association.

Bishop, P., & Downes, J. M. (2008). Engaging curriculum for the middle years. *Curriculum Matters, 4*, 52-68.

Boomer, G., Lester, N., Onore, C., & Cook, J. (Eds.). (1992). *Negotiating the curriculum: Educating for the 21st century*. London, England: Falmer Press.

Brazee, E. N. (1997). Curriculum for whom? In J. L. Irvin (Ed.), *What current research says to the middle level practitioner* (pp. 187-201). Columbus, OH: National Middle School Association.

Brinegar, K., & Bishop, P. (2011). Student learning and engagement in the context of curriculum integration. *Middle Grades Research Journal, 6*(4), 207-222.

Brown, D. F. (2011). Curriculum integration: Meaningful learning based on students' questions. *Middle Grades Research Journal, 6*(4), 193-206.

Brown, D. F., & Canniff, M. (2007). Designing curricular experiences that promote young adolescents' cognitive growth. *Middle School Journal, 39*(1), 16-23, 37.

Brynjolfsson, E., & McAfee, A. (2011). *Race against the machine: How the digital revolution is accelerating innovation, driving productivity, and irreversibly transforming employment and the economy.* Lexington, MA: Digital Frontier Press.

Buckingham, D. (2007). *Beyond technology: Children's learning in the age of digital culture.* Malden, MA: Polity.

Cook-Sather, A., & Alter, Z. (2011). What is and what can be: How a liminal position can change learning and teaching in higher education. *Anthropology and Education Quarterly, 42*(1), 37-53.

Cook-Sather, A., & Youens, B. (2007). Repositioning students in initial teacher preparation: A comparative descriptive analysis of learning to teach for social justice in the United States and in England. *Journal of Teacher Education, 58*(1), 62-75.

Dewey, J. (1998). *Experience and education* (60th anniversary ed.). West Lafayette, IN: Kappa Delta Pi.

Downes, J. M., Nagle, J., & Bishop, P. A. (2010). Integrating student consultation into teacher professional development: The Middle Grades Collaborative. *Current Issues in Middle Level Education, 15*(1), 36-44.

Drexler, W. (Producer). (2008). The networked student. [YouTube Video] Retrieved from http://www.youtube.com/watch?v=XwM4ieFOotA

Fielding, M. (2001). Students as radical agents of change. *Journal of Educational Change, 2*(2), 123-141.

Fletcher, A. (2010). *Examining the meaning of student involvement: The ladder of student involvement in school.* Retrieved from http://www.soundout.org/ladder.html

Howe, J. (2009). *Crowdsourcing: Why the power of the crowd is driving the future of business.* New York, NY: Three Rivers Press.

Ito, M., Horst, H., Bittanti, M., Boyd, D., Herr-Stephenson, B., Lange, P., ... Robinson, L. (2008). *Living and learning with new media: Summary of findings from the Digital Youth project.* Chicago, IL: The John D. & Catherine T. MacArthur Foundation.

James, C. (1974). *Beyond customs: An educator's journey.* New York, NY: Agathon Press.

Johnson, L., Adams, S., & Haywood, K. (2011). *The NMC horizon report: 2011 K-12 edition.* Austin, TX: The New Media Consortium.

Kuntz, S. (2005). *The story of Alpha: A multiage, student-centered team—33 years and counting.* Westerville, OH: National Middle School Association.

Lipka, R. P. (1997). Enhancing self-concept/self-esteem in young adolescents. In J. L. Irvin (Ed.), *What current research says to the middle level practitioner* (pp. 31-39). Columbus, OH: National Middle School Association.

Mertens, S. B., Flowers, N., Anfara, V. A., Jr., & Caskey, M. M. (2010). What research says: Common planning time. *Middle School Journal, 41*(5), 50-57. Retrieved from http://www.amle.org/Publications/MiddleSchoolJournal/Articles/May2010/Article9/tabid/2212/Default.aspx

Mitra, D. L. (2008). *Student voice in school reform: Building youth-adult partnerships that strengthen schools and empower youth*. Albany, NY: State University of New York Press.

Pate, E., & Nesin, G. (2011). How two university professors organize their curriculum. *Middle Grades Research Journal, 6*(4), 235-244.

Project Tomorrow. (2010). *Creating our future: Students speak up about their vision for 21st century learning*. Retrieved from http://www.tomorrow.org/speakup/pdfs/SU09NationalFindingsStudents&Parents.pdf

Richardson, W., & Mancabelli, R. (2011). *Personal learning networks: Using the power of connections to transform education*. Bloomington, IN: Solution Tree Press.

Rudduck, J. (2007). Student voice, student engagement, and school reform. In D. Thiessen & A. Cook-Sather (Eds.), *International handbook of student experience in elementary and secondary school* (pp. 587-610). Dordrecht, The Netherlands: Springer.

Schlechty, P. C. (2001). *Shaking up the schoolhouse: How to support and sustain educational innovation*. New York, NY: Jossey-Bass.

Schultz, B. D., & Banks, P. (2011). A shorty teaching teachers: Student insight and perspective on "keeping it real" in the classroom. In W. H. Schubert & M. F. He (Eds.), *Listening to and learning from students: Possibilities for teaching, learning, and curriculum* (pp. 45-59). Charlotte, NC: Information Age.

Siemens, G. (2010, February 16). *Teaching in social and technological networks* [Blog post]. Retrieved from http://www.connectivism.ca/?p=220

Springer, M. (2006). *Soundings: A democratic student-centered education*. Westerville, OH: National Middle School Association.

Stevenson, C. (2002). *Teaching ten to fourteen year olds* (3rd ed.). Boston, MA: Allyn & Bacon.

Tung, R. (2010). *Including performance assessments in accountability systems: A review of scale-up efforts*. Boston, MA: Center for Collaborative Education.

Warlick, D. (2009). Grow your personal learning network: New technologies can keep you connected and help you manage information overload. *Learning and Leading with Technology* (March/April), 12-16.

CHAPTER 16

FROM TEXTBOOKS AND TESTS TO PROBLEMS AND PROJECTS

Brianne L. Reck

At precisely 11:00 A.M. the bell sounds and Mr. Douglas' seventh grade science class begins its usual routine. Carlos dutifully copies the objectives from the board into his notebook, takes out his homework assignment, and settles in for the duration. The chapter on watersheds will be on the next test his teacher tells him. He watches the slides that flash on the screen, listens to the teacher's explanations, and completes the questions from the textbook chapter assigned. In the quiet of the classroom his mind wanders and he wonders about what the cafeteria will be serving for lunch.

Across town Sophia and her classmates in Ms. Keylor's class at PS 106 are gathering in their expert groups. They have been working to understand the impact that the runoff from the school playground might be having on the stream that leads to the wetlands behind the school. Sophia has just come from math class where she and her classmates were measuring the surface area of the hard top to calculate the volume of water that might have flowed in to the stream given different amounts of rain that have fallen during the last month. Today they will develop questions to ask the representative from the Environmental Protection Agency office

Middle Grades Curriculum:
Voices and Visions of the Self-Enhancing School, pp. 271–291
Copyright © 2013 by Information Age Publishing
All rights of reproduction in any form reserved.

when he comes to talk to the class on Friday. Ms. Keylor checks in with Sophie's group, listening to their progress report and providing some suggestions before moving on to talk with the group of students using the classroom computers to access a website to learn about pollutants that adversely affect wetlands.

These two classrooms in the same school district with the same state standards, the same mandated curriculum, the same statewide assessments, and the same district provided materials are at the same time worlds apart. Sophia's teachers have embraced a constructivist framework that acknowledges the unique characteristics of their learners, and they have employed strategies to engage them in authentic learning activities that provide opportunities to develop as learners. They have moved from an instructional approach that relies almost exclusively on textbook materials and activities and assessment using pencil and paper tests to an integrated approach to learning that engages students in active inquiry, collaborative problem solving and project based assessments that relate to the students and to the world around them. While Sophia and Carlos will both need and may both achieve acceptable scores on the end of course assessment tests, their journeys will be very different, and their notions of self and ownership of their learning may well be a telling factor in their future success. And so, while standards will appropriately form a framework for their learning experiences, a standards-driven curriculum does not necessitate the use of standardized instruction. In a self-enhancing middle school like PS 106, rigor, relevance, and relationships meet in innovative instructional practice that places the learner in the center of the learning process.

CALLS FOR RELEVANT CURRICULUM, INSTRUCTION AND ASSESSMENT

Over several decades researchers have identified specific characteristics of early adolescents that have a direct relationship to their learning and development during the middle grades years (Alexander & George, 1993; Carnegie Council on Adolescent Development, 1989; Eichorn, 1966; Wiles & Bondi, 1989). The developmental changes that occur during adolescence are varied and dramatic. Physical changes affect the development of adolescents' self-esteem and sense of identity. The social-emotional quest for independence and self-identity frames their relationships with peers and adults. The intellectual development of adolescents accompanies an emergent curiosity about the world around them, and their ability to think critically and engage in problem solving and decision-making blossoms. All of these changes must be factored in to the development of curriculum and instruction that meets their needs.

Since the early 1990s when middle level education began to receive attention as part of the larger school reform conversation, we have seen marked progress in the ways in which curriculum and instruction are developed and delivered. But, despite the rhetoric that proclaims that we will leave no child behind, traditional practices employed in the education of middle grades learners continue to do just that. By failing to address the characteristics and needs of diverse young adolescents, we most certainly place them at risk. Currently 80% of public schools in the United States are labeled as failing, and by 2014 given the current trajectory and criteria, some have suggested that it is likely that 100% may be so designated (Ratvitch, 2010). Clearly, by many measures, current practice is not supporting our lofty goal of high levels of achievement for all students.

The call for developmentally appropriate curriculum and instruction as a means to improve student learning has come from many quarters. Carnegie Corporation's 'Turning Points' emphasized the need for improving student learning in part through creating supportive learning environments that value all learners and engage them in planning and managing their own learning (Carnegie Council on Adolescent Development, 1989). In its policy statements and most notably in its publication *This We Believe,* the Association for Middle Level Educators, formerly National Middle School Association), has advocated for curriculum and instructional practices that are responsive to the unique characteristics and developmental needs of young adolescents (National Middle School Association, 2010). Specifically, they identify four characteristics or attributes that define responsive programs:

1. **Developmentally responsive**: using the distinctive nature of young adolescents as the foundation upon which all decisions about school organization, policies, curriculum, instruction, and assessment are made.

2. **Challenging:** ensuring that every student learns and every member of the learning community is held to high expectations.

3. **Empowering:** providing all students with the knowledge and skills they need to take responsibility for their lives, to address life's challenges, to function successfully at all levels of society, and to be creators of knowledge.

4. **Equitable:** advocating for and ensuring every student's right to learn and providing appropriately challenging and relevant learning opportunities for every student (p. 15).

Significantly, Beane and Lipka (1986), have suggested that curriculum, instruction and assessment that is designed to meet the young adolescent's needs will be characterized by concepts and methods that are congruent with their self-perceptions and likely to enhance them. By focusing instructional content, activities and assessments on concepts and ideas that reflect a balance between cognitive, affective and psychomotor domain objectives, these authors and others assert that not only will students realize significant growth and development, but that they will increase clarity and quality in their self perceptions. The notion of developmental appropriateness and the principles of the self-enhancing school are at the core of most models and recommendations for middle grades educational reform.

Therefore, developmentally responsive, rigorous, socially equitable, and empowering curriculum, instruction and assessment constitutes our best hope of reframing schools to address the unique needs of diverse middle level learners. The fundamental shift that must occur is to place the learner in the center of the learning equation. The paradigm shift needed to affect this change is a shift from textbooks and tests to problems and projects.

RELEVANT CURRICULUM, INSTRUCTION AND ASSESSMENT

Based upon the developmental characteristics of young adolescents and what we know about the characteristics of effective middle school curriculum, Beane (1993, 1997), Bracey (1998), Caskey (2002) Caskey and Anfara (2007), Paris, Lawton, Turner, and Roth (1991), Pate, Homestead, and McGinnis (1997), Williamson, Johnson and Kanthak (1995), and others have made the case for relevant middle school curriculum, instruction, and assessment. This relevance is situated in the nexus between the interests and needs of the students, and the larger social issues of the world around them. Effective middle level curriculum must enable students to explore and grapple with questions that they have about themselves and the world in which they live. It must not only address the curriculum targets set by state and national standards and common core curricula, but if it is to engage young adolescents it must also allow them to learn to think about ideas and concepts that cross disciplines and help them learn about themselves and to prepare for the world beyond school. The curriculum must be challenging and engaging, should be exploratory and integrative, and must be delivered by educators who value their young adolescent learners and are well prepared to meet their cognitive and social learning needs.

Instructional practice in a self-enhancing school must connect students directly to curriculum. Teachers must engage in an ongoing process of defining and refining the curriculum, working with students to construct their learning. At the core of the design processes teachers must consider the students themselves, who they are and how they best learn (Bransford, Brown, & Cocking, 1999; Jackson & Davis, 2000; Tomlinson & Eidson, 2003; Wiggins & McTighe, 1998; Zemelman, Daniels, & Hyde, 1998). Given the nature of the young adolescent learners and their varied learning styles, strengths, and differences, variety is also critical to successful instruction (Andrews & Morfield, 1991; Jackson & Davis, 2000; Tomlinson, 2001, 2005). The key is for instruction to bring the curriculum to life with learning approaches that will build upon students strengths, offer them choice and voice as well as engage students in the process of learning to learn.

Instruction must build upon what students already know, scaffolding them to deeper and more sophisticated understandings of content (Bransford, Brown, & Cocking, 1999). It should also prepare students specifically for performances that demonstrate the knowledge and skills they have gained, not simply for exercises that test factual knowledge (Wiggins & McTighe, 1998). Most importantly, instruction must respond to the developmental needs and characteristics of young adolescents, who are best served by experiences that account for their cultural, experiential, and personal backgrounds (NMSA, 2010).

Appropriate assessment must be developed to reflect the ways in which students will demonstrate what they have learned, not simply in traditional pencil and paper tests, but in ways that honor the nature of the learner and the learning. In the current high stakes accountability driven assessment era, the possibilities and purposes of assessment have become dangerously narrow. In order to satisfy the terms of state and federal initiatives, we have moved to a model of assessment of learning, neglecting the notion of assessment for learning. This shift has resulted in decreased emphasis on formative assessments needed to support student learning in favor of a focus on summative assessment that may be more limited in its diagnostic utility in current practice. Assessment at its best should provide "ongoing, useful feedback, to both students and teachers, on what students have learned" (Jackson & Davis, 2000, p. 54). That feedback should guide instruction so that it addresses any gaps in learning that assessment results reveal (Strebinsky & Ross, 2005). If we seek to develop the metacognitive skills and capacity for self-monitoring in adolescent learners, students must be actively involved in assessing their own progress. They must work "with their teachers to make critical decisions at all stages of the learning enterprise, especially goal-setting, establishing evaluation criteria, demonstrating, learning, self-evaluation, peer evaluation and reporting" (Vars, 2001, p. 79). Failure to do so may lead students to equate learning with test scores, leaving them ill prepared to manage and monitor their own continued learning.

Teachers must learn to employ a broad range of classroom assessments (Stiggins, 2001; Wiggins & McTighe, 1998) as well as a variety of assessment methods, "ranging from informal to formal, in the same way a court of law accepts evidence ranging from circumstantial to concrete" (Jackson & Davis, 2000, p. 55). Routine assessments should be appropriate to the nature of the learning to be demonstrated. In this way traditional paper-and-pencil assessments are appropriately used to demonstrate factual knowledge and open-ended, complex, and authentic performance tasks and projects are used to assess conceptual knowledge—the "enduring understandings" that educators want students to remember long after the course has ended (Wiggins & McTighe, 1998). It is difficult to imagine such enduring knowledge emerging from a steady diet of what students may experience as 'multiple guess' and 'mystical choice' quizzes and tests.

PRACTICE THAT HOLDS PROMISE

A problem or project based approach provides the best opportunity to provide high quality educational opportunities to all middle grade learners. Project-based learning is a systematic approach to learning based upon a foundation of authentic learning activities that engage students' interests by challenging them to answer a question or solve a problem that relates to their own lives and to life outside school. According to Thomas (2000), there are five primary criteria that define project-based learning: (a) "Projects are central, not peripheral to the curriculum"; (b) "projects are focused on questions or problems that 'drive' students to encounter (and struggle with) the central concepts and principles of the discipline"; (c) "projects involve students in a constructive investigation"; (d) "projects are student-driven to some significant degree"; and (e) "projects are realistic, not school-like." Inherent in his criteria is a sixth principle or criteria: collaboration.

The opportunity to explore a topic in depth using an interdisciplinary approach affords the individual authentic learning experiences that place him or her in the center of the concentric circles of the process. As students work cooperatively they have the opportunity to build upon and reflect upon their own ideas and conceptions of the world around them, exercise choice, and develop an ability to engage in self-assessment (Barron, et. al., 1998). The collaborative nature of the activities helps them build social skills and leadership, and the authentic assessment enables them to demonstrate mastery of challenging content in ways that are compatible with their own learning strengths and the demands of a rigorous curriculum.

This type of inquiry oriented instruction is grounded in the research in constructivist learning, content mastery, and critical thinking. Inherent in the design are rigor, relevance and relationships that are at the heart of the recommendations for educational reform. Such an approach holds promise for the self-enhancing school. It is helpful to examine this approach in terms of the developmental responsiveness, rigor, student empowerment and equity.

DEVELOPMENTALLY RESPONSIVE PRACTICE

An inquiry oriented project approach is by nature developmentally responsive to the middle grades learner. As middle grades students transition from childhood into adolescence, they begin to develop curiosity about the world beyond themselves. As their brains continue to develop, they are not only able, but are often more willing to explore relevant new ideas, knowledge and skills. That relevance can be found in situations where students are given opportunities to make meaning from information related to something that they already know, is at an appropriate level of difficulty, and connects to their lives beyond the school (Willingham, 2009). As they develop and define their sense of self and define themselves in relationship to their peers and others, they need to be provided meaningful opportunities to explore curriculum that helps them answer questions they have about themselves and the world around them.

An exploratory curriculum responds to the developmental needs of young adolescents by allowing students "to explore new arenas of interest, both as specific courses and as methodology within courses" (Bergman, 1992, p. 179). It provides an extension of the curriculum students typically encounter (Curtis & Bidwell, 1977; George &Alexander, 2003), and lets students try out various areas of interest (Briggs, 1920). When students are actively engaged in constructing curriculum that relates to their interests, not only will they develop the content knowledge, but they will continue to develop their sense of self as a learner.

Given what we know about the developmental needs of adolescent learners, orientation of classroom learning environments oriented toward specific performance outcomes and measurement of one's ability in relationship to that of others makes little sense. This appears to be particularly true for students who struggle most and whose self-perception and motivation are at risk in an environment that focuses on and catalogs their learning faults and flaws rather than helping them develop a realistic self-evaluation of their strengths and areas for growth (Paris et al.,

1991). Greater levels of active engagement are clearly linked to increased student achievement (Anderman, Maehr, & Midgley, 1999; Brewster & Fager, J., 2000; Fenzel & O'Brennan, 2007; Haselhuhn, Al-Mabuk, Gabriele, Groen, & Galloway, 2007). Therefore instruction that meets the needs of middle grades learners must provide opportunities to participate in meaningful hands-on activities rather than remaining in the role of passive recipients of information.

Students learn best by doing, especially in collaborative efforts with their peers. Self-perception of academic ability is a factor that has a significant impact on student motivation. Given the developmental levels of middle school students they are likely to doubt their own capacity (Heller, Calderon, & Medrich, 2003). Adolescents look to comparative measures that signal success in school as they develop their sense of self-worth and come to understand their own competences as learners. With a significant emphasis on social comparison linked directly to test results and grades, students are likely to become more anxious about how they stack up against their peers, more competitive, and more skeptical about the value and importance of the evaluation tools we use (Paris et al., 1991). Not surprisingly, the negative impact on the motivation, anxiety levels, and disillusionment among low achieving students is disproportionately harsh. The result of our current practice is likely to be a student less motivated to take the risks associate with giving maximum effort, one with heightened text anxiety, and one whose negative self-perceptions interfere with his or her willingness to engage (Paris et al. p. 14). Reframing curriculum, instruction, and assessment to focus on constructed meaning and collaborative learning addresses adolescents' levels of social anxiety and their need to build positive social relationships with their peers. Shifting the focus from isolating and competitive practices and aligning learning experiences with developmentally appropriate curriculum and assessments gives us the best opportunity to develop students who exhibit persistence, engage appropriate strategies for learning and demonstrating their learning.

Well-constructed projects allow students to interact with real world challenges and problems through hands-on engagement in gathering data, exploring ideas, creating, experimenting and organizing information. In these ways they develop not only their cognitive skills, but engage in appropriate social and emotional growth as well. As they make real connections to people, problems and events in their communities and beyond, they can engage with and find relevance in the learning within the curriculum. The active processes of communicating and sharing their processes and products with authentic audiences provides a level of quality control and feedback that supports their learning development. This type of hands on engagement with the world both within and beyond the walls of the school helps prepare students for participatory citizenship—one of the values we espouse for them. To the extent that relevant connections can be made, such learning engages students and fosters their critical thinking skills as well.

CHALLENGING CONTENT AND EXPERIENCES

If we are to help each young adolescent realize his or her fullest potential, we must hold high expectations for all learners. Engaging in authentic tasks with a real world orientation opens learners to opportunities to demonstrate competence that goes beyond the successes measured by traditional assessments. A common misconception that often attaches to multidisciplinary project-based approaches to learning is that there is a lack of rigor inherent in the approach. As standards are generally grounded in discrete academic disciplines, this thinking is reinforced. What is clear, however, is that students learn best when their learning is situated in 'big ideas' or concepts rather than grounded in the traditional focus on learning isolated facts, figures and names (Bransford, Brown, & Cocking, 1999). Integrated curriculum addresses young adolescents' need for authentic learning experiences and can afford opportunities for choice and voice in learning that leads to ownership and achievement.

The power of authentic learning is well established. Blumenfeld and colleagues (1991), and others have demonstrated that the best way to help students become problem solvers is to simulate the conditions under which experts master subject matter and become proficient at conducting investigations. Newmann, Marks, and Gamoran (1995) advocate for authentic instructional practices to engage learners and offer three criteria for authentic instructional practices: construction of knowledge, disciplined inquiry, and value beyond the school.

If we are to support students' construction of knowledge we must first acknowledge students' existing understandings and experiences. Identifying students' preconceptions and initial understanding is critical to the learning process. "If students' preconceptions are not addressed directly, they often memorize content (e.g., formulas in physics), yet still use their experience-based preconceptions to act in the world" (Donovan & Bransford, 2005, p. 5). Providing opportunities for students to address these misconceptions and gain experiences that will allow them to access new knowledge is essential.

Second, we must provide structured activities to facilitate disciplined inquiry. Meaningful engagement is critical to the construction of knowledge (Marzano, 2003; Newmann, Marks, & Gamoran, 1995) describe this process as building on the learner's prior knowledge to develop a deeper understanding, integrating new information, and using the knowledge in new ways.

The third criterion for authentic instructional practices is value beyond school (Newmann, Marks, & Gamoran, 1995). This may entail connecting content to personal or public issues as well as the demonstration of understanding to an audience beyond the school. Such activities include writing persuasive letters to the city council to advocate for a skate park, interviewing community members for an oral history project, or communicating the impact of a development project using scientific concepts. Newmann and his colleagues have a conception of authentic instructional practices requires that all three criteria be met, but this does not preclude the use of "repetitive practice or memory drills" which might support students as they construct the knowledge, skills and dispositions that might later serve as the basis for authentic performance (p. 4). Scaffolding the learning experiences is a critical dimension of authentic learning.

EMPOWERING EDUCATION

Adolescent learners often experience alienation in a world of rules and regulations imposed on them by adults who seem not to understand them or their world. The physical and emotional changes they experience are a further source of feelings that they have no control over their lives (Learning Point Associates, 2005, p. 5). Restoring a sense of ownership and control to the learning experience is critical if they are to develop the quality and clarity of self-perception. The low-risk self-directed environment of project-based learning provides opportunities for choice in middle level classrooms that will motivate and engage learners. Giving students opportunities to select a topic or text acknowledges young adolescents' need to exercise more decision-making power. The sense of ownership that this provides is an important component of developing a sense of self as a learner.

Given the young adolescent's need for authentic learning experiences and participation in decisions, curriculum that crosses subject boundaries and connects to real world is well situated to give students voice in what is learned and how (Pate, Homestead, & McGinnis, 1997). Teachers can help provide choices to learners by supplying a variety of text options including age-appropriate books at various reading levels, digital media, newspapers, and magazines, as well as multiple options to demonstrate mastery of content. A variety of authentic learning tasks or assessment options aimed at the same objective can give students a choice in activities or demonstrations of learning that empowers. This practice is central to the differentiation and individualization of instruction that leads to student growth.

Assessment must also serve as a tool for empowering young adolescent learners. If we are to ensure that students develop the ability to monitor and regulate their learning, something essential to the goal of creating lifelong learners, they must be actively involved in assessing their own learning. When we teach students how to assess their own progress and engage them in self-evaluation—judging the quality of their work based on evidence and explicit criteria, for the purpose of doing better work in the future—they develop a sense of ownership of their own learning and of their own success. Evidence about the positive effect of self-evaluation on student performance is particularly convincing, especially as it relates to difficult tasks (Arter, Spandel, Culham, & Pollard, 1994; Bond, Herman, & Arter, 1994; Maehr & Stallings, 1972), and among high need pupils. Self-evaluation is a potentially powerful technique because of its impact on student performance through enhanced self-efficacy and increased intrinsic motivation, key concerns for middle level learners.

Therefore, engaging students in the development of curriculum, instruction and assessment are all important considerations if we are to achieve our goal of fostering capable, self-regulated learners. Young adolescents are more likely to engage in the classroom when they connect content and learning tasks with life beyond the classroom walls (Caskey & Anfara, 2007; Learning Point Associates, 2005). Insofar as that life is rarely organized in subject or discipline specific ways, the notion of integrating curriculum and engaging students in interdisciplinary or multidisciplinary learning support their transfer of knowledge. Researchers and practitioners describe examples of effectively integrated curriculum, and note its significant power for student learning (Bergstrom, 1998; Caskey, 2002; Pate, Homestead, & McGinnis, 1997; Stevenson & Carr, 1993; Vars, 1997; Zemelman, Daniels, & Hyde, 1998). By infusing relevance, authenticity, and choice into the curriculum and learning activities, educators can make learning more purposeful.

EQUITABLE OPPORTUNITIES FOR SUCCESS

Consistent with calls for reforms that address 21st century skills and the advice from the Association of Middle Level Educators the literature on teaching for social justice calls for integrated curriculum and learning environments to benefit all learners, has brought into focus the challenges associated with differentiating our curriculum, instruction and assessment in the current standardized high-stakes accountability atmosphere (Darling-Hammond, French, & Garcia-Lopez, 2002; Hunt, 1998;

Lewison, Flint, & Van Sluys, 2002). If we are to support the success of all students, we must consider the impact of our practice particularly on those students who are and have been persistently underserved by traditional practice.

Over the past 2 decades progressive educators following in Dewey's lead have produced an extensive body of literature that provides powerful argument for more socially just practices to support the learning of traditionally marginalized students. A variety of scholars have addressed the unique learning needs of student for whom English is not a first language (Lopez, Gonzalez, & Fierro, 2005; Portes & Hao, 2004; Rolstad, Mahoney, & Glass, 2005), non-White students (Ladson-Billings, 1994, 1995, 2001), students identified as "at-risk" (Slavin, 2002, Wasik, Bond, & Hindman, 2002), and students with learning differences (Friend & Bursuck, 2006). We have also seen a proliferation of literature that illustrates and substantiates the effectiveness of differentiated instruction (Tomlinson, 2001; Tomlinson & Allan, 2000; Tomlinson & Reis, 2004). And yet the impact that this body of knowledge has had on practice appears to be limited by the current approaches to accountability that reinforce a traditional pedagogical approach that ignores both the cultural and developmental characteristics of middle level learners and much of what we know about effective instructional practices. Indeed, research examining highly successful programs and practices in middles schools (Willingham, 2009), shows us that those programs that are most successful use direct instruction less frequently, use cooperative learning more often, use inquiry-based teaching strategies more frequently, and place a higher emphasis on critical thinking. These results are particularly significant for students who are traditionally underserved, and provide every indication that these strategies are reasonably calculated to have positive impact on students across all groups.

A project based approach to learning opens the door to accommodating the needs of diverse learners within the context of a common learning experience and a rigorous and relevant curriculum. Authentic, personalized and individualized differentiated instruction honors the unique strengths and characteristics of each learner. The immediacy of connections to the world beyond school, the world that fascinates the young adolescent, results in a high level of engagement and provides opportunities to affirm cultural identity development and empower learners. Therefore, consistent with the calls from the profession and from a variety of scholars who advocate the adoption of a curriculum that is challenging, exploratory, integrative and relevant to our students, and instructional practices that engage students in authentic learning experiences and self-assessment, we must consider the possibilities of a new paradigm, and the costs of clinging to outdated practice.

PROBLEMS IN CURRENT PRACTICE

Despite the promise of these promising practices, most middle school students travel through their six or seven period day without seeing any relationship between or among the learning activities or content in their discipline-based courses. They have been taught to equate learning with recalling isolated facts on paper and pencil assessments, and many have difficulty seeing themselves as partners in the learning process. Given the structures and practice in which we engage, this is not surprising. An approach that is largely discipline oriented, focused upon content standards and cognitive objectives to the exclusion of affective and psychomotor developmental considerations is not likely to produce learners with a coherent sense of self or of their learning. This disjointed approach to learning that focuses on isolated facts rather than concepts and ideas, appears to be exacerbated by our current response to accountability pressures and an entrenchment of outdated conceptions of teaching and learning that serve as barriers to reform.

There are a number of factors that may suggest reasons that current practice does not conform to what we know about effective, developmentally appropriate teaching and learning. First, the traditional preparation, role expectations, and tools used to evaluate teachers present barriers to implementing meaningful inquiry based instruction. The notion of the teacher as the dispenser of knowledge remains strong, and coupled with the high stakes associated with mandated assessments creates a context in which it is unlikely that teachers will be encouraged to give up what they perceive to be control of their classrooms to assume the role of facilitator of learning and colearner alongside their students. The companionable learning (side-by-side) that developmentally appropriate instruction requires may be experienced as a threat to the teacher's authority. The risks involved in relinquishing or sharing control may appear to outweigh the reward for the teacher who knows that her or his continued employment and compensation are tied to student performance on high stakes assessments.

Teachers also tend to replicate their own educational experiences as they plan for instruction. Given the fairly traditional, subject-centered educational experiences and programs from which they have emerged, this makes the transition to different types of curricula based on different instructional philosophies challenging (Ball, 2002; Boaler, 1997). Add to that the inherent content focus, teacher dominated, test oriented, high stakes environment in which they work. And, add the extent to which appropriate resources and professional development and supervision are available. Given these realities, it is easy to understand why a move toward a more constructivist approach to teaching and learning is so difficult.

Likewise, despite the assertions of publishers and district level textbook adoption committees, there is sufficient evidence across grade levels and across disciplines to strongly suggest that textbooks continue to play a significant role in defining curriculum and framing instructional practice. Tyson-Bernstein and Woodward (1991) described the role of textbooks as "ubiquitous" in American schools, pointing to them as a driving force in determining what children have an opportunity to learn. Despite the development of new curricular standards and assessments, this appears to remain the case. Beyond that, Robitaille and Travers (1992) suggest that, to a large extent, teachers are the primary decision-makers regarding what it taught, and how it is taught. They make daily determinations about how to teach content and the exercises and activities assigned to their students. Those decisions, they argue, are largely determined by the content of the textbook authorized and assigned for the course (Robitaille & Travers, p. 708). Regardless of school or district level pacing guides and curriculum maps, there is ample evidence to suggest that for many if not most teachers, their textbooks serve as the de-facto scope and sequence guides determining what is taught (Tarr, Chavez, Reys, & Reys, 2006; Weiss, Pasley, Smith, Banilower, & Heck, 2003). It is apparent that teachers often "pick and choose" units to use and replace components of the curriculum with content provided by their texts (Seeley, 2003). Unfortunately, whether they make wholesale or selective use of these materials, the result is a focus on content and assessment that is restricted to subject-centered curriculum and cognitive objectives that may or may not align to the broader curricular goals or to the nature and needs of their learners.

Finally, in many school districts current accountability efforts have led to an almost pathological focus on raising standardized test scores by any means. Lipka (2005, p. 371) suggests that the uses and abuses of high stakes standardized tests stem from flawed assumptions about the nature and degrees of standardization in the students, conditions, and other factors that may impact student performance on often used measures. Assuming the playing field to be level, teachers, administrators, parents and politicians see state tests as the single most important indicator of school improvement or lack thereof. In response to the enormous stakes attached to the assessments, there is a predictable narrowing of the curriculum to match the content covered by the tests, and not surprisingly, teaching begins to resemble the multiple choice formatting of the all-important assessments. And while some would argue that "teaching to the test" simply implies a focus on the mandated curriculum content, one might question whether the improvements measured might not be more closely related to students' test taking skills rather than their overall academic performance. What is most likely an increased focus on memorizing isolated facts rather than developing higher order thinking and problem-solving skills.

There is no doubt that the traditional pencil and paper assessments common to most school settings can provide helpful diagnostic information. But, sadly the current use and practice seems to yield little useful data. And while there is little argument that accountability is critical, the use of testing data for teacher evaluation and accountability and for student promotion and retention decisions in most settings is at best flawed. As Bracey (1998) suggests, school provides a minimal percentage of students' overall experience and learning, and accounts for as little as 9% of the variance on standardized tests. Therefore it makes little sense to directly link instructional practice and outcomes on narrowly focused assessments, and illogical to use them in ways that define and often limit educational opportunities for the least privileged students in our schools. Reform efforts have focused primarily on political and psychometric concerns without regard to the potentially negative impact on students (Paris et al., 1991). As educators we must acknowledge the public expectations for standardized and comparable test data, and the need to ensure validity and reliability in our measures. However, if we are to shift the paradigm from a narrow focus on assessment of learning to a more robust model of assessment for learning, we must adopt a developmental approach. Paris and colleagues suggest that assessment must be collaborative and authentic to promote learning and motivation, longitudinal to provide information about cumulative patterns of progress, and multidimensional to address the interactive nature of learning, motivation and achievement (p. 18). If our pedagogy is to be driven by our assessments they must be aligned in ways that support student growth and learning over time. We must know more about them than how they perform on a test. We must understand how they experience learning and testing, what impact the results have on their self-concepts and their motivation to learn and to perform.

Due to a variety of factors, most students experience a curriculum centered around cognitive objectives, delivered through subject oriented texts and assessed through pencil and paper tests and activities. They learn to see their role as that of passive recipient of information disseminated by their teachers. This traditional subject-oriented approach may not only fail to engage his or her energies and attentions, but may well engrain the notion that life in the classroom is entirely separate from their own lives and interests. The ways in which we assess their learning may also have an impact on students' perceptions of themselves as learners and their willingness to engage. Even if we use relevant content and socially collaborative pedagogy, when we then revert to individualistic measures that foster notions of social comparison, competition and negative self-perceptions, we create a disconnect. Current practice not only fails to account for the content and process of dynamic growth and development that are so naturally and so prominently part of middle grades students' reality, but it sets up a notion that learning is something separate and apart from the "real world."

CONSIDERING WHAT IS AT STAKE

And so for Sophia, Carlos, and for so many children like them, much hangs in the balance. Closing achievement gaps and serving the needs of equity and justice requires that we accommodate diverse learners and build programs that recognize and capitalize upon the characteristics they bring with them to the learning experiences we provide. If we are to create schools that support the learning of all students, we must first orient our curriculum, our pedagogy, and our assessment to the students themselves. Given the critical task of equipping students with the tools and motivation to become effective continuous learners, the documented benefits or an inquiry-oriented approach are many. Effective schools give students opportunities to explore topics and problems in depth rather than perpetuating the inch deep, mile wide superficiality of the traditional 'coverage' approach. When we approach teaching and learning with the developmental needs of our students in mind and provide students with authentic learning opportunities, relevant curriculum, and appropriate assessment, we have the opportunity to increase their motivation and perceptions of themselves as learners. Students who are appropriately challenged and engaged as partners in the learning experience have the opportunity to gain a sense of efficacy, ownership and self-regulation that form the foundation for future success.

If we accept the proposition that an alignment of curriculum and materials, instructional practice, and school environment with a coherent and consistent philosophy that places the nature and needs of the learner at the center of the teaching and learning process, then we must address current practice if we are to enhance young adolescents' self-perception and self-concept. From a philosophical and pedagogical perspective project-based learning addresses the key elements and characteristics of effective middle grades instruction. What distinguishes this approach is the position of the learner in the process and the fundamental assumptions about how we, as educators, organize our schools and plan our instruction to support their collaboration in the decision-making about and implementation of developmentally appropriate curriculum instruction and assessment. Failing to align our curriculum, instruction and assessment to what we know about our early adolescent learners and what we aspire to help them achieve in terms of the cognitive, social and emotional development will continue to exact an enormous toll on the young people we are charged to serve.

REFERENCES

Alexander, W. M., & George, P. S. (1993). *The exemplary middle school* (2nd ed.). New York, NY: Hot, Rinehart, & Winston.

Anderman, E., Maehr, M., & Midgley, C. (1999). Declining motivation after the transition to middle school: Schools can make a difference. *Journal of Research and Development in Education, 32*(3), 131-147.

Andrews, R. L., & Morfield, J. (1991). Effective leadership for effective urban schools. *Education and Urban Society, 23*(3), 270-278.

Arter, J., Spandel, V., Culham, R. & Pollard, J. (1994, April). *The impact of training students to be self-assessors of writing.* Paper presented at the annual meeting of the American Educational Research Association, New Orleans, LA.

Ball, J. (2002). Learning from teaching: Exploring the relationship between reform curriculum and equity. *Journal for Research in Mathematics Education. 33*(4), 239-258.

Barron, B. J. S., Schwarts, D. L., Vye, N. J., Moore, A., Petrosino, A., Zech, L., … The Cognition and Technology Group at Vanderbilt. (1998). Doing the understanding: Lesson from research on problem- and project-based learning. *The Journal of the Learning Sciences, 7*, 271-311.

Beane, J. A. (1993). *A middle school curriculum: From rhetoric to reality* (2nd ed.). Columbus, OH: National Middle School Association.

Beane, J. A. (1997). *Curriculum integration: Designing the core of democratic education.* New York, NY: Teachers College Press.

Beane, J. A., & Lipka, R. P. (1986). *Self-concept, self-esteem, and the curriculum.* New York, NY: Teachers College Press.

Bergman, S. (1992). Exploratory programs in the middle level school: A responsive idea. In J. L. Ivin (Ed.), *Transforming middle level education: Perspectives and possibilities* (pp. 179-192). Boston, MA: Allyn & Bacon.

Bergstrom, K. L. (1998). Are we missing the point about curriculum integration? *Middle School Journal, 29*(4), 28-37.

Blumenfeld, P. C., Soloway, E., Marx, R. W., Krajcik, J. S., Guzdial, M., & Palinscar, A. (1991). Motivating project-based learning: Sustaining the doing, supporting the learning. *Educational Psychologist, 26*, 369-398.

Boaler, J. (1997). *Experiencing school mathematics: Teaching styles, sex, and settings.* Buckingham, England: Open University Press.

Bond, L. A., Herman, J., & Arter, J. (1994). Rethinking assessment and its role in supporting educational reform. In *Laboratory Network Program, A tool kit for professional developers: Alternative assessment.* Portland, OR: Northwest Regional Educational Laboratory.

Bracey, G. W. (1998). *Put to the test: An educators and consumers guide to standardized testing.* Bloomington, IN: Phi Delta Kappa.

Bransford, J. D., Brown, A. L., & Cocking, R. R. (Eds.). (1999). *How people learn: Brain, mind, experience, and school.* Washington, DC: National Academy Press.

Brewster, C., & Fager, J. (2000). *Increasing student engagement and motivation: From time-on-task to homework.* Portland, OR: Northwest Regional Educational Laboratory. Retrieved from http://www.nwrel.org/request/oct00/textonly.html

Briggs, T. H. (1920). *The junior high school.* Boston, MA: Houghton Mifflin.

Carnegie Council on Adolescent Development. (1989). *Turning points: Preparing youth for the 21st century.* New York, NY: The Carnegie Corporation of New York.

Caskey, M. M. (2002). Authentic curriculum: Strengthening middle level curriculum. In V. A. Anfara, Jr. & S. L. Stacki, (Eds.), *Middle school curriculum, instruction, and assessment* (pp. 103-117). Greenwich, CT: Information Age.

Caskey, M. M., & Anfara, V. A., Jr. (2007). *Research summary: Young adolescents' developmental characteristics.* Westerville, OH: National Middle School Association. Retrieved from http://www.nmsa.org/Research/ResearchSummaries/DevelopmentalCharacteristics/tabid/1414/Default.aspx

Curtis, T. E., & Bidwell, W. W. (1977). *Curriculum and instruction for emerging adolescents.* Reading, MA: Addison-Wesley.

Darling-Hammond, L., French, J., & Garcia-Lopez, S. P. (Eds.). (2002). *Learning to teach for social justice.* New York, NY: Teachers College Press.

Donovan, M. S., & Bransford, J. D. (Eds.). (2005). *How students learn: History, mathematics, and science in the classroom.* Washington, DC: National Academies Press.

Eichorn, D. H. (1966). *The middle school.* New York, NY: Center for Applied Research in Education.

Fenzel, M. L., & O'Brennan, L. M. (2007, April). *Educating at-risk urban African American children: The effects of school climate on motivation and academic achievement.* Paper presented at the annual meeting of the American Educational Research Association, Chicago, IL.

Friend, M., & Bursuck, W. (2006). *Including students with special needs: A practical guide for classroom teachers* (4th ed.). Boston, MA: Allyn & Bacon.

George, P. S., & Alexander, W. M. (2003). *The exemplary middle school.* Florence, KY: Thomson Learning Cengage.

Haselhuhn, C. W., Al-Mabuk, R., Gabriele, A., Groen, M., & Galloway, S. (2007). Promoting positive achievement in the middle school: A look at teachers' motivational knowledge, beliefs, and teaching practices. *Research in Middle Level Education, 30*(9). Retrieved from http://www.nmsa.org/portals/0/pdf/publications/RMLE/rmle_vol30_no9.pdf

Heller, R., Calderon, S., & Medrich, E. (2003). *Academic achievement in the middle grades: What does research tell us? A review of literature.* Atlanta, GA: Southern Regional Education Board. Retrieved from http://www.sreb.org/programs/hstw/publications/pubs/02V47_AchievementReview.pdf

Hunt, J. A. (1998). Of stories, seeds, and the promise of social justice. In W. Ayers, J. A. Hunt, & T. Quinn (Eds.), *Teaching for social justice* (pp. xiii-xv). New York, NY: The New Press and Teachers College Press.

Jackson, A. W., & Davis, G. A. (2000). *Turning points 2000: Educating adolescents in the 21st century.* New York, NY: Teachers College Press.

Ladson-Billings, G. (1994). *The dream keepers: Successful teachers of African American children*. San Francisco, CA: Jossey-Bass.

Ladson-Billings, G. (1995). But that's just good teaching! Toward a theory of culturally relevant pedagogy. *American Educational Research Journal, 32*(3), 465-491.

Ladson-Billings, G. (2001). *Crossing over to Canaan: The journey of new teachers in diverse classrooms*. San Francisco, CA: Jossey-Bass.

Learning Point Associates. (2005). *Using student engagement to improve adolescent literacy (Quick key 10 action guide)*. Naperville, IL: Author. Retrieved from http://www.learningpt.org/pdfs/qkey10.pdf

Lewison, M., Flint, A. S., & Van Sluys, K. (2002). Taking on critical literacy: The journey of newcomers and novices. *Language Arts, 7*(5), 382-392.

Lipka, R. P. (2005). Testing. In V. A. Anafara, Jr., P. G. Andrews, & S. B. Mertens (Eds.), *The encyclopedia of middle grades education* (pp. 368-372). Greenwich, CT: Information Age.

Lopez, G. R., Gonzalez, M. L., & Fierro, E. (2005). Educational leadership along the U.S.-Mexico border: Crossing borders/embracing hybridity/building bridges. In C. Marshall & M. Oliva (Eds.), *Leadership for social justice: Making revolutions in education* (pp. 64-84). Boston, MA: Pearson.

Maehr, M., & Stallings, R. (1972). Freedom from external evaluation. *Child Development, 43*,177-185.

Marzano, R. J. (2003). *What works in schools: Translating research into action*. Alexandria, VA: Association for Supervision and Curriculum Development.

National Middle School Association. (2010). *This we believe: Keys to educating young adolescents*. Westerville, OH: National Middle School Association.

Newmann, F. M., Marks, H. M., & Gamoran, A. (1995). *Authentic pedagogy: Standards that boost student performance*. Issues in Restructuring Schools (Issue Report No. 8). Madison, WI: Center on Reorganization and Restructuring of Schools. Retrieved from http://www.wcer.wisc.edu/archive/cors/Issues_in_Restructuring_Schools/ISSUES_NO_8_SPRING_1995.pdf

Paris, S. G., Lawton, T. A., Turner, J. C., & J. L. Roth. (1991). A developmental perspective on standardized achievement testing. *Educational Researcher, 20*(5), 12-20, 40.

Pate, P. E., Homestead, E. R., & McGinnis, K. L. (1997). *Making integrated curriculum work: Teachers, students, and the quest for coherent curriculum*. New York, NY: Teachers College Press.

Portes, A., & Hao, L. (2004). The schooling of children of immigrants: Contextual effects on the educational attainment of the second generation. Proceedings of the National Academy of Science. doi:101:11920-27

Ratvitch, D. (2010). *The death and life of the great American school system*. New York, NY: Basic Books.

Robitaille, D. F., & Travers, K. J. (1992). International studies of achievement in mathematics. In D. Grouws (Ed.), *Handbook of research on mathematics education* (pp. 687-709). New York, NY: Macmillan.

Rolstad, K., Mahoney, K., & Glass, G. (2005). The big picture: A meta-analysis of program effectiveness research on English language learners. *Educational Policy, 19*(4), 572-594.

Seeley, C. L. (2003). Mathematics textbook adoption in the United States. In G. Stanic & J. Kilpatrick (Eds.), *A history of mathematics education* (Vol. 2, pp. 957-988). Reston, VA: National Council of Teachers of Mathematics.

Slavin, R. E. (2002). The intentional school: Effective elementary education for all children. In S. Stringfield & D. Land (Eds.), *Educating at-risk students* (Vol. 101, pp. 111-127). Chicago, IL: University of Chicago Press.

Strebinsky, A., & Ross, S. M. (2005). Assessment: Formative evaluation. In V. A. Anafara, Jr., P. G. Andrews, & S. B. Mertens (Eds.). *The encyclopedia of middle grades education* (pp. 122-126). Greenwich, CT: Information Age.

Stevenson, C., & Carr, J. F. (1993). *Integrated studies in the middle grades: Dancing through walls.* New York, NY: Teachers College Press.

Stiggins, R. (2001). *Student-involved classroom assessment* (3rd ed.) Upper Saddle River, NJ: Merrill Prentice-Hall.

Tarr, J., Chavez, O., Reys, R. & Reys, B. (2006). From the written to enacted curricula: The intermediary role of middle school mathematics in shaping students' opportunity to learn. *School Science and Mathematics, 106*(4), 191-201.

Thomas, J. W. (2000). *A review of research on project-based learning.* Retrieved from http://www.bie.org/files/reserachreviewPBL.pdf

Tomlinson, C. A., (2001). *How to differentiate instruction in mixed-ability classrooms* (2nd ed.). Alexandria, VA: Association for Supervision and Curriculum Development.

Tomlinson, C. A. (2005). Instructional methods: Differentiated instruction. In V. A. Anafara, Jr., P. G. Andrews, & S. B. Mertens (Eds.), *The encyclopedia of middle grades education* (pp. 248-251). Greenwich, CT: Information Age.

Tomlinson, C. A., & Allan, S. D. (2000). *Leadership for differentiating schools and classrooms.* Alexandria, VA: Association for Supervision and Curriculum Development.

Tomlinson, C. A., & Eidson, C. (2003). *Differentiation in practice: A resource guide for differentiating curriculum.* Alexandria, VA: Association for Supervision and Curriculum Development.

Tomlinson, C. A., & Reis, S. (Eds.). (2004). *Differentiation for gifted and talented students.* Thousand Oaks, CA: Corwin Press.

Tyson-Bernstein, H., & Woodward, A. (1991). Nineteenth century policies for 21st century practice: The textbook reform dilemma. In P. G. Altbach, B. P. Kelly, H. G. Petrie, & L. Weis (Eds.), *Textbooks in American society* (pp. 91-104). Albany NY: State University of New York Press.

Vars, G. F. (1997). Effects of integrative curriculum and instruction. In J. L. Irvin (Ed.), *What current research says to the middle level practitioner* (pp. 179-186). Columbus, OH: National Middle School Association. (ED 427 847).

Vars, G. F. (2001). Can curriculum integration survive in an era of high-stakes testing? *Middle School Journal, 33*(2), 7-17.

Wasik, B., Bond, M. A., & Hindman, A. (2002). Educating at-risk preschool and kindergarten children. In S. Stringfield & D. Land (Eds.), *Educating at-risk students* (Vol. 101, pp. 89-110). Chicago, IL: University of Chicago Press.

Weiss, I. R., Pasley, J. D., Smith, P. S., Banilower, E. R. & Heck, D. J. (2003). *Looking inside the classroom: A study of K-12 mathematics and science education in the United States.* Chapel Hill, NC: Horison Research.

Wiggins, G., & McTighe, J. (1998). *Understanding by design.* Alexandria, VA: Association for Supervision and Curriculum Development.

Wiles, J., & Bondi, J. (1989). *Curriculum development: A guide to practice.* Boston, MA: Routledge & Kegan Paul.

Williamson, R. D., Johnston, J. H., & Kanthak, L. M. (1995). The agenda: The achievement agenda for middle level schools. *Schools in the Middle, 5*(2), 6-9.

Willingham, D. T. (2009). Why don't students like school? *American Educator, 33*(1), 7.

Zemelman, S., Daniels, H., & Hyde, A. (1998). *Best practices: New standards for teaching and learning in America's schools* (2nd ed.). Portsmouth, NH: Heinemann.

CHAPTER 17

MOVING THE MIDDLE GRADES CURRICULUM INTO OUR DYNAMIC WORLD

Edward N. Brazee

SCENARIO—A VIRTUAL MIDDLE SCHOOL

Sylvia and Mary had worked on their project for 1 month designing a new space for a nonprofit organization that had contracted with them. Their task as outlined by the executive director of Food For All, was to redesign the food intake, storage, and distribution areas for this well-known food bank. Their task was complex and began with a tour of the food bank's building, meeting with the Board of Directors, and observing how the operation actually worked at various times of the day. After that day on-site, the rest of the work had been done online, for Mary and Sylvia lived 100 miles apart. They communicated regularly via Skype using many Web 2.0 tools such as Google Docs, wikis, screen sharing, and Sketch Up that allowed them to work collaboratively and effectively. The shared Google Doc, for example, served as the "home base" for the project allowing them to work simultaneously on one documents with ideas and plans that both could access at any time.

This morning they had set aside a 2-hour block to put the finishing touches on their plans thus far. They were preparing for a midpoint, face-to-face meeting with Food For All's Board of Directors and staff to outline the plans and the process of how their proposal would work. Before they could finish the work, Mary and Sylvia needed some feedback from the Directors and the actual people who would be using their food distribution system. To date they had studied and visited similar food banks online in various towns and cities across the U.S.; interviewed managers of several other food banks; conferred with an architect about potential renovation plans, and; met with a contractor to begin to get some idea of the extent of physical changes needed. But now they needed some feedback on their ideas before they could move ahead.

Both Mary and Sylvia attend a virtual middle school in their state but they knew each other from the summer camp they had both attended since they were five. Nonetheless, they often worked together on their studies and when it came time for their 8th grade year-end project, they were happy to work together once again.

Mary and Sylvia are pretty typical young adolescent girls interested in music, sports, drama, and making a difference. The decision to leave their local middle school at the end of their 7th grade year was not an easy one for them or their parents. Separately, each girl felt she was not learning what she was interested in and was much more self-directed than the middle school allowed her to be. Both appreciated the flexibility to engage in projects that allowed them to be creative and to pursue answers to questions they had about themselves and the world. Yes, they took online classes that were more traditional and looked much like the classes from their former schools, but overall, the opportunities to direct their own learning and move ahead at their own pace far outweighed any disadvantages.

Does this scenario look like any middle grades schools you know? Or, does it sound like a "fantastical" notion of what middle grades curriculum could be in the future? Can you determine what the curriculum is? If so, is this a curriculum that you would be interested in teaching, learning from, or studying? In this chapter, we will explore the middle grades curriculum that young adolescents need. We'll look at where the middle grades curriculum has been, what it has looked like, what the experts say it should be, and why. Then we'll consider a vision for the present and the future based on the 17 dimensions of the self-enhancing school (Beane & Lipka, 1986). Finally, we will explore the essential reasons why we must provide a progressive curriculum for young adolescents and how more schools can get there.

But first, consider my central thesis: technology is now and will continue to be the key change factor in middle grades curriculum. But not technology as we often think of it in terms of adding more hardware and software to the school day or somehow mysteriously "integrating" technology into the curriculum. No, this is definitely not about technology, but the opportunities that digital learning has opened up to our students, one could say, "once again."

TECHNOLOGY IS CHANGING EVERYTHING ...
BUT NOT IN THE WAY WE MIGHT THINK

Whether it is happening at your school yet or not, technology is changing everything. Technology has changed some schools significantly in the past 20 years, while others have felt little influence. That is in itself amazing given the rapid developments in technology especially in the last 10 years. Consider these examples: In 2002, Maine began the Maine Learning Technology Initiative (MLTI), known more informally as the "Laptop Program" where laptops were assigned to every 7th and 8th grade student and teacher in the state. Every middle level school was wired for wifi access and professional development was provided for every teacher. To say that learning in Maine's middle level schools has changed with the advent of MLTI is a huge understatement. Of course, many school districts have followed Maine's lead and one-to-one programs are now common across all 50 states. Incredibly, there are still large numbers of schools where students have little access to digital learning. Those schools that do not embrace either the opportunities or challenges of the digital age will simply become redundant and most likely, obsolete.

But let's be clear about what we mean by technology. It isn't the bells and whistles of technology per se, not the hardware and gadgets, apps and software, or the "gee whiz" factor of the many great tools that allow us to be wildly creative, or even those tools that challenge us because we can spend so much time on them with little reward. So, if it isn't the ever-changing laptops, tablets, mobile devices, if it isn't the 500,000 apps for iPads and iPhones, if it isn't the Web 2.0 tools such as wikis, podcasts, videoconferencing, blogs, and so much more, and it isn't even social media such as Facebook, Twitter, or Pinterest, what does make a difference?

The promise of digital learning is that it allows middle grades schools to achieve its goals and gives an entire new focus to many of them. It is what technology allows our students to do that will continue to change middle grades curriculum. Four key themes for middle grades curriculum have emerged: New opportunities to collaborate; new opportunities to learn; new opportunities to create and showcase talents, and; new opportunities to balance technology and learning. Each of these themes existed before technology but now their influence on the middle grades curriculum is even more critical, immediate, and long lasting. But, before we consider these themes, let's look back at the history of middle grades curriculum development of the last 25 years to see what has worked, what directions curriculum has taken, and where middle grades work has stalled.

A LOOK BACK AT CURRICULUM IN THE MIDDLE GRADES

Where do we stand today? Do middle grades educators know about the work, even the relatively recent past work, discussions, and implementation of middle grades curriculum? For those of us involved in middle level education since at least the 1980s (if not longer), we are well aware that middle grades curriculum was not a major focus of the early development of the middle grades. In James Beane's words middle school curriculum was "the absent presence" in discussions of middle school development (Beane, 1990, p. 1), well behind both structural and organizational components such as advisory programs, interdisciplinary teaming and others. It wasn't that attention to the overall issues of the curriculum was unimportant, perhaps middle level schools needed to get their own houses in order before they could pay attention to critical issues like curriculum. Or maybe, just maybe, focusing on the curriculum might have been too contentious for middle schools to survive their early years.

Fortunately, a small book by James Beane, *A Middle School Curriculum— From Rhetoric to Reality* (1990) published by National Middle School Association (NMSA) (now Association for Middle Level Education [AMLE]) and the work of many middle grades pioneers—John Lounsbury, Gordon Vars, Conrad Toepfer, Chris Stevenson, John Arnold, Tom Erb and many, many others—brought the curriculum issue to the forefront. For the next few years books, articles, presentations at state and national conferences, and most importantly, a number of schools focused as never before on the larger question of what a middle school curriculum should and could be. A number of these schools like Brown Barge Middle School (Florida), Solon Elementary School (Maine), The Watershed Program (Pennsylvania) and many others (Brazee & Capelluti, 1995; Springer, 1994; Stevenson & Carr, 1993) were also active presenters at conferences and wrote about their experiences. This helped greatly to expand their influence.

In the 1990s, these resources and the many "curriculum conversations" they started shined a bright light on the middle grades curriculum, a light that dimmed and went out almost completely with the advent of the standards movement, standardized testing, and ultimately the restrictive curriculum environment of the No Child Left Behind legislation (http://www2.ed.gov/nclb/landing.jhtml). Then, only the hard-core progressive curriculum folk were left. The curriculum conversations moved from integrated curriculum, democratic ideals, social meaning, and student-involvement to something very different. The curriculum conversations that helped spark innovation in middle grades curriculum in the 1990s fell by the wayside once the standards movement hit, followed by the curriculum narrowing requirements of No Child Left Behind, followed by heavy testing requirements, and now further restricted by the Common Core State Standards. No wonder the middle grades curriculum was stopped in its tracks ... and moved backwards in many schools.

The questions about what the middle grades curriculum should and could be have not been answered and may even be more critical today in our digital world—a world characterized by increasing environmental uncertainties and political processes that promote division and mistrust. I believe that these questions still matter. What should middle grades curriculum be? Why should it be? Who should it include? What is its role in middle school philosophy? How does it connect with elementary and high school curricula? What influence did the "curriculum conversations" of the 1990s have on middle grades curriculum? And how should a curriculum align with the current standards? Or more accurately, what is the role that the Common Core State Standards play when developing middle grades curriculum?

What happened to the progressive middle level curriculum work after 1995? Did the standards movement, increased testing, and ultimately, No Child Left Behind, signal the end of a relatively brief "golden age" of middle grades curriculum attention? At least in the 1990s, middle grades educators talked about curriculum with a capital "C", the big picture, not just pieces and parts of the curriculum (lower case "c" intended). Once again, after an all-too-brief focus on a more progressive look at a curriculum that middle level students needed and a moving away from the traditional separate subject curriculum, we found ourselves "back to the future" with students in their seats preparing for standardized tests with few opportunities for inquiry or exploration and definitely not in a democratic setting. Why does the traditional curriculum seem to have so much staying power?

In too many classrooms, the integrative curriculum work done in the early 1990s was erased when schools returned to separate subject teachers, textbooks, reduced planning time for interdisciplinary teams, and organizational structures where "teams" looked and functioned more like high school departments than the collaborative and interdisciplinary teams they were meant to be.

Why is it so difficult for middle grades schools to invent, implement, and sustain a middle grades curriculum that does what we've been talking about for a very long time—a curriculum that meets the needs of young adolescents and prepares them for their futures? Are we any closer to a vision of the middle grades curriculum than we were 25 years ago? Fifty years ago?

These questions are even more compelling when we consider the solid empirical evidence about what comprises an excellent middle school curriculum. In the midst of so much status quo curricula are numerous examples of middle schools programs with spectacularly responsive curricula, doing exactly what the authors of this book advocate for young adolescents. And finally, vision statements from a variety of professional associations in addition to AMLE's *This We Believe: Keys to Educating Young Adolescents* (NMSA, 2010), *Breaking Ranks in the Middle* (National Association of Secondary Schools, 2006), *Turning Points 2000* (Jackson & Davis, 2000), the National Forum's Comprehensive School Reform project, its Schools to Watch criteria, and its Vision Statement (http://www.middlegradesforum.org) are all useful guides to middle school reform. "These organizations and their publications "speak with one voice" to provide a vision, a conceptualization of schooling, descriptions of practice, and evidences of success to guide those who desire to improve the education of young adolescents" (AMLE, 2012, p. viii).

A PERSONAL PERSPECTIVE ON CURRICULUM

In 1971 I began my teaching career as one of 20+ English teachers in a grades 10-12 high school with 2200 students. On my first day of teaching, I was given the "official" English curriculum of the school, an oversized three-ring notebook of more than 300 pages! As large as the curriculum guide was, it was not particularly useful, at least to a rookie teacher, and I don't remember ever opening it. Instead, I depended on my new colleagues for assistance and spent an inordinate amount of time inventing my own curriculum to meet the needs of my students.

In the early 1970s schools experimented with what high school English and social studies departments called, Phase Elective Programs, a process of allowing students considerable choice of short courses. Those were heady years when we worked hard to find topics that were interesting, appealing, and meaningful to our students. At my high school, I remember teaching 6-week courses in Consumer Reading, Science Fiction, Film Study, Filmmaking, and Sports Literature to name a few. The traditional curriculum was shown the door ... no more English 9, 10, 11, and 12 ... as we developed a blend of modular courses that we hoped would appeal to our students. While all of these short courses may not have had the rigor that traditionalists wanted to see, they certainly engaged the students in ways the regular curriculum had not. Later these Phase Elective Programs were eliminated as another round of conservative initiatives hit schools.

Several years later I found my niche in a progressive middle school in Colorado—but it wasn't the language arts curriculum that pulled me in.

The draw was most definitely the young adolescent age group, children one day, teens the next. Playing with dolls and toy cars one moment and wanting to ride in real cars while pretending to be 5 years older than their real age. These 10 to 15-year-olds were fun, interested in learning what they cared about, maddening when you tried to teach them ideas that adults thought they needed to know, talented, willing to try out new things, responsive to adult enthusiasm, mischievous, and very, very funny. As much as I enjoyed teaching high school students, there was something about middle school students that caught my attention and kept it.

I was very fortunate that my teaching career was in two schools where I had great flexibility to create the curriculum to meet the needs of students as I saw fit. No standards in those days, except those that my colleagues and I set as professionals, very little testing, and lots of focus on what was meaningful for students. Like many new teachers, I had little idea what the "formal" curricula was and how it came to be—two parts tradition, one part textbook, and hopefully, at least one part responsiveness to my students. I soon discovered that devising a responsive curriculum was much more complicated and much more complex than my teacher preparation program led me to believe. The real curriculum of the classroom depended heavily on understanding what students were all about, including their perceptions of the world they live in and the world they would know as adults.

What did I learn? First of all, I learned that curriculum is much more than textbooks, lesson plans, teachers' guides, and easily drawn plans for a group of students. Curriculum is about the people that inhabit classrooms, particularly the students who bring a wide variety of skills, talents, background knowledge, interests, and expectations. But also about the teachers who bring all of the same. I learned very early on that content, skills and knowledge, the traditional bread and butter of curriculum, is important but insufficient for determining what the curriculum should be.

I also learned that the traditional curriculum development process did not work as neatly as many textbooks describe. Not that the ideas of conducting needs assessments, formulating objectives, selecting and organizing content, selecting and organizing learning experiences, and determining what to evaluate and how to do so isn't important (Taba, 1962). But this process was rarely followed. Let's be honest, traditional curriculum development did little to inspire teachers. Too little time, too many tasks to accomplish, too many requirements from local, state, and federal officials, all made curriculum development less real and less formal than it might otherwise be.

So, asking the same question again. *What has happened in middle grades classrooms in the last 25 years?* While many might say, "Not much", that isn't entirely fair either. There are hundreds (perhaps thousands) of truly excellent middle grades classrooms that use the qualities *This We Believe* (NMSA, 2010) and similar documents describe. And there are a number of schools that follow the same patterns. But it is also accurate to say that the vast majority of middle grades classrooms are still stuck in the traditional model, continuing to depend on a traditional separate-subject, teacher-directed, do the same old things in the same old way, approach (McEwin & Greene, 2011). Optimistically, I would like to say that we've learned something in the last 25 years (as well as the 100 years previously) about a curriculum for the middle grades, but I'm not entirely sure that is true.

We wonder, *what holds us back?* Certainly we would be remiss if we didn't mention the numerous impediments to change that constantly hold middle grades schools and classrooms from implementing the curriculum that young adolescents need and want. Of course there are huge barriers to change, not the least of which is the tremendous inertia from tradition. Just about everyone has been to school and no matter where they lived, experienced a system with more similarities than differences. Bells, 47-minute periods, separate subjects, straight rows of desks, teacher-directed learning, moving from grade to grade, testing, testing, and more testing, and so much more. Moving such a monolith of a system is difficult if not impossible, particularly when our memories and perceptions of "what worked" when we were students changes over time. No wonder so many schools have a hodge-podge curriculum.

And we haven't even mentioned the different points of view of the many school constituencies that weigh in—parents, community members, administrators, school boards, outside experts, and even students. And what about the role that politics plays in forming schools' agendas. Yes, we may give lip service to democracy, equity, and fairness, but how often are those values seen in schools when outside the school door those same values are turned on their head. The vision for too many middle schools is too narrow.

PART II—A VISION FOR THE (PRESENT AND) FUTURE OF MIDDLE GRADES CURRICULUM

Am I wrong about this? I maintain that there are teachers in nearly every school who recognize that the traditional curriculum does not work for all. These teachers work very hard to offer their students' opportunities to pursue meaningful learning in a variety of ways. While most middle level classrooms stick to the traditional curriculum more and more people are calling for something different—problem-based learning, technology and learning, differentiated instruction, individualized instruction, hands-on/minds-on learning. The list goes on and on. Very few people advocate for MORE direct instruction! So, why is there such a disconnect between what research suggests the middle grades curriculum should be (Jackson & Davis, 2000; Caskey, Davis, Bishop, Capraro, Roe, & Weiss, 2010; Roney, Anfara, & Brown, 2008) and what real middle grades schools actually have for their curriculum (McEwin & Greene, 2011)?

Furthermore, has the vision of middle grades curriculum by progressive leaders actually changed all that much? I don't think so. Look at Gordon Vars' work with CORE (not the Common Core) (http://www.corestandards.org/). John Lounsbury's 50-year advocacy for involving kids in the curriculum (Smith & McEwin, 2011), Jim Beane's articulate and forceful explanations of integrative curriculum (Beane, 1995), or Heidi Hayes Jacobs' essential question, "What year are you preparing your students for? 1973? 1995?" (Jacobs, 2010). Today the literature references problem-based learning, student-centered learning, mass-customized learning, active learning, experiential learning, expeditionary learning, and many more. While each of these approaches has a slightly different take on learning, underlying each is the realization that studying separate subjects in a largely teacher-directed fashion is not the effective model that our students need to become engaged in their learning ... and learn at high levels.

Let's return for a fuller explication to the four themes mentioned earlier that should have a significant influence on middle grades curriculum today ... and well into the future.

HOW TECHNOLOGY IS CHANGING LEARNING

New Opportunities to Collaborate

Collaboration has always been a key element in middle grades schools. Beginning with interdisciplinary teams of students and teachers working together; teachers working within and across teams; a leadership team comprised of teachers, administrators and students to provide direction for the school. Each of these teams depends on close working relationships, implicit trust, and long-term commitment. Excellent middle level schools also work hard to connect with parents, caregivers, and the community and these collaborative efforts promote student learning and closer connections with parents. Digital tools change the way we communicate with each other and open up possibilities for wider connections with other people.

Many examples of communicating exist—student to student; teacher to student; teacher to parent, and; to the school board. For example using a "classroom cam" so that school board members can see what a middle grades classroom actually does. Student podcasts of daily activities and learning, wikis that are open to parents so they can see the work their young adolescents are doing.

Each of these connections is as important as ever, but digital tools now allow us to make and maintain contacts with people across the world. Opportunities to talk with experts, peers, connections anywhere and anytime promotes learning as never before. Students learning from people with different cultures and customs. Skype and other video conferencing systems are amazing for making these kinds of face-to-face connections, but also writing blogs, developing websites, recording podcasts are all effective ways to connect and collaborate.

New Opportunities to Learn 24/7

Never before have we had opportunities to access content and skills as we do today. The traditional curriculum is too often limited by the teacher's control over what is studied, focused on, and occasionally, learned. Contrast that with the learning that begins at 3:00 p.m. when students exit the school doors and are immediately on their own to access the Internet through their computers or smart phones. Here they have access to the world, looking at content that far surpasses the content found in their textbooks and other school materials. At the Middle School in Kennebunk, Maine we read

> students have combined lessons from art, math, science, and English as they gradually redesign every room of The Nonantum Resort on a tight budget and with environment-friendly principles in mind. The students' MLTI laptops come in handy for planning the design, comparing prices, making purchases, and publicizing their work. (Maine Department of Education, 2012)

On the skill side students have access to a wide variety of resources and possibilities. Devising personal learning plans, accessing tutorials on virtually any subject, participating in video lessons, watching TED Talks (www.ted.com/talks), completing lessons at the Kahn Academy (www.khanacademy.org/) and similar sites. The possibilities are limitless. And many of our students already take advantage of them. In schools where student involvement is ubiquitous and expected the lines between learning in school and learning on their own are diminishing. In those schools that consciously set up barriers so students cannot use the power of these online tools, students learn that school is the "interrupter in their day" until school ends and they can get back to the tools that allow they to learn.

New Opportunities to Create and Showcase Talents and Learning

Let me count the ways to do this. In the olden days, students' work was often displayed on bulletin boards, in the hallway trophy case, or possibly in the school newsletter. Today, students write their own blogs, write or contribute to novels, produce movies, podcasts, and art work and display each of these online. They also start their own organizations or businesses, communicate with people around the world, and in so doing, accumulate a sizable digital footprint that future employers, college admissions officers, and many, many others have access to. For example,

> This spring, nearly 300 students from 24 schools participated in Maine History Day at the University of Maine at Augusta, where they confidently discussed the wide range of historical themes they had researched. They used documentaries, live performances, poster exhibits and other media to present their work. (Maine Department of Education, 2012)

New Opportunities to Balance Technology and Learning

Perhaps the single most important lesson to be learned in this push-pull of technology and learning is NOT how to use technology effectively, but WHEN to use it. And, when to turn it off. Those who wish to control technology use, particularly for young adolescents, often cite their concern with students who depend on technology, don't know how to live without it, or actually become "addicted" to it. That is the point. The curriculum must address these issues, teaching students how to use technology productively, how to pose and solve problems, and how to balance social and entertainment use as well. Why are we surprised that young adolescents (as well as high school students) have gravitated to texting, social media, and games? Knowing what we do about growth and development, each of these areas merely allows young adolescents to do what they have always done and what is valuable to them—stay connected with their peers, be social, and have fun. With the Internet and digital tools, each of these things is more easily (and instantaneously) accomplished.

A good part of learning about technology is learning when to turn it off and knowing what to do when you step away from technology. This is as true for teachers and other adults as it is for our students. In schools considerable discussion centers around the idea that technology controls us—not the other way around. Teachers are concerned that if students have laptops, smart phones, or tablets in front of them that they will be distracted from learning. Hint—watch any meeting of adults with their phones and see how many are checking texts or emails or simply surfing for anything interesting. The essential point is that we must teach our students when to use technology. When to have a web browser open during a lesson to check out information that students can contribute to the discussion, when to look at images that further their learning in a lesson, when to define a word that a student doesn't know, or when to respond to a back channel discussion that everyone in the class is participating in.

Learning how to use digital tools efficiently, effectively, and ethically involves smart searching, an entire subset of skills and abilities that are both useful and complex. While many simply use the ubiquitous "Google search", smart searching is much more in-depth and requires students to be highly savvy searchers using operators, file-types, removing invasive results, using OR, and much more. In earlier days these kinds of tools were part of the curriculum under library skills or in English classes. But today they need to be included in every class. Certainly, learning the "rules of the road" also includes learning about digital citizenship "the norms of behavior with regard to technology use" (Ribble & Bailey, 2007). The diversity we find in the world can be present in the lives of middle school youngsters. For example, in Waterville, Maine, recently

> 250 eighth-grade girls attended Future Focus, where they learned about the careers of 50 women who have pursued a variety of career paths. To start the day, the eighth graders heard from Hannah Potter, a Yarmouth High School senior who used her MLTI laptop to connect her classmates with students in Iraq. Hannah used Skype to connect the 250 eighth-grade girls with an Iraqi friend so they could discuss what they have in common—and the differences between life in Iraq and the United States. (Maine Department of Education, 2012)

The Self-Enhancing School and Middle Level Education

Given that involving technology will be an ever present context as we consider the ideas presented thus far, let's look at the self-enhancing school (Beane & Lipka, 1986) as a useful framework for addressing middle grades curriculum, the heart of any school. Beane and Lipka suggest 17 "FROM—TO" dimensions that help us develop a clearer vision of curriculum and how it should work in middle grades schools. Not surprisingly, this vision from their work in 1986 is consistent with many other models including Association for Middle Level Education's, *This We Believe* series (NMSA, 1982, 1995, 2003, 2010) and *This We Believe in Action* (AMLE, 2011).

Anyone working on middle grades improvement or transformation would be well served by considering these dimensions. They clearly point in the direction for a student-oriented, democratic, humanistic, and progressive curriculum, what the middle grades has said we wanted all along. The costs of staying in the FROM positions should be clear ... a continuation of the status quo where students are acted upon rather than given opportunities to learn in ways described earlier in this chapter. The benefits for moving to the TO position are even clearer and supported by the research and opinions found in this very volume.

PART III—LET'S DO THIS!

I find my chapter to be in concert with my fellow contributors to this volume. Now is the time to place these knowledge, skills, and dispositions into practice in our middle grades. My assigned dimension in this book, "From maintenance of the status quo to continuous development", provides us with the lens to guide our plans of action. That all of us enter the school with unique characteristics and concerns that are subject to continuous change as a function of the dynamic society in which we live. That any school that has a program totally fixated upon the past risks becoming an anachronism in contemporary life. We cannot face change by "running for cover" or crying out for the "good old days". Rather change must be met with a continuous process of thoughtful planning, careful experimentation, and action research/evaluation. "In the end the school itself must become a growing, developing, reflecting environment, much like that which characterizes healthy self-perceptions. It is a place where self-enhancement is not just a technique, but a way of life" (Beane & Lipka, 1986, p. 188).

In short to do anything else shortchanges and diminishes our obligations as professionals. Shortchanges and diminishes the obligations we have to the young people in our schools. Shortchanges and diminishes the roles and duties our young people should assume as adults in our society.

REFERENCES

Association for Middle Level Education. (2011). *This we believe in action: Implementing successful middle level schools* (2nd ed.). Westerville, OH: Author.

Beane, J. A. *(1990). A middle school curriculum—From rhetoric to reality.* Columbus, OH: National Middle School Association.

Beane, J. A. (1995). *Toward a coherent curriculum: Yearbook of the Association for Supervision and Curriculum Development.* Alexandria, VA: Association for Supervision and Curriculum Development.

Beane, J. A., & Lipka, R. P. (1986). *Self-concept, self-esteem, and the curriculum.* New York, NY: Teachers College Press.

Brazee, E. N., & Capelluti, J. (1995). *Dissolving boundaries: Toward an integrative curriculum.* Columbus, OH: National Middle School Association.

Caskey, M. M., Davis, P. G., Bishop. P. A., Capraro, R. M., Roe, M., & Weiss, C. (2010). *Research and resources in support of This We Believe.* Westerville, OH: National Middle School Association.

Jackson, A. W., & Davis, G. A. (2000). *Turning points 2000: Educating adolescents in the 21st century.* New York, NY: Teachers College Press.

Jacobs, H. H. (2010). *Curriculum 21: Essential education for a changing world.* Alexandria, VA: Association for Supervision and Curriculum Development.

Maine Department of Education, Commissioner's Update. (2012, March 29). Retrieved from https://mail.google.com/mail/?hl=en&tab=wm#inbox/1365e4710d1e336f)

McEwin, K., & Greene, M. (2011). *The status of programs and practices in America's middle schools: Results from two national studies.* Westerville, OH: Association for Middle Level Education.

National Association for Secondary Schools. (2006). *Breaking ranks in the middle: Strategies for leading middle level reform.* Reston, VA: Author.

National Middle School Association. (1982). *This we believe.* Columbus, OH: Author.

National Middle School Association. (1995). *This we believe: Developmentally responsive middle level schools.* Columbus, OH: Author.

National Middle School Association. (2003). *This we believe: Successful schools for young adolescents.* Westerville, OH: Author.

National Middle School Association. (2010). *This we believe: Keys to educating young adolescents.* Westerville, OH: Author.

Ribble, M., & Bailey, G. D. (2007). *Digital citizenship in schools.* Eugene, OR: International Society for Technology in Education.

Roney, K., Anfara, V. A., Jr., & Brown, K. M. (2008). *Creating organizationally healthy and effective middle schools: Research that supports the middle school concept and student achievement.* Westerville, OH: National Middle School Association.

Smith, T. W., & McEwin, C. K. (2011). *The legacy of middle school leaders in their own words.* Information Age.

Springer, M. (1994). *Watershed: A successful voyage into integrative learning.* Columbus, OH: National Middle School Association.

Stevenson, C., & Carr, J. F. (1993). *Integrated studies in the middle grades: Dancing through walls.* New York, NY: Teachers College Press.

Taba, H. (1962). *Curriculum development: Theory and practice.* New York, NY: Harcourt, Brace & World.

EPILOGUE

What Have We Learned, and What Must We Do

Richard P. Lipka and Kathleen Roney

WHAT WE HAVE LEARNED

In reflecting upon the contributions of our authors, what have we learned and what must we do? In terms of what we have learned, please consider the following.

Schools must be warm, inviting places that focus upon intellectual development, but not at the expense of the learners' self-perceptions of their goals, aspirations and future contributions to a civil society. The school's warm, inviting climate must include strategies that place parents and families and the larger community in an instrumental role in the education of their child. That the *good* that their child learns in school will be valued and reinforced in the home and community.

The leadership in schools must be skilled in building trusting relationships with all who cross the doorways, be it students, teachers, staff, parents, families, and community members at large. School leaders must realize the potential that they have to create the cognitive and affective oasis in their communities. That the intellectual approach to problem

Middle Grades Curriculum:
Voices and Visions of the Self-Enhancing School, pp. 307–309
Copyright © 2013 by Information Age Publishing

solving valued in their schools may be utilized in solving real problems in their communities. School leaders must engender a view in their teachers that true professional growth can involve making mistakes as long as learning from these mistakes comes forthwith.

Teachers must feel comfortable and equipped to educate the diversity that we find in our nation, and they must believe that their words and views count for something when involved in the planning process for their school. Furthermore teachers must clearly understand that cognitive learning is hard won by someone whose life is in affective disarray. Teachers must understand that it is difficult to process content when one is scared, tired and hungry.

Students must view their schools as safe, sane environments that provide them with opportunities to be heard. That the process of growing up is a process of making mistakes. And that all efforts will be directed to learning from one's mistakes and not be punished for their efforts. They must sense schools as places where adults know them and care about their well-being and growth as young people.

WHAT WE MUST DO

Globally

We must keep the views expressed in this volume on the front burner of discussions involving teacher education and public schools in the United States. For teacher educators, Brazee (Chapter 17) makes a good point—the real curriculum of the classroom depends heavily on understanding what students are all about, and teacher education programs need to prepare teachers for the complicated and complex task of devising responsive curricula. Teacher candidates must be involved in coplanning with their teacher educators. Teachers—prospective and practicing—must develop skills as expert facilitators and curriculum negotiators.

When teachers are given state assessment tools and core curricula, they must know and understand that these provide partial pictures of what should be done in terms of working with their students in curriculum and assessment. The Association for Middle Level Education (NMSA, 2010) directs all those committed to working with young people in middle level schools to adopt the sixteen characteristics as a whole package. Five of the sixteen characteristics directly address curriculum, instruction and assessment in developmentally responsive middle level schools.

Specifically

This is the first volume in what we envision to be a three-volume series. Round one, volume one represents well-reasoned thoughts about the middle level school curriculum. Volume two is designed to take these thoughts into action by having people construct and use resource units predicated upon the concepts in volume one and place these resource units into practice in their classrooms and schools. We envision volume two to be a collection of resource units in a depository we set up and make available on the Web. Imagine the power if we can find schools willing to use all of these resources—we will have created a self-enhancing school.

Volume 3 will then be reflections upon those actions (resource unit) by having people under take research and evaluation studies of the resource units in practice to ascertain their effectiveness in terms of a variety of teacher and student outcomes, impact on leaders, and parents in both the cognitive and affective domains.

The editors of this volume, rooted in many years and experiences with young people and their schools, are up to the challenges represented in volumes two and three. Any reader of this volume (Volume 1) who considers themselves up to the challenge would be warmly welcomed by us.

REFERENCE

National Middle School Association. (2010). *This we believe: Keys to educating young adolescents.* Westerville, OH: Author.

ABOUT THE EDITORS

Kathleen Roney is professor of middle level education in the Department of Elementary, Middle Level and Literacy Education at University of North Carolina Wilmington. She has over 30 years in teaching and administration at the elementary, middle grades, secondary, and higher education levels. Among her professional affiliations is membership in the American Educational Research Association, Middle Level Education Research Special Interest Group of AERA, Association of Middle Level Education, North Carolina Association of Professors of Middle Level Education, and North Carolina Middle School Association for which she serves as editor of the *North Carolina Middle School Journal*. She has published in a variety of research journals, and has co-authored and/or edited three books: *The Developmentally Responsive Middle Level Principal: A Leadership Model and Measurement Instrument* (NMSA, 2006), *Creating Healthy and Effective Middle Schools: Research That Supports the Middle School Concept and Student Achievement* (NMSA, 2008), and, *An International Look at Educating Young Adolescents* (Information Age, 2009). Additionally, she has presented her research in middle level education at many international, national, and regional conferences.

Richard P. Lipka is distinguished professor at St. Bonaventure University. A graduate of the State University of New York College at Buffalo (BS, MS) and the University of Illinois (PhD), he taught sixth grade as a member of a four person team in Amherst, New York. His research interest is affective development with an emphasis upon self-concept and self-esteem. To that end, he served as coeditor of *Self-Perceptive Across the Life-Span* (1992 with Brinthaupt) and coauthor on *When the Kids Come First: Enhancing Self-Esteem* (1987 with Beane) and *Self-Concept and Self-Esteem and the Curriculum* (1986 with Beane). He serves as coeditor for numerous volumes in the Suny Press series, *Studying the Self*. In his role at

311

St. Bonaventure University he has the distinct pleasure of mentoring fellow faculty colleagues who are trying to finish degrees and/or get their works published. He continues to present at both regional and national conferences.

AUTHOR INDEX

Abdal-Haqq, I., 129
Abwender, D., 121
Adams, S.K., xiv, 115, 258, 260, 266
Ahmed, M., 106
Akiva, T., 200, 202
Akos, P., 105, 106, 108, 109, 112
Alexander, W.M., 35, 36, 42, 245, 272,
    277
Allan, S.D., 39
Al-Mabuk, R., 111, 112, 278
Alter, Z., 264
Alverman, D.E., 214
Amanti, C., 133
Ames, C., 196, 197
Amrein, A.T., 230
Anderman, E.M., 144, 145, 148, 149,
    150, 186, 187, 198, 278
Anderman, L.E., 144, 145, 148, 149,
    150, 187
Anderson, A., 126
Andrew, C., 195
Andrews, P.G., 35, 301
Andrews, R.L., 275
Anfara, Jr., V.A., 214, 265, 274, 281,
    301
Ansalone, G., 114
Apple, M.W., 256
Arel, S., 200, 202
Arellano, B., 129

Aronson, J., 186
Arowosafe, D.S., 228
Arseneault, L., 184
Arter, J., 281
Association for Middle Level Education
    (AMLE), 119, 120, 122, 228,
    229, 296, 298, 305
Augustine, C.H., 80

Baer, R.A., 184
Bailey, G.D., 304
Bailey, J.M., 261
Balanguer, I., 79
Ball, D.L., 195, 255
Ball, J., 283
Bandura, A., 161, 175, 185
Banilower, E.R., 284
Banks, P., 257
Baron, R., 145
Barradas, D., 125, 134
Barron, B.J., 276
Barrett, H.C., 261
Barth, R.S., 170, 173, 174
Bates, J., 120
Bauch, J.P., 129
Baumeister, R.F., 4
Baumert, J., 38
Beane, J.A., ix, x, xiv, xv, xviii, xix, 1, 2,
    3, 4, 6, 8, 10, 13, 33, 34, 37, 41,

43, 46, 47, 54, 55, 58, 62, 63, 64, 90, 91, 92, 96, 100, 101, 105, 106, 108, 109, 110, 143, 145, 146, 179, 204, 214, 227, 228, 229, 230, 231, 242, 243, 244, 245, 255, 256, 257, 259, 274, 294, 296, 301, 304, 305
Beaty-O'Ferrall, M.E., 235
Bedeian, A.G., 66
Beers, J., 184
Beery, S., 121
Belgrad, S., 261, 262
Bell, C.V., 112
Belsky, D., 184
Benn, R., 200, 202
Benson, J., 55
Beranek, M.L., 117
Berckemeyer, J., 261
Bergman, S., 277
Bergstrom, K.L., 281
Berliner, D.C., 230, 232
Beru, Y., 38, 39
Bidwell, W.W., 277
Biegel, G.M., 203
Billups, M., 40
Binkley, R., 215
Birman, B., 195
Bishop, P.A., 254, 256, 257, 267, 301
Bittanti, M., 261
Bjork, R., 11
Blackwell, L.S., 7, 186
Blais, M.R., 243
Blanck, H., 125
Blewitt, P., 109
Blum, R.W., 54, 215
Blumenfeld, P.C., 279
Blyth, D.A., 4, 228
Boaler, J., 283
Boelter, C.M., 110
Boisvert, C., 106
Boland, Jr., R.J., 97, 100
Bond, L.A., 283
Bond, M.A., 282
Bondi, J., 272
Boomer, G., 256
Boon, R.T., 115
Borich, G., 233

Bosker, R.J., 192
Boyd, D., 261
Bracey, G.W., 274, 285
Bradshaw, C.P., 105
Brainard, E., 54
Bransford, J.D., 182, 200, 275, 279
Braun, C., 144
Brazee, E.N., 256, 296, 308
Brewster, C., 278
Brière, N.M., 243
Briggs, T.H., 277
Brighton, C.M., 229, 234
Brigman, G., 112
Brinegar, K., 254, 257, 267
Briner, R., 201
Brinthaupt, T.M., 4, 228, 232, 233, 234, 236
Broderick, P.C., 109, 203
Brodrick, M., 249
Bromell, L., 124
Broom, J., 193
Brophy, J.E., 144, 145, 146, 147, 148, 243
Broughton, J., 77
Brown, A.L., 275, 279
Brown, B., 108
Brown, D.F., xiv, 19, 22, 25, 230, 257, 267
Brown, K.M., 301
Brown, K.W., 203
Brown, M.C., 53
Br?ll, M., 38
Brynjolfsson, E., 265
Buchanan, C.M., 244
Bucher, K.T., xiv, 43
Buckingham, D., 255
Burke, K., 261, 262
Burk-Braxton, C., 4, 10
Burgner, R., 217
Bursuck, W., 282
Busch, S., 192

Calderon, S., 278
Caldwell, J.S., 43, 45
California Department of Education, 53
Campbell, C., 112

Campbell, J.D., 4
Campbell, W.K., 6, 9, 12, 13
Canniff, M., 257
Capelluti, J., 296
Capraro, R.M., 301
Carlson, K.S., 6
Carnegie Council on Adolescent
    Development, 272, 273
Carr, J.F., 281, 296
Carter, E.W., 234
Caskey, M.M., 91, 214, 265, 274, 281,
    301
Caspi, A., 8, 184
Castellino, D., 120
Cerezno, N., 37, 233
Chandler, K., 121
Chang-Schneider, C., 7, 8, 14
Charles, P., 112
Charness, N., 184
Chavez, O., 284
Chen, X., 122
Chiu, D., 38, 39
Chisnal, K.F., 56, 57, 58, 59, 60, 61, 62,
    63, 64, 65, 66, 67, 68
Chrispeels, J., 129
Christenson, S., 129
Church, K., 133
C.I.A., 81
Clark, L.A., 122
Clayton, J., 126
Cleary, T.J., 113
Coccia, M.A., 201
Cocking, R.R., 275, 279
Coffield, F.C., 11
Cohen, D.K., 195, 255
Cohen, G., 186
Coie, J.D., 71
Colby, A., 79
Cole, M.S., 66
Coleman, J.S., 96
Collaborative for Early Adolescence,
    127
Collay, M., 173, 174
Collins, K.M., 36, 40
Common Core State Standards
    Initiative, 245, 246, 249
Compton, 245

Connell, J.P., 55, 193
Constant, L., 80
Cook, C.M., 228, 230, 231, 232
Cook, J., 256
Cook-Sather, A., 256, 264, 267
Cooley, C., 234
Cooley, V., 112
Cooper, H., 125, 128, 144, 145
Cope, M., 215
Costello-Daugherty, M., 249
Cousins, L.H., 131
Cox, N.D., 27
Craven, R.G., 7, 13
Crawford, B., 78
Crockett, L., 109, 110
Cronginger, R.G., 67
Crooks, T., 79
Cuban, L., 192, 245
Culham, R., 281
Cullen, M., 180, 201
Curtis, T.E., 277
Cushman, K., 25

Daddis, C., 108
Dali Lama, 182, 205, 250
D'Aluisio, F., 219
Darling-Hammond, L., 182, 200, 281
Dariotis, J., 203
Daniel, L., 43, 96
Daniels, H., 45, 232, 275, 281
Davies, J., 40
Davies, G.A., 37, 89, 142, 145, 148,
    275, 276, 298, 301
Davis-Kean, P., 76, 77
Debelak, C., 114
Deci, E.L., 77
Dejitterat, K., 187
DeLeon, A.P., 244
Dervarics, C., 123, 124
De Saint-Exupery, A., 250, 251
Desimone, L., 195
Dewberry, C., 201
Dewey, J., 73, 76, 91, 98, 246, 254, 255,
    257, 258
Diamond, A., 190
Diamond, J., 145
Dickinson, T.S., 29, 35, 51, 143

Dickson, N., 184
Doda, N.M., 24, 36, 96, 97, 101
Dodge, K.A., 71, 120
Doherty, J., 217
Doll, B., 62
Dollins, C., 133
Donnellan, M.B., 8, 9
Donovan, M.S., 279
Doty, G., 11
Doubet, K.J., 44
Dounay, J., 131
Downes, J.M., 254, 256, 267
Drexler, W., 261
DuBois, D.L., 4, 8, 10
Duchesne, S., 120, 125, 127
Duda, J.L., 79
Duflo, E., 39
DuFour, R. (Rebecca), 169
DuFour, R. (Richard), 169
Dufrene, B.A., 115
Dupas, P., 39
Durlak, J.A., 184
Dustin, E.R., 54, 55, 57, 67
Dweck, C.S., 7, 12, 13, 78, 184, 185,
    186, 191, 198, 204
Dymnicki, A.B., 184

Eaker, R., 169
Ebbeck, V., 233
Eberly, J.L., 132
Eccles, J.S., 19, 71, 76, 77, 78, 127,
    144, 145, 198, 228, 234, 244
Ecclestone, K., 11
Eggen, P., 150, 231
Eichorn, D.H., 272
Eidson, C., 275
Eisenberg, N., 110
Ekman, P., 201
Elbaum, B., 55
Elmore, R., 45, 68
Ellis, A.K., 242, 243
Englund, T., 121
Epstein, J.L., 122, 128, 129, 133
Ergün, A., 44
Ericsson, K.A., 184
Erikson, E.H., 179, 193
Erikson, L.H., 242

Evans, C., 126
Ewell, K., 121

Fabes, R., 110
Faeth, M., 25, 28
Fager, J., 278
Faircloth, C.V., 215
Farrell, A.D., 120, 126
Faulkner, S.A., 228, 230, 231, 232
Feldlaufer, H., 244
Fenstermacher, K., 129
Fenzel, M.L., 278
Ferguson, C.J., 6, 133
Fielding, M., 266
Fierro, E., 282
Finders, M., 127
Finn, J.D., 78
Fisher, 44
Fitzsimmons, P., 229, 231
Flanagan, C., 244
Flay, B.R., 8
Fleming, M., 108
Fletcher, A., 266
Flint, A.S., 282
Flohr, L.L., 40
Flook, L., 203
Flowers, N., 265
Fogarty, R., 261, 262
Foltz, C., 201
Ford, M.P., 43, 45
Foster, R., 95
Frankl, V.E., 205
French, J., 281
Frenzel, A., 38
Frey, N., 44
Friedman, T., 183, 190
Friend, M., 282
Fulton, J., 125

Gabriele, A., 111, 112, 114, 278
Galassi, J.P., 27, 106, 107
Galla, B.M., 203
Galloway, S., 111, 112, 114
Gamoran, A., 39, 46
Garcia, J., 58
Garcia-Lopez, S.P., 281
Gardner, H., 11, 40, 50

Gardner, J., 40
Garet, M., 195
Galloway, S., 278
Gamoran, A., 39, 46, 279, 280
Gehlbach, H., 77, 197
Gentile, B., 6
George, P.S., xiv, 35, 36, 42, 272, 277
Gest, S., 108
Gestsdottir, S., 109
Gezer, K., 44
Gibbs, J.C., 80
Gibbons, S.L., 233
Gillath, O., 201
Gillies, R.M., 44
Gingerich, E.F.R., 231
Giroux, H.A., xix
Gjerde, P.F., 6
Gladwell, M., 9
Glass, G., 282
Goddard, B., 175
Goleman, D., 182
Gomez, M., 111
Gonzalez, M., 129
Gonzalez, M.L., 282
Good, T., 143, 144, 145, 146, 147, 148
Goodman, A., 132
Goodman, J.F., 22
Goodwin, B., 164
Gottfredson, D.C., 106
Gotz, T., 38
Gould, J., 231
Gould, L.F., 203
Graham, S., 55
Green, A., 235
Green, M.W., 35, 300, 301
Green, V.P., 45
Greenberg, M.T., 184, 200, 201, 202, 203
Griffin, D., 106
Groen, M., 111, 112, 114, 278
Grzetich, J., 128
Guerra, N.G., 105
Gullatt, D., 233
Gulledge, S.A., 27
Guskey, T.R., 261
Guthrie, I., 110
Guzdial, M., 279

Hall, C.J., 229
Hall, E., 11
Hall, L., 231
Hallam, S., 37, 40
Halpin, G., 55
Hammon, A., 111, 113, 114
Hamre, B.K., 196
Hancox, R.J., 184
Hanna, F., 235
Hao, L., 282
Harackiewicz, J.M., 188
Harber, K.D., 39
Harkevy, I., 22
Harmin, M., xv
Harper, G.W., 66
Harrington, H., 184
Harris, A.R., 200, 202, 203
Harter, S., 4, 13, 20, 78, 198, 228, 234
Haselhuhn, C.W., 111, 112, 114, 278
Haynes, H.L., 45
Haywood, K., 258, 260, 266
Heckman, J.J., 182, 183, 184
Hecks, D.J., 284
Hedt, M., 217, 218, 219, 222
Heller, D.A., 167, 173
Heller, R., 278
Hempel-Jorgensen, A., 235
Henderlong, J., 7
Henry, D.B., 120, 126
Henson, R.K., 160, 162, 164, 175
Heredia, R.C., 13, 131
Herman, J., 281
Herrold, K., 132, 133
Herr-Stephenson, B., 261
Hess, C., 111, 113, 114
Hiatt-Michael, D.B., 122, 131, 132
Hicks, L., 186, 198
Higgins, A., 72, 83
Hill, N., 120, 124, 128, 130, 133
Hill, P.L., 6
Hindman, A., 282
Hines, V.A., 245
Hlebowitsh, P.S., 244
Hofman, R.H., 192
Homestead, E.R., 89, 274, 280, 281
Honkomp, B., 231
Hopkins, J., 184

Horn, D.R., 115
Horner, J., 126
Houts, R., 184
Horst, H., 261
Howard, E.R., 54
Howe, J., 259
Howell, B., 54
Hoy, W.K., 162, 165, 194, 195, 196
Hsieh, Y.P., 187
Hu, W., 42
Hubbard, L., 43
Huber, R.A., 231, 234
Huhman, M., 125
Hulleman, C.S., 188
Hundley, S., 215
Hunt, J.A., 281
Hurly, C., 129
Hyde, A., 232, 275, 281

Immordino-Yang, M.H., 25, 28
Ingram, N., 112
Intrator, S.M., 214, 215
Ireson, J., 37, 40
Irvin, J., 114
Ishijima, E., 203
Ito, M., 261
Iver, D.M., 244

Jackson, A.P., 113
Jackson, A.W., 37, 89, 102, 142, 145,
    148, 275, 276, 298, 301
Jacobs, H.H., 246, 301
Jacobson, L., 39, 51, 143
James, C., 253
James, W., 199
Jansorn, N.R., 133
Jarrett, R.L., 130
Jarvis, J.M., 229, 234
Jenkins, D.M., 29, 35, 45, 231
Jenkins, K.D., 35, 45
Jennings, P.A., 184, 200, 201
Jensen, E., 27
Jensen, M.K., 45
Johnson, A.M., 37
Johnson, D.W., 75, 184, 188, 191, 233
Johnson, H., 37, 45
Johnson, L., 258, 260, 266

Johnson, R.T., 75, 184, 188, 191, 233
Johnston, H., 45
Johnston, J.H., 274
Jones, M., 36, 40
Jordan, A., 126
Joshi, A., 132
Jussim, L., 39
Juvoven, J., 80

Kabat-Zinn, J., 180, 184, 188
Kacker, H.Z., 128
Kaiser Family Foundation, 126
Kaiser Greenland, S., 203
Kaganoff, T., 80
Kalvin, C., 108
Kanthak, L.M., 274
Kaplan, A., 199
Kasak, D., 41, 44
Kasari, C., 203
Kauchak, D., 150, 231
Kaura, S., 109
Keefe, J.W., 54
Keiser, M., 215
Kemeny, M.E., 201
Kelchtermans, G., 232
Kellough, R.D., xiv
Kellough, N.G., xiv
Kernis, M.H., 19
Kessinger, R., 38, 39, 48
Killin, T.E., 37
Kinney, P., 261
Kitayama, S., 205
Kitil, M.J., 203
Kliebard, H.M., 246
Klute, C., 108
Knapp, M., 231
Knowles, T., xiv, 24, 25, 230
Kohlberg, L., 72, 79, 83
Kohn, A., 7, 26, 161
Koller, O., 38
Konzal, J., 132
Koran, C.M., 54
Kose, S., 44
Kowalski, P., 198
Krajcik, J.S., 279
Krauthammer, C., 5
Krechevsky, M., 11

Kremer, M., 39
Krietemeyer, J., 184
Kronenberg, J., 215, 217
Krueger, J.I., 4
Kuhn, J., xiv, 115
Kuntz, S., 256
Kulik, C.A., 37, 39, 46, 49
Kulik, J.A., 37, 39, 46
Kunter, M., 55
Kuntz, S., 100
Kunzman, R., 214, 215
Kupersmidt, J.B., 71

Lachuk, A., 111
Langer, E.J., 188, 196
Landson-Billings, G., 282
Lane, K.L., 234
Lange, P., 261
Lanphar, E., 229, 231
Lansford, J., 120
Lan Yong, F., 55
Lapp, D., 44
Lareau, A., 122, 130
Latta, M.M., 37
Lau, S., 19, 186, 243, 244
LaVoi, N., 78
Lawlor, M.S., 203
Lawton, T.A., 274, 277, 278, 285
Layell, K., 111, 114, 215
Leaf, P.J., 203
Learning Point Associates, 280, 281
Leonard, G., 230
Leary, M.L., 5, 12, 13, 14
L'Esperance, M., 37, 41, 213, 214
Le, V., 80
Lee, J., 130
Lee, K., 190
Lee, V.E., 67, 191, 197
Leffert, N., 97
Lemov, D., 161
Leo, J., 1, 5
Lepper, M.R., 7
Lerner, J., 108
Lerner, R., 109
Lester, N., 256
Lewis, C., 127
Lewis, K., 186

Lewison, M., 282
Li, Y., 108
Lieberman, A., 196
Liesveld, R., 160, 171
Liu, J., 108
Licata, J.W., 66
Lintz, A., 43
Lipka, R.P., ix, x, xiv, xviii, xix, 1, 2, 3,
     4, 6, 8, 13, 33, 34, 37, 43, 44, 46,
     54, 55, 58, 62, 64, 90, 100, 101,
     105, 106, 108, 109, 110, 141,
     143, 145, 146, 179, 204, 214,
     224, 227, 228, 233, 234, 242,
     245, 253, 255, 274, 284, 294,
     304, 305
Lipsitz, J., 22
Lipton, M., 146, 149, 150
Litwack, S., 120, 125, 126
Lloyd, C.A., 193, 194
Locke, J., 203
Lockwood, A.T., 34
Loeber, R., 121
Lohman, B., 109
Lomax, R., 126, 130
Lomos, C., 192
Lopez, E., 132
Lopez, G.R., 282
Lopez, S.J., 164
Lord, S., 71, 228
Lounsbury, J.H., xiv, 92, 114, 176, 245
Loveless, T., 35, 36, 39, 42
Lowe, C., 145
Ludewig, J.W., 204
Ludtke, O., 38, 55
Luskin, F.M., 201
Luther, S., 127
Lynch, 108
Lyons, K.E., 200

MacDonald, E., 196
MacLaury, S., 26, 27
MacNeil, A.J., 192
Maehr, M., 187, 199, 278, 281
Mahoney, K., 282
Maine Department of Education, 302,
     303, 304
Mancabelli, R., 260, 261

Mann, H., 76
Manning, M.L., xiv, 43
Marachi, R., 77, 197
Marchant, G.J., 235
Markham, E., xi
Marks, H.M., 279, 280
Markus, H.R., 205
Marsh, H.W., 7, 13, 36, 37, 38
March, R.S., 36
Marx, R.W., 279
Marzano, J.S., 111, 235
Marzano, R.J., 111, 235, 279
Mastropieri, M.A., 115
Matusmoto, H., 205
Mays, S.A., 120, 126
McAfee, A., 265
McBride, O., 78
McCaffrey, K., 37
McClarty, C.L., 7, 8, 14
McCloskey, W., 186
McCombs, B.L., 231, 233
McCuddy, M.K., 231
McDaniel, M., 11
McDowelle, J.O., 192
McElrath, M., 145, 215
McEwin, C.K., 29, 35, 231, 300, 301
McGehee, P., 5
McGinnis, K.L., 274, 280, 281
McIntyre, D.J., 231, 234
McLaughlin, M.W., 197
McLean, K.C., 204
McNeal, R., 130
McNutt, M.R., 115
McTighe, J., 275, 276
Medrich, E., 278
Mee, C.S., 27
Meece, J.L., 144, 145, 146, 147, 150,
    161, 187
Mehan, H., 43
Mendelson, T., 203
Menzel, P., 219
Mertens, C., 54, 55, 57, 67
Mertens, S.B., 265
Metz, S., 203
Mickelson, R.A., 131
Middle Level Curriculum Project, 41

Midgley, C., 19, 71, 77, 78, 145, 186,
    187, 197, 198, 228, 244, 278
Miller, D., 45
Miller, J., 120, 125, 126, 128
Miller, J.A., 165, 171
Miller, L., 196
Miller, M.D., 165
Mills, L.B., 192
Mind and Lite Education Research
    Network, 180, 182, 190, 191,
    200, 203
Mitra, D.L., 267
Mo, Y., 120
Moffitt, T.E., 8, 184
Mohler, L.J., 115
Moll, L., 133
Molloy, L., 108
Montrosse, B., 186
Moon, T.R., 229, 234
Mooney, K., 186
Moore, A., 276
Moorman, E., 120, 125, 126
Moos, D.C., 231
Morfield, J., 275
Morgan, A., 122
Moseley, D.V.M., 11
Mounts, N.S., 121, 127
Mousley, J., 41
Murphy, B., 110
Murphy, J., 132
Murray, G.C., 54, 55, 57, 67
Muth, K.D., 37

Nagle, J., 267
Najake, S., 106
Naslund, A., 250
National Association of Secondary
    Principals, 142
National Association of Secondary
    Schools, 298
National Commission on Excellence in
    Education, 74
National Forum to Accelerate Middle-
    Grades Reform, 142
National Governors Association Center
    for Best Practices, 246

National Middle School Association, xiii, xiv, xix, 24, 25, 36, 41, 47, 77, 97, 110, 111, 113, 142, 145, 152, 213, 247, 250, 273, 275, 296, 298, 300, 305, 308
National School Reform Faculty, 93
Navarro, C., 96
Needles, M., 231
Neff, D., 133
Neff, K.D., 5, 184, 187
Nesin, G., 92, 267
Newkirk, C., 130
Newman, B., 109
Newmann, F.M., 279, 280
Nicholls, J.G., 78, 79
Nichols, S., 230, 232
Niemiec, C.P., 54, 59
Nguyen, J.T., 235
Noddings, N., 182, 190
Noeth, R.J., 131
Nolly, G., 58
Norasakkunkit, V., 205
Nothern Illinois University, 127
Notah, D.J., 37
Nowlin, P., 120

Oakes, J., 34, 36, 40, 146, 149, 150
O'Brennan, L.M., 278
O'Brien, E., 123, 124
O'Donnell, K., 132, 133
Okagaki, L., 11
Olafson, L., 37
Olinsky, S., 40
Olmi, D., 115
Onore, C., 256
Ormrod, J., 143, 148
Orthner, D., 112
Osgood, D.W., 126
Ozturk, M., 114

Pajares, F., 53, 54, 159, 161, 163, 164, 165
Palardy, G.J., 130
Paley, V., 72, 81, 82, 83, 84, 85
Palinscar, A., 279
Palmer, P.J., 165
Pape, S.J., 165

Paris, S.G., 274, 277, 278, 285
Park, N., 107
Parker, A.K., xiv, 33
Parker, J.W., 38
Parker, W., 72, 73
Pashler, H., 11
Pasley, J.D., 284
Pasupathi, M., 204
Patall, E., 125, 128
Pate, P.E., 89, 93, 96, 267, 274, 280, 281
Patel, N., 133
Paterson, J., 101
Patmor II, G.L., 231, 234
Pawlson, S.E., 235
Pecks, S.C., 180, 199, 200, 202, 203
Pelletier, L.G., 243
Petrash, J., 249
Petrilli, M., 44
Petrosino, A., 276
Pianta, R.C., 196
Pickering, D.J., 235
Pierson, M.R., 234
Pinar, M., 231
Pintrich, P., 144, 145, 146, 147, 150
Piper, W.E., 66
Pollard, J., 281
Pomerantz, E., 120, 125, 126
Porter, A.C., 195
Porter, S., 195
Portes, A., 282
Poulton, R., 8
Powell, J.V., 96
Powell, R., 35, 36, 45
Powell, S.D., xiv, 35, 36, 111, 167, 168, 173, 174
Power, A.M.R., 83, 85
Power, F.C., 72, 78, 83, 85
Prater, D.L., 192
Preckel, F., 38
Prescott, D., 245
Project Tomorrow, 261
Putnam, R., 108

Quennerstedt, A., 121

Raffaelli, M., 109, 110
Randolph, A., 145

Ratelle, C., 120, 125, 127
Raths, L.E., xv
Ratvitch, D., 273
Raywid, M., 36
Ream, R.K., 130
Reeves, D.B., 167
Reis, S., 282
Reisener, C.D., 115
Reuman, D., 244
Reynolds, G.P., 5, 45
Reys, B., 284
Reys, R., 284
Rhoades, B.L., 202
Rhodes, J., xiv, 115
Rhodes, R.W., xiv
Ribble, M., 304
Richardson, A.M., 66
Richardson, W., 260, 261
Rivera, A., 38, 39
Robitaille, D.F., 284
Robins, R.W., 8, 9
Robinson, J., 125, 128
Robinson, L., 261
Robinson, V.M.J., 193, 194
Roberts, B.W., 6
Roe, M., 301
Roeser, R.W., 19, 76, 77, 180, 184, 186,
    190, 193, 196, 197, 198, 199,
    200, 201, 202, 203, 243, 244
Rogers, L., 25
Rogers, R., 129
Rogoff, B., 124
Rohrer, D., 11
Rolstad, K., 282
Roney, K., 301
Rosenberg, M., xv
Rosenthal, R., 39, 143, 144, 146, 147
Roseth, C.J., 184, 188, 191
Ross, S.M., 275
Ross, W.E., 244
Roth, J.L., 274, 277, 278, 285
Rothlisberg, B.A., 235
Rouse, W.A., 192
Rowe, K.J., 193, 194
Rowley, S., 126
Rudduck, J., 257
Rulison, K., 108

Ryan, R.M., 54, 55, 59, 77
Ryan, T., 182, 206

Sachs, J.D., 182, 205, 206
Sahin, A., 44
Salinas, K.C., 128, 133
Sameroff, A.J., 193, 198, 199, 244
Sampson-Cordle, A.V., 96
Sanders, M.G., 122, 123
Sands, D., 62
Sarason, S.B., 192, 193, 196
Scales, P.C., 97
Schellinger, K.B., 184
Scheurich, J.J., 58, 68
Schiefele, U., 76, 77, 88
Schlechty, P.C., 256
Schmidlein, P., 38, 39
Schmidt, J.A., 128
Schneider, B.H., 195
Schonert-Reichl, K.A., 203
Schoeny, M.E., 120, 126
Schooler, J.W., 189
Schubert, C.M., 203
Schultz, B.D., 257
Schunk, D., 144, 145, 146, 147, 150
Schunk, D.H., 53, 54, 159, 161, 163,
    164, 165
Schwarts, D.L., 276
Scott, C.G., 54, 55, 57, 67
Scott, L., 233
Scruggs, T.E., 115
Seeley, C.L., 284
Seiffge-Krenke, I., 25
Seitsinger, A.M., 113
Selman, R.L., 71, 77, 79
Senecal, C.B., 243
Senko, C., 188
Sexton, C., 127
Shaffer, J., 126
Shapiro, S.L., 203
Sheehan, K., 78
Shiefele, U., 76, 77
Shen, Y.L., 109, 110
Shepard, S., 110
Sheridan, S., 129
Shirley, D., 196
Shotsberger, P.G., 231, 234

Shulkind, S., 132
Shumow, L., 120, 125, 126, 128, 130
Siemens, G., 261, 264
Silk, J., 125, 126
Simmons, R.G., 4, 228
Simon, B.S., 133
Simon, S.B., xv
Simson, E., 38, 39
Simpson, F., 45
Singh, K., 120
Skaalvik, E.M., 161
Skaalvik, S., 161
Skinner, E.A., 55, 184
Skoog, G., 45
Skrla, L., 58, 68
Slavin, R.E., 39, 44, 75, 282
Smalley, S.L., 203
Smallwood, J., 189
Smith, G.T., 184
Smith, J., 197
Smith, M.C., 126, 130
Smith, P.A., 195
Smith, P.S., 284
Smith, R.W., 231, 234
Smith, T., 126, 130, 145
Smith, T.W., 215, 301
Snowberg, K.E., 201
Soloway, E., 279
Sousa, D.A., 17, 21
Spandel, V., 281
Spencer, V., 115
Spillane, J., 145
Springer, M., 256, 296
Stallings, R., 281
Stang, K.K., 234
Steele, C.S., 172
Steer, D., 233
Steinberg, L., 121, 125, 126
Steiner, R., 247
Sternberg, R.J., 11
Stevens, R.J., 44
Stevens, S., 133
Stevenson, C., 253, 296, 281
Stiggins, R., 276
Stipek, D., 22, 23
Stott, K.A., 113
Stouthamer-Loeber, M., 121

Strahan, D.B., 37, 41, 111, 112, 114,
    145, 213, 214, 215, 217, 218,
    220, 222
Strebinsky, A., 275
Strill-Rever, 250
Stringer, S.J., 45
Sullivan, P., 41
Sutton, V., 22
Swan Jr., W.B., 7, 8, 14
Sweetland, S.R., 195

Taba, H., 299
Talbert, J.E., 197
Talbott, E., 115
Tarr, J., 284
Taylor, L., 126
Taylor, R.D., 184
Taylor, R.V., 97, 100
Tevendale, H.D., 4, 10
Thomas, J.W., 276
Thompson, K.F., 93
Thurston, A., 45
Tieso, C.L., 43
Tom, D., 144
Tomlinson, C.A., 43, 44, 111, 113, 114,
    275, 282
Toney, L., 184
Toole, C., 145, 215
Topping, K., 45
Trautwein, U., 38, 55
Travers, K.J., 284
Trzesniewski, K.H., 7, 8, 9
Tsai, Y., 55
Tschannen-Moran, 162, 165, 166
Tsikalas, K.E., 130
Tuinstra, C., 132
Tung, R., 261, 262, 267
Turner, J.C., 274, 277, 278, 285
Twenge, J.M., 6, 9, 12, 13
Tyack, D.B., 192
Tyler, K.M., 110
Tyson, D.F., 120, 124, 128, 130, 133
Tyson-Bernstain, H., 284

UNICEF, 81
Urdan, T.C., 198

U.S. Department of Education, 121, 122

Vagle, M.D., 115
Vallerand, R.J., 243
Vallieres, E.F., 243
Van der Wal, M., 235
Van Hoose, J., 37, 213, 214
Van Sluys, K., 282
Van Voorhis, F.L., 128, 129, 133
Vars, G.F., 245, 276, 281
Vaughn, S., 55
Veenman, S., 95, 98, 99, 100
Velasco, A., 131
Venkatakrishnan, H., 39
Vernberg, E., 121
Villanueva, I., 43
Virtue, D.C., 112
Vohs, K.D., 4
Vye, N.J., 276

Waas, G.A., 81, 82
Wahlstro, N., 121
Walberg, H.J., 183
Wallace, B.A., 201
Walsh, D., 20, 25
Walter-Thomas, C., 38
Wang, M.C., 183
Warlick, D., 260
Warren, L.L., 37
Warsik, B., 282
Waslander, S., 235
Watley, E., 38, 29
Way, J.W., 45
Wehby, J.H., 234
Weiss, C., 301
Weiss, H., 132
Weiss, I.R., 284
Weissberg, R.P., 183, 184
Wellborn, J.G., 55
Wentzel, K.R., 235
Wheelock, A., 34, 36

Whinery, B., 91
Whitesell, N.R., 198
Wigfield, A., 38, 39, 76, 77, 144, 145, 244
Wiggins, G., 275, 276
Wiles, J., 272
William, D., 39
Williams, B., 131
Williams, E.L., 245
Williams, R.L., 37
Williamson, R.D., 274
Willingham, D.T., 277, 282
Willis, J., 114
Willower, D.J., 54, 55
Wilson, D.B., 106
Wilson, J.L., 112
Wimberly, G.L., 131
Winzelberg, A.J., 201
Wisenbaker, J., 45
Wittgenstein, L., 99
Woodward, A., 284
Woolfolk, A., 164, 165, 169, 171
Woolfolk Hoy, A., 165, 165, 166, 175
Wright, V., 129
Wubu, S., 38, 39

Yaksic, D., 96
Yetkin, I.E., 112
Yonezawa, S., 36, 40
You, S., 235
Youens, B., 256, 267

Zarett, N.R., 127
Zech, 276
Zehr, M.A., 42
Zelazo, P.D.R., 196, 199, 200
Zemelman, S., 232, 275, 281
Zevenbergen, R., 40, 41
Zimmerman, B.J., 113, 183
Zins, J.E., 183
Zoder-Martell, K., 115

SUBJECT INDEX

21st century educational outcomes, 183

ability profiling, 40
achievement gap,
   Large Gap (LG), 56
   Small Gap (SG), 56
advisories, 26-27
apprenticeship, 76
appropriate assessment, 275
authentic instructional practices, 279-280
autonomy, 108-109

barometric self, xv
baseline self, xv
big-fish-little-pond effect (BFLPE), 37-38
brain development processes, 25

caring, 22
   explicit behaviors, 21
climate (*see also* school climate), 99
   custodial, 54
   humanistic, 55, 100
      themes supportive of, 68
   mutual respect, 23
cognitive abilities,
   growth, 109
collaborative decision making, 28

collaborative learning structures, 44
collective efficacy, 175
cooperative learning, 44
Common Core State Standards, 245-246
crowdsourcing,
   concept of, 259
culture,
   (of) exclusion, 80
   just community, 71
   moral community, 72
   school, 21
curriculum (*see also* teacher-exclusive planning and teacher-student planning), 299
   development with student participation, 265
   life-centeredness, 242-243
      four primary advantages, 246
   subject-centeredness, 242-243
   Waldorf, 247, 248-249
curriculum integration, 91, 255
   planning process of nine steps, 92

daily stress, 19
democratic citizenship, 73
development,
   Stage 2 morality, 80
   Stage 3 morality, 80

developmental needs of young adolescents, 213
developmentally responsive practice, 277
differentiated instruction, 43-44
differentiation, 113-114

effective middle level educators, 26
ego-skepticism, 5
electronic portfolio, 261, 262
    assessment, 261
emotional well-being, 25
exploratory learning, 112
expectancy-value theory, 144
expectations (see also teacher expectations),
    principles for positive expectations, 151
    theory behind, 143

field, 40
foundational skill argument, 9
four essential attributes, xiii

grouping,
    attribute (see also tracking), 34, 41
    multiage, 45, 90
    heterogeneous, 114
    variable, 34, 41
        detracking, 42-43, 45
    within-class reading group, 45

habitus, 40
high stakes testing, 229, 232, 235
    state testing, 18

identity (see also self)
idiocy, 72
instruction,
    building upon, 275
    instructional practice, 275

knowledge work, 100-101

labeling,
    effects, 38

leadership,
    consistency, 66
learning, 29-30
    constructs, 228
    rigor in, 29-30
    self-directed, 64
learning management systems (LMS), 263
locus of control,
    internal, 55

meaningful curriculum, 111
middle adolescence, 4
middle level teachers, 19
mindful,
    classroom cultures, 196
    middle school, xx
        conceptualization, 180-181, 191
    school culture, 194
    school leadership, 192
mindfulness, 180
    programs for educators, 200-201
    program for adolescents, 202
    training programs, 199-200
mindset,
    developmental mindset, 193
    fixed mindset, 184-185
    improving mindset, 185
    malleable mindset, 184-185
    proving mindset, 185
multiage, 45, 90
    community of knowing, 96
        perspective making, 97
    community of learners, 95
    interactions strategies, 92
        chalk-talk, 93
            procedures, 94
        class meetings, 92
        Consensus Building, 93, 95

narcissism, 6, 10-11
    teaching about, 13
Need Polarities, 253
No Child Left Behind, 2, 29, 296-297

opportunity centers, 29

out of school curriculum,
  self-perception, 9-10

parent engagement (*see also* parental
      involvement),
  academic enrichment at home, 129
  at-home, 124
  at-school, 131
    types, 131
      as volunteers, 132
      attending events, 133
      conferences, 132
      decision-making, 133
    parental management, 127
    socialization, 125
  with educational planning, 130-131
  with homework, 127
parental involvement (*see also* parent
      engagement),
  guidelines for engaging parents, 122
  parental disengagement conse-
      quences, 120
  why parental engagement matters,
      120
parenting style, 125
peer tutoring, 115
Personal Learning Networks (PLN),
      260
Play Like a Champion Today, 78-79
practice of self-related skills, 9
praising students, 7
predictors,
  general, 7
  specific, 7
prevention mindset, 106
professional learning community
      (PLC), 169-170
  six characteristics, 170
project based,
  approach, 282
  learning, 276
puberty, 73

relevant curriculum, instruction, and
      assessment, 274
  four attributes that define responsive
      programs, 273

risk-taking, 20

school climate (*see also* climate),
  definition of, 54
  two types, 54
school connectedness,
  research with students, 215
self, 14
  development of,
    early adolescence, 4
    middle adolescence, 4
  identity, 10
  preoccupations of, 5
  teaching psychology of, 10
  teacher training programs on, 13
self-compassion, 5
  definition of, 187
self-concept, 2, 33, 38
  definition of, xiv
  global self-concept,
  domain-specific self-concepts,
  multidimensional, 33
self-efficacy,
  and self-perception defined, 159
  characteristics of high self-efficacy,
      163
  definition of, 160
  impact of high self-efficacy in stu-
      dents, 164
self-enhancement,
  definition of, 204
self-enhancing school, ix
  model, xv-xix
self-esteem, xv, 2, 33
  enhancement program, 4-5, 9
    developmental, age, or grade peri-
        ods, 10
  global, 7, 8
    raising of, 12
self-fulfilling prophecy, 38-39, 143-144
self-identity,
self-perception, 3
  and self-efficacy defined, 159
  curriculum, 9
    informed by empirical research, 13
  definition of, 159
  enhancing student, 3

middle level school recommendations, 11
three major arguments, 3
enhancement program,
do's and don'ts, 12-14
extreme and inaccurate, 5
specific academic competencies and
abilities, 12
specific outcome, 7
self-regulation, 109
self-regulatory skills, 189
self-talk, 5
self-transcendence, 204, 205
separate-subjects approach, 241
service learning, 113
shared norms, 83
difference from rules, 83
social challenges, 24
social consciousness of puberty, 72
social comparison and competition, 19
social relationships, 108
socialization,
experiences, 26
skills, 26
development of, 24
strengths promotion approach, 107
student-centered strategies, 230

teach (to) the test, 230, 232
teacher,
efficacious teacher characteristics,
163
increasing teacher efficacy, 165
professional development, 166
effective professional development, 168
relationships among teachers, 173-
174
self-efficacy, 161
teacher-student relationships, 111
teacher-exclusive planning,
definition of, 254-255

teacher expectations, 110
conveying through four primary
means, 144
definition of, 144
impact of negative, 148
individual expectations factors, 145
socioeconomic status, 145
strategies for positive expectations,
147
five strategies for positive classroom expectations, 150
teacher-student planning, 255, 256
Ladder of Student Involvement in
School, 266
student benefits, 257
teacher benefits, 257
Teachers' Sense of Efficacy Scale, 165-
166
teaching,
highly social experiences, 22
technology,
communication through digital
tools, 301-302
four themes for curriculum, 295
when to use and when not to use,
303
technological trends, 258
four promising directions, 259
tracking (see also attribute grouping),
34-35
achievement, 39
arguments for, 35
arguments against, 35
expectancy effects, 38
labeling effects, 38
research into, 39-41
self-perceptions, 37
true middle school, xiii

vague/specific continuum, 228

You Can't Say You Can't Play, 81

CPSIA information can be obtained at www.ICGtesting.com
Printed in the USA
LVOW01s0120030915

452596LV00002B/2/P

9 781623 962272